ASPECTS
OF
INDOLOGICAL STUDIES

(Classical Literature, Dharmaśāstra and Epics-Purāṇas)

By
Prof. Dr. M.L. Wadekar
General Editor/Professor,
Oriental Institute,
M.S. University of Baroda
VADODARA

BKP

BHARATIYA KALA PRAKASHAN
DELHI (INDIA)

First Edition : 2001

Published by **C.P. Gautam**
BHARATIYA KALA PRAKASHAN
3421-A, IInd Floor, Narang Colony, Tri Nagar,
Delhi-110035. Phone : 7153083

ISBN : 81-86050-68-X

Laser Type Setting by
A-ONE GRAPHICS
X-4, Street No. 2, Brahmapuri, Delhi-110053
Phone : 218 3470

Printed in India

PREFACE

"Aspects of Indological Studies" is in fact an outcome of incessant research endeavours of the present researcher for last more than a decade. Being associated with the world famous Oriental Institute of Baroda, there was a scope for ample research on the valuable treasure of more than 27000 Mss. He could dive deep into that ocean and find out gems in the form of little-known works based upon rare manuscripts. This incidently was a reason for most of the research papers, written by him to be found in this collection, published in several esteemed research journals. At several occasions, he was also invited to present research papers on various topics at different regional, national and international seminars and conferences. The present book incorporates many of such research papers of diverse subjects pertaining to different *śāstras* like *Vedānta*, Classical literature, *Purāṇa*, *Dharmaśāstra* and Technical literature. The papers, therefore, are classified accordingly, under different heads for the interested scholars. The researcher humbly wishes to present his research outcome, before the world of scholars, through the form of this book.

The author is indebted to all the editors and publishers of different journals from which the papers in this book are reprinted. He is also thankful to those scholars and institutions, which made him to think and present papers on the diversified topics. He is also indebted to his colleagues especially, Prof. R.I. Nanavati, Shri P.H. Joshi and Dr. S.Y. Wakankar for their constant encouragement and co-operation.

The Publisher Shri Chandraprakash Gautam of Bharatiya Kala Prakashan also deserves thanks for his prompt and neat production of the book.

M.L. Wadekar
Author

ACKNOWLEDGEMENTS

The author acknowledges his indebtedness to the editors and publishers of the following Research Journals from which the papers in this collection are reprinted.

1. Journal of the Oriental Institute, M.S. University of Baroda, Vadodara.
2. Annals of Bhandarkar Research Institute, Pune.
3. Adyar Library Bulletin, Adyar, Chennai.
4. Journal of Ananthacharya Indological Institute, Mumbai.
5. Vishvabandhu Indological Journal, Vishveshvaranand Vishvabandhu Indological Institute, Hoshiarpur, (Punjab).
6. Vinayatoshini, B. Bhattacharya Centenary Volume, Calcutta.
7. Meerut University Sanskrit Research Journal.
8. Surabharati, Annual Magazine, Baroda Sanskrit Mahavidyalaya, Vadodara.

CONTENTS

Articles *Page No.*

PHILOSOPHY

EPICS & PURĀṆAS

TECHNICAL LITERATURE

CLASSICAL LITERATURE

I

GAṆEŚALAHARĪ OF GOPĪNĀTHA— A RARE AND LITTLE— KNOWN STOTRAWORK

Introductory

In the diversified and extensive field Sanskrit Literature, *Stotras* occupy a very important and indispensable place, as poetic pieces, exuberant with poetic imagination, devotional sentiment and different figures of Speech. There are several kinds of *Stotras*, composed by eminent poets in praise of their favourite deities. The *Stotras* of Śaṅkarācārya are the most famous among them, due to their simplicity of diction, depth of philosophical thought and immensity of devotional sentiment. Not only Śaṅkarācārya, but several other poet-stars like Jagannātha Paṇḍita, Mayūra, Bāṇa and others, of the galaxy of Sanskrit Literature also have made the entire field reslpendant with the lustre of their devotional songs, of different varieties, superb with the inmost feelings. Among such *Stotras*, there are also numerous *Kāvyas*, that are styled as *Laharīkāvyas*. The most famous among them are the *Saundaryalaharī* of Śaṅkarācārya and the *Gaṅgālaharī* of Jagannātha Paṇḍita. Composed on similar lines, the present work, namely *Gaṇeśalaharī* is a small but rare *Stotra* written by Gopīnātha.

Gaṇeśalaharī Specified :

The present paper is written with a view to introducing the *Stotra* namely the *Gaṇeśalaharī* of Gopīnātha. In the *New Catalogous Catalogorum*[1], there is the entry of the

Gaṇeśalaharī but it is noted there that the *Gaṇeśalaharī* is the same as *Herambacaraṇāmṛtalaharī* of Accyutarāya Moḍaka. Thus here the reference is to the work *Herambacaraṇāmṛtalaharī*, (and not to the *Gaṇeśalaharī*) the manuscripts of which are available at *Bhārata Itihāsa Saṁśodhaka Maṇḍaḷa* Library of Poona, as mentioned in the NCC. In the *Gaṇeśakośa*[2] of Shri Amarendra Gadgil, the *Stotra,* named *Gaṇeśastutilaharī,* also known as the *Gaṇeśalaharī,* composed by Khaṇḍarāja is found which incorporates some Vedic *mantras* and contains fifty-four verses in all. Similarly, while describing *Gaṇeśagranthas,* the author has also dealt with one Sanskrit work, namely the *Gaṇeśatattvasudhālaharī,* composed by the poet Nīla-kaṇṭha Śāstrī, containing totally 246 verses in two *taraṅgas.*[3] There is also reference to the *Gaṇeśalaharī* on page 123, in the enumeration of names of the books, found in the list namely *Gāṇapatyopayogī Pustakānām Saṅgrahaḥ*, published by Chintamanarao Balakrishna Dhadaphale (Deshmukh) (of Kashi). But, unfortunately, excepting some works of the list, most of them are rare and even the author himself could not consult them. Though there is reference to the *Gaṇeśalaharī* here, it is not quite clear which work is referred to by it, as there is no mention of the author of the said *Stotra*. Thus it is evident that though there are several works styled as *Gaṇeśalaharī*, the one, written by Gopīnātha, dealt with in the present paper, is quite a different one. The reference to Allahabad and Kavīndrācārya, found under the entry of the *Gaṇeśalaharī* in *NCC* is also vague, as it is not clear which work is referred to and who is the author of the said work. In the entry of Gopīnātha, in NCC, there is no reference to the author of the *Gaṇeśalaharī*.

Gaṇeśalaharī of Gopīnātha—Quite A Rare _Stotra_ :

It was mentioned previously that the *Gaṇeśalaharī* of

Gopīnātha is not specifically referred to in the *New Catalogous Catalogorum*. There is no mention of it in the *History of Classical Sanskrit Literature* of Dr. M. Krishnamachariar.[4] It is also not found in the printed collection of *Stotras* and the *Gaṇeśakośa*, already referred to. Thus the *Stotra* is quite rare and little-known. The present research paper is written with a view to introducing this forgetten, obliterated *Stotra*, based upon the study of the rare and original manuscript, available in the Oriental Institute of Baroda. In fact, this paper is an attempt to salvage this rare *Stotra* from going into complete oblivion.

The Rare Manusript in the Oriental Institute :

The Oriental Institute of Baroda has a vast and valuable treasure of several important and rare manuscripts, on a variety of subjects. The *Gaṇeśalaharī* of Gopīnātha is also one of the rarest works, found in the extensive collection of mss. in the Oriental Institute. It has been noted previously that neither the work nor its manuscript is referred to in the *NCC*. It is deposited in O.I. with its ACC No. 11763. This manuscript contains the *Gaṇeśalaharī* in folios 47 to 50. It is complete in its form in the said folios of the manuscript, written in *Devanāgarī* Script, with quite clear and readable handwriting. The *Granthasaṅkhyā* of the work is about 170. The *Stotra* is copied on a country-made paper of 29 cms. X14 cms. size, written on both sides, with about 29 letters to a line and 27 lines to a page or one side of the folio.

The Scribe and his Peculiarities :

The name of the scribe as evident from the post-colophon entry is Nandikeśvara, who was resident of Navīnapura and was most probably a descendant of a Brahmin family. He begins with a salutation to *Gaṇapati* and *Dakṣiṇāmūrti* and solicits benediction at the end with the words, '*Śubhaṁ Bhavatu*'. There are some marginal corrections and additions, which suggest fidelity and conscientiousness of the scribe. As regards the peculiarities of writing, it is note-worthy that sometimes letters are doubled *i.e. Nāryyaḥ* and *Anusvāra* is always used for nasals, without resorting to *parasavarṇa* rule. The date of the scribe is not found.

The Author—Gopīnātha :

In the verse no. 51, the name of the author of the present work, namely *Gaṇeśalaharī* is explicitly mentioned as Gopīnātha. The author has also mentioned some personal information and date, place and general nature of the work (verse 49 to 52). He was resident of the *Viśveśvara nagarī* i.e. modern Benares. The present *Stotra* was composed by him in V.S., 1785 i.e. 1729 A.D.; writtein in *Śikhariṇī* metre, it was completed by him on the Full-moon day of the Bright fortnight in the month of *Caitra*.

Regarding the *Stotra* and his ability of composing it, the poet has some important remarks. The concept is: The Lord was sporting in the ocean in the form of Vedas. A drop of good verses was thrown upon the poet by the Lord. This is in the form of the present *Stotra*. The sweet tones of small children exhilarate the minds of the people. This praise of *Gaṇapati*, composed through His Grace only may also similarly be accepted by Him. He assures that the devout reciter of this *Stotra* can obtain success, virtue and wealth, because nothing is inaccessible for a person, with whom the God becomes pleased.

Summary of Contents :

The *Stotra,* as suggested by its very title, is in praise of the favourite deity of the poet namely *Gaṇapati*. The very titling of it as *Laharī* can clearly suggest that the poet had an idea of composing this *Stotra* for eulogizing Lord Gaṇeśa, in the style of the other *Stotras* like the *Saundaryalaharī* or the *Gaṅgālaharī*. The metre, used here is as usual *Śikhariṇī,* having four lines, with seventeen letters in each. Totally there are fifty-two verses in the same metre.

In the beginning, the poet eulogizes Him in the most general manner as the bestower of all kinds of happiness, most benevolent, compassionate Lord, captivating minds of scholars etc. Then His physical features are referred to. His temples are wet with the incessant flow of *dāna* and decorated with ornaments and the necklace of jewels. In the four huge arms, *Varadamudrā*, lotus, noose and goad are held. With wide buttocks, but comparative small feet, He appears very strange in form, yet is capable of bestowing happiness to His devotees. His beauty is very captivating and attractive and his glance is for the benefit of the world. His miraculous appearance is inconceivable even by the Vedas. Through the greatness of His side-glance, the wise obtain all the aims of life, by overcoming all difficulties. His magnificent *dhāma* (Abode) in the *maṇidvīpa* and His Shining Home are also described. He is sitting on the lustrous jewelled throne, fanned by a group of ladies. His armed followers, standing on all doors are always intent on removing calamities of devotees. There is no epithet that is not meaningful in his respect. His huge belly seems to incorporate the infinite *Brahmāṇḍa* in it, hence his epithest *Lambodara* is found. He is the Lord of *gaṇas* i.e. *tattvas*, hence he is *Gaṇapati*. With golden vessels, Gods offered water to Him, which became later on the water of holy *tīrthas* (religious places), as it is sanctified due to its contact with the body of the Lord. Though he is enclosed with the garment in the form of Vedas, he happily accepts the garment offered with devotion by his devotees. The musk-deers whose musk has been applied to the Lord's body have obtained good *gati* being already sanctified. Even wind due to his service at the feet of the great God, has become the Soul of the entire world. He is so compassionate that though he has been worshipped by Gods, with the offering of divine flowers at His feet, He is also pleased with the offering of simple *dūrvā* grass with devotion. In separate verses, the offering of fragrant *dhūpa, dīpa, bhakṣya* (eatable food etc.), fruits, *tāmbūla,* holy-water of Ganges, *puṣpāñjali* and dance by beautiful ladies, has been eulogized. His greatness is evident from the fact that the Divine pairs like *Lakṣmī* & *Viṣṇu, Pārvatī* & *Śaṅkara, Rati* & *Madana* and *Avanī* & *Vanavarāha* are residing in places nearby Him. Some describe the Lord to be the Primordial Supreme Puruṣa, while others talk of Him as beyond three *guṇas* still others call Him *saguṇa*. In fact He is indescribable, undertaking different forms for the benefit of His devotees. He himself is in the form of different Gods, like Viṣṇu, Indra, Vāyu, Sūrya etc. The devotees worship Him in different places like heart, the head etc. But once they enjoy the taste of bliss in His devotion, they become quite pleased in His service. The entire world has sprung from Him. He is the originator even of the *māyā,* having three *guṇas.*

The ordinary person, with his limited knowledge can not know the infinite *līlās* of God. Even the Serpent Ananta, possessing infinite mouths is praising His virtues, everyday, at all times, yet there is no end to his act. For destroying the demon Sindūrāsya, He took the mouth of elephant. It is not at all miraculous or strange that he wrote the entire *Mahābhārata* and gave it to Vyāsa, because the entire mass of *Veda* is in the form of His breathing. Then the poet refers to a sacrifice in which the 108 *apūpas* are offered with devotion. The person becomes wealthy as a fruit of it. Nothing is impossible, when the God is compassionate upon His devotee.

Some Remarks :

The entire *Stotra* is no doubt replete with devotional sentiment, yet there is some tinge of *Śṛṅgāra* rasa also in Verses (26-28), in which we find very picturesque and vivid description of the beauty of Divine damsels. There are also several verses that contain poetic imaginations and ideas of superb quality (e.g. verse 13, 16, 17, 36, 41, 49, 50 etc). The *rūpaka* in verse 19, regarding the ever-shining *dīpa* for the Lord is also quite noteworthy. The episodes of killing of *Sindūṛāsya* demon and writing of the *Mahābhārata* for *Vyāsa* are referred to. Though the poet has tried his best for making it perfect, there are sometimes metrical defects (for example verse 40 line 1). There seems to be some influence of *Saundaryalaharī* on the text as the poet seems to have written some verses (e.g. 29, 37, 39, 42) on the model of similar verses found in the *Saundaryalaharī*.

Conclusion :

It would be clear from the above exposition, that by composing this *Laharī* in praise of *Gaṇapati*, the poet Gopīnātha has made an important contribution to the Classical Sanskrit Literature in general and to the *Stotra* literature in particular. By the present research paper, the researcher has made an attempt to bring to light, an otherwise forgotten, contribution of the said poet.

।। श्रीः ।।

गणेशलहरी।

(गोपीनाथविरचिता)

श्रीगणेशाय नमः।

श्रीदक्षिणामूर्तये नमः।

सदानन्दाकारं सकलसुखकर्तारममलं
महोदारं तारं विबुधपरिवारं सुरवरम्।
कृपापारावारं श्रुतिनुतविहारं सुमनसां
मनोहर्तारं त्वां गजवदनमात्मन्परिणुमः।।1।।

सदादानस्त्रावस्नपितविलसद्गण्डयुगलं
लुलल्लोलव्यालाभरणमणिमालाविलसितम्।
प्रचण्डैर्दोर्दण्डैर्वरकमलपाशाङ्कुशधरै-
र्लसन्तं श्रीमन्तं गजमुखमनन्तं परिणुमः।।2।।

चलत्कर्णोपान्ते श्रुतिरुचिररावो मधुलिहां
विना तारं नायं प्रभवति सुखाय श्रुतमपि।
विमृश्यैवं विघ्नावलिहरणशीलेन भवता
महाशुण्डादण्डः प्रणवसमतापैव(यै वि) लिपितः।।3।।

स्वभावे बालेन्दुद्युतिरमलकुम्भस्थलयुगा-
त्स्त्रवत्स दा(सद्दा)नाम्भःपरिमलमनोहारिवर(द)नात्।
क्वणत्काञ्चीदामाभरणमणिमुक्तातिरुचिरा
तवेयं सन्मूर्तिर्वरद वरदा नः सुखयतु।।4।।

लसत्सद्ब्रह्माण्डद्वयशकलकुम्भस्थलरुचां
दिशां प्रान्तोद्भासच्छ्रवणमरुणाभेभवदनम्।
नराकारं चाद्यः पृथुलकटिभारं मृदुपदं
विचित्रं त्वद्रूपं प्रभवति मुदे किं न भजताम्।।5।।

त्वदीयं सौन्दर्यं सुहृदयमनोहारि भगव-
न्कटाक्षोऽयं लोकेष्वनुपमविभूत्यै सुविदितः।
विचित्रं चित्रं[5] ते श्रुतिभिरवितर्क्यं मुनिवरैः
सदा ध्यातं युष्मच्चरणयुगलं नः सुखयतु।।6।।

त्वदीयापाङ्गेनावगतपुरुषार्थाः सुमनसो
निहत्य प्रत्यूहान्निखिलकृतसत्कर्मनिचयाः।
स्थिता युष्मत्पार्श्वे परमसुखसिद्धिं ह्युपगता
न ते भूयः स्वर्गेष्वपि जननमायान्त्यवशतः।।7।।

लसत्स्वर्णेलायां तरलिततरङ्गेक्षुजलधौ
मणिद्वीपे दिव्य[6]द्रुमनिकरकुञ्जेऽरुणरुचि।
कृपासिन्धो भव्यं किमपि विमलं धाम भवतो
विभाति प्राणेश प्रभवतु मुदेऽस्माकमिह तत्।।8।।

चतुर्द्वारोपेतं सकलसुखसंपत्तिसहितं
करं स्वर्णस्तम्भावलिविलसितं रत्नखचितम्।
लसद्भानोर्भाभिः सदृशमणिमालाभिरमल-
प्रभाभिर्भास्वद्यो [द्यद्] गृहमपि च मन्दं स्फुरति ते।।9।।
प्रवालस्तम्भाढ्ये वरकनकवस्त्रास्तरणके
लसन्नारीवृन्दे परिरचितबालव्यजनके।
लसच्छत्रोपान्ते विशदमणिपीठे प्रतिदिनं
भवन्तं भूतानामधिपमभिवन्देऽरुणतनुम्।।10।।
प्रतिद्वारस्था ये विपुलमतयस्तेऽनुसरिणो
महोदारा भक्तव्यसनविनिवारायुधधराः।
वदन्तस्त्वामेवं निजजनममुं पालय विभो
नमस्कुर्मस्तेभ्यस्तव विमलभक्तिं ददतु मे।।11।।
भवेयुर्मे प्रीत्यै शतधृतिमुखास्तेऽप्यनिमिषाः
प्रसन्नाः श्रीमन्तः सुभगवदनाश्चारुवपुषः।
विधाय त्वत्पूजां विमलबहुपूजोपकरणैः
स्तुवन्ति त्वामीशं सकलजनसौख्याय सततम्।।12।।
अनन्तब्रह्माण्डोद्वहनमुदरं भाति भवत-
स्ततो देवैर्गीतस्त्वमसि वर लम्बोदर इति।
गणानां तत्त्वानामधिपतिरतस्त्वं गणपति-
र्न चानर्था काचिज्जगति भवदाख्यातिरुदिता।।13।।
इदं येषामम्भः कनककलशेनामरगणै-
स्त्वदर्थं सद्भक्त्या विविधमनुना नीतमपि यत्।
अघौघं संहर्तुं तव सुतनुसङ्गात्सुरपते
सुतीर्थानां तेषामभवदमलं वारि सकलम्।।14।।
सुराधीशे भानूदयरुचिरकान्तौ त्वयि विभो
महच्छ्रीच्छन्दोमयवसनमाभाति नियतम्[7]।
तथापि त्वं भक्त्यार्पितवसनमादाय भगवन्
श[8]शीव प्रीणासि प्रणयितमिमं सेवकजनम्।।15।।

त्वदीयाङ्गे येषां मृगमदविलेपो मृगगणाः
पवित्रीभूतास्ते शुभगतिमियन्तस्त्ववशः।
समीरोऽभूद्युष्मच्चरणपरिचर्याचरणतो
जगत्प्राणस्तस्मा[9]त्तव चरणभक्तिर्भवतु मे।।16।।
कृपासिन्धो दिव्यैर्कुसुमनिचयैः कोमलतरैः
सुगन्धाढ्यैर्नित्यं रुचिररुचिभिः पूजितपदः।।
तथापि त्वं भक्त्यर्पितविमलदूर्वाङ्कुरदलैः
प्रसन्नस्तस्मान्नो त्वमिव सुरपूज्यस्त्वमसि मे।।17।।
कृपासिन्धो स्वामिन्विविधसुरभिद्रव्यसहितः
सुगन्धाढ्यो दिव्यः पुरुघृतसिताद्यैर्विरचितः।
सुराणां संस्तुत्यः परमसुखदस्ते प्रतिदिनं
पुरस्ताद्धूपोऽयं सुरवर भवन्तं सुखयतु।।18।।
धरित्री सत्पात्रं जलधिविमले स्नेहसहितं
सुमेरुः सद्वर्ति द्युमणिरपि यस्य द्युतिरिति।
अखण्डोऽयं दीपः सुखयति भवन्तं सुरपते
तथैवायं दीपः प्रवणरचितस्त्वां सुखयतु।।19।।
पुरस्ते यद्भक्तैर्व्युपहृतमिदं भक्ष्यममलं
दधि क्षीरं चाज्यं मधु लवणमिक्षोर्घनरसम्।।
सुमृष्टं संस्निग्धं विविधरसमास्वादसहितं
सितासिक्तं चाज्यं सुखयतु भवन्तं तदखिलम्।।20।।
रसालाख्यं द्राक्षाफलममृतकल्पं च कदली-
फलं तद्वज्जम्बूफलमपि तथान्यानि भवता।
फलानि स्वादूनि त्रिभुवनपते यानि कृपया
गृहीतानि श्रेयस्तव भजनशीले विदधतु।।21।।
इदं यत्ताम्बूलं त्रिभुवनपते हर्षजनकं
लवङ्गैलापूगीफलमृग[10]मदाद्यैर्विरचितम्।
त्वदर्थं चानीतं वदनरुचिकृत्सौख्यजनकं
त्वया भुक्तं भव्यं व्यसनविनिवाराय भवतु।।22।।

इदं गाङ्गं वारि त्रिभुवनमनोहारि विमलं
पवित्रं पावित्र्यं जनयति जनानामविरलम्।
मयानीतं भक्त्या वरकनककुम्भेन भगवँ-
स्त्वदर्थं पेयं तद्भवतु तव तुष्ट्यै प्रतिदिनम्।।23।।

भवत्पादाम्भोजे कमलकरवीरादिकुसुमैः
सदूर्वाबिल्वाम्राङ्कुरकनकपुष्पैर्विलसितम्।
समर्प्येमां पुष्पाञ्जलिमनुपमां देव भवतो
मुदे नित्यं सन्तु प्रणतय इमा मे विरचिताः।।24।।

रणत्तालं वीणामुरजमपि वेण्वादिकमिदं
गृहीत्वा या नार्यः कमलनयनाश्चारुवदनाः।
पुरस्ते कुर्वन्ति त्रिभुवनपते नृत्यमतुलं
नमस्कुर्मस्ताभ्यो वरद तव भक्तिं ददतु मे।।25।।

गलद्वेणीबन्धस्त्रवदमलगन्धाढ्यकुसुमा-
श्चलद्वस्त्रप्रान्तश्रमितभृकुटीलोलनयनाः।
क्वणत्काञ्च्यो हर्षात्स्थगितगतयश्चारुवदना-
स्त्वदीया नर्तक्यो मयि विमलभावं विदधताम्।।26।।

स्थिता युष्मत्पार्श्वे वरकनकदिव्याम्बरधरा
लसत्पीनस्निग्धस्तनजघनभाराश्च सुभगाः।
कृशोदर्यः श्यामास्तडित इव ता देववनिता
नमन्ति त्वामीशं तव विमलभक्तान्सुखयितुम्।।27।।

लसन्नीव्यो देव्यश्चिकुरनिकरान्सुन्दरतरा-
न्समाकुञ्च्यापीनस्तनयुगलमाच्छाद्य ललितम्।
त्वदीयास्तीव्राद्या नव परिमिताः शक्तय इमा
वहन्त्यस्ते पीठं मम हृदयपद्मे विदधतु।।28।।

सदानन्दं बिन्दुः कलयतु मदन्तः सुगुणतां
त्रिकोणं षट्कोणं षडरिविजयं ते वसुदलम्।
सुराणामैश्वर्यं नृपदलमिदं षोडशकला
त्रिवृत्तं वेदास्त्रस्त्रितयमपि सर्वार्थनिचयम्।।29।।

यदग्रं देवानां सुरभिरनुभागे सुवनिते
तयोः पार्श्वे पुत्रौ निधिरपि पुरो यस्य विपुलः।
यदग्रे गोधीशा विबुधनिकराः सायुधकरा
नमस्तस्मै तुभ्यं शरणद शरण्यं सुखय माम्।।30।।

त्वदग्रे सद्बिल्वीद्रुमतलनिवासातिमुदिती
रमाविष्णू एतौ सितजलजनीलाम्बुजनिभौ।
सरोजे[11] बिभ्राणौ सितवदनपीताम्बरधरौ
विभूत्यै मे स्यातां त्वदभिमुखमास्थाय सततम्।।31।।

सदोदारावेतौ वरद तव तौ दक्षिणरतौ
वटाधोवासीनौ वरकनककोद[12]ण्डसदृशौ।
सुराधीशौ नेत्रत्रितयविलसच्चारुवपुषौ
शिवेशावानन्दं विमलमनसा मे कलयताम्।।32।।

सुखासीनावेतौ त्वदनुवरबोधिद्रुमतले
सरोजे पुष्पेषून्धनुरपि दधानौ विजयिनौ।
त्रिलोकीदर्पघ्नौ रतिमदनदेवौ मम विभो
शिवायैव स्यातां वरकनकवैदूर्यवपुषौ।।33।।

कृपासिन्धोर्वामे वरकनकसिंहासनरतौ
प्रियङ्गुच्छायायां नवजलदनीलाम्बुजनिभौ।
विधातारौ देवौ सितवसनपीताम्बरधरौ
मयि प्रेमप्रेम्णावनिवनवराहौ कलयताम्।।34।।

स्थिता युष्मत्प्राश्र्वे वरदवर वैनायकगणाः
प्रमोदाद्याः सिद्ध्यष्टकसहितषट्कोणनिलयाः।
त्वदीयेभ्यो नृभ्यः सकलसुखमानन्दमतुलं
वहन्तस्ते नित्यं तव चरणभक्तिं ददतु मे।।35।।

क्व चाहं ते मायागुणगणसमुद्भासितवपुः
क्व च त्वं मायेशो निरवधिसुखस्यैकशरणम्।
तथापि त्वं दीनोद्धरणबिरुदोऽसीत्यविरलं
सुखं धत्से दीने मयि भजनहीनेऽतिकृपया।।36।।

वदन्ति त्वामाद्यं परमपुरुषं वेदविविदो
गुणातीतं केचित्सगुणमपरे भक्तिरसिकाः।
परं तत्त्वं कस्ते कथयितुमिह स्यात्त्रिभुवने
यतो जातोदारं जयति तव सद्धाम विमलम्।।37।।

तवेदं रूपं चेद्यदि न हि भवेद्भक्तिजनकं
तदासक्तः को वा भवति भजने किंचिदपि ते।
कृपासिन्धो दिव्यान्यनुपमसरूपाणि भगव-
न्नतस्त्वं भक्तानामनुपमसुखार्थं प्रकुरुषे।।38।।

हृदिस्थं त्वां केचिद्विपुलमतयो लब्धसुदृशो
यजन्त्यन्ये मूर्ध्नि स्थितमजमनन्तामृतरसम्।
यथानन्दस्वादानुभवमपि जानन्ति भगवँ-
स्तथा युष्मत्सेवामुदितमनसो भक्तिरसिकाः।।39।।

यथा हि काश्यां ते वसति सकलं वस्तु विमलं
तथैवेदं विश्वं त्वयि महति रूपे सुविमलम्।
तवाद्यं ते माध्यं तव निरवसानं सुरपते
प्रवक्तुं कः शक्तः प्रभवति नरो वा नरपतिः।।40।।

अनन्तास्ते लीला ललितवपुषा या विरचिताः
कथं ज्ञातुं शक्या वरद मनुजैरल्पनिगमैः।
अनन्तोऽनेकास्यैरनुदिनमिमास्ते गुणगणा-
न्वदन्वारंवारं तदपि तु न वारं स लभते।।41।।

त्वमीश त्वं विष्णुस्त्वमसि च विरिञ्चिः सुरपते
त्वमिन्द्रोऽर्को वायुस्त्वमसि परमं दैवतमपि।
इदं त्वत्तो जातं जगदखिलमुद्भाति भगवन्-
यतस्त्वं मायायास्त्रिगुणजनिताया जनयिता।।42।।

यदा जातः पद्मासनवदनतो जृम्भणवशा-
द्विभो सिन्दूरास्यः सुरपतिरिपुर्दैत्यगणपः।
अजेयोऽन्यै रूपैरिति सपदि संहत्य भवता
करीन्द्रास्यं धृत्वा निजजनमुदेऽसौ विनिहतः।।43।।

कृपासिन्धो कश्चिद्वदति यदि पुंसामपि पुर-
स्तदैवास्मिँल्लोके सपदि लभते सोऽर्थमखिलम्।
भवद्द्वारिस्थोऽहं मयि कुरु कृपामित्यनुदिनं
वदाम्युच्चैः स्वामिन्नुचितमिदमस्ति त्वयि तु किम्।।44।।
प्रभो पूर्वं प्रेम्णा वरद वरदं तेन भवता
लिखित्वा व्यासायार्पितमिद(ह) महाभारतमिदम्।
न तच्चित्रं यत्ते श्वसितमिदमस्ति श्रुतिकुलं
त्वदिच्छाचिच्छाक्ति(क्ती) रचयति जगज्जालमखिलम्।।45।।
त्वदीयं बीजं यो भजति सततं भक्तिसहितः
प्रभो तीर्थान्सर्वान्भवदनुभवादाशु लभते।
अतः सर्वे युष्मद्विमलमनवः कल्पतरवो
वरिष्ठाः संतुष्टाः सकलसुखदाः सन्ति भजताम्।।46।।
अयि प्राणेशस्त्वं प्रणयिनि मयि प्रेमसहितं
कृपापाङ्गालोकं विरचय विभोऽनन्तमहिमन्।
यथा भूयो भूयो भवदमलभक्तिं विरचय-
न्कृतार्थस्तस्यां तत्त्वरितमनुशाधि त्वमिह माम्।।47।।
अपूपान् यो भक्त्या मृदुतरमधुस्वादुसहिता-
ञ्जुहोत्यग्नावब्दं शतपरिमितांस्त्वष्टसहितान्।
चतुर्थ्यामर्थार्थो धनपतिरिवाढ्यः स भवति
प्रभो नैतच्चित्रं तव करुणया किं न भवति।।48।।
जलक्रीडां कर्तुं निगमजलधौ संविहरतां(ता)
दयासिन्धोश्छन्दोमयविमलसुश्लोककणिका।
त्वया क्षिप्ता यस्मिन्मयि विनयिनी प्रेमसहिता
जनानां सानन्दं जनयतु सदानन्दलहरी।।49।।
मायाकारि स्वामिँस्तव वरदमूर्तेर्भगवतः
कृपातः कापीयं वचनरचनाभिः स्तुतिरिह।
त्वमङ्गीकुर्वेनामपि च सततं प्रीतिमनया
यतो लोकः स्वान्तं सुखयति शिशूनां कलरवैः।।50।।

इति श्रीब्रह्मादिस्तुतवरदमूर्तेः स्तुतिमिमां
शुभां गोपीनाथार्पितविमलपद्यां च ललिताम्।
पठेद्यो वै भक्त्या स भवति यशोधर्मधनभाक्
कृपासिन्धौ तुष्टे किमपि न भवेद्‌दुर्लभमिति।।51।।
स्तुतिस्त्वेषा विश्वेश्वरनगर्यां निवसता
शरेभागेन्द्वब्दे विलसति विभो विक्रमशकात्।
मधौ मासे शुक्लेऽभवदमलतिथ्यां विरचिता
मया युष्मत्प्रीत्यै सुखयतु सदास्माञ्छिखरिणी।।52।।

।। इति श्रीगणेशलहरी [स्तोत्रं] संपूर्णम्।।

।। शुभं भवतु।।

लिखितं(ता) नवीनपुरमध्ये भटनन्दकेश्वरेणैषा। ।। श्रीः।।

FOOTNOTES

Paper published in Journal of the Oriental Institute, Baroda, Vol. 39. Nos. 1-2, Sept.-Dec., 1989 Issue, pp. 83-95.

1. *New Catalogus Catalogorum*, University of Madras, Vol. V, 1969, p.280, Vol.1, 1949, p.61, Vol. VI, 1971, pp.160-165.
2. Gadgil, Amarendra: *Gaṇeśakośa*, Shriganeshkosh Mandal, Pune, Second ed., 1968, p. 470.
3. *Ibid.*, p. 124.
4. Krishnamachariar, M. : *History of Classical Sanskrit Literature*, Motilal Banarasidass, Delhi, Third ed., 1974.
5. चित्रं in marg.
6. Before corr. °च्यु
7. before corr. °ताम्
8. before corr. °री°
9. °स्मा° in marg.
10. before correction °द°
11. after correction °ज°
12. before correction °दि°

II

SAUBHĀGYALAHARĪ OF *ŚAṄKARASOMANĀTHA*— A LITTLE-KNOWN *LAHARĪ-KĀVYA*

Introductory

The Sanskrit Literature has a rich and varied treasure of several kinds of *Kāvyas*, poetic compositions. Besides the *Mahākāvyas* and *Khaṇḍakāvyas*, written by the greatest poets of the galaxy of Sanskrit Literature, there are also other smaller poetic compositions, containing short but good specimens of poetry. *Stotras*, written in praise of favourite deities, are also such poems that are replete with devotional sentiments. Among several varieties of such devotional songs or *stotras,* those known as *Laharīkāvyas* are also in great number. The *Saundaryalaharī* of Śaṅkarācārya and the *Gaṅgālaharī* of Jagannātha Paṇḍita are the most famous among them. In the present paper, an attempt is made to introduce the *Laharīkāvya*, entitled *Saubhāgyalaharī*, a rare and quite little-known one, composed by a scholar, Śaṅkarasomanātha of 1644 A.D.

A Rare work

Several *stotra*-works have been published in different *stotra*-collections like the *Stotārṇava,* the *Stotraratnākara* etc. But the present *Laharīkāvya* is not found in them. In the *Catalogus Catalogorum*,[1] there is mention of a *stotra*, named *Saubhāgyalaharī,* but it is a different work, composed by the poet Gopālakṛṣṇa, who is evidently quite different from the author of the work under consideration. Similarly,

Prof. Krishnamachariar[2] also refers to the same *Kāvya*, which is mentioned by Aufrecht in his Catalogue. The present work of Śaṅkarasomanātha has not been taken notice of by these scholars. Thus it is very rare and little-known *stotra*-work, composed by a forgotten poet of Sanskrit literature, namely Śaṅkarasomanātha.

Two Mss. in the Oriental Institute

The *Saubhāgyalaharī* of Śaṅkarasomanātha is available in two Mss. of the Oriental Institute, Baroda (with Acc. Nos. 5099 and 7153), of which the Ms. No. 5099 contains the work in its incomplete form, while fortunately the other Ms. No. 7153 has preserved it in its complete form. But the Mss. are so much corrupt that it is very difficult to edit the said work on the basis of these available Mss. However, we get a very good idea about the entire *stotra* from them.

Both the Mss. have recorded in the colophon that it is a work called *Saubhāgyalaharī*, composed by Śaṅkarasomanātha. The Ms. No. 5099 has totally eleven folios having eight lines on each page with 41 letters to a line. Written on countrymade paper of 23 cms. × 10 cms. size, the Ms. is fairly readable, owing to its good handwriting. The first folio contains *Kālyaṣṭaka* of Viṣṇu. The second one is missing. Only the folios from 3 to 11 are available. The third folio begins the *stotra* from '*Śivacayamudagrā dadatu me*' in 13d. Moreover, the portion of the *stotra* from 47^b to 55^b is also missing. The Ms. has preserved the work in a very corrupt and incomplete form.

The other Ms. No. 7153 contains the work in its complete form. It also has totally eleven folios, with about 12 lines on each page and about 29 letters to each line. Written on country-made paper of 24 cm × 14 cms. size, the Ms. is readable, but the hand writing is not good. It is also very corrupt at several places. But we get the complete idea of the contents of the *stotra* from this Ms. From the post-colophon entries, we get some information about the scribe and the date of copying the Ms. The name of the scribe seems to be Kāmeśvara. He has written this Ms. on eleventh day in the dark fortnight of the month of *Āśvina* in *Vikrama Saṁvat* 1798 (i.e. 1742 A.D.).[3] Thus this is a complete and dated manuscript of the work, under consideration.

Author

As is evident from the last verse (No. 101) of the *Stotra*[4] the author of the *stotra, Saubhāgyalaharī* is Śaṅkara, the son of Somanātha. But the colophon records that *Paṇḍita* i.e. Scholar Śaṅkarasomanātha, is servant at the feet of Śaṅkarī (i.e. Goddess) and is an ornament to the entire family of poets.[5] Thus the poet was not only a scholar and devout worshipper of Goddess, but was also quite well-versed in the field of poetry, obtainng highest distincitons and reputation among the assembly of poets.

In the last verse (101), the author also refers to the date of composition of this *stotra,* which is 1556 (whether it is *Śaka* or *Saṁvat* is not explicitly mentioned.[6] It may be either 1566+78=1644 A.D. or 1566-56=1510 A.D.). It was perhaps composed at the occasion of a great sacrifice in Kāśī, hosted by Prabhākara.[7]

Regarding his place of residence, we get some information in the said verse (101)[8] and in verse (46)[9]. From the verse No. 46, it seems that he was a Mahārāṣṭrian, as he refers to himself as a *Mahārāṣṭraśiśu.* Moreover, in verse No. 101, he refers to Vijayapura, which may be present Vijāpur[10]. In this light, we may again consider the point about the date of the poet. If he is belived to be a Mahārāṣṭ rian, the reference to the date in verse No. 101, must be to *Śaka* era and not the *Vikrama Saṁvat,* as *Śaka* era is generally followed by the Mahārāṣṭrians. Hence the date of the author must be 1644 A.D. from this point of view. Thus the poet was probably the contemporary of Jagannātha Paṇḍita, whose literary activity (according to Mm. P.V.Kane)[11] lies between 1620 A.D. and 1660 A.D.

About his ability and the efficiency of composition of poetry, the poet humbly and politely implores that the Goddess should forgive him for the faults and defects, just as the prattling of the child rejoices others or just as a master listens the indistinct words of a parrot with great curiosity, after training it before-hand.[12] Moreover, it is the wish of the Goddess Herself that makes him talk in Her praise.[13]

The *Stotra*—General Remarks

This *stotra* has totally 101 verses, written in the *Śikhariṇī* metre (which is mostly found in the *Laharīkāvyas*). In this *stotra*, the poet has eulogised his favourite deity—the Mother Goddess. Therefore, the entire *stotra* abounds in devotional sentiment, fanciful imaginations and figures of speech.[14] The poet has good mastery over prosody, grammar and the language, in the absence of which it is impossible to compose such a long *stotra* of 101 verses. However, some verses are defective from the point of view of grammar and metre.[15] The Mss. are so corrupt that sometimes it is very difficult to decide, whether these are grammatical irreguliarities or scribal errors only. There is great influence of the *Saundarya-laharī* of Śaṅkarācārya, as there are verses, having similarity in words, phrases and ideas.[16]

Thus the *Saubhāgyalaharī* is a rare, but an interesting and important *stotra,* written by a poet of 17th century. The present research paper is written with a view to introducing this rare *stotra*-work to the world of scholars. It is an attempt to salvage the said *stotra,* from going into complele oblivion and bringing to light the said contribution of the poet to Sanskrit literature in general and to the *Laharīkāvyas* in particular.

FOOTNOTES

Paper published in Journal of the Oriental Institute, Baroda, Vol. 40, Nos. 1-2, Sept-Dec., 1990 Issue, pp. 83-87.

Paper read at the 16th Annual conference of Gujarat State Uni. and College Sk. Teachers' Association, held at Shamalaji 27-29 March 1991.

1. Aufrecht, Theodor : *Catalogus Catalogorum*, Franz steiner verlag, GMBH, Wiesbaden, 1962, Part I, p. 738.
2. Krishnamachariar, M. : *History of Classical Sanskrit Literature*, Motilal Banarasidass, Delhi, Third ed., 1974, p. 518, fn. 5.
3. संवत् १७९८ वर्षे आश्विनमासे कृष्णपक्षे ११। लिखितं व्र. कामेश्वरः। श्रीः।।
4. सुतः सोमेशस्य प्रथितकमठाणद्विजपते–
   रसाङ्गेषूर्व्यब्दे सविजयपुरे शङ्करसुधीः।
   महः काश्यां प्राभाकरमलघुलब्धाशुफलदां
   नभस्यास्थानङ्गेऽरचयदिह सौभाग्यलहरीम्।।101।।
5. इति श्रीमत्सकलकविकुलललामशङ्करीचरणकिङ्करीभूतशङ्करसोमनाथपण्डितविरचितः सौभाग्यलहरीस्तवः समाप्तः।।
6. Cf. fn. 4 above
7. *Ibid.*
8. *Ibid.*
9. तदीयाङ्के शङ्के हरगृहिणि पङ्केरुहदृशां
   जनीनां साध्वीनां जननि खनिरस्तीति निभृतम्।
   अदः स्मारादारात्सकृदपि महाराष्ट्रशिशुना–
   प्यमत्तं स्त्रीरत्नं सपदि समवाप्यङ्कविषये।।46।।
10. Cf. fn. 4; Joshi, Mahadev Shastri : *Bhāratīya Saṁskṛtikośa*, Poona, 1974, See P. 670 *Vijāpura*.
11. Kane P.V.: *History of Sanskrit Poetics*, Bombay, 1951, p. 312.
12. हरीशाजस्तुत्ये मम कृतिमिमां संशृणु यतः
    प्रसूः श्राव्यं हित्वा शिशुकलपनैर्हर्षतितमाम्।
    स्वयं संशिक्ष्याथ प्रभव इह सत्पञ्जरशुकं
    तदीयामस्पष्टां गिरमपि हि शृण्वन्ति कुतुकात्।।100।।
13. अविद्यापद्यायां त्रिजगदनवद्याङ्गि सकलं
    परिभ्रान्तं तत्त्वं तव किमपि नो वेत्ति जननि।
    तथापि त्वत्पादाम्बुजरतिरियं मे प्रतिलवं
    त्वदिच्छातः स्तोतुं मुखरयति दोषो न हि मयि।।2।।
14. गिरो नान्दीपाठः करणचयकौशीलवगणं
    नटोऽहं मच्चित्तं विरचयति वैदुष्यककृतिः।

नटी बुद्धिर्मेता (में सा) त्वमयुगदृशा नाटकमिषाद्
अहं यद्यत्कुर्वे तदखिलमुमे तेऽस्तु यजनम्।।6।।
त्वदीयं वन्देऽहं चरणयुगलं यत्र गिरिजे
सरस्वत्याच्छन्ना वसति नु सदालक्तकमिषात्।
यतस्त्वत्पादाब्जागतजलपिपासोरपि मुखात्
सगद्या सत्पद्या व्रजति नवविद्याजलनदी।।28।।
भवत्सेवा नौका भवति भवती नाविकगुरु-
स्तथा सत्क्षेपिण्यौ जननि भवदाजानुचरणौ।
ययोर्ध्यानादेव प्रबलमपि संसारजलधिं
जनस्तीर्त्वा गच्छत्यपि च शिवसायुज्यपदवीम्।।42।।
गले तिस्रो रेखास्तव ननु महेशानमहिले
सदा नः कल्याणं प्रतनु कलयन्तां जननि ताः।
वपुष्मन्तो वेदास्त्रय इह वसन्तीति कलये
त्वदाज्ञां ब्रह्माद्या दधति हि शिरोभिर्यदनिशम्।।68।।
तमस्ते धम्मिल्ले रविरपि च सीमन्तफलके
मुखे चन्द्रो मातस्त्वदधरदले लोहिततनुः।
दृशांपाते सौम्यो वचसि गुरुकाव्यौ ग्रहमयि
स्मिते मन्दः सा त्वं भव मयि सदा सद्ग्रहवती।।96।।

15. e.g. तृतीया ते दृष्टिः परमशिवकल्याणकरि सा। verse 79.
भ्राती वन्दे मातस्तव सुचिरमाकाशकुहरम्। verse 80.

6

सौभाग्यलहरी	सौन्दर्यलहरी
1 अहं यद्यत्कुर्वे तदखिलमुमे तेऽस्तु यजनम्। —6	सपर्यापर्यायस्तव भवतु यन्मे विलसितम्। —27
2 भयेभ्यः संत्रातुं फलमपि च दातुं बहुविधम्। —38	भयात्त्रातुं दातुं फलमपि च वाञ्छासमधिकम्। —4
3 अदः स्मारादारात्सकृदपि महाराष्ट्रशिशुना। —46	दयावत्या दत्तं द्रविडशिशुरास्वाद्य तव यत्। —75
4 शिवस्त्वं जीवस्त्वं क्षितिमुखमहत्तत्त्वनिवह- स्त्वमेव त्वं चेतः प्रभृतिकरणं त्वं हि सकलम्।— 23	मनस्त्वं व्योम त्वं मरुदसि मरुत्सारथिरसि त्वमापस्त्वं भूमिस्त्वपि परिणतायां न हि परम्। —35
5. नितम्बे पृथ्वी त्वं मनसि च दयार्द्रा जलमयिं महो रूपा भाले समदृशि जगत्प्राणसुभगा। वियन्मध्ये चेत्त्वं जननि सकलं तत्त्वमसि सा मम स्वान्ते शान्ते परमशिवकान्ते वस सदा।। —94	अराला केशेषु प्रकृतिसरला मन्दहसिते शिरीषाभा चित्ते दृषदिव कठोरा कुचतटे। भृशं तन्वी मध्ये पृथुरुरसिजारोहविषये जगत्त्रातुं शम्भोर्जयति करुणा काचिदरुणा।। —92

Acharya, Ram Narayan : *Saundaralaharī of Śaṅkarācārya*, Nirnaya-sagar Press, Bombay, 1961.

III

THE *RUKMIṆĪSVAYAMVARAM OF PT. JAGANNATH PADESHASTRI* A UNIQUE METRICAL COMPOSITION*

Introductory :

Baroda has contributed a lot to the Modern Sanskit Literature. It has obtained the reputation as '*Choṭī-kāśī*' i.e., small Kāśī, on account of the great scholarship exhibited in different lores by its scholars. Among such eminent Paṇḍitas, the names of Pt. Badarīnātha Śāstrī, Pt. Maṇiśaṅkara Upādhyāya and Pt. Śrīdhara Śāstri Pade are at the top due to their expertise in the varied fields of knowledge. The late Pt. Jagannātha Śrīdhara Padeśāstrī is also one of such versatile and profound erudites of Baroda. His contribution to the Modern Sanskrit Literature deserves to be taken notice of. Here in this paper, an attempt is made to present the details about his biography, scholarship, contribution and especially his unique metrical composition i.e., the *Rukmiṇīsvayaṁvaram*, composed by the scholar during his college days i.e., in his teenage.

Biography :

This great Indologist, who also possessed the uncommon poetic genius was born in Vadodara on the 26th April 1912, in the family of well-known traditional scholars. In view of their traditional study of the Vedic texts in the form of '*Padapāṭha*', the family came to be traditionally known as 'Padapāṭhaka' or Padepāṭhaka' and later on simply as 'Pade' or even more popularly known as Padeśāstrī. The family ancestors firstly came from Pohe-gaon in Ahmednagar district of Maharashtra to Narayanagaon near Pune and from there to Vadodara. The father of Jagannātha Padeśāstrī, *Vedaśāstra-sampanna* Pt. Śrīdharaśāstrī Pade was also a versatile scholar, well-versed in different fields like the *Vedas,* the *Smṛtis, Dharmaśāstra, Āyurveda, Jyotiṣa, Vyākaraṇa* and *Saṅgīta.* He was *adhyāpaka* (a teacher) in both the then *Rajakīya Saṁskṛta Pāṭhaśālā* and *Saṅgītaśālā*. He was a disciple of Pt. Rajaram Shastri Topale and had obtained great distinctions of the '*Vaiyyākarāṇa-Kesarī*' and the '*Vaidyapañcānana*'. The mother of him was Kashibai and his maternal uncle Bhikaji Rahurkar also was famous for his practice in Ayurvedic medicine.

Education :

Thus being brought up in the atmosphere of traditional scholarship Pt. Jagannath Padeshastri also obtained right from his childhood traditional training in all the different fields. He possessed the expertise in the *YajurvedaSaṁhitā,* the *Vedāṅgas, Vyākaraṇa, Dharmaśāstra, Jyotiṣaśāstra, Āyur-veda, Saṅgīta. Darśanaśāstra* and *Sāhitya.* He also took active part in the *'Vāda'*debates arranged by the Sanskrit Vidvat-sabha, Vadodara and exhibited his scholarship in different fields therein.

Besides the traditional knowledge, it is an uncommon feature that such a versatile *Paṇḍita* had training and education in the Modern type of educational system also. After passing the Matriculation examination, he joined the Baroda College and took his degree of B.A. (with Skt. principal) in 1937 and M.A.(with grammar as a special *Śāstra*) in 1939 from the University of Bombay. He secured the S.R. Bhandarkar Prize of Bombay University for obtaining the highest number of marks at M.A. in the subject of the Sanskrit Grammar.

Service :

As Pt. Padeshastri was a pious devotee of Rāma and an ardent follower of Vedic culture, he did not wish to leave Vadodara (where he has a Rāma-temple in his house), and go out of Vadodara for service. Hence, he had to start his career in 1940 as a clerk in the Gaekwar Baroda State Railways and then in 1941, he joined the State Police Department. During these days, the Oriental Institute was also housed in the premises of the Kothi-building, just neighbouring the Police Department. Dr. Benoytosh Bhattacharya, the then Director of the Oriental Institute, could properly recognise the telents and scholarship of Pt. Jagannath Padeshastri and got him tansfered first to the Oriental Institute as a Superintendent of the Printed Section in 1944. In 1952, he was promoted to the position of the Superintendent of the Manuscript Section, where he could make a meticulous and thorough study of the rare books and Mss. and enrich himself more with the research aptitude. In 1953, he was recognised as a Post-graduate Teacher in Sanskrit and in 1957, he was awarded the rare honour of recognition of a Guiding Teacher for researches in all *Śāstras* (though he himself did not have a Ph.D. Degree). From 1958, he was given the designation as a Research Officer, the position which he adorned till his retirement in 1973. He left his mortal body on the 9th December 1982.

His contribution :

During his tenure in the Oriental Institute, he edited four important works on the basis of very rare and moth-eaten Mss.

1. *TĀBŪLAMAÑJARĪ* : This was based upon a single, rare and moth-eaten manuscript and was published as M.S. University of Baroda Oriental Series No.1 in 1957. It is a model of Critical Edition of ancient texts. This work is relating to the eating, preparation and ingredients of *Tāmbūla*.

2. *VĪṆĀLAKṢAṆAM AND VĪṆĀPRAPĀṬHAKAḤ* : These two small works were based upon rare and single manuscripts. These were published in the world-famous Gaekwad's Orinetal Series as No.131 in 1959. These contain the texts regarding playing of *Vīṇā*.

3. *NĀṬYAŚĀSTRAM OF BHARATA* : (with the *Abhinavabhāratī* commentary of Abhinavagupta) Vol. IV. This was published as Gaekwad's Oriental Series No. 145 in 1964.

4. *PRAŚNAVIDYĀ OF BĀDARĀYAṆA*: (with the commentary of Utpala). This was also based upon a very rare manuscript and was published as the M.S. University Oriental Series No.10 in 1972. This is evidently a work on *Jyotiṣa*.

Thus he had edited these works relating to four different *Śāstras*, i.e., *Āyurveda*, *Saṅgīta, Nāṭyaśāstra and Jyotiṣa*.

5. *DHARME SARVAṀ PRATIṢṬHITAM* : His long scholarly essay of about 29 articles in Sanskrit was published serially in a monthly magazine '*Sūryodaya*' of Varanasi, (1968-1973). This incorporated his own thesis regarding *Dharma-vāda* to be the only path, ever-sustaining the entire world and envisaging the *Samanvaya*-synthesis of both the *Mīmāṁsās—Pūrva* and *Uttara*. This is published in a book form by Bharatiya Kala Prakashan, Delhi, 2000.

6. Besides the above works, he has written more than 35 (besides 29 in Sanskrit, mentioned above) research papers in different languages i.e., Sanskrit, Gujarati, Marathi and English etc.

7. *RUKMIṆĪSVAYAṀVARAM* : An excellent piece of Modern Sanskrit Poetry, containing sixtysix verses in sixtysix different metres (each verse composed in different metres), with the name of that particular metre, (interwoven in the verse) was written by him during his college days. It was

serially published in the then Baroda College Magazine during 1933 to 1937.

8. His numerous reviews of Books on Indology, published in the Journal of the Oriental Institute are also full of research outlook and critical remarks.

9. His scholarly lectures on the *Bhagavadgītā*, explaining the *Pada* and *Padārtha* (entity indicated by the *pada*), exhibiting his objective approach to the text, were attended by a great number of scholars—professors and seekers of truth-from Baroda. Nearly for seven years, he delivered lectures on every Saturday for one hour, in the Rāma-temple at his residence.

10. He has guided scholars for their Ph.D., Post-Doctoral & other researches. He was in fact a living encyclopaedia of all *Śāstras*. Prof. George Cardona (Professor of Linguistics, University of Pensylvania, Philadelphia) has had the fortune to learn the basic Sanskrit grammar at his feet. Prof. Cardona has dedicated one of his volumes on Pāṇini to Pt. Jagannath Padeshastri. He has also made great social service by helping the needy and the oppressed. He would prepare horoscopes and guide people free of charge at large with his foresighted prognostications, which proved accurate. He also served the diseased people by giving the Ayurvedic medicines free of charge. The present writer has had the great fortune of being brought up in his family from his early childhood, due to loss of his father at the early infancy. It is with his able guidance and constant encouragement that the present writer could complete his Ph.D. thesis within the stipulated period.

Present Poem—*Rukmiṇīsvayaṁvaram*

As is clear from the title itself, the present poem composed by Pt. Jagannātha Śrīdhara Padeśāstrī is small modern poem of sixtysix verses, describing the Pauranic

Legend of marriage of Rukmiṅī with the Lord, Śrīkṛṣṇa. Rukmiṇī was a daughter of Bhīṣmaka of Vidarbha. She was betroded by her father to Śiśupāla, but she secretly loved Śrīkṛṣṇa and sent a letter, praying him to take her away. Kṛṣṇa with Balarāṃa came and snatched her off, after having defeated her brother in battle. She bore to Kṛṣṇa, a son named Pradyumna. This is the Pauranic Legend.

After describing the beautiful form of Lord Śrīkṛṣṇa, possessing garland *(sragdharā)* in the first verse, the poet begins the legend by first delineating the greatness of the king, Bhīṣmaka of Kundinpur, the city, the capital of Vidharbhas. He was a formidable king like the thunderbolt of Indra *(upendravajrāyudhabhīmavīryaḥ)*. He had a daughter, well-known as Rukmiṇī and five great sons, who were powerful like the thunderbot of Indra (*devendravajrāyudhadehasārāḥ*). One of them was Rukmī, who was an enemy of Kṛṣṇa and was very haughty. Then the poet has devoted about seven verses to describing the beauty of Rukmiṇī in ascending order starting from the feet upto her hair on the head (6 to 12). The king became anxious about her marriage as to which virtuous king she was to be given in marriage. He having respected and worshipped the brahmins as per the procedure of *Śruti* and *Smṛti*, implored them gladly to find out an appropriate match for her.

The brahmins immediately opined that Śrīkṛṣṇa alone to be such an appropriate *vara* (bridegroom) for her. Then they first describe the city Dvarka and praise the virtues of the lord Śrīkṛṣṇa. The Brahmins then went home and king was very happy on listening to them. He thought Śrīkṛṣṇa to be the most proper *vara* (bridegroom) for Rukmiṇī. But her brother Rukmī was against this, which was a great obstacle in this good cause. Rukmiṇī was dejected on hearing the desire of her brother in this resepect. So she sent a brahmin to Dvarka with a letter addressed to Śrīkṛṣṇa.

The Brahmin went to Dvarka and saw the magnanimity of the city of Dvarka. The Brahmin went to Śrīkṛṣṇa and was greeted and respected warmly by Śrīkṛṣṇa. Śrīkṛṣṇa asked him about his well-being and whereabouts. At this occasion, the Brahmin talked about the daughter of Bhīmasena namely Rukmiṇī and gave him the letter sent by her. Śrīkṛṣṇa went through the letter, message of which is related in the following seven verses. The main import of which is—

मन्दाक्रान्तां त्वयि विगणय मां नाथ गाढं सतृष्णाम्।

and suggests him to choose her by the *āsura* form of marriage. The messenger Brahmin also requested lord Śrīkṛṣṇa to go to Kundinpur very urgently. Lord Śrīkṛṣṇa replied him positively and started with him on his chariot and entered the city on an auspicious day. As per the wish of his son, the king arranged the auspicious marriage of Rukmiṇī with the Caidya king, Śiśupāla, but Rukmiṇī was engrossed in the thoughts of Śrīkṛṣṇa alone:

तरला द्विजस्य वीक्षणे सरला भुजंगसङ्गता।
पतिता विचारसागरे महिला मुकुन्दलालसा।।

There were evil omens, when the son of Damaghoṣa (i.e. Śiśupāla) arrived the city. Rukmiṇī also knew that Śrīkṛṣṇa had also entered Kundinpur very silently like a snake. She gave a jewel as a gift to the Brahmin, who carried her message to Śrīkṛṣṇa.

Balarāma also followed Śrīkṛṣṇa along with his soldiers. The king worshipped them both, who had come to his city. Rukmiṇī went to the temple of Goddess, Durgā and praised her with hope that "*Kṛṣṇo bhūyān mama patiḥ.*" when she was coming out of that temple, Kṛṣṇa immediately carried her off, after conquering the troop of soldiers, attending her. But the son of king became very angry and obstructed him with his army. But Śrīkṛṣṇa conquered him with his arrows and bound him. Buton the request of Rumiṇī, he was released by Śrīkṛṣṇa. Then Śrīkṛṣṇa and Rukmiṇi went to their capital in a very happy mood.

Evaluation :

Thus here we find the Pauranic narrative in the composition beginning from the description of the king Bhīṣmaka, his daughter Rukmiṇī, Sending of message by her to Śrīkṛṣṇa and ultimately, Śrīkṛṣṇa conquering the battle and carrying her away and marrying her in *āsura* form of marriage. This episode of her *svayaṁvara* is depicted in these sixtysix verses. Though there is no significant diversion from the Pauranic account, the peculiarity lies in its presentation in the poetic form. Besides the usual poetic embelishments of easy-flowing language and the use of a variety of figures of speech, the poet has most significantly utilized the sixty six different metres in the sixty-six different verses, each verse, incorporating the name of that respective metre, appropriately interwoven in the composition. The sixty-six metres, utilized in sixtysix verses are *Sragdharā, Pṛthivī, Upendravajrā, Indravajrā, Rukmavatī, Praharṣiṇī, Śālinī, Madhyakṣāmā, Mañjubhāṣiṇī, Mandākinī, Mālati, Gajagati, Vasantatilakā, Rucirā, Pramāṇikā, Śārdūlavikrīḍita, Svāgata, Vilokitā, Samānikā, Vidyunmālā, Pramitākṣarā, Tāmarasā, Vaiśvadevī, Maṇi-mālā, Sragviṇī, Vaṁśastanita, Jaladharamālā, Tvaritagati, Maṇimadhyā, Paṅkti, Kanyā, Somarājī, Drutavilambitam, Madhumatī, Madalekhā, Vidyullekhā, Anuṣṭubh, Tanu-madhyā, Śaśivadanā, Mattā, Śikhariṇī, Hariṇī, Bhrama-ravilasitam, Mandākrāntā, Sarasī, Aparājitā, Nandanā, Mañjarī, Rathoddhatā, Candravartmā, Upajāti, Kalahaṁsā, Jaloddhatagati, Mattamayūrī, Māṇavakam, Bhujaṅgaśiśubhṛtā, Bhujaṅga-saṅgatā, Dodhaka, Toṭaka, Bhujaṅgaprayāta, Kṣamā, Sambādhā, Praharaṇakalikā, Vāsantī, Tṛṇaka* and *Mālinī.*

This not only exhibits his mastery over the prosody but also his scholarship in Sanskrit language and the Pauranic literature at his teenage. The prevailing sentiment is *Śṛṅgāra* but is not much developed as having very little scope in the small narrative. There is no doubt *Kāvyacamatkṛti, Ramaṇīyārtha, Lalitapadavinnyāsa* etc. in great abundance. The poet was well-versed in grammar even in his teen-age and had traditional training in grammar from his father, who was also a versatile scholar. Hence there is no grammatical or meterical defect in the poem. There is great influence of Kālidāsa's style on the poet as he himself has suggested in one of his verses, composed in another context -

भवनीश्रीकण्ठप्रबलपरिचर्यानवफला
महाकाव्याभ्यासाल्ललितपदविन्यासुसुभगा।
स्मृतिश्रेयोवादाकलितसुरवाग्रम्यविभवा
कृतिर्जागन्नाथी जयति विबुधामोदजनका।।

The poet has very nicely decorated the poem with the use of various *Śabdālaṅkāras* and *Arthālaṅkāras* like *Anuprāsa, Yamaka, Upamā, Utprekṣā, Rūpaka, Vyatireka, Atiśayokti, Bhrāntimān, Ullekha, Annyonya* etc. The description of Rukmiṇī is made in ascending order (*ārohakrama*) i.e. *Pādadikeśānta* and not in the descending order (*avarohakarama*) i.e. *keśādipādānta* (as in the description of the Goddess in the *Saundaryalaharī*). He has made use of both the forms of words, as per the need of the metre like *Dhariṇī/Dharaṇi, Pṛthivī/Pṛthvi, Avanī/Avani, Bhujaga/Bhujaṅga-* all being grammatically correct. The word *Patra* or *Patrikā* is used in the sense of a letter (in Marathi, a letter is called *Patra*). On the whole, the lotus is the most favourite *Upamāna* of the poet, which is met with in most of the verses of the poem. The entire poem is printed herewith for the benefit of scholars, interested in Modern Sanskrit Literature.

The poem deserves to be taken notice of as a unique specimen of metrical composition and an outstanding contribution of a scholar from Baroda to Modern Sanskrit Literature.

।। रुक्मिणीस्वयंवरम् ।।

कवि :— ज० श्री० पदेशास्त्री०, वटपत्तनम्

1

वर्षानीलाभ्रमालारुचिभरनिवहोत्सेकसंहारयित्री
वीणामाधुर्यभिन्नस्वरमुखमुरलीमूर्च्छनामुन्नयन्ती।
वृत्तालङ्काररत्नद्युतिनिकरपरिद्योतमाना समन्ता-
देषा श्रीकृष्णमूर्तिः क्षणमपि मनसः **स्रग्धरा** नापयायात्।।

2

पुरन्दर इव श्रिया परिवृत्तो मृगाङ्कच्छविः
कुशेशयनिभाननो नयविदां मतीनां पतिः।
सदार्थिसुरपादपः पितृसमः प्रजावत्सलो
बभूव **पृथिवी**पतिः प्रथितविक्रमो भीष्मकः।।

3

स कुण्डिनं कुण्डिनतुल्यशोभ**मुपेन्द्रवज्रा**युधभीमवीर्यः।
श्रिया च धीवत् परिदीप्यमानो धिया च श्रीवच्चिरमध्युवास।।

4

एतस्य राज्ञः किल रुक्मिणीति नाम्ना प्रसिद्धा तनया बभूव।
पञ्चाभवन्नुग्रतराः सुताश्च दे**वेन्द्रवज्रा**धिकदेहसाराः।।

5

कृष्णरिपू रुक्मी बहुगर्वो रुक्मरथो रुक्माधिकबाहुः।
रुक्मकचो रुक्माधिकमाली **रुक्मवती** कन्या किल धन्या।।

6

आबाल्यादनवरतं **प्रहर्षिणी** सा
रूपेणाप्रतिमगुणैर्विरोचमाना।
यत्पादोपमविभवं सहस्रपत्रं
खिन्ना यद्गतिमवलोक्य राजहंसाः।।

7

वृत्ते जङ्घे श्रीजितेभेन्द्रशुण्डादण्डोत्सेकं शोभनं चोरुयुग्मम्।
काञ्चीस्थानं सर्वलोकैकरम्यं धत्ते लीलाशालिनी भूपबाला।।

8

मध्यक्षामा पृथुकुचयुगभारानम्रा
बाहुद्वन्द्वं सुभगमृदुलपुष्पश्रीकम्।
पीवग्रीवां जलजसहजकम्बुच्छायां
रम्यं बभ्रे जितसरसिजगर्वं वक्त्रम्।।

9

स्मितकौमुदीकिरणहृष्टबान्धवा
श्रुतिवल्लकीनिनदमञ्जुभाषिणी।
मदिरेक्षणा नृपतिभीष्मकात्मजा
नयनाम्बुजेन मधुरेण वीक्षते।।

10

अधररुचिसरस्वतीसङ्गता हरितमणिनवप्रभामूर्च्छिता।
सुतनुदशनकान्तिमन्दाकिनी जनयति वदनं प्रयागद्युतिम्।।

11

चिकुरसमूहसमूढमालतीकुसुमसमाहृतषट्पदावलिः।
पतति विभिन्नसरोजविभ्रमात् स्मितमहिते ननु रुक्मिणीमुखे।।

12

गजगतिर्नृपसुता गुणवती समुदिता।
उपचिता सुललिता सुमहिता किमु लता।।

13

फुल्ला वसन्ततिलका नववल्लरीव
सा रुक्मिणीगुणगणैरुपचीयमाना।
देया कथं गुणवते नृपसत्तमाये-
त्याप प्रजाहितपरो नृपतिः स चिन्ताम्।।

14

निशम्य तां धरणिसुरास्तपस्विनो
वदाम्यतामतिरुचिरां प्रजावितुः।
विभास्वरं सुरपतिमन्दिरश्रिया
दिने दिने नृपसदनं ययुर्मुदा।।

15
श्रुतिस्मृतिप्रमाणिकां विधाय भूसुरार्हणाम्।
प्रपूर्य तन्मनोरथान् मुदा जगाद भीष्मकः।।
16
रामः शस्त्रधरैर्यमो रिपुगणैः शार्दूलविक्रीड़ितैः
कन्दर्पो वरवर्णिनीभिरचलाकल्पद्रुमो याचकैः।
ब्रह्मण्यो विबुधैः स्वधर्मनिरतः पौरैःश्च यो वीक्ष्यते
कः पृथ्वीपतिरीदृशो विजयते भूमण्डलेऽस्मिन् द्विजाः।।
17
प्रश्न एष उचितस्तव राजन् कन्यकावत इति द्रुतमुक्त्वा।
स्वागतामुदितमानसविप्रा भीष्मकं सपदि चोत्तरमूचुः।।
18
दैत्येन्द्रवंशाग्निरहो विराजते श्रीकृष्ण एकः खलु मेदिनीतले।
नूनं तदीयार्णवगा विलोकिता द्वारावती चेत् किममर्त्यराट् पुरा।।
19
सिन्धुना पुरी विभाति सागरस्तया विभाति।
श्रीः समानिकाऽनया न कुत्रचिन् महीतलेऽस्ति।।
20
अन्या कान्तिर्लक्ष्मीरन्या कीर्तिश्चान्याऽन्यत् सामर्थ्यम्।
अन्या विद्युन्मालादीप्तेः श्रीकृष्णस्य प्रज्ञा लोके।।
21
न भवेत्समाप्तिरनन्तः कथयेद्यदि देवकीसुतगुणान् नृपते।
इयमस्मदीयभणितिः सुतरां प्रमिताक्षरा ननु कथं प्रभवेत्।।
22
इति वनमालिगुणान् कथयित्वा स्फुटमुखतामरसं नरपालम्।
अवनिसुराः प्रययुर्निजगेहं वियति ममौ न धरापतिमोदः।।
23
मेने गोविन्दं रुक्मिणी योग्यकान्तं
तस्याः सम्पन्नाऽऽराधना वैश्वदेवी।
लक्ष्मीः सौन्दर्यं तस्य वीर्यं च लीला
तस्या हि स्वान्तं संचकर्षैव नूनम्।।

24

राजा बहु मेने कृष्णं गुणराशिं कन्यामणिमालायोग्यं जलजाक्षम्।
रुक्मी प्रतिकूलश्चैद्यं नृपवर्यं नूनं गुरुकार्ये विघ्नप्रतिघातः।।

25

रुक्मिणोत्पादितं विघ्नमाज्ञाय सा
दुःखिता रुक्मिणी श्रीर्ननु स्रग्विणी।
चिन्तयित्वा द्विजं पत्रयुक्तं मुदा
द्वारकां सत्वरं शार्ङ्गिणे प्राहिणोत्।।

26

महीसुरोऽसौ समुपेत्य तां पुरीं
सुश्राव्यवंशस्तनितानुकर्षिणीम्।
ददर्श तूर्णं किल विस्मयावहं
मुकुन्दसौधं विधुमण्डलस्पृशम्।।

27

तस्मिन् सौधे कृतपदपद्मन्यासः
क्षोणीदेवः स्मितमुख ईक्षाञ्चक्रे।
गाढं नीलां जलधरमालामन्या-
मध्यासीनां मणिमयपीठं रम्यम्।।

28

अवनिसुरेक्षणमुदितो मुदिररुचिर्यदुकुलजः।
त्वरितगतिः परिजगृहे दुरितहरौ द्विजचरणौ।।

29

तं मणिमध्यं पीठमधिष्ठाप्य मुरारिर्विप्रवरम्।
स्नेहयुतः पूजां विदधे सज्जनमान्यो मेघरुचिः।।

30

भूसरवर्यः पङ्क्तिपवित्रः।
काममभुङ्क्त श्रीहरिगेहे।।

31

वीक्ष्य प्रीतिं कंसारातेः।
सिद्धं मेने कन्याकार्यम्।।

32
द्विजं सोमराजीव्यपेताखिलाघम्।
उपस्थातुकामो मुकुन्दोऽभ्युपेतः।।

33
अभिमृशन् द्विजपादसरोरुहं
सरज आशु रजस्ततिवारणम्।
द्रुतविलम्बितमञ्जुपदोक्तिभिः
सविनयं तमपृच्छदधोक्षजः।।

34
विबुध मधुमतीसुकृतविलसितम्।
तदपि जयति ते व्यपगतविपदम्।।

35
यत्रासौ मदलेखा किञ्चिन् नो बहुदोषा।
सन्तुष्टिः परिपूर्णा तं वन्दे द्विजराजम्।।

36
कच्चित् क्षोणीपालाल्लोकत्राणासक्तेः।
विद्युल्लेखादीप्ते धर्मात्मन् ते क्षेमम्।।

37
किमर्थमत्र सम्प्राप्तो निःशङ्कं ब्रूहि मेऽखिलम्।
अनुष्टुभ्नामि विपदं कृतार्थो भव भूसुर।।

38
एवं परिपृष्टो वृत्तं तनुमध्याम्।
कन्यामधिकृत्य प्रोचे द्विजराजः।।

39
अथ मुरहन्त्रे प्रणयमनोज्ञम्।
अददत पत्रं शशिवदनायाः।।

40
श्रुत्वा वृत्तं द्विजवरगीतं मत्तारातिद्विपमृगराजः।
ईक्षाञ्चक्रे किल वनमाली सोत्कण्ठं तद्वरतनुपत्रम्।।

41

गुणानां वृन्दं ते हृदयपरितापप्रशमनं
नितान्तं सौन्दर्यं भुवनरमणीविस्मयकरम्।
निशम्याजस्रं मे नृपशिखरिणीजातिसुलभां
विहायाशु व्रीडां त्वयि विशति चेतो मुररिपो।।

42

नलिननिलया दासीभूता त्वदीयपदाम्बुजं
त्यजति न मनाङ् मेघश्याम त्वयि प्रचुरादरा।
जलजनयनः सौदर्येणाधरीकृतमन्मथो
हृदयनिलयः कस्या न स्याद् भवान् हरिणीदृशः।।

43

स्मारं स्मारं तव गुणनिवहं ध्यायन्त्यास्त्वां ननु मम कुरुते।
पादाम्भोजे तव रसरुचिरे लीनं चेतो भ्रमरविलसितम्।।

44

योऽयं देवो विहितमतिभिर्दुर्लभो योगिवृन्दै-
राशाबन्धो गगननलिनीतुल्यतां याति तस्मिन्।
भूयो भूयो मधुरमधुरैः प्रार्थयन्तीं वचोभि-
र्मन्दाक्रान्तां त्वयि गणय मां नाथ गाढं सतृष्णाम्।।

45

परिचररक्षितां वद कथं भवतीमवरोधवर्तिनी-
मनिहतसोदरः परिणयामि बलदिति युक्तिरुच्यते।
कृतनवमङ्गला सह पुरन्ध्रिगणैः सरसीरुहेक्षण
व्रजति समर्चितुं नववधूर्वरदां तुहिनाद्रिकन्यकाम्।।

46

सुनिभृतमपराजिताशु समेत्य तद्-
हिमनगतनयालयं हि ससैनिकः।
रिपुकुलमथनं विधाय निराश्रया-
मुपयमविधिनासुरेण वृणीष्व माम्।।

47

व्रतनियमार्हणाभिरसकृत् सुसेविता देवता

विभवबलादमोघफलदा दृढव्रतिनां सदा।

अवसर एष पूर्वसुकृतैरुपस्थितः प्रार्थये

यदुकुलनन्दन कुरुत मे सरोजनेत्रं पतिम्।

48

इति रुक्मिणीप्रहितपत्रिकां मध्वरि-

र्मधुमञ्जरीमधुरवर्णविद्युत्वतीम्।

सदयः पठन् प्रणतरक्षणैकादरो

जयमङ्गले मुदितमानसः सम्बभौ।।

49

लोकमोहनगुणैरथोद्धता रुक्मिणी त्वयि दृढादरा पुनः।

प्राह भूसुरवरस्तदा हरिं याहि कुण्डिनपुरं मया द्रुतम्।।

50

चन्द्रवर्त्मगमनैः सुरनिवहैः पूजितोऽयमवनित्रिदशवरम्।

प्राह विष्णुरमलं हृतहृदयो रुक्मिणीपरिगतैः सुरसगुणैः।।

51

राजन्यपापापसदोपजातीरुन्मथ्य युद्धे तरलायताक्षीम्।

तामानयाम्याशु निबद्धरागामपारसौन्दर्यविलासलक्ष्मीम्।।

52

कलहंसकण्ठोनिनदो द्विजराजं

प्रतिसन्निगद्य सह तेन रथाग्र्यम्।

जवनैस्तुरङ्गमवरैरनुयुक्तं

द्रुतमारुरोह सुदृढं यदुवर्यः।।

53

विचार्य निपुणं विवाहसुदिनं स राजदुहितुर्विलोक्य विपदम्।

जलोद्धतगतिः सुरारिमथनो विवेश तरसा विदर्भविषयम्।।

54

तत्रापश्यन् मत्तमयूरीकृतलास्यं
मध्येमार्गं वैरिनिहन्ता जलजाक्षः।
हित्वा सर्वं संशयजातं विजयाप्तौ
प्रीतः पौरैः कुण्डिनवासैः परिणूतः।।

55

पुत्रमते योग्यवरं चैद्यनृपं माणवकम्।
वीक्ष्य नृपस्तद्दुहितुर्मङ्गलकं संविदधे।।

56

यदुपतिवरलाभः स्यादिति नृपवरपुत्री सा।
भुजगशिशुभृतामस्तौत् सततमवहिता गौरीम्।।

57

तरला द्विजस्य वीक्षणे सरला भुजङ्गसङ्गता।
पतिता विचारसागरे महिला मुकुन्दलालसा।।

58

श्रीहरिसङ्गमलास्यविभावा स्वेष्टमनोरथपूरणकामा।
अभवन् मङ्गलदोधकभावा भूपसुता शुभनेत्रविनामा।।

59

नृपसङ्कुलिते गजराजगते दमघोषसुते नगरोपगते।
करपीडनतोटकवृत्तकराः परितो जनिता भयदाः शकुनाः।।

60

हरेः कुण्डिने वाडवोक्त्याऽश्रृणोत् सा
भुजङ्गप्रयातानुकल्पं प्रवेशम्।
स्वलेखार्थसंवाहकाय प्रहृष्टा
द्विजेन्द्राय रत्नं ददौ राजबाला।।

61

रिपुभयचकितो नीलवासास्तदा
मुररिपुमनुयातो बलैरन्वितः।
निजनगरमुपेतौ क्षमायाः पति-
र्विपुलकुशलपूर्णोऽर्चयामास तौ।।

62
वीरेन्द्रैर्गुप्ता नरपतिदुहिता दुर्गां
गत्वा पद्भ्यां मङ्गलनिलयगतां देवीम्।
नत्वाऽसम्बाधा सुतपतिसहितामस्तौत्
कृष्णो भूयान्मम पतिरिति शुभाशंसा।।

63
हिमनगदुहितानवमणिनिलयाद्
वलति सुवदना नरवरतनुजा।
व्यथयति च सुमप्रहरणकलिका
नरपतिहृदयं विकसितवदना।।

64
वीरैर्गुप्तां राजदुहितरं निष्क्रामन्तीं
गौरीगेहान् मङ्गलवसनां मुक्ताहाराम्।
तूर्णं जित्वा रक्षकनिवहं कंसारति-
र्वामामाहार्षीच्छ्रियमिव वासन्तीं वीरः।।

65
माधवेन सङ्गतां विलोक्य राजकन्यकां
सेनया रुरोध रोषितो नृपात्मजो बली।
तूणकाच्छरैर्विजित्य तं बबन्ध माधवः
पादयोर्निपत्य मोचयाम्बभूव रुक्मिणी।।

66
यदुपतिरथ देवी मालिनी रुक्मिणी सा
विकसितवदनौ स्वां जग्मतू राजधानीम्।
धृतपरिणयभूषौ रेजतू दम्पती तौ
परमसुखसमृद्धामक्षयां प्राप्य लक्ष्मीम्।।

FOOTNOTES

Paper published in Journal of Ananthacharya Indological Institute, Mumbai, Vol. II, pp. 137-154.
Paper presented at the 39th session of All-India Oriental Conference, held at Oriental Institute, Baroda—13th-15th Octo. 1998.

IV

THE RARE MANUSCRIPT OF JHĀRU PAṆḌITA'S COMMENTARY ON THE *KUMĀRASAMBHAVAM OF KĀLIDĀSA*

Introductory :

The Oriental Institute of Baroda is one of the greatest Indological Institute of India. It was conceived (in 1893) and established (in 1927) by the fore-signted Maharaja Sayajairao Gaekwad of Baroda. It has a valuable treasure of more than 27000 Mss., which incorporate the scholarly original works or commentaries on some works, on diverse subjects written in different scripts. Many mss. of the collection are quite rare and works, they incorporate are mostly little-known. The Oriental Institute has so far published in the famous Gaekwad's Oriental Series more than 178 original works, based on such rare and valuable Mss. Still there are numerous works on different subjects, which are lying hidden in the form of Mss. in the Institute. Some of them are singular codices of certain works (*codex unicum*), the other copies of which are very difficult to be obtained elsewhere. In this paper, An attempt is made to introduce to the world of scholars, a rare and valuable Ms. of the commentary of a Jain scholar Jhāru on the famous *Mahā-kāvya*, the *Kumārasambhavam* of Kālidāsa. The work has still remained unedited and unpublished and Ms. also has been unnoticed, being available perhaps only in the Oriental Institute.

The Rarity of the Comentary and Its Ms. :

The *New Catalogus Catalogorum*[1], has recorded more

than sixty four commentaries on the *Kumārasambhavam of Kḁlidāsa*, only few of them have been published. No mention of Jhāru's commentary on the *Kumārasambhavam* is found there. Similarly, among the thirtyeight commentaries, mentioned by Krishnamachariar[2], Jhārupaṇḍita's commentary is not noticed. The commentary *Pañjikā* of Vallabhadeva is edited and published by Prof. Gautam Patel[3]. He refers to other four published commentaries on the *Kumārasambhavam*[4]. K.G.Ambika[5] refers to six Sanskrit commentaries from Kerala and gives details about two unpublished Keralite commentaries in one article, published in Shri Venkateshwar University Oriental Journal. Unfortunately, the Ms. of Jhāru Paṇḍita's commentary has not received any attention of scholars writing about the *Kumārasambhavam*.

About the Manuscript :

The manuscript of commentary of Jhāru Paṇḍita on the *Kumārasambhavam* is available in Oriental Institute of Baroda, bearing acc.No. 2099 i.e. a very early collection of the Institute, during Sir Sayajirao Maharaja (III)'s Royal regime. It is on an old countrymade brownish paper, with total sixty folios, written in *pṛṣṭhamātrā* on both sides of folio in *Devanāgarī* script. The size of the Ms. is 11 cms.×26 cms. There are about 17 lines to a page and about *60* letters in a line. The *granthasaṅkhyā* or extent of the ms. is about 2400. On the last page, it is noted that this is a copy of Muni Kuśalavijaya, who was disciple of Pt. Śāntivijaya Gaṇi[6]. The scribe begins the ms. with *Om Namo Vītarāgāya*, which indicates Jain origin. The middle portion of each page has artistic design, made by keeping blank space. This is also a Jain peculiarity. The *supra* and *infra* margins are of equal measure. The *Recto & verso* margins are also of equal measures, with four lines drawn on each side. The ms. is written by a single scribe in a good hand writing. No date is found anywhere in the ms., but the ms. seems to be old of about 14th or 15th century A.D. from the paper and style of writing. There are many *lacunae* in the manuscript. Moreover the ms. is very very corrupt. These facts indicate ignorance of the scribe regarding the Sanskrit language. From the colophons to the cantos, the name of commentator Jhārupaṇḍita and the name of commentary *Yaśodharanandinī* are known. The title *Yaśodharanandinī* also indicates Jain influence and most probably the commentator Jhārupaṇḍita may be a Jain scholar. The Beginning of the ms. is as follows:

।। द० ।। ॐ नमो वीतरागाय। अस्त्युत्त० ।। हिमालयो नाम हिमालय इति प्रसिद्धो नगाधिराजो भूभृतां नाथोऽस्ति अद्यापि वर्तते। यद्यद्यापि वर्तते तर्हि कुत्र वर्तत इत्याशङ्कायामाह। उत्तरस्यां दिशीति।

The colophon to the first *sarga* is in the following form-

इति झारुपंडितविरचितायां कुमारसंभवटीकायां यशोधरनंदिन्यां प्रथमः सर्गः ।। 1 ।।

The concluding portion of the ms. is as follows—

इति श्रीझारुपंडितविरचितायां कुमारसंभवटीकायां अष्टमः सर्गः समाप्तः। शुभमस्तु लेखकपाठकयोः ।। 6 ।।श्री ।।

The ms. contains the commentary only on one to eight *sargas* on the *Kumārasambhavam* and it is complete. The commentator seems to have commented only on eight *sargas* of the *Kumārasambhavam*. Moreover, the text of the verses, commented is not fully presented but only the *lemma* or the *pratīka* only of the verses commented is mentioned.

The Commentator and Commentary :

It will not be out of place here to give some preliminary details about the commentator and the commentary which would enhance the importance of the rare ms. As with other scholars, no personal/biographical information is available about the commentator. As mentioned previously, from the title of the commentary namely, "*Yaśodharanandinī*", it may be presumed that he was a Jain scholar. He has referred to Vallabhadeva at some places in his commentary, which indicates his posterity to Vallabhadeva (first quarter of tenth century as mentioned by Prof. Gautam Patel[7]). The work of studying and copying down the ms. is in progress. So far, Besides Vallabhadeva, the following authors and works are found referred to by the commentator.

Authors : *Paṇini, Amara, Daṇḍī, Durga, Madinīkāra*. Works-*Rāmāyaṇa, Nirukta, Bhagavadgītā, Harivaṁśa, Malatīmādhava, Bhāgavata, Mādhavanidāna, Viśva* or *Viśvalocana, Kaṇṭhābharaṇa*. Among these, the mention of the *Kaṇṭhābharaṇa* (1100 A.D.) and of *Medanīkāra* (1200-1275 A.D.) are important for determining his date, which set his upper limit to 13th century A.D.

The scholarship of the commentator is evident from the various sources quoted and referred to by him. He often gives grammatical explanations, quoting Pāṇini. He explains the metres and figures of speech. Daṇḍin's *Kāvyādarśa* is frequently quoted for explaining figures of speech. In the first verse, the commentator reads "*Vigāhya*" as against "*Vagāhya*" read by Mallinātha. The verses from the *Harivaṁśa* are quoted for explaining the mythology in the second verse-"*Pruthūpadiṣṭām duduhur dharitrīm*". The commentator gives a romantic explanation of the thickness of breasts of the vergin Pārvatī—*stanyarāhityāt kāṭhinyam*.

Concluding Remarks

The work of styding, copying down & editing the commentary is still in progress. The researcher has simply tried to bring to the notice of scholars this rare manuscript of the little-known commentary, available in the Oriental Institute of Baroda.

FOOTNOTES

Paper read at All-India Oriental Conferenc, 40th Session, Deptt. of Skt. Chennai, 28-30th May 2000.

1. Raghavan, V.: *New Catalogus Catalogorum*, Uni. of Madras, Madras, Vol. IV, 1968, pp. 211-220.
2. Krishnamachariar, M. : *History of Classical Sanskrit Literature*, Motilal Banarasidas, Delhi, 1970, p. 118.
3. Patel, Gautam V.(ed.) *Kumārasambhavam of Kālidāsa*(with the commentary of Vallabhadeva), Ahmedabad, 1986.
4. *Ibid.* page 26: (1) *Prakāśikā*- Aruṇagirinātha (2) *Vivaraṇa*-Nārāyaṇa (3) *Śiśuhitaiṣiṇī*-Caritravardhana (4) *Sañjīvanī*-Mallinātha
5. Ambika K.G. : "Two Unknown Keralite Commentaries on Kumārasambhavam of Kālidāsa", *Shri Venkateshvara University Oriental Journal,* vol. XL, 1997, part 1 & 2, pp. 107-113.
6. Ms. Oriental Institute No. 2099 folio 60 : पंडितश्रीशांतिविजयगणिशिष्यमुनिकुशलविजयस्य कृतिरेषा।
7. *Op. cit.,* p. 18.

DHARMAŚĀSTRA

V

UTSAVANIRṆAYAMAÑJARĪ—A RARE AND UNPUBLISHED WORK OF GAṄGĀDHARA, A SCHOLAR FROM GUJARAT

Introductory

The *Utsavanirṇayamañjarī* is a rare and unpublished work on *Dharmaśāstra,* written by a scholar, Gaṅgādhara, who was residing in Gujarat, during 17th century A.D. This monumental work contains descriptions of several festivals, occurring throughout the year, from the standpoint of *Dharmaśāstra*. This work is quite unique as it is written in a special and peculiar style by the author. Unlike the other digests on *Dharmaśāstra,* it incorporates elucidation of festivals of the year in verses of several metres, composed mostly by the author himself, expatiating those festivals and giving the author's own opinions and decisions, regarding their observance, without generally referring to or quoting the views of other scholars, as is generally met with in other *Dharmaśāstra*-works. Secondly, it is quite rare and important work, the complete manuscript of which is available in the Oriental Institute of Baroda. Thirdly, being the treatise of a scholar from Gujarat, it naturally contains exposition of peculiar religious observances of Gujarat and of *Vaiṣṇava* cult. This fact also enhances the importance and significance of this unknown and unpublished work.

Description of the manuscript

The rare manuscript of this work is available in the

Oriental Institute of Baroda (its accession No. being 2375). It is a complete manuscript, written in *Devanāgarī* Script, containing twenty-one folios. The *grantha saṅkhyā* of this work is about 700. It is copied on a paper of 28 cms. x 15 cms. size, written on both sides, with about 42 to 46 letters to a line and about 15 to 17 lines to a page or one side of the folio. There is a mistake in the numbering of the folios, which total twentyone (but not twenty as noted by the scribe). There is a repetition of number four in numbering the folios by the scribe. In the margin there is reference to the work in short-form as Ti. Ma. (i.e. *Tithimañjarī*) or sometimes as Ti. Ni. Ma. (i.e *Tithinirṇayamañjarī*). Similarly in the Introductory verse and colophons to some *adhyāyas*, the work is referred to as *Nirṇayamañjarī*,[1] while in colophon to some *adhyāyas* and the concluding *śloka*, the work is explicitly referred to as *Utsavanirṇayamañjarī*.[2]

The Scribe and his Date

In the post-colophon entries,[3] there is explicit mention of the scribe, the copyist of the manuscript, along with his name and reference to his home and date of copying the manuscript. He was a scholar from Gujarat, residing in Gauḍala (probably present Goṇḍala). His name was Lakṣmīdhara and his father's name was Īśvara. In the writing of the scribe also, there is some kind of impression of the characters of the Gujarati script. Sometimes the scribe has preserved *lacunae* in the text, which indicate his fidelity and faithfulness. The copying of the manuscript was completed by the scribe on Wednesday of second day of bright half of *Āśvina* month in *saṁvat* 1866 (*śake* 1731 i.e. 1810 A.D.). This clearly shows the time of the scribe.

The Author Gaṅgādhara

In the concluding verses of the work, the author has described in brief his family background, the period of composition of the text and the nature of the text. He was a scholar named Gaṅgādhara, son of Nṛsiṁha, born in the highly cultured family of Brāhmaṇas of *Bhāradvāja Gotra* and *Vālakhilya* family.[4] From his *Gotra*, it appears that he was a follower of *Yajurveda*, because *Vālakhilya Brāhmaṇas* of *Bhāradvāja Gotra* are the followers of *Yajurveda Saṁhitā*[5],. There was a happy union of *Śrī* (wealth) and *Sarasvatī* (scholarship) in his family. The present work is composed by him in three-hundred and eleven (311) verses, expounding *Sacchāstra* (the auspicious science), with the grace of Lord Śrīkṛṣṇa.

In the other concluding verse,[6] the author has referred to his home and the period of the composition of the text. He mentions in clear terms, that he was residing in an auspicious city, situated on the bank of the heavenly river, created by Kaśyapa. He has completed this work on Wednesday of ninth Day of the *Caitra* month in the *Śālivāhana Śaka* 1545 (i.e. 1623 A.D.) and dedicated it to the Lotus-feet of Lord Hari.

As mentioned previously, the author was residing in a city, situated on the bank of the heavenly river, created by Kaśyapa. There is a description of a *suranadī*, brought to the earth by Kaśyapa, in the *Sābhramatī-māhātmya* of the *Padma Purāṇa* (*Uttara*. 135).[7] It is quite evident that Sābhramatī described there, is most probably the present Sābaramatī river. The author may be presumed to be a resident of Ahmedabad.

The work—*Utasavanirṇayamañjarī*

The work, as suggested by its very title, contains exposition of several festivals of the year in totally 311 (three hundred eleven) *ślokas*, composed mostly by the author himself, in several metres. He has given his own decisive opinions regardng the time or period of the observance of those festivals, without referring to or discussing the views of others. Corresponding to the twelve months of the year, there is elucidation-in twelve *adhyāyas* of important festivals of each month, beginning from the *Caitra* upto the month of the *Fālguna*. The observances and vows of the *Adhika* or *Puruṣottama-māsa* are dealt with in the 13th *adhyāya* and in the last i.e the 14th *adhyāya*, some vows, common to all the months and those observed on the peculiar lunar days are also delineated. The work is concluded with two important verses, giving ample information, regarding the author, his time, his place of residence and his family-background and the present metrical work on *Dharmaśāstra,* composed by him.

Influence of Vaiṣṇava Cult

There are several evidences in the text that reflect upon the influence of the *Vaiṣṇava* cult on the author. He has praised the lotus like feet of the Lord Śrīkṛṣṇa in the beginning and concluding verses.[8] The lotus like feet of Śrikṛṣṇa are not only the bestowers of *Dharma*, *Artha* and *Kāma* but also are the destroyers of the threefold miseries of the devotee. With the Grace of the said Lord only, the author has composed the *Nirṇayamañjarī*, awakening understanding regarding the auspicious religious duties. Similarly, the author has dedicated the present work to the lotus-feet of Lord Śrīkṛṣṇa in the concluding verse. Thus the author has explicitly shown his dedication to the Lord Kṛṣṇa, indicating his leaning towards *Vaiṣṇava* cult.

In the exposition of festivals also, he has described several festivals, that are purely related to *Vaiṣṇava* cult. e.g. *Vallabhotsava*, *Rādhāṣṭamī*, *Rāsotsava, Gokulanāthotsava, Viṭṭhaleśotsava, Govardhanodhāraṇāgamanotsava, Viṣṇorāndolotsava, Viṣṇnordolotsava, Puṣpamaṇḍallyutsava* etc. The description of all these *Vaiṣṇava* festivals suggests that the author had great acquaintance with such *Vaiṣṇava* festivals. He might be a follower of the *Vaiṣṇava* cult.

Some Remarkable Peculiarities

The author has very vividly and accurately described the festivals namely, the *Śītalāsaptamī* and the *Pārvatīvrata*, which are most significant as they are practised in Gujarat only, in the manner, described by him.[9] The eating of stale and cold food on *Śītalāsaptamī* day and worship of Goddess Pārvatī, during *Gorā* festival are the most peculiar observances in Gujarat. Nevertheless, the eludidation of the *Maṅgalāgaurī Vrata*[10] is remarkable, as it is observed especially by Maharastrians on the day and manner, depicted by the author. The name *ajāpratipat* reminds us of the Marāṭhī term *ājepāḍavā*, employed for the same festival. Generally, there is a practice of following *Vikrama Saṁvata* in Gujarat, but the author has referred specifically to the *Śālivāhana Śaka* in the concluding verse.[11] These facts may indicate that the author was definitely a scholar influenced by and acquainted with Maharastrian customs and practices.

The text of this monumental work of the author is presented herewith. There are numerous grammatical and metrical defects in it, but it is after all a metrical work, not of a grammarian, but of a *Dharmaśāstra* scholar, who according to his knowledge and ability has tried his best to present the scholarly *Dharmaśāstra* matter in compositions of different metres. The author really deserves great praise and compliments for such a novel attempt.

गङ्गाधरकृता

उत्सवनिर्णयमञ्जरी

।। प्रथमोऽध्यायः ।।

श्रीमत्त्रिपुरसुन्दर्यै नमः।

अथ निर्णयमञ्जरी।

श्रीमत्कृष्णपदारविन्दयुगलं धर्मार्थकामप्रदं
ब्रह्मेन्द्राद्युप[1]कल्पितं च भजतां तापत्रयोन्मूलनम्।
वन्दे तत्कृपया करोमि सकलां सत्कर्मसंबोधिनीं
श्रीमन्निर्णयमञ्जरीं च विदुषां सौख्याय धर्माय वै।।1।।

अथ चैत्रमासस्य मासेश्वरादीनाह—

चैत्राधीश्वरविष्णुवाक्यविधिना भानुवि (विं)यन्मण्डलं
पौलस्त्योदितवेदमन्त्रविभवाच्छ्रीवासुकीभ्यां सह।
संचाराध्वनि वाद्यवादनपरः स्यात्तुम्बरुर्नृत्य(नर्त)की
नृत्यन्वै सुकृतस्थलीति विभवान्मासं नयन्ति ध्रुवम्।।2।।

संवत्सरारम्भनिर्णयः—

चैत्रे या प्रतिपत्तिथिश्च धवले सूर्योदयव्यापिनी
ग्राह्या वै विबुधैश्च [2]निश्चलधिया संवत्सरारम्भके।
व्याप्ता युग्मदिनेऽथ नो भवति चेत्पूर्वा हिता नापरा
तद्वारस्तु सभापतिर्भवति वै मासेऽधिसंज्ञेऽपि च।।3।।

इति वर्षपतिनिर्णयः

अथ संवत्सरारम्भव्रतम्—

वर्षारम्भतिथौ व्रतं वितनुयात्सत्सौख्यलाभाय वै
धातारं सुविधानवेदविधिना संपूजयेद्भक्तिमान्।
तस्यां निर्जलभूमिमार्गविषये कुर्यात्प्रपारम्भणं
लक्ष्म्या हीनजनैस्तु धर्मघटको विप्राय संदापयेत्।।4।।

इति प्रपा।

अथ नवरात्र्युत्सवः—

चैत्रे चण्डिविधानके च प्रतिपद्ग्राह्या द्वितीयान्विता
शुद्धा नवरात्रिके तिथिलयो वृद्धिर्न दोषाय वै।
अष्टाम्यां हवनं च पूजनविधी(धिस्) तत्पारणे भोजने
स्वाचारान्नवमी तथैव दशमी पूर्वान्विते तेपिते।।5।।

विद्याप्रतिपद्व्रतम्—

वर्षाद्यप्रतिपद्दिने च विबुधैः कुर्याच्च विद्याव्रतं
तीर्थस्नानविधिं उपोषितनरो ब्रह्माणमाब्जे दले।
वेदादीन्विधिनार्चयेद्विभवतो मासे च मासे पुन—
र्वषान्ते द्विजभोजनं च सुरभि(भी)दानात्सुविद्यान्वितः।।6।।

आरोग्यप्रतिपद्—

चैत्रस्याद्यदिने व्रतं वितनुयादारोग्यसंज्ञं व्रती
स्नात्वा पद्मजले रवेश्च यजनं होमं पयाढ्यैः फलैः।
दध्नापूपसितान्वितैर्द्विजवरान्संतोष्य विप्राज्ञया
ग्रासं वा सुजलं ग्रहेत विधिवदारोग्यसौख्याय वै।।7।।

अथ तिलकव्रतम्—

चैत्रस्याद्यदिने व्रतं सुतिलकं कुर्यान्नरैर्नारिभिः
स्नात्वा तीर्थजलैः सुगन्धविरजैः कृत्वा सुदेहाकृतिम्।
वर्षाद्यैस्तु सुनाममन्त्रविभवैः संपूज्य तच्चूर्णयुक्
श्रीखण्डं तिलकं चरेत्य(द)नुदिनं दुर्विघ्नविध्वंसनम्।।8।।

अथ सौभाग्यशयनव्रतम्—

चैत्रे या तृतिया सिताप्युदयगा तस्यां च नारीजनैः
सौभाग्यं शयनं व्रतं वितनुयाद्गौरीश्वरं पूजयेत्।
सौभाग्याष्टकदानभक्षणपरा शुक्लतृतीयासु वै
पूर्णेऽब्दे शयनीं च हेमप्रतिमादानं सुसौभाग्यदम्।।9।।

अथ गौर्या दोलोत्सवम् (वः)—

चैत्रे वै गिरिजातिथौ व्रतवती गौरीश्वरं पूजये-
दान्दोले विनिधाय चोत्सवपरा नारी सुपुत्रं लभेत्।
तस्मिन्नेव दिने ह्यरुन्धतिवसिष्ठं पूजयेत्प्रार्थये-
त्सा सौभाग्यमखडितं लभति वै तुर्ये हि होमार्चनम्।।10।।

अथ मत्स्यजयन्ती—

शुक्ला गौरितिथौ मधौ दिनमुखव्याप्तासु कुर्याद्व्रतं
मत्स्याख्यं सुहरिं पराह्णसमये संपूजयेत्तद्व्रती
सा मन्वादिकसंज्ञिता च परमा पित्र्यर्चने तृप्तिदा
मासे वै पुरुषोत्तमे यदि भवेच्छ्राद्धं च मासद्वये।।11।।

अथ कल्पादितिथिः—

या पञ्चमी चैत्रसिते विभागे
कल्पादिका स्यात्सवितोदयाढ्या।
स्नाने च दाने द्विजभोजने च
सुरार्चने चाक्षयपुण्यदा स्यात्।।12।।

अथ अशोकाष्टमीव्रतम्—

चैत्रे या धवलाष्टमी परयुता तस्यां सुदेव्योत्सवं
सौख्यानन्दसमृद्धयेऽपि च पुनर्वस्वृक्षजाढ्या यदा।
आशोकीं कलिकां पिबेत्तु मनुजो शोकादिनाशार्थये
तस्यां स्नानविधानतो हि लभते श्रीवाजिमेधोद्भवम्।।13।।

अथ रामजन्मनवमी—

[3][अथ प्रस्तावाद्दशावतारजयन्त्युत्सवानाह।
द्वादश्यैकादशी या बटुझषकमठो बुद्धकल्याख्यदेवौ
भाद्रे मार्गे च पौषे [4]*[शु]चि नभसि सिते माधवे रामसिंहौ।
वह्नौ भूते वराहः सितदिन[5] **[हुत]भुक् फाल्गुने श्रावणे च
कृष्णाष्टम्यां च कृष्णो रघुपतिरभवच्चैत्रशुक्ले नवम्याम्।।14।।

चैत्रे वै नवमी सिता भवति या सूर्योदयव्यापिनी
तस्यां विष्णुपरयणैस्तु विबुधैः कुर्याद्व्रतं वैष्णवम्।
मध्याह्नेऽपि तथा पुनर्वसुयुता चेद्वै महापुण्यदा
ज्ञेया जागरणे व्रते च विधि[6] *****(वद्दानार्पणे) मुक्तिदा।।14।।

अथ व्रतविधिः —

रामाख्या नवमी तिथि(थिर्) हि वृणुयाद्विप्रान् चतुःसंमिता-
न्गेहं मं[7]*********प्राग्द्वारसंसेविते।
मध्ये चाष्टदलाब्जके ससुहृदं रामं सुहेमोद्भवं
संपूज्यादपरेऽह्नि पायसघृतैर्होमं च पीठार्पणम्।।15।।

अथैकादशीव्रतविधिनिर्णयस्तु षड्भिवृत्तैः —

विद्धैकादशि या चतुर्विधमता संकीर्तिता पण्डितैः
स्पर्शः पञ्चयुगाधिका कृतयुगे त्याज्या तु सा वैष्णवैः।
पञ्चाशद्घटिकाधिका भवति या साङ्गेति त्रेतायुगे
शल्याख्या शरबाणतोऽप्यधिकगा सा वर्जयेद्द्वापरे।।16।।

विद्धा षट्शरतोऽधिका कलियुगे सा वै चतुर्धा त्यजे-
द्व्याकुल्या त्रिजटा च भासुरतिका ज्ञेया क्रमान्मोहिनी।
लक्ष्मीपुत्रकलत्रधर्मनिचयान्निघ्नन्ति तासां व्रता-
त्तस्मात्तां(ताः) परिवर्जयन्ति विबुधाः सर्वेषु मासेष्वपि।।17।।

शुद्धा मिश्रा दशम्या क्वचिदपि च ततो द्वैधमेकादशीयं
प्रत्येकं च त्रिधासौ पुनरपि समतान्यूनताधिक्ययोगात्।
पक्षाः प्रत्येकभिन्नाः पुनरपि षडमी द्वादशीन्यूनताद्यैः
संबन्धादेवमष्टादश खलु मिलिताः कल्पनाः संभवन्ति।।18।।

संपूर्णैकादशी या न भवति परतः सा समा वासमा वा
न्यूना वा नास्ति वाच्यं व्रजति हरिदिनं द्वादशी सापि चोर्ध्वम्।
सर्वे कुर्युः परस्तादुपवसनमथ द्वादशी नोर्ध्वमेति
प्राव्राडत्वद्वितीयामुपवसतु जनः पूर्वमन्ये च सर्वे।।19।।

यद्येषा पूर्वविद्धा भवति परतः सा समा वासमा वा
सर्वे कुर्युर्द्वितीयामथ हरिदिवसः पूर्वविद्धोऽपि यायात्।
द्वादश्यां रात्रिसंस्पृग्यदि भवति परं मोक्षिणः पूर्वमन्ये
यद्वा विद्धा न चोर्ध्वं परमुपरि भवेत्तत्र सर्वे पुरस्तात्।।20।।

पूर्वा विद्धा[8] असौ चेन्न भवति परतो द्वादशी नापि चोर्ध्वं
कुर्यात्तत्रोपविष्टान्मुनिजननिकरः पूर्वमन्ये च सर्वे।
विद्धं प्रातर्दशम्यां हरिदिनमथ चेद्द्वादशी रात्रिदोषे
सर्वः पूर्वे तदानीमुपवसतु जनः प्रीतये केशवस्य।।21।।

एकादशीनिर्णयस्तम्भः।

1	2	3	4	5	6
10 र. 58	10 र. 58	10 र. 58	10 र 58	10 र. 59	10 र. 58
11 चं. 57	11 च. 57	11 चं. 57	11 चं. 60	11 चं. 60	11चं. 60
12 मं. 56	12 मं. 60	12 मं. 60	12 मं. 59	12 मं. 61	12 मं. 61
7	8	9	10	11	12
10 र. 61	10 र. 59	10 म. 1	10 र. 1	10 र. 1	10 र. 1
11 च. 60	11 चं. 60	11 बुध. 3	11 चं. 58	11 चं. 58	11 चं. 60
12 मं. 61	12 मं. 59	12 गु. 0	12 मं. 57	12 मं. 60	12 मं. 58
13	14	15	16	17	18
10 र. 1	10 र. 1	10 र. 1	10 र. 1	10 र. 1	10 र. 1
11 चं. 60	11 चं. 60	11 चं. 60	11 चं. 2	11 चं. 1।।	11 चं. 2
12 मं. 60	12 मं. 61	12 मं. 61	12 चं. 60	12 चं. 57	12 चं. 61

अथ स्थूलतया सुगमप्रकारेणैकादशी—

या स्याद्विष्णुतिथी रवेरुदयगा मुहूर्तमात्रापि सा
ग्राह्या युग्मदिनोदये यदि तदा स्याद्द्वादशीसंयुता।
लुप्तैकादशिवित्तदा व्रतपरैर्ग्राह्या व्रते द्वादशी
कुर्यात्कामतिथौ हि पारणविधिं सत्कर्मधर्माय वै।।22।।

स्वादेकादशिसुव्रते यदि तदा तत्पारणं भोजनं
द्वादश्यां हरिवासरादिरहितां कुर्यात्सदा वैष्णवैः।
योऽन्नं वै हरिवासरेऽथ सुव्रते भुक्त्वा तमिस्त्रं व्रजे-
च्छुक्ला वा परपक्षगा हरितिथिर्न्यूनाधिका सा न हि।।23।।

अथ पद्मललितैकादशी—

चैत्रे वै धवले च पद्मललिता संज्ञेति विष्णोस्तिथि-
स्तस्यां वै नियमेन संयुतव्रती विष्णुं घृतेनैव तु।
संसिच्यान्निशि जागरादिविधिना नीत्वा च सूर्योदये
होमः क्षौद्रतिलैश्च वेदविदुषे शाल्यर्पणं स्वर्गदम्।।24।।

अथ विष्णोर्दोलोत्सवम् (वः)—

मधौ शुक्लपक्षे च वैकुण्ठतिथ्यां
हरिं पूजयेद्दोलकारोहणस्थम्।
ततः सार्धमासं सुपुष्पोत्कहर्म्ये
हरिं स्थापयेद्वैष्णवैर्मुक्तिहेतोः।।25।।

इति पुष्पमण्डल्युत्सवम् (वः)।

अथ दमनारोपणोत्सवः—

चैत्रे द्वादशिका तिथिर्धवलगा [9]चेन्दूदयव्यापिनी
तस्यां यन्त्रघटस्थितं दमनकं संपूजयेद्वैष्णवैः।
नाम्ना कामवसन्तयोः सुविधिना संप्रार्थ्यते नैव तु
विष्णोः संपरिपूजनाच्च सफला पूजा भवेद्वार्षिकी।।26।।

अथ अनङ्गत्रयोदशीव्रतम्—

चैत्रे सिता स्मरतिथिः सवितोदयाद्या
तस्यां व्रतं वितनुयान्नरनारिभिश्च।
कामं वसन्तसहितं विधिनार्चयन्ति
ते वै सदा सुरसुरूपसमन्विताः स्युः।।27।।

अथ चैत्रीपौर्णिमा—

चैत्रे पूर्णा पराद्या भवति च सदा मन्दसूर्येज्यवारै-
र्युक्ता चित्रान्विता साप्यतिसुकृतकरा स्नानदानादिकृत्ये।
ग्राह्या सा देवकृत्ये दमनविधिवशात्पूजयेत्सर्वदेवा-
न्सा वै मन्वादिसंज्ञा विहितविधिकरा पितृणां तृप्तिदात्री।।28।।

अथ वैशाखस्नानम्—

चैत्र्यां मेषगते रवौ वितनुयात्स्नानं सदा माधवे
तीर्थे वा सुजलेऽरुणोदयगते सद्ब्रह्मचर्यान्वितः।
कुर्याद्वै मधुसूदनस्य यजनं यावत्सिता पौर्णिमा
भूशय्या च हविष्यभोजनपरो नक्तैकभक्तोऽथवा।।29।।

अथ वैशाखस्नानानन्तरकर्माह—

स्नाने माधवसंज्ञके मधुरिपुं लक्षैकवृन्दादलै-
र्यो वै[10] अर्चयते स मुक्तिफलभाक् सौख्यान्वितो मानवः।
योऽश्वत्स्थः परिसिञ्चयेज्जलघटैः कुर्यात्परिक्रामणं
सोऽपि मोक्षफलं लभेच्च सततं सौख्यं सुरेन्द्रोपमम्।।30।।

अथ वैशाखस्नानोद्योपनविधिः —

वैशाख्यां च शुभेऽह्नि मासव्रतवान्सन्मण्डपे मण्डले
कुम्भस्थं मधुसूदनं सह रमां संपूजयेज्जागरम्।
कृत्वा सद्घृतपायसेन हवनं त्रिंशद्द्विजान्भोजये-
च्छय्याछत्रमुपानहौ सुकलशान्दद्यात्स सायुज्यभाक्।।31।।

अथ कल्पादितिथिः —

चैत्रे कृष्णे पञ्चमी या तिथिस्तु
कल्पाद्या वै सा पराह्णान्वितायाम्।
यद्यद्दानं पूजनं वा जपं वा
तत्तत्सर्वं चाक्षयं स्यान्नराणाम्।।32।।

अथ चण्डीव्रतम्—

कृष्णाष्टम्यां चैत्रमासे विदध्या-
न्नारीभिस्तु चण्डिकाख्यं व्रतं च।
तीर्थस्नानाच्चण्डिपूजोपवासा-
त्सौभाग्यं स्यात्पुत्रपौत्रादियुक्तम्।।33।।

अथ वैरूथिन्येकादशीव्रतम्—

चैत्रे कृष्णविभागके हरितिथिर्वैरूथिनीसंज्ञिता
तस्यां वै सुघृताभिषेकविधिना विष्णुं समभ्यर्चयेत्।

द्वादश्यां हवनं मधुघृततिलैर्दत्त्वाढकस्तन्दुला-
नग्निष्टोमफलं लभेद्बहुगुणं यो भुञ्जते सुव्रती।।34।।

अथ श्रीमद्वल्लभोत्सवः —

चैत्रे चापरपक्षगा हरितिथौ शुद्धाधिकायां तु वै
श्रीमद्वल्लभदेवमार्गगजनैर्जन्मोत्सवं कारयेत्।
विद्धायां च तिथिक्षयेऽथ दिवसस्यार्धे हरिं पूजये-
च्छ्रीमद्वै गुरुपादुकां स्वविभवैः पूजोपहारादिभिः।।35।।

अथ वरुणपर्वमा(र्व आ)ह—

चैत्रस्यापरपक्षगा स्मरतिथिः पाश्यर्क्षपंगुशुभै-
र्युक्ता कोटिरविग्रहोपमफला पर्व भवेद्वारुणम्।
स्नात्वा सत्सरितेऽर्चयेच्च वरुणं गोहेमभूम्यर्पणं
कुर्यात्सौख्यसमृद्धयेऽतिसुकृताँल्लभ्येत गाङ्गं नरः।।36।।

अथ प्रेतत्वमोचनपर्वः (र्व)—

कृष्णा चतुर्दशिमधौ मनुजां हिताय
संनिर्मिता च विधिना सुकृतप्रदात्री।
स्नात्वा सुतीर्थसलिले शिवसन्निधौ यः
प्रेतत्वदोषमपहाय सुरोत्तमः स्यात्।।37।।

अथ स्वर्गप्रदपर्वः (र्व)—

चैत्रेऽमा पूर्वविद्धा पितृतिथिरमा स्यात्सदा दर्शकृत्ये
सा चेच्चन्द्रार्कवारे क्रियमगतरवौ रेवतीवैधृताढ्या।
योगः स्वर्गप्रदोऽसौ दशरविग्रहणैस्तुल्यता स्यान्नराणां
तीर्थस्नाने च दानेऽप्यथ पितृयजने भोजने वै द्विजानाम्।।38।।

अथ संक्रान्तिपर्वः (र्व)—

संक्रान्तिकालः समयो हि सूक्ष्मः
पुण्यप्रदः पापहरो नराणाम्।
धर्मार्थकामामृतसाधनानां
सिद्धिप्रदो मुक्तिफलस्य हेतुः।।39।।

संक्रान्तिकालात्परपूर्वभागे
पुण्या घटी षोडश षोडशैव।
सदौषधिस्नानमथार्कपूजा
श्राद्धं विपिण्डं विहितं च दानम्।।40।।

या पूर्वभागा[11] द्विचरेत्प्रभाते
चेत्पुण्यदा स्यात्परनाडिकासु।
परार्धया स्याद्यदि भास्करास्ते
पूर्वासु पुण्येति च गौणकालः।।41।।

यदा निशीथे रविसंक्रमः स्या-
द्दिनद्वयं पुण्यफलप्रदं च।
स्नानं च दानं सुरार्चनाद्यं
रात्रौ निषेधात्परिचिन्तनीयम्।।42।।

संक्रान्तौ वर्ज्यकर्माणि

सूर्यस्य संक्रान्तिदिनं विवर्ज्यं
विवाहमौञ्ज्यादिकमङ्गलेषु।
गोलायने चाथ दिनार्धमात्रं
क्रत्वान्तरेऽन्यासु परा परा च।।43।।

अथोत्तरगोलपर्वः (र्व)—

स्यात्सोम्यगोलरजभे रविसंक्रमाच्च
पूर्वा परा दश दशेति घटीस्तु पुण्या।
स्नानं सुतीर्थसरितादिषु सूर्यपूजां
श्राद्धं सुखाय क्रियदानविधिर्नराणाम्।।44।।

इति निर्णयमञ्जर्यामुत्सवव्रतादिकथनं नाम प्रथमोऽध्यायः।।1।।

।। द्वितीयोऽध्यायः।।

अथ वैशाखमासस्येश्वरादीनाह—

राधे वै मधुसूदनस्य वचनात्तेजोनिधिस्त्वर्यमा
पुलहेनैव सहायतो विचरति पद्माह्वनागेन तु।

तुर्यं वाद्यति नारदोऽत्र समये नृत्यन्ति पुञ्जस्थला
मासं माधवसंज्ञकं नयति वै सत्कर्मपुण्यप्रदम्।।1।।[12]

अथाक्षय्यतृतीयानिर्णयः—

राधे या तृतीयाक्षयेति धवला रव्यूदयव्यापिनी
ग्राह्या वै परमा तु सा कभयुता ज्ञेन्दुद्युयुक्तापि चेत्।
तस्यां चन्दनसौरभादिव्यजनैः संपूजयेन्माधवं
सा वै सा तु युगादिका बहुगुणा कल्पादिकृत्येऽपि सा।।2।।[13]

अथाक्षय्यतृतीयायां कृत्यमाह—

सा वै चाक्षयसंज्ञिकेति तृतीया तस्यां सुतीर्थोदके
स्नात्वा यः सुयवान्नतो हि विधिना संपूजयेन्माधवम्।
होमं प्राशनमर्पणं शुचिकरं कुर्यात्तु कुम्भोदकं
शक्तुग्रीष्मजसस्यपुष्पसफलान्दद्यात्सुखार्थी नरः।।3।।

तस्यां परशुरामजयन्तीव्रतम्—

वैशाखे तृतिया सिता निशिमुखे तस्यां सुजन्मोत्सवं
कुर्याद्युग्मदिनोपगाः परयुताश्चान्यत्र पूर्वास्तथा।
स्नात्वा तद्व्रतवान् यजेत्सुविधिना रामं तथा रेणुकां
जमदग्निं स तु पुण्यभाग्भवति वै कोट्यश्वमेधाधिकः।।4।।

अथ गाङ्गसप्तम्युत्सवः—

या सप्तमी माधवशुक्लपक्षे
दिनार्धजायां मनुजो जितात्मा।
स्नात्वा सुतीर्थे यजतीह गङ्गां
मुक्तिं लभेत्किल्बिषसंयुतोऽपि।।5।।

मोहिन्येकादशी—

शुक्लैकादशि माधवे भवति या सा मोहिनीसंज्ञिता
तस्यां वै मधुसूदनं च विधिना क्षीराभिषेकेण तु।
वह्नौ चैव घृताहुतिं वितनुयात्कुम्भं घृताढ्यं ददे-
द्धुङ्क्ते यः स व्रती फलं च लभते यद्वाजिमेधोद्भवम्।।6।।

अथ पुण्यप्रदपर्वम् (र्व)—

सिंहस्थौ गुरुभूमिजौ क्रियगते सूर्ये सिता द्वादशी
वैशाखे व्यतिपातहस्तभयुते तस्यां सुपुण्याभिधम्।
पर्वेऽस्मिन्सलिलं च गौतमिसमं विप्रस्तु ब्रह्मोपमः
स्याद्गोभूकनकार्पणैस्तु पुरुषो मुच्येन्महापातकात्।।7।।

अथ नृसिंहचतुर्दशीव्रतम्—

वैशाखस्य चतुर्दशी धवलगा मित्रोदयव्यापिनी
ग्राह्या स्वातिशशान्विता च परमा काभान्विता सा त्यजेत्।
तस्यां वै सुव्रती दिनान्तसमये हैमं नृसिंहं यजे-
त्पूर्णायां द्विजभोजनं च गुरवे पीठार्पणं मुक्तिदम्।।8।।

अथ वैशाखीपौर्णिमाकृत्यम्—

वैशाखी पौर्णिमा या शिवतिथिसहिता वाथ सार्धत्रियामा
तस्यां स्नात्वा सृतान्त्रं[14] जलयुतकलशान्दापयेत्सौख्यहेतोः।
हेमं वस्त्रं सिताज्यं गुडमधुसतिलान्वाथ कृष्णाजिनं च
गोदानं वा स्वशक्त्याखिलदुरितविनाशाय दद्याद्द्विज्येभ्यः।।9।।

अथापरैकादशीव्रतम्—

कृष्णैकादशि या परेति कथिता मासे सुवैशाखके
तस्याराधनतत्प[15]रो मधुरिपुं क्षीराभिषेकेण तु।
होम(मं) साज्यतिलैर्विधाय सघृतं कोशोद्भवं दापये-
द्भूमेर्यस्तु (त्तु) परिक्रमोद्भवफलं संप्राप्यते मानवः।।10।।

अथ वैशाखी अमा—

या माधवे दर्शतिथिः सुपुण्या
सार्धत्रियामान्वितपूर्वविद्धा।
स्नाने च दाने च सुरार्चने च
पित्र्यर्चनेऽनन्तफलप्रदात्री।।11।।

अथ वृषसंक्रान्तिः—

ग्रीष्मर्तुः संनिवेशो भवति हरिपदी संज्ञिता वै वृषार्के
तत्संचाराच्च पूर्वा नृपमतिघटिका(:) पुण्यदा(:) पुण्यकाले।

तस्यां स्नानं सुतीर्थे श्रुतिहितविधिना पूजनं भास्करस्य
श्राद्धं विप्रादिभोज्यं शतदशगुणितं स्यात्तथा धेनुदानम्।।12।।

इत्युत्सवनिर्णयमञ्जर्यां वैशाखमासव्रतनिर्णयः।।2।।

।। तृतीयोऽध्यायः।।

अथ ज्येष्ठमासेश्वरादीनाह—

ज्येष्ठे त्रिविक्रमनिदेशवशाच्च पित्रोः
संगच्छते गुरुबलेन सतक्षकेन।
हाहेति वाद्यविधुरोऽध्वनि मेनकाख्या
नृत्यन्नयन्ति भृगुमासदिवानिशं च।।1।।[16]

अथ रम्भाव्रतम्—

ज्येष्ठे वै तृतिया सिताथ नभसि शुक्ला च भूताभिधा
राका माधवमासकार्तिकगता स्यात्पूर्वविद्धा तु सा।
स्वाचारात्कदलीव्रतेषु विबुधैर्ग्राह्याप्यनस्तं गते
शुक्रे वा सुरपूजिते च विबले चन्द्रे कुयोगोक्तिगे।।2।।

अथ रम्भाव्रतविधिः—

या रम्भाव्रतकारिणी च युवती स्नाता विभूषान्विता
प्रेमानन्दभरेण शास्त्रविधिना रम्भाद्रुमं रो[17]पयेत्।
गेहे पूजनमम्बुसिञ्चनविधिं कुर्यात्फलाढ्या यदा
हेमोत्थां कदलीं सुपीठसहितां दद्यात्सुपुत्रा भवेत्।।3।।

[18]********वृषगते सूर्ये गिरानन्दक्रे
पाते हस्त[19]बुधान्विते दशहरा पर्वं सुपुण्यप्रदम्।
या काचित्सरितोदके सुविधिना स्नात्वा च गङ्गां यजे-
द्गोभूहेमतिलार्पणैस्तु मनुजो मुच्येन्महापातकात्।।4।।

अथ दशहरापर्वे (र्वणि) तीर्थविशेषात्फलविशेषः —

योगेऽस्मिन्दशके च सेतुपुलिने रामेश्वरस्यार्चना-
न्मुच्येत्पातकराशितो हि मनुजः स स्वर्गसौख्यं लभेत्।

गङ्गां यां (यो) मनुजस्तु पुण्यनिचयाल्लभ्येत चेद्वै तदा
मुच्येद्वै दशजन्मपापनिचयाद्गाङ्गव्रतान्मुक्तिभाक् ।5।।

अथ निर्जलैकादशी—

ज्येष्ठे शुक्लविभागके हरितिथिः सा निर्जला संज्ञिता
तस्यां शर्करया सुधेनुपयसा संस्नापयेद्विक्र[20]मम्।
द्वादश्यां घृतपायसैस्तु हवनं हेमान्नकुम्भोदकं
दद्याद्वै नरमेधजं स लभते पुण्यं व्रतेनैव तु।।6।।

अथ ज्येष्ठपूर्णिमापर्वम् (र्व)—

ज्येष्ठे वै खलु पूर्णिमा शिवतिथि वि(र्वि)द्धा च दानार्पणे
सा सूर्योदयगामिनी च विबुधैर्ग्राह्या च मन्वादिके।
ऐन्द्रर्क्षेन्दुगुरूकभे च सविता ज्येष्ठान्विता पौर्णिमा
योगेऽस्मिन्महती सुदानविषये स्नानेऽर्चने दुर्लभा।।7।।

वटसावित्रीव्रतम्—

ज्येष्ठे पूर्णतिथिर्गजेन्दुघटिका भूतान्विता सा त्यजे-
त्पूर्वा वाथ परान्विता व्रतविधौ सावित्रिके स्यात्सदा।
तस्यां वै त्रिदिनव्रताद्युवतिभिर्न्यग्रोधमूलेऽर्चये-
त्सावित्रीं त्रिसमान्तके च प्रतिमादानात्सुसौभाग्यभाक्।।8।।

अथ स्नानयात्रोत्सवम् (वः)—

ज्येष्ठे ज्येष्ठासंयुता पूर्णिमायां
शुद्धायां वा पञ्च पीयूषभिर्यः।
सूक्तैर्विष्णोः शीतनीराभिषेकं
कुर्याद्भक्त्या भुक्तिमुक्तिं लभेत।।9।।

अथ योगिन्येकादशीव्रतम्—

ज्येष्ठे कृष्णैकादशी योगिनी स्या-
त्तस्यां क्षीरासेचनं विक्रमस्य।
प्रातर्होमं पायसेनैव कुर्या-
त्पक्वान्नं वै दापयेन्मुक्तिहेतुः।।10।।

ज्येष्ठी अमावास्यापर्वणी—

ज्येष्ठे कुह्वां कर्मनिष्ठैर्मनुष्ये(ष्यैस्)
तीर्थस्नानं देवपित्र्यर्चनं च।
कुर्याद्भक्त्या नीरकुम्भं सधान्यं
दत्त्वा भुङ्क्ते स्वर्गसौख्यं सभोगः।।11।।

अथ मिथुनसंक्रान्तिः—

षडशीतिमुखसंज्ञिता मिथुनभे[21] आदित्यसंचारतो
नाड्यस्तु परभागिका नृपमिता(:) पुण्या(:) सुपुण्यक्रतौ।
स्नानं सत्सरितादिपुण्यसरसि भक्त्या च सूर्यं यजे-
त्सद्वस्त्राभरणानि वेदविदुषे दद्यात्सुसौख्यार्थये।।12।।

इति निर्णयोत्सवमञ्जर्यां ज्येष्ठकृत्यम्। तृतीयोऽध्यायः।।

।। चतुर्थोऽध्यायः।।

अथ आषाढमासेश्वरादीनाह—

आषाढेश्वरवामनस्य वचनाद्गच्छेद्द्वियन्मण्डलं
तिग्मांशुर्वरुणो वसिष्ठविभवात्सुश्रावनागेन तु।
हूहूर्वाद्यसुघोषवादनपरो नृत्यन्ति रम्भाशरा
मासं वै शुचिसंज्ञकं विनयति रात्रिदिवाभागतः।।1।।

अथ रथयात्रोत्सवम् (वः)—

शुचौ सिते पुण्ययुता द्वितीया
शुद्धा तिथिर्ऋक्षविभागके च।
तस्यां रथस्थं च हरिं समर्च्य
यात्रोत्सवान्मुक्तिवतो मनुष्यः।।2।।

मन्वादिराह—

आषाढमासे धवले च पक्षे
सूर्योदयव्यापिनिका दशम्याम्।
सनीरकुम्भं सुफलान्नदानं
सुखार्थदं सापि मनोस्तिथिस्तु।।3।।

अथ देवशयन्येकादशी—

आषाढे धवले च देवशयनी विष्णोस्तिथिः कीर्तिता
तस्यां वै पयसाभिषेकविधिना संपूजयेद्वामनम्।
होमं सघृतदुर्वया वितनुयाच्छ्रीनालिकेरार्पणं
कृत्वा विप्रवराय सस्तु लभते श्रीवाजिपेयोद्भवम्।।4।।

देवशयनोत्सवमाह—

शयन्येकादश्यां भुजगशयनीं हेमप्रतिमां
हरेस्तां संपूज्य पयदधिसितासर्पिमधुभिः।
सुपर्यङ्के स्थाप्या शयनविधिना सुव्रतधरो
नरो वा नारी वा लभति सुमहामुक्तिपदवीम्।।5।।

चातुर्मास्यव्रतारम्भः—

कर्केऽर्केऽप्यथवा सुषुप्तिसमये वा पौर्णमास्यां बुधै-
श्चातुर्मास्यव्रतं तथैव नियमान्प्रारम्भयेद्भक्तितः।
अस्ते वा गुरुशुक्रयोस्तु मकरे सिंहस्थितेज्ये तथा
वक्रे वाप्यतिवारकेऽरिभगते मासाधिकेऽपि तथा।।6।।

चातुर्मास्ये नियमानि(माः)—

शाकं वै नभसंज्ञिके दधि तथा भाद्रेऽश्विने वै पयः
ऊर्जेऽन्नं द्विदलं त्यजेत्तु बदरं [22]वार्ताककूष्माण्डके।
धात्रीमूलकबीजपूरकपटोलंबीरकौलत्थका-
न्खट्वारोहणमद्यमांसविषयाँस्तुर्येषु मासेष्वपि।।7।।

चातुर्मास्यव्रते फलोदयम् (यः)—

स्याद्वै सुस्वरवान्गुडव्रतधरो(रस्) तैली सुरूपाकृति-
र्योगाभ्यासरतो हि ब्रह्मपदवीं ताम्बूलिको भोगवान्।
लावण्यं च घृतवती कुशनिरात्पुत्रान्नयाची सुखं
नक्तैकान्तरमौनपत्रमशनैर्मुक्तिं हविष्याद्व्रतम्।।8।।

व्रतपारणानिर्णयः—

शयन्येकादश्यां व्रतयुतनरैः पारणविधिं
विदद्यादद्वादश्यां सुकृतहरमित्रर्क्षवियुता।

वियुक्तालाभे वै प्रथमपदमिर्त्रक्षघटिका-
वियोगान्ते कुर्याद्व्रतफलसमृद्ध्यर्थविबुधैः ।।9।।

अथ[23] गोपद्मव्रतम्—

कार्यं वै शयनीदिनात्प्रतिदिनं यावत्प्रबोधो हरे-
र्गोपद्माख्यव्रतं सतीयुवतिभिर्गोष्ठे शुभे मण्डले।
पद्मानि सुरसंमितानि रचयन्संपूजयेत्केशवं
तत्संख्यावयनार्पणैश्च नतिभिः पञ्चाब्दिकं मुक्तिदम् ।।10।।

अथ पार्वतीव्रतम्—

आषाढे धवले त्रयोदशितिथिमारभ्य पञ्चाह्निकं
नारीभिर्विविधं सुपार्वतिव्रतं वैधव्यविध्वंसनम्।
कुर्यात्पार्वतिपूजनं सहहरं यं(यत्)पञ्च पञ्चाब्दिकं
षष्ठेऽह्नि सकलत्रकान्द्विजवरान्संपूज्य संतोषयेत् ।।11।।

अथ विष्णोरान्दोलोत्सवम् (वः)—

शुचौ शुक्लविश्वाह्नि[24] गोविन्दधिष्ण्ये
सुलग्ने हरेर्दोलकारोहणं वा।
पराह्णे सदा गीतवादित्रघोषै-
र्विधेयोत्सवः श्रावणीपौर्णिमान्तम् ।।12।।

अथ कोकिलाव्रतम्—

भूताद्याषाढिकायां सुमतियुवतिभिः कोकिलाख्यं व्रतं य-
न्मासस्नानोपवासात्कलिकलुषहरं कोकिलापूजनेन।
तस्यां वै पार्वतीशं शयनविधिवशात्पूजयेत्स्वार्थकामा-
न्कार्यं वा व्यासपूजाश्रुतिमुखविदुषैः पूर्वविद्धां विहाय ।।13।।

अथ स्वस्तिकव्रतम्—

आषाढाद्वा देवसुप्तिव्रताद्वा
कुर्यान्नारी तुर्यमासैर्व्रताद्या।
देवागारे स्वस्तिकान्पञ्चवर्णा-
न्सकृल्लक्षान्भुक्तिमुक्तिप्रदाँश्च ।।14।।

[25]अथ परमाषाढीयोगः—

पूर्वाषाढासंयुता शुक्लयोगे
सोमे पूर्णा दुर्लभा पुण्यकृत्ये।
या पूर्वाह्णव्यापिनी पूर्णिमा च
तस्यां स्नानं दानमन्वादिकृत्यम्।।15।।

[26]इति मन्वादिः तिथिः।

प्रसङ्गाद्वायूनाह—

आषाढ्यां भास्करास्ते सुरपतिककुभं वायुवाते सुवृष्टिः
सस्यार्धं संप्रकुर्याद्यदि दहनदिशा मन्ददृष्टिर्यमेन।
नैर्ऋत्यां मध्यमा स्याद्वरुणबहुजला वायुना वायुकोपैः
कौबेर्यां सस्यपूर्णा भवति वसुमती तद्वदीशानवाते।।16।।

इति तिथिप्रसङ्गाद्वायुपरीक्षा।

अथ कामिकैकादशी—

कृष्णा विष्णुतिथिः शुचौ भवति या सा कीर्तिता कामिका
तस्यां यः पयसा घृतेन व्रतवाञ्छ्रीवामनं सिञ्चयेत्।
वह्नौ धान्यघृताहुतिं वितनुयाद्दध्यन्नदानं तथा
पक्वान्नैर्द्विजभोजनं च स लभेद्यत्कोटिभोज्योद्भवम्।।17।।

[27]अथ आषाढी अमा—

[28]आषाढे चेद्द्विह्नियुक्ता कुहुश्च
ग्राह्या दैवे पैतृके चैव दाने।
सार्पर्क्षे सा भौमचन्द्रार्कवारे
पाताढ्या चेद्दुर्लभा पुण्यकृत्ये।।18।।

आषाढे वै प्रतिपद्द्विह्नियुक्ता
कुहुश्च ग्राह्या देवकर्मे च दाने।
सा पाताढ्या मन्दचन्द्रार्कवारे
स्नाने दाने दुर्लभा विप्रभोज्ये।।18।।

कर्कसंक्रान्तिः—

स्याव्द्याम्यायनसंज्ञिका भवति वै वर्षर्तुसंवेशके
कर्कसंक्रमणाद्रवेस्तु घटिकाः पूर्वाश्च त्रिंशन्मिताः।
पुण्या कोटिप्रदेति कथिता तस्यां नरो भक्तिमा-
न्स्नात्वा पुण्यजलेऽर्कपूजनपरो दद्याद्घृतं सौरभीम्॥19॥

इत्युत्सवनिणर्यमञ्जर्यामाषाढमासकथनं नाम चतुर्थोऽध्यायः॥4॥

॥ पञ्चमोऽध्यायः॥

अथ श्रावणमासस्येश्वरादीनाह—

मनोधीश्वरः[29] श्रीधरस्यानुदेशा-
च्चरेदिन्द्रनामाङ्गिरा वीर्यतश्च।
राह स्रोतसा नृत्यकृत्प्रम्लुचाख्या
सुवाजि(दि)त्रकर्ता हि विश्वावसुश्च॥1॥

अथ बिल्वरोटकव्रतम्—

मासे वै नभसाद्वये च धवले पूर्वेन्दुवारे व्रतं
कुर्याद्रोटकसंज्ञकं सुधनदं स्नात्वा हरस्यार्चनम्।
माहात्म्यश्रवणं च कार्तिकसिते भूतासु संपूजनं
कृत्वा रोटकपञ्चकैः सुविधिना दानार्पणं भोजनम्॥2॥

अथ[30] मङ्गलागौरीव्रतम्—

गौरीमङ्गलिकाव्रतं नभसिगे स्त्रीभिः कुजेऽह्नि सिते
स्नात्वा गौरिहरार्चनं च गुडयुग्गोधूमसंसेवनात्।
अन्त्येऽह्नि निशि जागरं युवतिनां संपूजनं तोषये-
त्सौभाग्यादिसमृद्धये च प्रतिमादानं च पञ्चाब्दिके॥3॥

मधुसुश्रवा तृतीयोत्सवः—

[31]या वै तृतीया श्रावणशुक्लपक्षे
मधुश्रवाख्या च सदा परैव।
ग्राह्या च तस्यां मनुजैः प्रहृष्टै-
र्महोत्सवं मङ्गलगीतघोषैः॥4॥

शुक्ला या तृतिया नभस्युदयगा सत्स्वर्णगौरीव्रतं
तस्यां वै मनुजैर्विधानचतुरैर्भक्त्या च गौरीं यजेत्।
स्तुत्या दोरकबन्धनं नृपमिते वर्षे तमुद्यापये-
द्दानाल्लक्ष्मिकलत्रपुत्रसहितं सौख्यं लभेच्चाक्षयम्।।5।।

इति स्वर्णगौरीव्रतम्।

अथ[32] गणपतिव्रते तिथिनिर्णयः—

शुक्ले या सुचतुर्थिका परयुता मध्याह्निकव्यापिनी
ग्राह्या चापरपक्षगा च विबुधैश्चन्द्रोदयव्यापिनी।
व्याप्त्यव्याप्तिगतावुभावपि दिनौ पूर्वान्विता सर्वदा
तस्यां स्वेष्टकरं गजाननव्रतं कुर्यात्सुपूजादिभिः।।6।।

दूर्वागणपतिव्रतम्—

दूर्वाविघ्नपसंज्ञकं नभसि या शुक्ला चतुर्थीतिथौ
कार्तिक्यामथवार्कवासरयुतां प्रारम्भयेत्सद्व्रतम्।
हैमीं सत्प्रतिमां तथा कनकजैर्दूर्वाङ्कुरैरासनं
कृत्वा मण्डलकुम्भगेऽर्चनविधिं पञ्चाब्दिकं सिद्धिदम्।।7।।

नागपञ्चमीव्रतम्—

शुक्ले पञ्चमिका तिथिः परयुता भाद्रेऽथवा श्रावणे
तस्यां वै विधिना व्रती स्वविभवैर्नागं च संपूजयेत्।
नैवेद्यं घृतमोदकैः सुपयसा मासे च मासे पुनः
कुर्याद्द्वादशवार्षिकं च प्रतिमादानार्पणाद्रोगदम्।।8।।

पुत्रदा नामैकादशी—

सितैकादशी पुत्रदा श्रावणे च
व्रती श्रीधरं पूजयेत्क्षौद्रदुग्धैः।
तिलाज्यैस्तु होमं सुवर्णस्य दानं
मनुष्यो लभेद्वाजिमेधोत्थपुण्यम्।।9।।

विष्णोः पवित्रारोपणोत्सवमाह—

या श्रावणैकादशी शुक्लपक्षे
विहाय विष्टिं व्रतिभिश्च तस्याम्।

कुर्यात्पवित्रैस्त्रिविधैस्तु विष्णोः
संपूजनं पुण्यफलस्य हेतोः।।10।।

पवित्राद्वादशीव्रतम्—

द्वादश्यां गुरवे सुमन्त्रविधिना कुर्यात्पवित्रार्पणं
शौचाद्यापदिके च भक्तिनियुतैः पूर्णासु हर्यर्क्षके।
अस्यामेव दधिव्रतं वितनुयादारोग्यसौख्येप्सुभिः
सन्नयमाम्य मनुजैस्तदर्पणविधि(र्वि)प्राय पूर्णे व्रते।।11।।

श्रावणीनिर्णयः—

श्रावण्यां श्रवणेऽथवा द्विजवरैः कुर्यादुपाकर्मकं
संक्रान्तिग्रहणादिदूषिततिथौ प्राग्रात्रिकाले यदा।
कार्यं श्रावणिका सिता च करभाढ्यां नागतिथ्यां बुधैः
श्रावण्यां विधिना च विष्टिरहिते सद्रक्षिकाबन्धनम्।।12।।

अशून्यशयनव्रतम्—

कृष्णा वै द्वितिया नभस्युदयगा रि(इ)न्दोरशून्यस्वपं
कुर्याद्वै जलपात्रगं सहरमाविष्णुं नरैः पूजयेत्।
भुक्त्वा सार्पियवान् तदर्पणविधिं मासे च मासे पुनः
कार्तिक्यां प्रतिमादिगोभूशयनीदानात्सुसौख्यार्थदम्।।13।।

अथ कज्जलिकाव्रततिथिनिर्णयः—

कृष्णा या तृतिया नभस्युदयगा तस्यां सु(स)स्यार्थिभिः
कुर्यात्कज्जलिकाव्रतं बहुगुणं गौर्यर्चनाज्जागरात्।
प्रत्येकान्नविभोजनात्सुविधिना पञ्चाब्दिकान्ते पुन-
र्वस्त्राद्याभरणैः स्वभोज्यविधिना स्त्रीणां समभ्यर्चयेत्।।14।।

बहुलाचतुर्थीव्रतम्—

कृष्णा चतुर्थि बहुलेत्यभिधानिका स्या-
त्तस्यां यवान्नमशनेन नितम्बिनीभिः।
सच्छ्रावणे निशियुता च सदा प्रशस्ता
वत्सार्चनं कलुषनाशकरं विधेयम्।।15।।

संकष्टचतुर्थीव्रतम्—

कृष्णे वै नभसार्कगे गणपतेस्तिथ्यां च चन्द्रोदये
संकष्टोत्तरणव्रती गणपतिं संपूजयेद्भक्तितः।
नैवेद्यं च सुमोदकैर्वितनुयात्सर्वेषु मासेष्वपि
स्वर्गाङ्क(21)प्रतिमे समासु हवनं दानार्पणं भोजनम्।।16।।

हलषष्ठीव्रतम्—

या कृष्णा हलषष्ठिसंज्ञिततिथिः सा सप्तमीसंयुता
ग्राह्या श्रावणिका च कार्षुकजनैः कुर्याद्व्रतं धान्यदम्।
समन्त्रैश्च हलाधिपं सुवृषभान्भूमिं समभ्यर्चये-
द्भुक्त्वा वै सुयवाँश्च वेदविदुषे सद्धान्यदानार्पणम्।।17।।

शीतलासप्तमी—

या सप्तमी श्रावणकृष्णपक्षे
षष्ठ्यन्विता शीतलिकाव्रते च।
तस्यां सुपुत्रार्थनीभिस्तु देवीं
संपूजयेच्छीतलभक्ष्यभोज्यैः।।18।।

दशफलाव्रतम्—

या कृष्णाष्टमि श्रावणे दशफला संज्ञा निशीथान्विता
तस्यामब्जदलैर्हरिं च सुव्रती वृन्दादलैः पूजयेत्।
स्तुत्या दोरकबन्धनं च दशमे घस्त्रे द्विजान्भोजये-
देवं वै दशमाब्दिके च हवनं पीठार्पणं मुक्तिदम्।।19।।

श्रीकृष्णजयन्तीव्रतम्—

मासे श्रावणकेऽष्टमी च बहुला चन्द्रोदयव्यापिनी
सा वै रोहिणिसंयुतेति परमा स्मार्तैर्जयन्तीव्रते।
तस्यां वै सुव्रती सुपूजनविधिं कृत्वाथ तत्पारणं
तिथ्यन्तेऽप्यथवा च भान्तसमये संभोज्य विप्राँस्ततः।।20।।

जन्माष्टमीतिथिनिर्णयः—

सा शुद्धाष्टमि केवला च नवमी ह्रासे तु जन्माष्टमी
ग्राह्या विष्णुपरायणैश्च विबुधैर्जन्मोत्सवे सद्व्रते।

कृत्वा पुण्यव्रतं निशीथसमये तस्यां च कृष्णार्चनं
कुर्यान्नन्दमहोत्सवं स्वविभवैः सत्संप्रदायादिभिः।।21।।

अथ तयोरुद्यापनविधिरा(मा)ह—

तदुद्यापनके तयोर्व्रतधरः सन्मण्डपे मण्डले
श्रीकृष्णं वसुदेवदेवकीयुतं संकर्षणं रोहिणीम्।
कुर्याद्वै विधिनार्चनं स्वविभवैर्नन्दादिगोपाँस्तथा
रात्रौ जागरणं सपीठप्रतिमादानात्सुसायुज्यदम्।।22।।

मन्वादितिथिः—

या पूर्वविद्धाष्टमि कृष्णपक्षे
मन्वादिका श्रावणमासिका च।
स्नाने च दाने सुरपूजने च
पित्र्यर्चने वै परमातिपुण्या।।23।।

अजा नामैकादशी—

नभैकादशी कृष्णपक्षे त्वजाख्या
व्रती सिञ्चयेच्छ्रीधरं गोघृतेन।
घृतेनैव होमं सु(व)स्त्रस्य दानं
ददेद्विप्रवर्याय मोक्षार्थसिद्ध्यै।।24।।

शिवमङ्गलाव्रतम्—

या वै चतुर्दशितिथिर्नभकृष्णपक्षे
तस्यां नरैर्वितनुयाच्छिवपूजनं च।
सद्वाद्यघोषनिशिजागरणादिभिश्च
सत्सौख्यदं व्रतमिदं शिवमङ्गलाख्यम्।।25।।

वरदलक्ष्मीव्रतम्—

मासे श्रावणकेऽन्त्यभार्गवदिने कर्कार्कयुक्ते तदा
कुर्याद्वै वरलक्ष्मिसंज्ञिकव्रतं धर्मार्थकामप्रदम्।
लक्ष्मीं धातुमयीं विधाय चतुरैः कुम्भस्थितामर्चये-
द्भक्त्या दोरकबन्धनं च वयनान्दद्यात्सुभक्त्यादिभिः।।26।।

अथ दर्भमोचिनीनिर्णयः—

या वै श्रावणिका कुहूः सुफलदा ग्राह्या च भूतान्विता
तस्यां वै विदुषैः सुमन्त्रविधिना कुर्यात्कुशोत्पाटनम्।
सा चेत्सूर्यकुजेन्दुवारसहिता पातान्विता पितृभे
सूर्ये वै परमातिदुर्लभतरा सत्स्नानदानादिषु।।27।।

सिंहक्रान्तिः—

संज्ञा विष्णुपदीति सिंहभरविः संचारतः पौर्विका
नाड्यः षोडश पुण्यदेति कथिता(स्)तासु सुखार्थी नरः।
स्नात्वा पुण्यजले रविं च विधिना संपूज्य विप्राय वै
छत्रं हेमसमन्वितं च विधिवद्द्यात्सुराज्यप्रदम्।।28।।

इति श्रीनिर्णयमञ्जर्यां श्रावणमासव्रतोत्सवतिथिनिर्णयो नाम पञ्चमोऽध्यायः।।5।।

।।षष्ठोऽध्यायः।।

अथ भाद्रपदमासस्येश्वरादीनाह—

भाद्राख्यमासि हृषिकेशनिदेशतस्तु
शुक्रप्रभावविबलेन चरेद्विवस्वान्।
सच्छङ्खपालसहनृत्यपरानुमोचा
वाद्यादिवादनपरः खलु उग्रसेनः।।1।।

हरितालिकाव्रतम्—

भाद्रे या तृतिया सिता उदयगा तस्यां च नारीजनैः
कुर्याद्वै हरितालिकाव्रतमिदं सत्पुण्यसौभाग्यदम्।
कृत्वा गौरिहरार्चनं च वयनान्दत्त्वा सुवस्त्रैः फलैः
पूर्णे षोडशवत्सरे द्विजवरान्सा[33]पत्यकान्पूजयेत्।।2।।

हस्तगौरीव्रतम्—

मासे भाद्रपदे सिता सुतृतिया हस्तर्क्षयुक्ता तिथौ
वैधव्यादिदरिद्रनाशनकरं सद्धस्तगौरीव्रतम्।

कुर्यात्सार्धत्रयोदशैस्तु कुसुमैर्गौरीहरस्यार्चना-
द्वर्षे वै मनुसंमिते सुविधिना पीठार्पणं भोजनम्।।3।।

कोटीश्वरीव्रतम्—

भाद्रे सिते वै तृतिया तिथौ च
व्रतं सुकोटीश्वरिसंज्ञकं स्यात्।
अखण्डितैः शालिभिर्वै युवत्या
गौर्यर्चनं पुत्रसुखाप्तिहेतोः।।4।।

मन्वादितिथिः—

पौर्वाह्णिकी या तृतिया च भाद्रे
मन्वादिकृत्ये परमा सिताख्या।
भाद्राद्यपक्षे करभे हितं स्या-
दुत्सर्गकर्म खलु सामागानाम्।।5।।

सिद्धिविनायकव्रतम्—

भाद्रे या सुचतुर्थिका सितगता मध्याह्नसंव्यापिनी
तस्यां सिद्धिविनायकस्य सुव्रतं सत्सौख्यलाभप्रदम्।
कुर्याद्वै सुगजाननं च विधिना संपूजयेन्मोदकैः
स्वर्गाङ्कप्रमितैस्ततो द्विजवरान्संभोज्य तद्दापयेत्।।6।।

चन्द्रदर्शनापवादः—

भाद्रे वै सितगा चतुर्थिदिवसे स्नानं च दानं तथा
भोज्यं वा द्विजभोजनं दशगुणं पुण्यं लभेन्मानवः।
तस्यां चन्द्रविलोकनेन मनुजो मिथ्याभिशापं व्रजे-
त्तद्बाधापहरं मणेश्च चरितं श्रुत्वा पठेद्वा बुधः।।7।।

अथ कपर्दीश्वरविनायकव्रतम्—

मासेऽस्तादिविवर्जितेऽर्कदिवसे शुद्धा चतुर्थीतिथौ
सन्मन्त्रैर्व्रतवान्कपर्दिगणपं संपूजयेद्भक्तितः।
सद्वर्ची बटवे वराटकगणं सत्तण्डुलैः संयुतं
दत्त्वैवं तु[34] चतुष्कभानुदिवसैः सर्वांश्च कामान्लभेत्।।8।।

ऋषिपञ्चमी—

या वै पञ्चमिका नभस्यसितगा सूर्योदयव्यापिनी
तस्यां सप्त ऋषीन्सुमन्त्रविभवैः संपूजयेत्सुव्रती।
स्वकृष्यान्नफलैस्तु विप्रयजनं कृत्वाब्दिके सप्तमे
सत्पूजादिविधानतोऽर्चनविधिः पीठार्पणं सौख्यदम्।।9।।

सूर्यषष्ठीव्रतम्—

षष्ठी तिथिः परयुता धवला च भाद्रे
सा सूर्यषष्ठिति हि पुण्यकरा च तस्याम्।
स्नात्वा सुतीर्थसलिले च रविं समर्च्य
यः पञ्चगव्यमशनं कुरुते स शुद्धः।।10।।

ललिताषष्ठी—

षष्ठी भाद्रपदे सिता च ललिता संज्ञेति तस्यां व्रती
पात्रे वंशमये सुवेलुजनितां सत्पञ्चपिण्डाकृतिम्।
कृत्वा वै ललितां स्मरन्सुकुसमैः संपूज्य सज्जागरं
सप्तम्यां सरितं नयेत्सुविधिना दानादिना सौख्यभाक्।।11।।

मुक्ताभरणी—

भाद्रे वै सितसप्तमीदिनदले कुर्यात्सुपुत्रार्थिनी
मुक्ताहेमविनिर्मिताङ्गुलियकं[35] सोमात्मकं पूजयेत्।
पश्चाद्दोरकबन्धनं व्रतवती मासे च मासेऽर्चनं
वर्षान्ते च समुद्रिकार्पणविधिं कुर्याद्द्विजान्भोजयेत्।।12।।

राधाष्टम्युत्सवम् (वः)—

शुद्धाष्टम्यां भाद्रशुक्ले प्रकुर्या-
च्छ्रीमद्राधाजन्मकालोत्सवं च।
मध्याह्ने वै वैष्णवैर्भक्तियुक्तैः
श्रीसूक्तेनासिञ्चनं मुक्तिहेतोः।।13।।

ज्येष्ठाव्रतम्—

ज्येष्ठे भाद्रपदेऽष्टमीसुरपती-ऋक्षान्वितायां व्रतं
ज्येष्ठाख्यं सुतसौख्यदं त्रिदिवसं वन्ध्यत्वदोषापहम्।

मैत्रे वै विनिमन्त्रयेच्छुभकरीं ज्येष्ठार्क्षगे पूजनं
कुर्याज्जागरणं विसर्जनविधिं मूलेऽर्कवर्षात्मकम्।।14।।

नीलज्येष्ठाव्रतम्—

सा वै सूर्यदिनान्विता यदि भवेत्तन्नीलज्येष्ठाव्रतं
पूर्वेद्युः सिकतां नयेत्सुप्रतिमां कृत्वाथ सन्मण्डले।
स्थाप्या तामपरेऽह्नि पूजनविधिं कृत्वाथ सौवासिनीः
संपूज्येदपरेऽह्नि पूजिततमान्दत्त्वाखिलार्थांल्लभेत्।।15।।

दूर्वाष्टमी—

सिंहार्केऽनुदिते मुनौ नभसि[36] या शुक्लाष्टमी पूर्विका
तस्यां वै सुफलैरनग्निपचितैरन्नैश्च दूर्वां यजेत्।
ज्येष्ठामूलयुता भवेद्यदि सकृद्भुक्तापि तामर्चये-
त्सौभाग्यादिसमृद्धये युवतिभिर्वन्ध्यं न नेयं दिनम्।।16।।

अथात्र प्रसङ्गादगस्त्योदयकालः—

उदेति याम्यां हरिसंक्रमाद्रवे-
र्वैकाधिके विंशतिमे ह्यगस्त्यः।
स सप्तमेऽस्तं वृषसंक्रमाच्च
प्रयाति गर्गादिभिप्यभाणीः(णि)।।17।।

उद्यानिका शिवपवित्रकमेघपूजा
दूर्वाष्टमी फलविरूढकजागराणि।
स्त्रीणां व्रतानि निखिलानि सजागराणि
कुर्यादगस्त्य—उदितेन शुभानि लिप्सुः।।18।।

अगस्त्यर्घः—

भाद्रे त्वगस्त्युदयगे प्रथमेऽह्नि भक्त्या
कृत्वा कुशस्य कुसुमैः प्रतिमा च रम्या।
स्थाप्या सुतीर्थसलिले च निशाविरामे
अर्घार्चनं नगदिनैर्विविधार्थदं स्यात्।।19।।

महालक्ष्मीव्रतम्—

या ज्येष्ठ्यार्क्षयुताष्टमी निशिदले तस्यां सुलक्ष्मीव्रतं
प्रारम्भेद्व्रतधारिणी नृपगुणं सूत्रं करे धारयेत्।

नित्यं पूजनतत्परा स्वविभवैर्यावत्सुकृष्णाष्टमी
तस्यां जागरणार्चनं च हवनं दानैः सुरैश्वर्यदम्।।20।।

दशावतारव्रतम्—

मासे च भाद्रे सितगे दशम्यां
स्नात्वा सुतीर्थे व्रतवान्मनुष्यः।
दशावतारान्विधिना समर्च्य
दशाब्दिकाद्विष्णुपदं प्रयाति।।21।।

पद्मा नामैकादशी—

भाद्रे शुक्लविभागके हरितिथिः पद्मेति सा कीर्तिता
तस्यां वै हृषिकेश्वरं सुपयसा संपूजयेत्सुव्रती।
होमं वै सचरुर्घृतेन मधुना गोधूमदानार्पणा-
द्द्वादश्यां लभते फलं बहुगुणं यद्ब्रह्ममेधोद्भवम्।।22।।

श्रावणद्वादशी—

नाभस्या सितगा हरेस्तिथिरसौ हर्यक्षयुक्ता तिथौ
विष्णुः शृङ्खलयोगके स्वविभवैः सन्मन्त्रपूजादिभिः।
पर्यावर्तनकं हरेर्वितनुयाद्भक्त्या निशाजागरा-
द्दानाद्यैर्द्विजभोजनैर्व्रतवतः सारूप्यमुक्तिं व्रजेत्।।23।।

वामनजयन्ती—

तस्यामेव दिने दिनार्धसमये श्रीवामनं पूजये-
द्विष्णुशृङ्खलके तु पूर्वदिवसे पूर्वाह्णि जन्मोत्सवम्।
कुर्याद्द्वादशिकामुपोष्य विधिना तत्पारणं सद्व्रती
हर्यक्षस्य च मध्यभागघटिका त्यक्ताथ मोक्षार्थिभिः।।24।।

शक्रध्वजस्थापनोत्सवम् (वः)—

यो वै वामनजन्ममङ्गलदिने शक्रध्वजं स्थापये-
द्देवानां सदने लभेत्स मनुजो सौख्यं सुरेन्द्रोपमम्।
अस्यामेव तिथौ पयोव्रतमिदं सप्ताह्निकं सद्गुणं
कुर्याद्वै हरिपूजनादिविधिभिर्गव्याशनाद्वर्जितैः।।25।।

गोत्रिरात्रजव्रतम्—

शुक्ले भाद्रपदे त्रयोदशितिथौ धेनोस्त्रिरात्रिव्रतं
कुर्यात्पुत्रसुखार्थिनी सुकलशे लक्ष्मीपतिं पूजयेत्।
धेनोरर्चनतत्परा निरशना सज्जागरेणान्विता
वर्षे वै तृतिये च वायनविधिर्गोधान्यपीठार्पणैः।।26।।

अशोकव्रतम्—

शुक्ले भाद्रपदे च मन्मथतिथौ कुर्यात्त्रिघस्त्रं व्रतं
सत्सौभाग्यसुखार्थिनी स्वविभवैराशोकवृक्षाङ्घ्रिके।
सीतालक्ष्मणसंयुतं रघुवरं संपूज्य तं प्रार्थये-
द्द्राक्षाद्यैः सुफलैः परिक्रमविधिस्तुर्येऽह्नि तत्पारणम्।।27।।

अनन्तव्रतम्—

भाद्रे शुक्लचतुर्दशी परयुता मुहूर्तमात्रापि सा
ग्राह्यानन्तव्रते विधानचतुरैः संकर्षणं पूजयेत्।
कृत्वा दोरकबन्धनं च यवनान्भोक्ष्यैः फलैर्दापये-
त्तदुद्यापनकं चरेन्मनुमिते वर्षेष्वभीष्टार्थदम्।।28।।

उमामहेश्वरव्रतम्—

राका भाद्रेपदे च भूतसहिता पूर्णा क्रतौ पुण्यदा
तस्यां वै तु[37] उमामहेश्ववरव्रती भक्त्या च तौ पूजयेत्।
ग्रन्थीपञ्चदशात्मकं दृढतरं सद्दोरकं धारये-
द्वर्षे पञ्चदशे तु मण्डलगतौ संपूजनादर्थदौ।।29।।

पितृपक्षारम्भे श्राद्धतिथिनिर्णयः—

राकाष्टादशनाडिगा च नभसी मासे तु तस्यां नरो
नान्दीश्राद्धविधानतः पितृगणान्नान्दीमुखान्संयजेत्।
पूर्वं वै तु तिलोदकादियजनं नित्यं ततोऽर्घ्यार्चनं
सव्यासव्यविधानतो द्विजवरान्संभोज्य पिण्डार्चनम्।।30।।

महालयनिर्णयम् (यः)—

भाद्रे मासि परे दले च सविता कन्यार्क्षगे मानवै-
राकाद्यैस्तु महालयं नृपदिनैः पितॄन्सुसंतोषयेत्।
तदशक्तैः स्वपितुर्विनाशकतिथिर्लुप्तासु वै यत्नतः
पिण्डाद्यर्चनविप्रभोज्यविधिभिस्तृप्तिर्भवेद्वार्षिकी।।31।।

अथ महालये पिण्डाधिकारिणः—

तातम्बातृती(त्रित)यं सपत्नजननी मातामहादित्रयं
स्वस्त्रिस्त्रीतनयादितातजननीस्वभ्रातरस्तत्स्त्रियः।
तातम्बात्मभागिन्यपत्यधवयुक् जायापिता सद्गुरुः
शिष्याप्ताः पितरो महालयविधौ तीर्थे तथा तर्पणे।।32।।[38]

इति महालयपिण्डाधिकारिणः।

बृहद्गौरीव्रतम्—

भाद्रे चापरपक्षगे च तृतीया चन्द्रोदयव्यापिनी
तस्यां सौख्ययशेप्सिनी व्रतधरा गौरीं बृहत्संज्ञिकाम्।
रेणूमण्डलगां समर्च्य विधिना सद्दोरकं धारये-
त्पक्वान्नैर्वयनादिभोजनविधिं वर्षे तु वै पञ्चमे।।33।।

चन्द्रषष्ठीव्रतम्—

षष्ठी प्रौष्ठपदे दले च बहुले चन्द्रोदयव्यापिनी
पूर्वाह्णा च परान्विता हितकरा स्याच्चन्द्रषष्ठीव्रते।
तस्यां वै मनुजोऽर्चयेद्व्रतधरश्चन्द्रं सुचन्द्रोदये
स स्थाल्योदनशर्करान्वितपयो दद्यात्सुसौख्यान्वितः।।34।।

कपिलाषष्ठी—

भाद्रे कृष्णदले कुजेऽह्नि विधिभे षष्ठी च पातान्विता
हस्तार्के कपिलाभिधा बहुगुणा स्नात्वा रविं पूजयेत्।
[39] *
दद्याद्वै कपिलां च वेदविदुषे मुक्तीप्सुभिर्मानवैः।।35।।

मातृनवमी—

या स्याद्भाद्रपदे च कृष्णनवमी ग्राह्या धृतिर्नाडिका
स्यादन्वष्टकिसंज्ञितार्चनविधौ श्राद्धं त्रिभिः पार्वणैः।
मातॄणां यजनेऽपि सा हिततमा जीवत्पितापि चरे-
त्पिण्डाद्यर्चनपूर्वकं द्विजवरान्पत्नीसहान्भोजयेत्।।36।।

इन्दिरैकादशीव्रतम्—

नभसि विष्णुतिथिः परगेन्दिरा
समधुना हृषिकेशविपूजनम्।
हवनकर्मविधिं मधुनाचरे-
ल्लभति पुण्यफलं यवदानतः।।37।।

द्वादशीश्राद्धम्—

संन्यासिनां वैष्णवानां जटीनां
वानप्रस्थानां च दिग्वस्त्रकाणाम्।
द्वादश्यां वै पितृपक्षे प्रकुर्या-
देकोद्दिष्टं तत्सुतैर्भक्तियुक्तैः।।38।।

त्रयोदशीश्राद्धम्—

भाद्रे कृष्णदले च मन्मथतिथिर्व्याप्ता पराह्णेति या
पुण्या स्यात्सुयुगादिकृत्यविषये स्नानेऽर्चने तर्पणे।
तस्यां श्राद्धविधानकं वितनुयात्सत्पुत्रसंवर्जितैः
सद्भ्रात्रैरनपत्यकाँश्च विधिवत्संस्कारहीनान् यजेत्।।39।।

अथ चतुर्दशीश्राद्धम्—

शस्त्रास्त्राग्निजलैः सरीसृपनखीदंष्ट्रीमगर्यादिभि-
र्विद्युत्पातमहीरुहादिपतनैः पञ्चत्वयातात्मनाम्।
एकोद्दिष्टविधानतो हि यजनं भाद्रेऽपरे पक्षके
भूतायां पुरुषत्रयेऽथ नशने दुर्मृत्युभिः पार्वणम्।।40।।

अथामावास्या च गजच्छाया—

मासे भाद्रे या कुहूः पूर्वविद्धा
पितृणां वै पूजने तृप्तिदात्री।
सा चेद्धस्तार्के च चन्द्रेऽतिपुण्या
ज्ञेया छाया [40]कौञ्जरी श्राद्धकाले।।41।।

अथाजाप्रतिपच्छ्राद्धम्—

दौहित्रः स्वविभवैरिषावाद्यघस्त्रे
प्रातः सुसङ्गवगते विधिनार्चयेद्वै।
मातामहादिपुरुषानथ विद्यमाने
सन्मातुलेऽपि स पितापि च जातमात्रः।।42।।

कन्यासंक्रान्तिः—

षडशीतिमुखसंज्ञिकेति कथिता शर्दर्तुसंवेशकः(ने)
कन्यायां रविसंक्रमान्नृपमिता नाड्यः परा(:) पुण्यदा(:)।
स्नात्वा पुण्यजलेऽर्चयेद्दिनकरं पितृन्सुरान्वै यजे-
द्वस्त्रं वा सुग्रहं द्विजाय विधिवद्दानं च स्वर्गप्रदम्।।43।।

इति श्रीनिर्णयमञ्जर्यां भाद्रपदस्य व्रतोत्सवनिर्णयं(यो)
नाम षष्ठोऽध्यायः।।6।।

।।सप्तमोऽध्यायः।।

अथाश्विनमासस्येश्वरादीनाह—

ईषोधीश्वरपद्मनाभवचनात्त्वष्टावियन्मण्डलं
जमदग्निविभवाच्चरेच्च सततं कम्बू(म्ब)लनागेण तु।
नृयन्ती[च] तिलोत्तमा च शतजित्तुर्याणि संवादय-
न्मासं ईषवसंज्ञकं नयति वै भागं दिवारात्रिजम्।।1।।

अथाश्विननवरात्रिषु दुर्गामहोत्सवव्रतम्—

शुक्ले या प्रतिपत्तिथीरिषवके मासेऽथ सूर्योदय-
व्याप्तायां कलशार्चनं सुविधिना देवीं च संपूजयेत्।

चित्रावैधृतिसंयुतेऽखिलदिने मध्याह्नगेऽर्के तद्,
कुर्याद्वै नवरात्रिकं व्रतमिदं प्रत्याब्दिकं मानवैः॥2॥

व्रतविधिर्वृत्तद्वाभ्याम्—

पूर्वाह्णे प्रतिपद्दिने च विधिवत्स्नात्वा व्रतारम्भणं
कुर्याद्वै सुफलैरनग्निपचितैरेकान्तरैः शक्तितः।
सद्वेद्यां यववापितां सुकलशे दुर्गां च संपूजये-
न्नित्यं भक्तियुतैश्चरित्रनिचयैः स्तुत्वाङ्घस्त्रान्नयेत्॥3॥

अथ शरदष्टमीकृत्यम्—

अष्टम्यां च नवाह्निकव्रतधरो होमं चरित्रैस्त्रिभिः
सद्द्रव्यैर्घृतपायसैर्वितनुयात्कौमारिकां पूजयेत्।
सद्भक्ष्यैर्नवमीदिने द्विजवरान्संतर्प्य तत्पारणं
स्वाचारान्नवमेऽथ वा च दशमे घस्त्रे विवर्जेत्ततः॥4॥

नवरात्रिव्रतकरणे फलश्रुतिः—

भक्त्या नवाह्निकव्रतं च शरदृतौ यः
प्रत्याब्दिकं प्रकुरुते मनुजस्तु देव्याः।
सो वै लभत्यनुदिनं धनरुद्धिसौख्यं
श्रीपुत्रभोग्ययशनैरुजतासमेतम्॥5॥

उपाङ्गललिताव्रतम्—

पञ्चम्यामिषवे सिते दिनदले पूर्वान्वितायां व्रती
सौवर्णीप्रतिमामुपाङ्गललितां देवीं च संपूजयेत्।
भूहस्तैर्वटकैश्च वायनविधिं कृत्वा च तान्प्राशये-
द्रात्रौ जागरणार्चनादिप्रतिमादानैस्तु सर्वार्थवान्॥6॥

सरस्वतीव्रतम्—

मासीषे धवले सरस्वतीव्रतं कुर्यात्सुमूलर्क्षके
संस्थाप्याथ सरस्वतीं सुविधिना सत्पुस्तकस्थां शुभाम्।
सत्पूजादिभिरर्चनं त्रिदिवसैर्भक्त्या तु हर्यर्क्षके
कुर्याद्वै सुविसर्जनं प्रतिसमास्वर्थाढ्यविद्याप्रदम्॥7॥

दुर्गानवमी—

मासीषे धवले च दुर्गनवमी संज्ञेति पूर्वान्विता
ग्राह्या वै विबुधैर्विधानविधुरैः श्रीभद्रकालीं यजेत्।
रात्रे जागरणे नवाहगणनान्खड्गादिकानायुधाँ-
श्छस्त्रादीन्विधिनार्चयेत्तु बलिभिः संतोषयेद्भक्तितः।।8।।

युगादितिथिः—

मासेऽश्विने वै नवमी सिता या
पूर्वाह्णसंव्यापि[नि]का मनोस्तु।
ज्ञेया प्रशस्ता द्विजभोजने च
स्नानेऽर्चने मन्त्रजपे च दाने।।9।।

विजयादशम्युत्सवः—

मासीषे विजयक्षणाढ्यदशमी कर्णान्विता सा नृप-
प्रस्थाने [41]विजया शमीतरुसमर्चायां श्रुतिर्नो यदा।
द्युद्वन्द्वेऽप्यपराह्णगा प्रथमयुक्कार्यापराह्णे न चे-
दन्येद्युर्दशमी मुहूर्तकमिताधीष्ट्यान्विता चापरा।।10।।

दशमीकृत्यम्—

ईषे शुक्ले दशम्यां नृपतिहितकरं पूजनं वाहकानां
शम्याश्चैवायुधानां विविधद्युतिमतां छत्रसिंहासनानाम्।
तुर्याणां वा विदध्यान्नृपतिरपि सदा मुख्यकालेऽथ गौणे
धानर्क्षं वर्जयित्वा रिपुविजयकरं प्रस्थितः सर्वदिक्षु।।11।।

अथ विजयादशम्यां खञ्जनावलोकनम्—

ऊर्ध्वं भ्राम्यति चार्थसिद्धिमतुलां शाक्रे हुताशे धनं
याम्ये रोगभयं सुरारिकलहं वित्तं समुद्रालये।
वायव्ये वरवस्त्रलाभमतुलं दिव्याङ्गना चोत्तरे
ईशाने मरणं ध्रुवं निगदितं दिग्लक्षणं खञ्जने।।12।।

पाशाङ्कुशैकादशी—

शुक्लैकादशी चाश्विने भवति या पाशाङ्कुशा सा मता
तस्यां वै पयसा विधानचतुरः श्रीपद्मनाभं यजेत्।

होमं व्रीहियवैस्तिलैस्तु विधिना कुर्याद्घृताढ्यो(ढ्यं) नरै-
र्दद्यात्क्षौद्रघटं लभेच्च सुकृतं यद्ब्रह्ममेधोद्भवम्।।13।।

अथ दानफलव्रतं वाचारतः प्राप्तमाह—

मासीषे धवलेऽन्त्यभानुदिवसादारभ्य माघे सिते
सप्तम्यावधि पुत्रसौख्यजननं सत्कन्दमूलैः फलैः।
कुर्याद्दानफलव्रतं रविदिने स्नात्वार्चयेद्भास्करं
द्रोणान्नं प्रतिमार्पणान्त्यदिवसेऽप्येवं तु पञ्चाब्दिकम्।।14।।

कोजागरव्रतम्—

कोजागर्तिव्रतं नरैर्वितनुयादीषानुमत्यां व्रती
पुष्पैः कौमुदिजैः सुपद्मदलगां लक्ष्मीं सुभक्त्यार्चयेत्।
को जागर्ति नरो धनार्थमतिभिर्लक्ष्मीं भ्रमन्तीं ब्रुवँ-
स्तस्माज्जागरणाक्षखेलविधिना [42]रात्रिं सुखार्थी नयेत्।।15।।

अथ रासोत्सवः—

राकायामिषमासके हरिरतै रासोत्सवस्थं हरिं
गोपीभिः सहितं यजेत्स्वविभवैः संगीतनृत्यादिभिः।
रात्रौ जागरणं कुमुद्वतिभवैः पुष्पैश्च संपूजये-
त्सन्मुक्तिं विभवं च सौख्यसहितं संप्राप्यते भक्तिमान्।।16।।

कार्तिकस्नानादिकर्माह—

राकायामथवा सिता हरितिथिमारभ्य मासेऽश्विने
ऊर्जस्नानविधायकं वितनुयाद्धर्मार्थमोक्षप्रदम्।
तस्मिन्वै दिवसे सुसौख्यजनकं सद्दीपदानार्चनं
धात्रीभूरुहपूजनं च तुलसीकाष्ठस्त्रजीधारणम्।।17।।

कार्तिकस्नानविधिमाह—

ऊर्जस्नानकरैः शुभे दिनमुखे स्नानं सुतीर्थोदके
कृत्वा सद्विधिना व्रतं वितनुयान्मासोपवासादिभिः।
नक्तैर्वाथ हविष्यभोजनरतैर्दामोदरं राधिकां
कुम्भस्थं विधिनार्चयेदनुदिनं पूजोपहारादिभिः।।18।।

अथ कार्तिकस्नानोद्यापनविधिः—

पूर्णे वै सुव्रते च कार्तिकसिते भूतातिथौ मण्डपे
वृन्दामूलविभागकेऽथ कलशे सन्मण्डलस्थेऽर्चयेत्।
विष्णुं सद्विभवैस्तु जागरविधिं कृत्वाथ सूर्योदये
होमं ब्राह्मणभोजनं च सुरभीं दत्त्वा नरो मुक्तिभाक्।।19।।

कर्कचतुर्थीव्रतम्—

कृष्णाख्या सुचतुर्थिकाश्विनगता चन्द्रोदयव्यापिनी
ग्राह्या वै कर्केतिसंज्ञिकतिथिस्तस्यां सुसौख्यार्थिनी।
भित्त्यां चित्रविमण्डले च सहरां गौरीं सुपुत्रान्वितां
पक्वान्नं करकैः समर्च्य करकान्विप्रेभ्य संपादयेत्।।20।।

रमानामैकादशी—

कृष्णैकादशि या रमेति कथिता मासीषवे संज्ञके
तस्यां द्रोणकमानकेन पयसा श्रीपद्मनाभं यजेत्।
होमं व्रीहितिलाज्यक्षौद्रसहितं सप्तान्नदानं तथा
दत्त्वा भुञ्जति यो नरः स लभते स्वर्गापवर्गं पदम्।।21।।

गोवत्सद्वादशी—

कृष्णा द्वादशिका प्रदोषसहिता गोवत्ससंज्ञेति या
मासीषे सुगुणां सवत्ससुरभीं तस्यां व्रती पूजयेत्।
दत्त्वार्घ्यं वटकं निवेद्य विधिवन्नीरञ्जयेत्प्रार्थये-
त्तैलं गव्यविवर्जनात्स लभते पुत्रं कुलोद्दीपनम्।।22।।

द्वादशीकृत्यम्—

या द्वादशी चाश्विनकृष्णपक्षे
तस्यां दिनान्ते विधिना सुदीपैः।
देवाँश्च विप्राँश्च तुरंगमाँश्च
नीराजयेत्पञ्चदिनेषु भक्त्या।।23।।

धनत्रयोदशी—

मासे चाश्विनके त्रयोदशि तिथौ सूर्यास्तकाले नरै-
र्दुर्मुत्युं वि(त्युर्वि)निवारकं यमहितं दद्यात्सुदीपं बहिः।

केचिद्वै तु निधित्रयोदशिरिति संज्ञेति तस्यां निधिं
सद्भूषादिसमन्वितां च पयसा संपूजयेत्सिञ्चयेत्।।24।।

रूपचतुर्दशी—

मासे चाश्विनसंज्ञके शिवतिथिः कृष्णासु चन्द्रोदये
व्याप्ताव्याप्तिगते च युग्मदिवसे पूर्वा हिता नापरा।
सा चेत्स्वातिभसंयुतातिपरमा ज्ञेया तु साभ्यञ्जने
तस्यां वै यमदण्डभीरुमनुजैः स्नात्वा यमं तर्पयेत्।।25।।

दीपोत्सवी—

या वै दर्शतिथिः प्रदोषसमये व्याप्ता तुलायां रवौ
ग्राह्या साश्विनमासकेऽतिपरमा दीपोत्सवे मानवैः।
तस्यां श्राद्धविधिं रमार्चनव्रतः सायाह्नि दीपोत्सवं
पितृदीपविधिं कुबेरयजनं चालक्ष्मिनिःसारणम्।।26।।

बलिराजप्रतिपदोत्सवम् (वः)—

ऊर्जे वै प्रतिपत्तिथिः कुहुयुता ग्राह्याथ शुद्धा तिथि-
श्चन्द्रालोकनवर्जिता क्रमगता तुर्याह्निका पण्डितैः।
तस्यां वै बलिपूजनं गिरिवरं गोपाँश्च गाः पूजये-
द्धेनोः क्रीडनकं तथैव च हरिं सदन्नकूटोत्सवैः।।27।।

तुलासंक्रान्तिः—

गोलो दक्षिणसंज्ञकस्तु तुलभे सूर्येऽस्य संचारतः
पूर्वा वै दशनाडिकेति च परा दिक्संमिताः पुण्यदाः।
स्नानं तीर्थजलेऽर्चयेद्दिनकरं दत्त्वा तिलान्गोरसं
विप्रेभ्यस्तु फलं सलक्षगुणितं स्यात्कर्मपाशापहम्।।28।।

इति श्रीनिर्णयमञ्जर्यामाश्विमासव्रतोत्सवनिर्णयकथनं
नाम सप्तमोऽध्यायः।।7।।

।। अष्टमोऽध्याय:।।

अथ कार्तिकमासस्येश्वरादीनाह—

श्रीदामोदरवाक्यतो विचरते विष्णुर्वियन्मण्डलं
नागेनाश्वतरेण प्रत्यनुदिनं श्रीकौशिकस्तेजसा।
रम्भा नृत्यति वाद्यवादनपर: श्रीसत्यजिद्वादको
मासं कार्तिकसंज्ञकं नयति वै धर्मार्थकामप्रदम्।।1।।

यमद्वितीयाव्रतम्—

ऊर्जे या द्वितिया सिता दिनदलव्या(प्ता)थ युग्मे दिने
युक्ता वा वियुता तदा परयुता ग्राह्या यमस्यार्चने।
तस्यां वै भगिनीगृहे च विधिवद्भुक्तासु भूषार्पणं
कृत्वा यस्तु नर: स सौख्यमतुलं लब्ध्वा सुमुक्तिं व्रजेत्।।2।।

कल्पादिसप्तमी—

या सप्तमी कार्तिकशुक्लपक्षे
पूर्वाह्णिकव्यापिनिका प्रशस्ता।
कल्पादिका सा परमा सुपुण्या
सत्स्नानदानार्चनभोजनेषु।।3।।

गोपाष्टम्युत्सवम् (व:)—

ऊर्जे सिताष्टमितिथि: सवितोदयाढ्या
गोपाष्टमीति विबुधै: कथिता च तस्याम्।
सद्गोपवेशवसनैस्तु हरिं समर्च्य
गोपार्भकाँश्च सगवा विविधैस्तु भोज्यै:।।4।।

युग्मा नवमी—

ऊर्जे सत्ययुगादिकाश्च [च] नवमी शुद्धासु सूर्योदये
तस्यां पिण्डविवर्जितं च विबुधै: श्राद्धं प्रकुर्यात्सदा।
आहारस्तु दिनत्रयं व्रतपरैर्विष्णुं तुलस्यन्वितं
सद्भक्त्या विभवैर्विवाहविधिभि: संपूजयेद्वैष्णवै:।।5।।

देवसंबोधिन्येकादशी—

शुक्लैकादशिकार्तिके भवति या सा देवसंबोधिनी
तस्यां दुग्धदधिःसिताज्यमधुभिर्दामोदरं पूजयेत्।
होमं क्षौद्रतिलैस्तु वेदविदुषे पक्वान्नदानार्पणं
पुण्यं तन्निशिजागरेण लभते यद्वाजिमेधोद्भवम्।।6।।

देवप्रबोधोत्सवः—

रात्रौ देवप्रबोधनाख्य[43]समये त्यक्त्वा च भद्रां नरै-
र्मन्त्रैर्गीतसुघोषभिश्च विधिवदुत्थापयेत्केशवम्।
सा[44] चेदश्विभचन्द्रवारसहितानन्तेति सा कीर्तिता
तस्यां दानजपादि[45]कर्मकरणेऽनन्तं फलं चाश्नुते।।7।।

प्रबोधिनीव्रते पारणम्—

ऊर्जे द्वादशिका च पौष्यभयुता त्यक्त्वाथ तत्पारणं
कुर्याद्वा विबुधैश्च भान्त्यचरणं तिथ्यर्क्षयुक्ते तथा।
तस्यां यो व्रतपारणे द्विजवरान्संभोज्य कुम्भार्पणं
कृत्वा मुक्तिफलं सुसौख्यसहितं विष्णोः पदं प्राप्यते।।8।।

मन्वादितिथिः—

ऊर्जे सिता द्वादशि पौर्णिमा च
मन्वादिके ते मुनिभिः प्रदिष्टे।
पूर्वाह्णिके ते विहिते सुकृत्ये
सत्स्नानदाने द्विजभोजने च।।9।।

अथ भीष्मपञ्चकव्रतम्—

ऊर्जे देवप्रबोधनादिदिवसादारभ्य पञ्चाह्निकं
कुर्याद्भीष्मव्रतं विधानचतुरैः पापौघविध्वंसनम्।
विष्णुः सद्विधिनार्चयेत्स्वविभवैर्होमं घृताक्तैर्यवै-
र्गव्यं प्राश्य शराह्णिके तिलजलैर्भीष्मं च संतर्पयेत्।।10।।

भीष्मपञ्चके पूजाविधानम्—

पद्मश्रीदलभृङ्गवाजिहननैः पुष्पैश्च गव्यैः पृथक्
पादौ जानुनि नाभिकां क्रमगतां स्कन्धं [च] संपूजयेत्।

पूर्णायामखिलैर्हरिं सुविधिना संपूज्य होमान्तके
लौहीं सत्प्रतिमां यमस्य सतिलां दद्याच्छराब्दे पुनः।।11।।

चातुर्मास्यव्रतोद्यापनविधिः—

चातुर्मास्यव्रतान्वितैस्तु पुरुषैः कुर्याद्व्रतोद्यापनं
ऊर्जे द्वादशिकातिथौ सितदले भक्त्या हरिं पूजयेत्।
यद्यद्द्रव्यविवर्जितं व्रतवतैस्तत्तत्सुविप्राय वै
दद्याद्दक्षिणयान्वितं द्विजवरान्संभोज्य भुञ्जेत्स्वयम्।।12।।

चातुर्मास्यव्रतोद्यापने दानान्याह—

नक्ते वस्त्रयुगं च भूमिशयने शय्यां च गोग्रासके
कृच्छ्रे गव्यव्रते च शाकफलकेऽप्येकान्तरादेश्च गाम्।
मौने वै घृतकुम्भवस्त्रयुगलं घण्टां च सद्दीपकां
दीपेऽभ्यञ्जनके तु तैलकलशं कांस्यं च पर्णाशने।।13।।
वार्ताकगृञ्जने मधुघृतघटौ देवालये पद्मके
पद्मं हेममयं च धान्यव्रतवान्स्वर्णं सुधान्यं तथा।
ताम्बूले च परिक्रमे सुवसनं दद्यात्सुविप्राय वै
चातुर्मास्यव्रती तु हेमप्रतिमां सद्ब्रह्मचर्यान्वितः।।14।।

प्रदोषव्रतम्—

ऊर्जे कामतिथिः प्रदोषसमये व्याप्ता प्रदोषव्रते
ग्राह्या वै शिवपूजने बहुगुणा पक्षे च पक्षे पुनः।
वर्षान्ते प्रतिमार्पणार्चनविधिं कुर्यात्सुभौमान्विता
दारिद्रोऽपि हरेन्दुशुक्रसहिता सत्सौख्यसौभाग्यदा।।15।।

शनिप्रदोषव्रतम्—

ऊर्जेऽनङ्गतिथिः शनिद्युसहिता शुक्ले प्रदोषान्विता
तस्यां पार्थिवपूजनं निशिमुखे लिङ्गस्थितं [46]चार्चयेत्।
भुञ्जीतस्तु ततो व्रती स्वविभवैः पूर्णे च हैमं शिवं
भक्त्या सद्यजनादिजागरविधिं दानं च सर्वार्थदम्।।16।।

वैकुण्ठचतुर्दशी—

वैकुण्ठख्यचतुर्दशी सितदले [47]ऊर्जे निशीथान्विता
ग्राह्या चेत्तु दिनद्वये व्रतवतैः सायं निशीथोभयः।
तस्यां सद्विभवैर्निशि मधुरिपुं सज्जागरैरर्चये-
त्प्रातर्वै द्विजभोज्यपारणविधिं कृत्वा लभेत्तत्पदम्।।17।।

वैकुण्ठाख्यतिथिः शिवार्चनव्रते ग्राह्या निशान्त्यान्विता
सा वै सोमसमन्विता तु परमा पुण्यप्रदा स्यान्नृणाम्।
काश्यां सा बहुपुण्ययोगनिचयैर्विश्वेश्वरस्यार्चने
लब्धा चेज्जननान्त्यभीतिहरणे किं वा परैः सुकृतैः।।18।।

कार्तिकपूर्णिमामहोत्सवः—

पुण्या कार्तिकपूर्णिमा परयुता ग्राह्या सुपुण्यक्रतौ
सा वै वह्निभसंयुता बहुगुणा द्वीशान्विते भास्करे।
योगो पद्मकसंज्ञकोऽर्चनविधौ सत्स्नानदाने नृणां
पुण्यौघाल्लभते सुपुष्करसरे पापौघविध्वंसनम्।।19।।

कार्तिक्यां कृत्यानि—

कार्तिक्यां त्रिपुरोत्सवं निशिमुखे कुर्यात्सुदीपादिभि-
र्दद्याद्वाथ सुरालयेषु विदुषैः सद्दीपवृक्षाणि च।
तस्यां सौख्यकरं विपत्तिहरणं स्कन्दार्चनं पुण्यदं
नीलोद्वाहविधिं सुमुक्तिकरणं पित्र्यर्चनं तुष्टिदम्।।20।।

कालाष्टमीव्रतम्—

ऊर्जे वै बहुलेऽष्टमी निशियुता कालाष्टमी संज्ञिता
तस्यां तद्व्रतधारिभिस्तु विधिना संपूजयेद्भैरवम्।
कुर्याज्जागरणं कथा सुचरितैः प्रातः पुनः पूजनं
विप्राणां यजनं च पारणविधिमाजन्मपापापहम्।।21।।

कालाष्टमीव्रतम्—

कालाष्टम्यां कालतीर्थोदके च
कृत्वा स्नानं तर्पणं धेनुदानम्।
कालाधीशं पूजयेद्वा विलोक्य
पितृणां वै मुक्तिदो मानवः स्यात्।।22।।

मोघ्नी नामैकादशी—

कृष्णैकादशी कार्तिके भवति या मोघ्नीति सा कीर्तिता
तस्यामिक्षुरसाभिषेकविधिना दामोदरं पूजयेत्।
होमं दाडिमपुष्पतण्डुलघृतैर्मृद्‌गस्य दानार्पणं
कृत्वा विप्रवराय सस्तु लभते पुण्यं नृमेधोद्भवम्।।23।।

गौरीतपोव्रतम्—

ऊर्जे गौरितपोव्रतं कुहुदिने सौभाग्यपुत्रेप्सिनी
कुर्याच्छोडशवार्षिकं बहुगुणं स्नात्वा सुपोषान्विता।
गौरीं रुद्रयुतां यजेत्सुविधिना दीपार्चनं जागरा-
त्प्रत्यब्दे क्रमगे तिथौ सहगते राकासु चोद्यापयेत्।।24।।[48]

वृश्चिकसंक्रान्तिनिर्णयः—

हेमन्तर्तुनिवेशनं हरिपदी संज्ञालिभे संक्रमा-
द्भानोः षोडशनाडिकेति प्रथमा पुण्यप्रदा स्यान्नृणाम्।
तीर्थस्नानविधिं रवेश्च यजनं दीपस्य दानं तथा
दद्याद्विप्रवराय सस्तु लभते पुण्यं सुसौख्यप्रदम्।।25।।

इति श्रीनिर्णयमञ्जर्यां कार्तिकव्रतोत्सवतिथिनिर्णयकथनं
नामाष्टमोऽध्यायः।।8।।

।।नवमोऽध्यायः।।

मार्गशीर्षमासस्येश्वरादीनाह—

मासाधीश्वरकेशवस्य वचनात्संगच्छते चांशुमान्
श्रीमत्कश्यपतेजसा च सुमहाशङ्खाह्वनागेन च।
नृत्यन्नुर्वशी कृत्यसेनकुशलस्तूर्यादिसंवादने
मासं यत्सहसंज्ञकं नयति वै मासाधिपोऽसौ स्मृतः।।1।।

पुनर्नागपञ्चमीव्रतम्—

या पञ्चमी शुक्लदले सहाख्ये
नागार्चने षष्ठियुता प्रशस्ता।
सत्स्नानदानार्चनपूजनाद्यैः
स्यान्नागलोकस्य विभूतिदात्री।।2।।

चम्पाषष्ठीव्रतम्—

शुक्ले मार्गशिरे च सप्तमियुता षष्ठीति चम्पाभिधा
पुण्या वारुणभेऽर्कवासरयुता मल्लारिसंपूजने।
तस्यां प्रावरणोत्सवादिविधिना संपूजयेत्केशवं
सा वै पञ्चमि संयुतातिफलदा स्कन्दार्चने वै नृणाम्।।3।।

गोकुलनाथोत्सवम् (वः)—

शुक्ले मार्गशिरे च सप्तमितिथिः सूर्योदयव्यापिनी
श्रीमद्गोकुलराजपूजनविधौ ग्राह्या सुभक्तैर्जनैः।
सिञ्चेन्मङ्गलद्रव्यकुङ्कुमजलैर्भोज्यादिभिः पूजये-
द्विष्णुं मङ्गलगीतशब्दनिचयैः कुर्यान्महानुत्सवम्।।4।।

कल्पादिकृत्यम्—

मार्गे सिते या नवमी तिथिश्च
सूर्योदयव्यापिनिका प्रशस्ता।
कल्पादिकृत्ये द्विजभोजने च
स्नानार्चने चाक्षयपुण्यदा स्यात्।।5।।

मोक्षदा नामैकादशी—

शुक्ला मार्गशिरे जनार्दनतिथिः सा मोक्षदासंज्ञिता
तस्यां वै पयसा सुवेदविधिना संपूजयेत्केशवम्।
होमं शुक्लतिलैश्च वेदविदुषे श्रीनालिकेरं घृतं
दद्याद्भक्तियुतो नरो हि लभते श्रीराजसूयं फलम्।।6।।

एकादशीव्रतोद्यापनकालमाह—

शुक्लैकादशिकाव्रतं सहगतादारभ्य[49] ऊर्जावधी
शुक्लायां क्रमतो यजेत्सुविधिना सद्धोमदानादिभिः।
कार्यं चेदभयाव्रतं त्रिदिवसं सर्वा उपोष्यास्तदा
मासेषु मधुसूदनार्चनविधिमुद्यापयेत्कार्तिके।।7।।

एकादश्युद्यापनविधिः—

पूर्णे विष्णुव्रते व्रती वितनुयादुद्यापनं सत्फलं
कृत्वा मण्डलकं विधाय कलशान्द्विघ्नाँस्तथा द्वादशान्।

तावद्वै प्रतिमाः सुवर्णरचिताः संपूज्य सज्जागरं
होमं ब्राह्मणभोजनं च सुरभीदानं सुमुक्तिप्रदम्।।8।।

पिशाचमोचिनी चतुर्दशी—

मार्गे सिते शिवतिथिर्धृतिनाडिकाढ्या
सा वै पिशाचहरिणी कथिता द्विजेन्द्रैः।
तस्या सुतीर्थसलिले च तिलोदकादि-
श्राद्धार्चनादिविधिभिर्लभते सुमुक्तिम्।।9।।

दत्तात्रेयोत्सवम् (वः)—

राकायां सहमासिके वितनुयात्सद्योगयुक्तैर्नरै-
र्दत्तात्रेयमहोत्सवं सुविधिना सु(सं)पूजयेत्पादुकाम्।
स्नानं दानजपार्चनं बहुगुणं कुर्यान्निशाजागरं
सद्भक्त्या द्विजभोजनं सुफलदं सर्वार्थकामप्रदम्।।10।।

सौभाग्यसुन्दरीव्रतम्—

सौभाग्यसुन्दरिव्रतं तनुयाद्युवत्या
मार्गे सिता दिनमुखोपगता तृतीया।
तामादिकृत्य गिरिजां विधिना यजेत
मासार्चनादिविभवैरखिलार्थयुक्तम्।।11।।

श्रीविट्ठलेशोत्सवम्(वः)—

मासे मार्गशिरे च कृष्णनवमी मित्रोदयव्यापिनी
तस्यां भक्तियुतैस्तु वैष्णवजनैः श्रीविट्ठलेशोत्सवम्।
कुर्याद्वै हरिपूजनादिविधिना घस्राद्ययामान्तके
श्रीमद्वै गुरुपादुकार्चनविधिः(धिं) संतोषयेद्भूसुरान्।।12।।

सफला नामैकादशी—

मार्गे वै कृष्णपक्षे हरितिथि(ः) सफला कीर्तिता ब्रह्मविद्भि-
स्तस्यां तीर्थोदकेन श्रुतिविधिपटुभिः स्नापयेत्केशवं च।
वह्नौ होमं घृतेन श्रुतिमुखविदुषे पायसं दापयेच्च
भक्त्या वै मानवा(व)स्तु लभति हि सुकृतं विष्णुयज्ञोद्भवं च।।13।।

वैतरणीव्रतम्—

कृष्णैकादशिका तिथिः सहगतादारभ्य सद्वार्षिकं
कुर्याद्वैतरणीव्रतं बहुगुणं तामिस्त्रदोषापहम्।
नक्ताढ्यैरसितां सुगां प्रतिदिनं भक्ष्यादिभिः पूजये-
च्छय्यालोहसतूलहेमसुरभीदानादि पूर्णेऽर्पयेत्।।14।।

धनुःसंक्रान्तिनिर्णयः—

षडशीतिमुखसंज्ञिताश्च धनभे सूर्यस्य संचारतो
नाड्यस्तु परभागिका नृपमिताः पुण्ये सुपुण्यप्रदाः।
स्नात्वा सत्सरितोदकेऽर्कयजनं वस्त्रान्नपानार्पणं
मासेऽस्मिन्सततं दिनादिमलवे(समये) कुर्यात्तु वै भोजनम्।।15।।

इति श्रीनिर्णयमञ्जर्यां मार्गशीर्षव्रतोत्सवतिथिनिर्णयकथनं नाम नवमोऽध्यायः।।9।।

।। दशमोऽध्यायः।।

पौषमासस्येश्वरादीनाह—

पौषेशनारायणवाक्यतो भगः
अत्रेः प्रभावाच्चरते निरन्तरम्।
नागेन कर्कोटकसंज्ञकेन
नृत्यन्ति पूर्वचित्तिरायुवाद्यैः।।1।।

पुण्याष्टमी—

पौषेऽष्टमी शुक्लदले बुधाढ्या
पुण्यप्रदा लक्षगुणा [50]प्रशस्ता।
तीर्थाप्लवे होमजपादिकृत्ये
दानेऽर्चने भूसुरभोजने च।।2।।

[51]पुत्रदानामैकादशी—

पौषे वै शुक्लपक्षे हरितिथिरिति या पुत्रदासंज्ञका स्या-
त्तस्यां नारायणं वै दिनदलसमये सिञ्चयेद्गोपयाद्यैः।
होमं कृत्वा घृतेन श्रुतिमुखविदुषे तण्डुलान्मुद्गयुक्ता-
न्दद्याद्भक्त्यान्वितैस्तु लभति च हुतभुक्ष्टोमजं सत्फलं हि।।3।।

मन्वादितिथिः—

सूर्योदयाढ्या मधुसूदनस्य
तिथिस्तु पौषस्य सिते विभागे।
मन्वादिकानन्तफलप्रदात्री
पित्र्यर्चने तीर्थविधानकृत्ये।।4।।

पौषीपौर्णिमापर्वम् (र्व)—

पौषे चानुमतिस्तिथिस्तु परमा देवेज्य-ऋक्षान्विता
सा चेद्वैधृतिभानुवारसहिता पर्वं भवेद्भास्करम्।
कोटिसूर्यग्रहोपमं सुफलदं स्नाने च सूर्यार्चने
गोदाने द्विजभोजनेऽर्चनविधौ सन्मन्त्रजाप्ये तथा।।5।।

माघस्नानम्—

पौषे वै मकरार्कगे हरितिथौ वा पौर्णमास्यां कुहौ
माघस्नानविधिं चरेत्सुविधिना रात्रौ विरामे नरैः।
माघे(घो) वाप्यधिको भवेद्यदि तदा स्नाने तु मासावुभौ
पूर्वे माघविधिं परेऽधिकविधिं कुर्यात्सुपुण्येप्सुभिः।।6।।

माघस्नानविधिः—

सत्तीर्थे च सरिज्जलेऽथ विधिवद्ध्यात्वा प्रयागोदकं
स्नायान्माधवपूजनं प्रतिदिनं कुर्यात्तिलस्यार्पणम्।
अभ्यङ्गाग्निकलत्रसेवनविधिं त्यक्त्वाथ कुर्याद्व्रतं
चर्यं नक्तहविष्यभोज्यविरसं मासोपवासादिभिः।।7।।

माघस्नानोद्यापनम्—

यो माघव्रतधारकस्तपगतायां चानुमित्यां सदा
स्नानोद्यापनकं च तत्सुविधिना श्रीमाधवं पूजयेत्।
होमं सघृतापायसैर्द्विजवरान्त्रिशन्मितान्भोजये-
द्गोभूहेमतिलार्पणैस्तु लभते मुक्तिं चतुर्धा शुभाम्।।8।।

षट्तिला नामैकादशी—

कृष्णैकादशि षट्तिलेति कथिता मासे च पौषद्वये
तस्यां वै सुव्रती[52] यजेत्सुपयसा नारायणाख्यं हरिम्।

होमं वै घृततण्डुलैश्च विधिना दद्यात्तिलान्सद्द्विजे
सो वै मुक्तिफलं लभेच्च सततं मुच्येन्महापातकात्।।9।।

स्वरूपद्वादशी[53]—

रूपद्वादशिका व्रतं च विबुधैः पौषे परे पक्षके
द्वादश्यां सुसरिज्जले च सरसि स्नात्वा मृदाद्यैर्नरः।
भक्त्या सत्तिलभाजने च प्रतिमां संस्थाप्य विष्णुं यजे–
द्रात्रौ जागरणं तिलाज्यहवनं दानात्सुरूपप्रदम्।।10।।

यमचतुर्दशी—

पौषे चतुर्दशि तिथिर्बहुले च पक्षे
चन्द्रोदये सुविधिना सरितोदके च।
स्नात्वा तिलोदककुशैर्यमतर्पणं च
कुर्याद्विमुच्यति नरः खलु पापसङ्घात्।।11।।

अमावास्यानिर्णयम् (यः)-अर्धोदयः—

पौषे दर्शतिथी रवेस्तू (रु) दयगा या स्यात्सुपित्र्यर्चने
सा चेद्विष्णुभपातभास्करयुता योगोऽयमर्धोदयः।
कोटीसूर्यग्रहोपमो भवति चेद्वारादिहीने पुनः
स स्यात्तैस्तु महोदयो बहुगुणः सत्स्नानदानार्चने।।12।।

अर्धोदयपर्वकृत्यम्—

पर्वेऽर्धोदयसंज्ञके च विबुधैः स्नात्वा च नद्योदके
ब्रह्माविष्णुमहेश्वरादिप्रतिमार(अ)भ्यर्च्य पुष्पादिभिः।
पात्रे पायसपूरितेऽष्टदलके पद्मे च ताः स्थापये–
द्द्याद्विप्रवराय पुण्यनिचयं भूदानजं प्राप्यते।।19।।

मकरसंक्रान्तिः—

स्यात्सौम्यायनसंज्ञिकात्तु शिशिरस्यावेशनं स्यान्मृगे
सूर्यः संक्रमणात्खवेदघाटिका(काः)(40) स्यादुत्तराः पुण्यदाः।
तस्यामौषधिभिस्तिलैश्च विधिना स्नात्वा रविं पूजये-
च्छ्राद्धं वै सगुडस्तिलाश्च हुतभुक्पात्रं स[54] कृष्णं ददेत।।14।।

संक्रान्तिव्रतान्याह—

संक्रान्तिव्रतधारकैस्तु विषुवे पुण्येऽथ सौम्यायने
स्नात्वा सत्सरितेऽष्टपत्रकमले भक्त्यार्चयेद्भास्करम्।
स्तुत्वा सद्व्रतवत्तु वेदविदुषे दद्यादुपोषान्वितैः
कुर्याद्द्वादशमासिकं व्रतमिदं सर्वासु संक्रान्तिषु।।15।।

अथ संक्रान्तौ कामद्रव्यैर्व्रतानि द्वाभ्याम्—

रूपं स्याद्घृतधेनुतोऽथ सुखदं कुम्भं गुडाद्यं तथा
कान्तिस्तेजकरं सदीपकरकं सत्तण्डुलाढ्यं नृणाम्।
सौभाग्याभरणं तु वस्त्रसहितं दानात्सुसौभाग्यदं
ताम्बूलार्पणतो सुपुत्रविभवं लक्ष्मीं च कुम्भोदकात्।।16।।

सौभाग्याष्टकतन्दुलार्पणविधिः सद्भोगसौख्यार्थदः
कांस्यात्क्षीरघृतान्वितात्तु निरुजं दीर्घायुषं प्राप्नुयात्।
धान्याद्वै धनधान्यवान्सलवणपात्राद्गुडस्यार्पणा-
त्सर्वान्वै सुमनोरथाँश्च लभते संक्रान्तिकोपासकी।।17।।

संक्रान्तिव्रतानामुद्यापनम्—

संक्रान्तिव्रतधारकैर्वितनुयात्पूर्णे तदुद्यापनं
कुर्याद्धेममयेऽम्बुजेऽर्कयजनं भक्त्या निशाजागरम्।
होमान्ते व्रतवस्तुदापनविधिं कृत्वाथ गोभूतिला-
न्कुम्भान्द्वादशसंख्यकान्सप्रतिमान्विप्रेभ्य संदापयेत्।।18।।

आज्यसिञ्चनव्रतम्—

गोले चायनसंक्रमेऽह्नि विबुधैः कुर्याद्घृतासिञ्चनं
विष्णोर्वाथ घृतार्पणेन मधुना मुच्येन्महापातकात्।
चेद्वै पातसमन्विते बहुगुणं कुर्याद्विशोकव्रतं
भक्त्या भास्करपूजनेन कपिलादानेन नैरुज्यदम्।।19।।

इति श्रीनिर्णयमञ्जर्यां पौषव्रतोत्सवनिर्णयो नाम दशमोऽध्यायः।।10।।

।। एकादशोऽध्यायः।।

माघमासस्येश्वरादीनाह—

माघाधीश्वरमाधवस्य वचनात्पूषा वियन्मण्डलं
नागेनैव धनंजयेन चरते श्रीगौतमाशीर्बलात्।
नृत्यन्वै सुपथि घृताचियुवती तुर्याणि संवाद्यते
गन्धर्वः सुरुचो नयन्ति फलदं मासं तपःसंज्ञिकम्।।1।।

तिलचतुर्थी—

माघे सिते तिलचतुर्थि निशी(शा)मुखाढ्या
तस्यां च नक्तव्रतवान्निशि जागरेण।
ढुण्ढार्चनं स्वविभवैः कुरुतेऽतिभक्त्या
शत्रोः पराजयभयं न भवेच्च तस्य।।2।।

कुन्दचतुर्थीव्रतम्—

माघे कुन्दचतुर्थिका निशिमुखव्याप्ता च कुन्दोद्भवैः
पुष्पैर्विघ्नहरार्चनं व्रतधरः कुर्यात्सुसंपत्तये।
तस्यां भोगसुखार्थदं बहुगुणं गौरीव्रतं पूजनं
सद्धूपादिभि(भिः) कुन्दपुष्पनिचयैः सौभाग्यदानादिभिः।।3।।

वसन्तपञ्चम्युत्सवम् (वः)—

पञ्चम्यां तपशुक्लिकां दिनदले कुर्याद्वसन्तोत्सवं
सौरभ्याढ्यरजैस्तु गन्धसलिलैः पुष्पैर्हरिं पूजयेत्।
यावत्फाल्गुनपौर्णिमा प्रतिदिनं मासेऽधिकेऽपि तथा
सद्गीतादिभि(भिस्)तुर्यवाद्यविभवैर्भक्त्यान्वितैर्वैष्णवैः।।4।।

श्रीपञ्चमी—

या पञ्चमी माघसिते विभागे
श्रीपञ्चमी सा कथिता सुतज्ज्ञैः।
तस्यां दिनार्धे विधिना श्रियं वै
संपूजयेल्लक्ष्मीसुखेप्सुभिश्च।।5।।

रथसप्तमी—

माघे वै रथसप्तमीति धवले ब्राह्मे मुहूर्ते नरै-
स्तस्यां तीर्थजले विधानचतुरैः स्नात्वा तु सन्मण्डले।
सूर्यं स्यन्दनसंस्थितं स्वविभवैः संपूज्य सज्जागरं
कुर्याद्दानविधानतो हि लभते राज्यं सुसौख्यान्वितम्।।6।।

स्नानसप्तमी—

माघे सप्तमिकारुणोदयगता स्नानेऽतिपापापहा
सा चेदर्कदिनान्वितातिपरमा कोट्यर्कपर्वोपमा।
तस्यां स्नानविधानतो हि मनुजो निष्पापतां संव्रजे-
द्गोभूहेमतिलार्पणैस्तु विभवं नैरुज्यसौख्यान्वितम्।।7।।

अचलासप्तमीव्रतम्—

माघे सा ह्यचलेति संज्ञिततिथिः स्नात्वा च दीपार्पणं
तस्यां त्वष्टदले व्रती स्वविभवैर्गौरीश्वरं पूजयेत्।
पूर्वादिक्रमतो रविं च विधिवत्पुष्पैः सुधूपादिभिः
सत्सौभाग्यकरं सुरूपजननं पीठार्पणं भोजनम्।।8।।

पुत्रसप्तमीव्रतम्—

माघे सप्तमिका सुपुत्रफलदा शुद्धे च तस्यां व्रती
स्नात्वा भास्करपूजनं स्वविभवैः कुर्यान्निशाजागरम्।
प्रातर्होमविधिस्तु भोजनविधिः शुक्लेऽथ कृष्णे दले
सप्तम्यां प्रतिमासिकं व्रतमिदमब्दे तमुद्यापयेत्।।9।।

मन्वादितिथिः—

माघे सिते सप्तमिका तिथिश्च
पौर्वाह्णिकी सा परमा प्रशस्ता।
मन्वादिका स्नानजपादिकृत्ये
पित्र्यर्चनेऽनन्तफलप्रदात्री।।10।।

भीष्माष्टमीकं व्रतम्—

भीष्माष्टमी माघसिते विभागे
पूर्वान्विता स्याद्विबुधैस्तु तस्याम्।

स्नात्वा सुतीर्थे च तिलोदकाद्यै-
भीष्मं यजेत्पापविनाशहेतोः।।11।।

जया नामैकादशी—

माघे शुक्लदले जया हरितिथिस्तस्यां व्रती मानवः
क्षीरेणैव घृतेन वेदविधिना श्रीमाधवं पूजयेत्।
वह्नौ वै ह्यमृताहुतिं च जुहुयात्पात्रं तिलस्यार्पणं
कृत्वैवं लभते फलं बहुगुणं श्रीवाजपेयोद्भवम्।।12।।

भीष्मद्वादशीव्रतम्—

या द्वादशी तपगता धवलाख्यपक्षे
भीष्मस्ति(ति)थिस्तु परमा धनसौख्यदात्री।
भीष्माय पूजनविधिश्च तिलोदकं च
सद्विप्रभोजनयुतं विदधीत तस्याम्।।13।।

कल्पादिः—

माघे त्रयोदशि तिथिः सवितोदयाद्या
कल्पादिकेति परमा खलु देवपक्षे।
तीर्थादिके च जनपूजनभोजनेषु
होमे च दानकरणेऽक्षयपुण्यदात्री।।14।।

माघीपौर्णिमापर्वम् (र्व)—

माघे चानुमतिस्तिथिर्बहुगुणा सत्स्नानदानेऽर्चने
सा चेत्पित्रभसंयुता शतगुणा पुण्यप्रदा स्यान्नृणाम्।
चेद्वै सिंहगतौ शशिसुरगुरू मन्दे च मेषस्थिते
सूर्ये विष्णुभगेऽप्यनन्तफलदा माघी महासंज्ञिता।।15।।

श्रीमद्गोवर्धनोद्धारणागमनोत्सवः—

माघे कृष्णे सप्तमी या तिथिश्च
तस्यां कुर्यादुत्सवं विष्णुभक्तैः।
सत्पूजाद्यैर्धूपदीपार्घदानैः
संगीताद्यैः पूजयेत्केशवं च।।16।।

शोककहराव्रतम्—

कृष्णाष्टम्यां माघमासे व्रताढ्यै-
रामं सीतां लक्ष्मणं वायुपुत्रम्।
सद्गन्धाद्यैः पूजयेद्भक्तियुक्तैः
[55]शोकश्चार्तिर्नाशमाप्नोति तस्य।।17।।

विजया नामैकादशी—

माघे कृष्णविभागके च विजया विष्णोस्तिथिर्या भवे-
त्तस्यामिक्षुरसेन सूक्तविधिना संपूजयेन्माधवम्।
द्वादश्यां हवनं तिलाज्य[56]सयवैः कुम्भाज्यदानार्पणं
कृत्वा वै द्विजभोजनं च व्रतवा[57]न्सद्भुक्तिमुक्ती लभेत्।।18।।

शिवरात्रिनिर्णयः—

माघे कृष्णचतुर्दशी निशिमुखव्याप्ता निशीथान्विता
तस्यां वै शिवपूजनादिविधिना कुर्याद्व्रतं शैविकैः।
पूर्वद्युस्तु निशीथिनीपरदिने युक्ता निशीथे तदा
ग्राह्यानङ्गयुता यदोभयदिने नोचेन्निशीथे परा।।19।।

शिवरात्रिव्रतोद्यापनम्—

शिवरात्रिव्रतधारकैर्मनुमिते वर्षे तदुद्यापनं
कुर्यान्मण्डल(प)मण्डलस्थकलशे हैमे शिवोमे यजेत्।
रात्रौ जागरणार्चनं च हवनं कृत्वा द्विजान्भोजये-
द्वस्त्रं गाशयनीं च पीठप्रतिमां दद्यात्सुमुक्तीप्सुभिः।।20।।

पयोव्रतम्—

माघे भूतसमन्वितान्त्यदिवसादारभ्य पुत्रार्थिनी
कुर्याद्वै हरिपूजनादिविधिना यावत्सिता द्वादशी।
एतद्वै तु पयोव्रतं च कथितं प्राचीनकैः पण्डितै-
र्विष्णुयज्ञसमं फलं हि लभते वन्ध्यत्वदोषापहम्।।21।।

युगादितिथिः—

माघे चैव युगादिसंज्ञिततिथिर्ग्राह्यापराह्णान्विता
तस्यां श्राद्धविधानतो हि विदुषैर्दद्याच्च पिण्डोदकम्।

सा वै कुम्भगते रवौ च वसुभे वा वारुणे चन्द्रमा-
योगेऽनन्तफलोऽतिदुर्लभतरः श्राद्धे च दानेऽर्चने।।22।।

कुम्भसंक्रान्तिः—

कुम्भेऽर्कक्रमणे भवेद्धरिपदी संज्ञेति तत्संक्रमा-
त्पूर्वा षोडशनाडिका सुकृतदा स्यात्पुण्यकल्पेषु च।
तीर्थस्नानविधी रवेस्तु यजनं श्राद्धार्चने वै गवे
दद्यादम्बुत्रणं च वस्त्रयुगलं विप्राय सौख्यार्थिभिः।।23।।

इति श्रीनिर्णयमञ्जर्यां माघमासस्य व्रतोत्सवतिथिकथनं नामैकादशोऽध्यायः।।11।।

।। द्वादशोऽध्यायः।।

अथ फाल्गुनमासस्येश्वरादीनाह—

गोविन्दस्य निदेशश्चरति वै सूर्यो वियन्मण्डलं
भारद्वाजबलेन प्रत्यनुदिनं नागाधिराजेन तु।
विश्वची पथि नृत्यसाधनपरा सद्वाद्यकृत्सेनजि-
न्मासं फाल्गुनसंज्ञकं नयति वै पुंसां स्मरोत्पत्तिदम्।।1।।

आमलक्येकादशीव्रतम्—

शुक्लैकादशीफाल्गुने भवति या धात्रीफला संज्ञिका
गोविन्दं पयसाभिषिच्य विधिना होमं तिलाज्यादिभिः।
द्वादश्यां च यवान्नमाढकमितं दत्त्वा सुविप्राय वै
भुञ्जेद्यस्तु व्रती नरः स लभते पुण्यं च गोमेधजम्।।2।।

नारायणोत्सवम्(वः)—

शुक्ले फाल्गुनमासके स्मरतिथी रव्यूदयव्यापिनी
वृन्दारण्यनिवासिनो हि कुरुते तस्यां महानुत्सवम्।
गत्वा क्षीरिणीवृक्षकेऽथ विधिना संपूजयेत्केशवं
नैवेद्यैः परितोषयेद्द्विजवरान्सौख्याय मोक्षाय च।।3।।

होलिकामहोत्सवम् (वः)—

फाल्गुन्यां वै प्रदोषे मनुजहितकरीं होलिकां दीपयेद्वै
भद्रान्ते वा सुपुच्छे यदि परदिवसे सार्धयामात्रयोने।
तस्माद्राकाधिका वै शिखितिथि(थिश्)च यदा वर्धमानेऽपरेऽह्नि
कर्तव्याथ प्रदोषे यदि गलिततिथौ वह्नियुक्ते प्रकुर्यात्।।4।।

फाल्गुन्यां ग्रहणं यदा भवति वै भद्रां विनार्कान्निशि
ग्रस्तश्चेदुदयेऽष्टपुच्छसमये संदीपयेद्धोलिकाम्।
मन्वादिरपि फाल्गुनीति कथिता ग्राह्या च पूर्वाह्णिकी
तस्यां तर्पणपिण्डदानविधिना तृप्तिः शताब्दी भवेत्।।5।।

वसन्तोत्सवः—

मासे फाल्गुनक(के) [तु] वह्नितिथिके प्रातर्वसन्तोत्सवं
कुर्याद्युग्मदिनोदये भवति चेत्पूर्वा हिता नापरा।
स्नात्वा तर्प्य सुराँश्च नूत्नकुसुमैः संप्राश्य होलां नमे-
त्तत्रैवार्यमभे हरिं सुविधिना दोलागतं पूजयेत्।।6।।

कल्पादिः—

या फाल्गुने गौरितिथिस्तु कृष्णा
कल्पादिकृत्ये परमा प्रशस्ता।
तीर्थाप्लवे मन्त्रजपे च दाने
पित्र्यर्चनेऽनन्तफलप्रदा स्यात्।।7।।

पापमोचिन्येकादशी—

कृष्णे फाल्गुनमासके हरितिथिः पापौघसंमोचिनी
गोविन्दं पयसाभिषिच्य सुकथासक्तो नयेद्वै निशाम्।
द्वादश्यां हवनं तिलाज्यसहितं विप्राय व्रीहिं ददे-
द्भुङ्क्ते यस्तु नरः सुखं स लभते मुच्येन्महापातकात्।।8।।

मन्वादितिथिः—

यामा फाल्गुनमासके भवति वै मन्वादिसंज्ञेति सा
पितॄणां चं सुतृप्तिदा बहुगुणा पिण्डादिदानादिभिः।

सा वै मीनगते रवौ च शशिनि पूषान्विते वैधृते
योगश्चाक्षयसंज्ञिकोऽतिफलदः स्नाने च दानेऽर्चने।।9।।

मीनार्कसंक्रमणम्—

षडशीत्याख्यविसंज्ञिका च कुसुमारम्भस्तु मीनार्कगे
संचाराद्घटिका परा नृपमिता पुण्यप्रदा स्यान्नृणाम्।
तीर्थस्नानविधिं रवेश्च यजनं श्राद्धं च विप्राय वै
मालां वै सुरसोद्भवां च सुग्रहं दद्यात्सुमोक्षाय वै।।10।।

इति श्रीनिणर्यमञ्जर्यां फाल्गुनव्रतोत्सवनिर्णयं(यो)
नाम द्वादशोऽध्यायः।।12।।

।। त्रयोदशोऽध्यायः।।

अधिमासस्येश्वरादीनाह—

भानोः संक्रमवर्जितोऽधिकमतः संक्रान्तियुग्मे क्षयो
मासौ तौ शुभकर्मणि परिहरेन्नित्ये च नैमित्तिके।
ग्राह्यो वै विबुधैस्तु मासिकविधौ श्राद्धे च मन्वादिके-
ऽप्याधानादिषु सप्तसंस्कृतिकृतौ स्नानोपवासादिषु।।1।।

अथाधिमासदेवतानाह—

मासेऽधिसंज्ञे पुरुषोत्तमः स्या-
न्मासाधिप[57] कोऽग्रिममासजस्तु।
पृथक्पृथग्घस्रपतिर्भवेद्वै
स्नानोपवासादिषु दुर्लभोऽयम्।।2।।

अधिमासव्रतविधिः—

मासे वै प्रथमे च भूतदिवसे कृत्वा निरन्नं व्रतं
संकल्पादिविधानतो व्रतपरः स्नायात्सुतीर्थोदके।
पद्मस्थे घटपात्रके प्रतिदिनं संपूजयेच्छ्रीहरिं
मासान्ते प्रतिपत्सु पायसघृतैर्होमं व्रतोद्यापनम्।।3।।

उपवासोऽथ हविष्यभोजनपरो नक्तैकभक्तोऽथवा
तीर्थस्नानपरो जितेन्द्रियनरः सद्ब्रह्मचर्यान्वितः।

य: कुर्यादधिमाससंज्ञकव्रतं सत्सौख्यस्वर्गप्रदं
मुच्येत्पातकराशितोऽपि स लभेन्मुक्तिं चतुर्धां शुभाम्।।4।।

स्नाने तीर्थविशेषमाह—

चैत्रे वै पुरुषोत्तमे च सरयु: सन्माधवे नर्मदा
ज्येष्ठे चैव सरस्वती च तपती स्वच्छे नभे कौशिकी।
भाद्रे रामह्रदं च शोणमिषवे ऊर्जेऽधिके पुष्करं
मार्गादित्रिषु जाह्नवी च तपनी [58]सर्व्या पुन (नर्) दुर्लभम्।।5।।

हरिवल्लभैकादशी—

मासेऽधिके वै हरिवल्लभाख्या
विष्णोस्तिथि: शुक्लविभागके च।
संपूजयेद्वै पुरुषोत्तमं च
घृताहुतिर्वै सुरभीप्रदानम्।।6।।

स्वर्गदैकादशी—

मासे वै पुरुषोत्तमे हरितिथि: कृष्णे च या स्वर्गदा
तस्यां वै पुरुषोत्तमं च विधिवत्क्षीराभिषेकादिना।
सद्गन्धादिभि(भि:)पूजयेच्च हवनं क्षीराज्यसत्तन्दुलै-
र्दद्याद्वै सुयवाश्च वेदविदुषे सत्स्वर्गसौख्यं लभेत्।।7।।

क्षयमास:—

मासो य: क्षयसंज्ञिकोऽतिभयदश्चन्द्राब्धिभूमिसमै-(141)
र्विश्लेषान्तरितेऽथवा नवकुभिर्वर्षै:(19) क्वचित्संभव:।
तन्मासाधिपतिर्गतागतपति: स्यात्पक्षयोश्चोभयो-
र्निन्द्यो वै शुभकर्मणि जनिमृतौ पूर्वापर: संज्ञित:।।8।।

इति श्रीनिर्णयमञ्जर्यां पुरुषोत्तममासव्रतकथनं नाम त्रयोदशोऽध्याय:।।13।।

।। चतुर्दशोऽध्याय:।।

अथाखिलमासप्रशस्तव्रतान्याह—

सर्वेषु मासेष्वपि या द्वितीया
चन्द्रोदयव्यापिनिका च तस्याम्।

चन्द्रं यजेदर्चनगन्धपुष्पैः
क्षीरार्घदानैः सुसुखार्थिभिश्च।।1।।

अङ्गारकचतुर्थी—

कृष्णा चतुर्थी कुजवारयुक्ता
सा लक्षमार्तण्डग्रहोपमा स्यात्।
स्नाने व्रते वै सुरपूजने च
तस्यां सुतार्थी कुसुतं यजेद्वै।।2।।

सुखषष्ठीव्रतम्—

मासेऽखिले च सुखषष्ठिव्रतं विदध्या-
न्नक्तेन वा निरशनेन फलाशनेन।
स्कन्दं यजेद्द्विजवराय सदन्नदाना-
त्संजागरात्कलुषनाशकरं हितार्थी।।3।।

भानुसप्तमी—

या सप्तमी भास्करवारयुक्ता
शुक्ला च सूर्यग्रहणोपमा सा।
स्नानेऽर्चने मन्त्रजपे व्रते च
दानादिषु चाक्षयपुण्यदात्री।।4।।

बुधाष्टमी—

या शुक्लाष्टमि सौम्यवारसहिता सर्वेषु मासेष्वपि
शस्ता कोटिरविग्रहोपमफला स्नाने च दानेऽर्चने।
तस्यां पुण्यव्रतं यमार्तिहरणं कुर्यात्सुतीर्थोदके
स्नात्वा चाष्टदले सुवर्णजनितं सौम्यं यजेन्मानवः।।5।।

बुधाष्टम्युद्यापनम्—

पूर्णे चाष्टमवर्षके स्वविभवैरुद्यापयेत्तं सुधीः
स्नात्वा मण्डपकेऽष्टपत्रकमले संस्थाप्य कुम्भाञ्छुभान्।
मध्यस्थः परिपत्रके च सगणं सौम्यं च संपूजये-
द्धोमं ब्राह्मणभोजनं च यव [वाय]नान्दत्त्वा सुमुक्तिं व्रजेत्।।6।।

आशादशमी—

आशाख्या दशमीव्रतं वितनुयात्सर्वेषु मासेष्वपि
शुक्लायां च दिनेश्वरादिसहितामाशां च संपूजयेत्।
चित्रस्थां प्रतिमासकेऽथ विधिवदुद्यापयेद्द्वादशे
मासे वै प्रतिमार्चनाच्च हवनाद्दानाच्च सर्वार्थदम्।।7।।

सोमवतीपर्वमा(पर्वा)ह—

सर्वेषु मासेष्वपि सोमवारे
भवेत्कुहुर्घस्त्रमुखाभिगामी।
सा कोटिसोमग्रहणोपमा स्या-
त्स्नाने च दाने द्विजभोजने च।।8।।
या सोमवत्यां व्रतधारका स्त्री
स्नात्वा सुतीर्थे कुरुते फलैस्तु।
अश्वत्थवृक्षस्य प्रदक्षिणा वै
सौभाग्यसौख्यं विविधं लभेत्सा।।9।।

प्रदक्षिणाफलम्—

जम्बीरैर्विभवं सुभोगमतुलं सद्दाडिमैः श्रीफलैः
सन्मानं क्रमुकैः सुरूपजननं तेजः सुतं मौक्तिकैः।
वैडूर्यादिभिराज्यसौख्यमतुलं मोक्षं तु रुद्राक्षजैः
सोमायां हरिपुंरुहार्चनविधौ भक्त्या स्त्रियः संलभेत्।।10।।

सोमवत्युद्यापनम्—

सोमाया व्रतधारकास्तु(तु) युवती त्रिंशन्मिते सुव्रते
कुर्यात्पूर्णविधिं सुसौख्यफलदं सन्मण्डपे मण्डले।
हैमाश्वत्थतले हरिं सहरमां संपूजयेद्वायना-
न्दद्यात्स्वस्वफलैः सुमन्त्रविभवैर्भक्त्या द्विजान्भोजयेत्।।11।।

अथ ग्रहणपर्वः(र्व)—

चान्द्रे सहस्त्रगुणितं च रविग्रहे च
पुण्यं चं लक्षगुणितं च जपादिकृत्ये।
चन्द्रग्रहः शशिदिनेऽर्कदिने रवेस्तु
चूडामणीति कथितोऽक्षयपुण्यदस्तु।।12।।

इति चूडामणियोगः।

यामत्रिकं शशिग्रहेऽथ चतुष्टयं च
सूर्यग्रहात्प्रथमतोऽप्यशने विवर्ज्यम्।
स्नानं जपं च हवनं सुरपूजनं च
दानं च मुक्तिसमयाप्लवनं क्रमेण।।13।।

अभ्राच्छादितमण्डले च विबुधैः शास्त्रोक्तकाले शुभे
स्नात्वा नित्यविधिं चरेत्स्वविभवैर्दानं च मुक्त्यूदिते।
बिम्बे दृष्टिगते तु भोजनविधिर्नैमित्तिकी सत्क्रिया
ग्रस्तास्तेऽपि तथैव सूतकयुतैर्मर्त्यैस्तु दानं ग्रहे।।14।।

इति शास्त्रार्थः।।

व्यतीपातपर्वः(र्व)—

उत्पाताभ्र[59]मणे तथैव पतने पाते त्रिभागात्मिकं
पुण्यं लक्षगुणं च कोटिगुणितं स्याद्वै तथा चाक्षयम्।
तेभ्यो वैधृतिसंज्ञके दशगुणं पुण्यं लभेन्मानव-
श्चेत्पादुत्क्रमगे जपार्चनविधौ सत्स्नानदानादिषु।।15।।

इति वैधृतिपर्वः(र्व)।

व्यतीपातव्रतं—

व्रती व्यतीपातदिनेऽवगाहये-
त्तीर्थे सुखाढ्योऽष्टदलस्थकुम्भे।
चन्द्रार्कपुत्रं विधिवद्यजेत
ह्युद्यापयेच्छक्रमिते सुपाते।।16।।

वारव्रतानि—

यो वै वारव्रती सुमन्त्रविधिना स्वे स्वेऽथ सन्मण्डले
ध्यानावाहनपूर्वकं सहगणं वारेश्वरं पूजयेत्।
तत्तन्मन्त्रजपं च ध्यानमशनं कृत्वाथ पूर्णे व्रते
होमं सत्प्रतिमादिदानविधिभिर्मुच्येदरिष्टान्नरः।।17।।

वारव्रते फलान्याह—

तेजस्वी निरुजान्वितोऽर्कयजनाच्चान्द्रात्सुकान्ति सुखं
स्त्रीपुत्रार्थयुतं कुजाद्बुधव्रतात्सन्मन्त्रसिद्धिं शुभाम्।

देवेज्यस्य व्रतादरिष्टहरणं साम्राज्यतां वै भृगो-
मन्दाच्छत्रुभयापहं बहुसुखं स्याद्राहुकेतोस्तथा।।18।।

व्रतारम्भे वर्ज्यकान्याह—

वर्षाधिक्षयगेऽथवाधिकतरे जीवे च नक्रे हरौ
वक्रे वाप्यतिचारगेऽरिगते तुर्याष्टरिष्फस्थिते।
उत्पाते शिखितोद्गमे सुरगिरौ शुक्रे तु मौढ्यत्वगे
बाल्ये वार्धगते व्रतं तु विबुधैर्नोद्यापयेन्नारभेत्।।19।।

एषां त्याज्यावश्यकमाह—

अष्टाविंशतिवासरान्सुरगुरौ वक्रातिचारे त्यजे-
त्सिंहेपञ्चनवांशकान्मृगगते नीचे तु पञ्चांशकान्।
मासं शत्रुभगे शिशुस्थविरयोः सप्ताहमुत्पातके
सर्वं चास्तगतं क्षयेऽधिकतरं संवत्सराद्यं शुभम्।।20।।

अथ व्रतारम्भविधिः—

सद्योगान्वितवासरे शुभतिथौ भक्त्याह्निकं कृद्व्रते
नत्वा वै स्वगुरुं धनं च विधिवत्संप्रार्थ्य तद्वाक्यतः।
गन्धाढ्यैः सुमनैः फलैश्च विधिवत्संपूज्य लम्बोदरं
गृह्णीयान्नियमान्वितं सुफलदं सत्कर्मयुक्तं व्रतम्।।21।।

अथ देवताप्राधान्ये मण्डलान्याह—

गौरीपूजनके तु गौरितिलकं शैवे तु लिङ्गोद्भवं
षट्कोणं गिरिजासुतेऽर्कयजने कुर्यात्तु चाष्टं दलम्।
नाभाङ्कप्रतिमं विधातृयजने स्वं स्वं ग्रहस्यार्चने
विष्णोः पूजनकेऽखिलार्चनाविधौ कुर्यात्तु भद्रं शुभे।।22।।

अथारम्भिकव्रते संकटप्राप्तौ शास्त्रार्थः—

रोगाद्यापदिके मिथो वितनुयात्स्त्रीकान्तयोः सद्व्रतं
पुत्रैर्वा त्वथ सूतकेऽप्यनशनं पूजा तु सद्ब्राह्मणैः।
अज्ञानादपि दैवयोगनिचयाद्भग्ने व्रते मानवः
प्राश्चित्तं कनकार्पणं जपविधिं कृत्वा चरेत्तद्व्रतम्।।23।।

ग्रन्थकर्तावर्णनम्—

भारद्वाजसगोत्रजो द्विजवरो यो वालखिल्ल्यान्वये
विद्या-ऋद्धियुतो नृसिंहतनयो गङ्गाधराख्यः सुधीः।
तेनेऽयं रचिता हरेश्च कृपया सच्छास्त्रसंबोधिनी[60]
ह्युत्सवनिर्णयमञ्जरीस्तु(तु) त्रिशतैर्वृत्तैस्तु रुद्राधिकैः।।24।।

श्रीमत्काशपनिर्मिता सुरसरित्तीरस्थसत्पत्तने
संस्थः सन्नृपशालिवाहनशके पञ्चाब्धिघस्त्रोन्मिते।
चैत्रे वै नवमीतिथौ बुधदिने पूर्णीकृता सा तु वै
भूयान्मङ्गलकारिणी सुखकरी हर्यङ्घ्रिपद्मेऽर्पिता।।25।।

इति श्रीमद्गङ्गाधरविरचितायामुत्सवनिर्णयमञ्जर्यां सार्वमासिकव्रतोत्सववर्णनं नाम चतुर्दशोऽध्यायः।।

समाप्तोऽयं ग्रन्थः।

गौडलवासिना ईश्वरसूनुना लक्ष्मीधरेणेदं लिपीकृतं स्वार्थे।

संवत् 1866 ना 1731 प्रवर्तमाने आश्विने शुद्धे द्वितीया सौम्ये।

लेखकपाठकयोः कल्याणं भूयास्ताम्।।

FOOTNOTES

Paper published in Journal of the Oriental Institute, Baroda, Vol.37, Nos. 1-2, Sept.-December, 1987 issue, pp. 89-125 & Vol. 37. Nos. 3-4 March-June 1988 issue pp. 253-284.

1. उत्सवनिर्णयमञ्जरी (उ. नि. मं.) text (Manuscript Acc. No.2375 of the Oriental Institute, Baroda) -1.1 and colo. to adh.1.
2. *Ibid*; colo. to adh. 2, and adh. 14; also 14.25.
3. *Ibid;* Scribe's note after adh. 14.
4. *Ibid*; 14.24.
5. Babaria Indraji Mulaji : trans. *Vālakhilya Purāṇa*, Bombay, 1894, adh. 12, p.50.
6. उ. नि. मं. 14.25.
7. Ksemaraj Srikrsanadas, ed. The *Padmapurāṇa*; Venk. ed., Bombay, *Śake* 1817, reprint by Nag Publishers, Delhi-7, Third part, *Uttara* and *Kriyā; Uttara* adh. 135.

8. उ. नि. मं. 1.1 and 14.25.
9. *Ibid;* 4.11 and 5.18.
10 *Ibid;* 5.3.
11. *Ibid;* 14.25.

Variants/notes to the Text

1. प्रतिजितं in marg.
2. निश्च in marg.
3. (.....) in marg.
4. Damaged
5. Damaged
6. Lacuna
7. Lacuna.
8. Note hiatus
9. before corr. मि for चे
10. note hiatus
11. गा in marg.
12. Scribe notes runuing no. 45 here.
13. Scribe records running no.46 and also 2 here.
14. before corr. न्मं
15. before corr. प्त
16. Scribe notes no.57 also.
17. before corr. पू (for रो).
18. Lacuna
19. स्त in marg.
20. before corr. त्रि
21. note hiatus.
22. वृन्ताक in marg.
23. अथ in marg.
24. before corr. त्रि.
25. अथ in marg.
26. इति... तिथिः in marg.
27. अथ in marg.
28. आषाढे....भोज्ये।।18।। in marg.
29. marg. gloss कामः.
30. अथ in marg.
31. before corr-reads या सा दिवै तृतीया श्रावणे.
32. अथ in marg.
33. दा marg. for सा.

34. before corr. सु
35. यकमिदं (be. corr.).
36. भसि in marg.
37. Note hiatus.
38. Scribe's mistake in numbering verses, from here upto the end of adh. 6 is corrected.
39. Line is missing.
40. Before corr. कुंजरी.
41. विज in marg.
42. before corr. रात्रौ.
43. marg. also दिवसे(for समये).
44. सविद्विश्विभ also in marg.
45. कर्म in marg.
46. या (also marg.) (for च).
47. note hiatus.
48. m. gloss—प्रत्यब्दक्रमगे तिथौ द्वितीयाद्यष्टादिषु प्रतिपदादिक्रमेण वर्धमानतिथौ व्रतं कुर्यादिति क्रमेण षोडशप्रत्यब्दव्रते मार्गपौर्णिमा स्यादित्यर्थः।
49. note hiatus.
50. पवित्रा in marg.
51. before corr. मोक्षदा.
52. before corr. सुरती.
53. ins. व्रतं in marg.
54. before corr. सकष्टं.
55. before corr. शोकस्याप्तिर्.
56. before corr. यवभिः.
57. marg. व्रतमान्.
58. before corr. सद्या
59. ब्रह्मणे before corr.
60. after corr. बोधान्विता.

VI

CONTRIBUTION OF GAṄGĀDHARA PĀṬHAKA—A 17TH CENTURY SCHOLAR FROM GUJARAT

Introductory

Sanskrit Literature is a vast and unfathomable ocean. Several works on different fields of Sanskrit Literature have been published. Still there is a large number of works of different fields, lying hidden in the manuscript libraries, not much noticed and hence little-known to the world of scholars. Gujarat has contributed a lot to several fields of Sanskrit Literature. Still the contribution of several scholars of Sanskrit Literature in different fields has remained less-noticed. Gaṅgādhara Pāṭhaka is one of such scholars of 17th century from Cambay, Gujarat, whose contribution of varied digests on *Dharmaśāstra* has not been taken notice of and all his works have remained only in manuscript form. In this paper, an attempt is made to introduce this unknown scholar from Gujarat and his contribution to *Dharmaśāstra* Literature.

Mm. P.V. Kane has given two exhaustive lists of authors and works on *Dharmaśāstra* at the end of the second part of the revised first volume of the *History of Dharmaśāstra*.[1] Here we get some important information under the title *Pravāsakṛtya*. It is clear from note that this work was composed by Gaṅgādhara Pāṭhaka, who was a resident of the Stambhatīrtha i.e. Modern Cambay. So I was very much interested in going through this particular work, connected with *Pravāsa*, written by a scholar from Gujarat. One manuscript of this work is deposited in the Asiatic Society of Calcutta. Hence when I was deputed to Calcutta for procuring mss. of the *Mārkaṇḍeya Purāṇa*, I was fortunate enough to get the xerox-copy of this small, but rare work of a scholar from Gujarat. While studying the above work, I could get authentic and detailed information about the biography of Gaṅgādhara and his contribution of several other works.

Biographical Details

His complete name is Gaṅgādhara Rāmacandra Pāṭhaka. His father was a *mahāyājñika*. He is said to be *trayīsāra-vivektā* (commentator of essence of three *Vedas*.). The name of the preceptor of his father was Hariśaṅkara, who was not only a great *Yājñika*, but was also *dīkṣita* (may be an *āhitāgni*). At the beginning of two of his works, namely the *Prakṛtivikṛtiyāgakālaviveka*[2] and the *Kātyāyanaśulvasūtra-bhāṣya*[3], he pays homage to both of them in verses, that are identical.

जयत्येको जगत्यां श्रीहरिशंकरदीक्षितः।
त्रयीसारविवेक्तृश्रीरामचन्द्रगुरोर्गुरुः।।
रामचन्द्रगुरुं नत्वा गर्गकर्कादियाज्ञिकान्।।

The colophons to all the three works namely the *Pravā-sakṛtya*, the *Prakṛtivikṛtiyāgakālaviveka* and the *Kātyāyana-Śulvasūtrabhāṣya* are also quite identical and supply some information, as noted previously. From the last portion of his commentary on *Śulvasūtra*, it is evident that it was completed by his son, whose name was Rāmakṛṣṇa, who is said to be belonging to *Nāgara* caste of Gujarat, but his son, Rāmakṛṣṇa was residing at Kashi.[4]

The name of his brother was *Yāgnika* Nārāyaṇa. It is quite possible that Balabhadra Pāṭhaka and his son Devabhadra Pāṭhaka may be scholars, belonging to the same Pāṭhaka family of Gujarat.

Date and Place of Gaṅgādhara

Unlike several scholars of Sanskrit Literature, fortunately enough, we get authentic information about the date and place of Gaṅgādhara, from his work *Pravāsakṛtya*. He clearly states—

वर्षे षोडशके त्रिषष्टिसमये वासन्तिके माधवे।
पूर्णेन्दौ रविवासरे...... गते मार्तण्डके मण्डले।
श्रीमद्गुर्जरमण्डले विजयते श्रीस्तम्भतीर्थे शुभे
श्रीमत्पाठकरामचन्द्रतनयो गंगाधरोऽलीलिखत्।।

Thus it is evident that the work was complete in 1663 in *Vasanta* i.e. spring season, & in *madhumāsa*-means the *Caitra* month, on Sunday, the Pūrṇimā day, when the Sun was in the Northern hemisphere. The year 1663, if taken as *Vikrama Saṁvat*, as he was a scholar from Gujarat, it would be 1606-1607 A.D. He has clearly mentioned his place of residence in the second part of the above verse. He was resident of Stambhatīrtha of the *Gurjaramaṇḍala* i.e. Modern Cambay or Khambhat of Gujarat. Thus he was from Gujarat. Moreover, he also belonged to *nāgara* caste, as is mentioned by his son Rāmakṛṣṇa in his commentary on the *Kātyāyana-śulvasūtra*.

Works of Gangādhara Pāṭhaka

He was mainly a scholar of *Dharmaśāstra* especially of its *śrauta* aspect. He has written about seven works on different *śrauta* aspects. Though he belonged to Gujarat, it is curious that most of his works have travelled far and wide and excepting only one, that too not in good condition, all have gone to different places like Ujjain, Lahore, Bengal, Benares, Trivendrum, Darbhangā etc. Hence I could not get much detailed information about them. Mss. of his works are thus available mostly in places, mentioned above. The name of his seven works[5] are—

1. *Pravāsakṛtya* 2. *Kātyāyanaśulvasūtrabhāṣya*
3. *Yāgakālaviveka* 4. *Parvanirṇaya*
5. *Yājamānapaddhati* 6. *Sarvatomukhapaddhati*
7. *Haviryajñakālaviveka.*

1. *Pravāsakṛtya*—This work deals with the subject of *Pravāsakṛtya* for *Agnihotrin.* When an *āhitāgni* is required to go outside, how he should maintain the fire-worship. The detailed treatment of this topic is made by considering views of different schools, commentators and other ancient *sūtra* works. It is in 149 *Anuṣṭubh Śloka-Kārikās*. He clearly states his purpose in composing this work at the beginning.

धनार्जने तथापत्तौ प्रवासे समुपस्थिते।
अग्नेर्भारं प्रतिष्ठाप्य पत्न्यामृत्विक्षु धर्मवित्।
प्रवसेद् विधिना सम्यक् तत्र कृत्यमिहोच्यते।

The rare and important manuscript of this work is available in the Asiatic Society of Calcutta (RASB II.1063).[6] I have procured the Xerox-copy of it for my research purposes. The manuscript has totally ten folios in a damaged condition.

2. *Kātyāyanaśulvasūtrabhāṣya*—There is a commentary on the *Kātyāyanaśulvasūtra* by Gaṅgādhara. Only two mss. of this work are available—one at Darbhaṅgā (Mithila IV.28) and another at Asiatic Society of Bengal, Calcutta, (RASB II. 973). From the penultimate portion of the work, it is known that it is completed by Gaṅgādhara's son, Rāmakṛṣṇa by name. This is one of the important works of the author, still little-known.

3. *Yāgakālaviveka or Prakṛtivikṛtiyāgakālaviveka*—The manuscript of this work only is available in the Oriental Institute, with Accession no. 10475. The manuscript contains fiftyseven folios and fifteen hundred *granthas*. It is in *Devanāgarī*. The manuscript is dated *Saṁvat* 1724 (i.e. 1668 A.D.), written by Śivadatta, son of Uddhava Śukla of

Śivapura. The subject, dealt with in this work is the detemination of the time of sacrifice, whether it is to be on Full-moon day or New moon day. One manuscript of it is said to be in Lahore Library.

4. *Parvanirṇaya*—The manuscript of this work is deposited in the Scindia Research Institute, Ujjain. No more information of it is available to me as it is a latest addition (N. 601).

5. *Yājamānapaddhati*—The manuscript of this work is said to be deposited at the Lahore Library (PUL II. App. p. 26), hence no more information could be obtained.

6. *Sarvatomukhapaddhati*—Only two manuscripts of this work are known. One is deposited in the Sanskrit College Library of Benares (no. 15) and another at Scindia Research Institute, Ujjain (Latest additions 600). I could get no more information of this work.

7. *Haviryajñakālaviveka*—The only manuscript of this work is available in the Travancore University Manuscript Library of Trivandrum (No. 1779). No more information is available.

Conclusion

It is evident from the above deliberation that Gaṅgādhara Pāṭhaka, a *nāgara* brahmin was a great scholar of 17th century from Cambay, Gujarat, whose contribution to *Dharmaśāstra* Literature has remained less-noticed.

FOOTNOTES

Paper published in *Vinayatośiṇī* B.Bhattacharya Centenary Volume, Culcutta, 1996.

1. Kane, P.V.: *History of Dharmaśāstra*, Bhandarkar Oriental Research Institute, Poona, Vol. I, Part II, pp. 1072-1073 & 1173.

2. Baroda Oriental Institute, Ms. Acc. No. 10475. Folio.1.
3. Banerjishastri, Anantaprasad : *A Descriptive Catalogue of Mss. in Mithila,* Vol. IV, The Bihar & Orissa Research Society, Patna, 1940 Vol. IV No.28. pp. 33-34.
4. *Ibid.*
5. *New Catalogus Catalogorum,* Deptt. of SK., University of Madras, 1969, Vol.5, pp. 203-204.
6. *New Catalogus Catalogorum,* Dptt. of SK, University, of Madras, 1991 Vol. 13, pp. 89-90 for some other mss. of this work.

VII

ADDITION TO THE *PULASTYASMṚTISAṄGRAHA*

The Reconstruction of Lost *Smṛti*-texts on the basis of quotations, found in the digests and commentaries on *Dharmaśāstra* has been a long-felt desideratum. Recently Prof. Smt. Krishna Kanti Gopal and Prof. Lallanji Gopal reconstructed the text of Pulastya and presented it in the form of a monograph entitled "*Pulastyamṛtisaṅgraha*" (Pub. by Rishi Publications, 79, Chandrika Colony, Varanasi-221 010, 1992, price : Rs.195.00). I have had the opportunity to review this book, in the Journal of the Oriental Institute (JOl Vol. 40 Nos. 3-4, March-June 1991, pp. 337-340). Some points, not covered in the said review, especally relating to additional verses, not included in the above book are specifically treated in this paper. The authors might have tried to be as exhaustive as possible in their attempt. However some verses, collected by me are not found in their book. Hence in this papers, the quotations/verses, not found in the collection of the authors, are collected and presented herewith for the benefit of scholars, with a view to making addition to the *Pulastyasmṛtisaṅgraha*.

Additional Verses

1. सन्निहत्यामुपस्पृश्य राहुग्रस्ते दिवाकरे।
   सत्रधर्मप्रविष्टस्य दानकर्मफलैषिणः।।

   —स्मृतिचन्द्रिका आशौचम् पृ. 78

2. दध्यादीनां विकाराणां क्षीरतः संभवो यथा।
   तथैवाशेषकामानां क्षीरस्नापनतो हरेः।।

3. स्नाप्य दध्ना सकृद्विष्णुं निर्मलं प्रियदर्शनम्।
विष्णुलोकमवाप्नोति सेव्यमानः सुरोत्तमैः॥

4 गवां शतस्य विप्राणां यद्दत्तस्य फलं भवेत्।
घृतप्रस्थेन तद्विष्णोर्भवेत्स्नानं न संशयः॥

5 पुष्पजातिषु सर्वासु सौवर्णं पुष्पमुत्तमम्।
त्रुटिमात्रप्रदानात्तु शक्रार्धासनमाप्नुयात्॥

—स्मृतिमुक्ताफलम्, आह्निककाण्डम् P. 387

6 एतद्विदित्वा यः संध्यामुपास्ते संशितव्रतः।
दीर्घमायुः स विन्देत सर्वपापैः प्रमुच्यते॥

—पराशरमाधवे (आचारकाण्डम्) अ. 1 कां. 1 P. 302

7 न ते शिष्या न ते पुत्रास्तर्पयन्ति न ते पितॄन्।
प्रायश्चित्तं न तेष्वस्ति गुर्वतिक्रमकर्तृषु॥

—बालम्भट्टी P. 541

8 सूतके च नरः स्नात्वा प्रणम्य मनसा हरिम्।
एकादश्यां न भुञ्जीत व्रतमेतन्न लुप्यते॥
मृतकेऽपि न भुञ्जीत ह्येकादश्यां सदा नरः॥

—स्मृतिमुक्ताफलम्—कालखण्डः 5, P. 848

9 संप्रवृत्तेऽपि रजसि न त्याज्यं द्वादशीव्रतम्।

—हेमाद्रिः, व्रतखण्डः अ. 15 P. 996

10 स्त्री(य)मनथास्तत्काले नासेध्या इति तु पौलस्त्याः।

—वीरमित्रोदये व्यवहारः P. 57

In the above mentioned book, namely the *Pulastya-smṛtisaṅgraha*, the authors, have also collected and presented in the chapter 7, called Appendix, 7 passages from some *Dharmaśāstra*-works and the *Mahābhārata*, wherein Pulastya is an interlocuter, expounding certain topics like *dāna, vrata* and *tīrthayātrā* etc. However, a long passage of 48 verses, found in Hemādri (*Dāna,* pp. 318-324) has failed to find a place in their collection.

पुलस्त्य उवाच

1. तत्रासीना मुनयः शौनकाद्या-
स्ते चारण्ये नैमिषे सत्रयागे।
सुखासीनं सूतसूनुं तदानीं
गत्वापृच्छन् यज्ञकर्मावसाने।।

2. उग्रस्रवः परिपृच्छामहे त्वां
किं कृत्वासौ पुरुषो वाथ नारी।
आयुश्च सर्वं लभतेऽथ रोगै–
र्विमुच्यते भूतिमुपैति चाग्र्याम्।।

3. दुःखप्रना(णा)शं ग्रहभीतिनाशं
दृष्टं तथा त्रिविधे चाद्भुते वा।
अथान्यद्वा भयदोषप्रशान्ति–
मभीष्टसिद्धिं प्रददाति कर्तुः।।

4. दानं व्रतं देवताभ्यर्च्य(र्च)नं वा
किं तत्कृत्वा कृतकृत्यो भवेत्ताः।
शुश्रूषवस्तव वाक्यं च यत्तु
वदास्माकं सूत दानातिविद्वन्।।

5. इत्येवमुक्तो मुनिभिस्तदानी-
मुग्रश्रवाः प्रत्युवाचाथ तेषाम्।
शृणुध्वं वः कथयिष्याम्यहं त-
त्त्वेवंभूतं पृथिवीपद्मदानम्।।

6. देवागारे नदनद्योस्तु तीरे
गृहेऽन्यस्मिन् पुण्यदेशे च कुर्यात्।
तडागे वा नन्दने वाथ कुर्या–
दारामे वा रमते यत्र चेतः।।

7. विप्रं गुरुं वेदपुराणदक्षं
संगृह्य वैतानि क्रमादरेण।
दद्यात्तु तस्मै गुरु(र)वेऽथ वासो
युगं शुभं काञ्चनभूषणानि।।

8. अलङ्कृतोऽसौ प्रकरोति सर्व-
मृते दानं किञ्चिदिहास्ति कार्यम्।
गव्येन भूमिं शकृता जलेन
चालेपयेद्विंशतिहस्तमात्राम्।।
9. कूटं वर्षातपत्राणां समं प्राक्प्लवमेव वा।
षोडशारन्तिमात्रं तु चतुरस्त्रं प्रकल्पयेत्।।
10. यथेष्टं तत्र कुर्याद्वै स्तम्भांश्च परिकल्पयेत्।
चतुर्द्वारसमायुक्तं चतुस्तोरणभूषितम्।।
11. दर्भमालापरिवृतं मङ्गलाङ्कुरशोभितम्।
वितानेनोपरिच्छन्नं शुभेन सितरूपिणा।
12. परितो लोकपालानां ध्वजाश्च परिकल्पयेत्।
वस्त्रैरावेष्टयेत् स्तम्भान् चतुर्दिक्षु विचक्षणः।।
13. लम्बयेत् पुष्पमालाश्च सर्वतः स्तम्भसन्धिषु।
प्रागुदक्प्रवणां भूमिं गोमयेनोपलेपयेत्।।
14. एवं कूटप्रपां चाथ पटं वा परिकल्पयेत्।
मध्ये व्रीहिमयं शैलं महामेरुं प्रकल्पयेत्।।
15. मध्यमं दशभारेण तुरीयांशेन चेतरान्।
मन्दरं पुरतः कृत्वा दक्षिणे गन्धमादनम्।।
16. विपुलं पश्चिमे शैलं सुपार्श्वं चोत्तरेऽचलम्।
विष्कम्भकपर्वतौ द्वौ तु पूर्वपश्चिमभागयोः।।
17. परितश्चान्तरे वर्षपर्वताः समुदाहृताः।।
18. जम्बुप्लक्षाह्वयौ द्वीपौ शाल्मलश्च तथापरः।
कुशं क्रौञ्चश्च शाकश्च पुष्करं चैव सप्तमम्।।
19. लवणेक्षुसुरासर्पिर्दधिदुग्धजलैः समम्।
एवं द्वीपाः समुद्रैश्च सप्त सप्तभिरावृताः।।
20. एवं व्रीहिमयान् शैलान् पत्रिणः कारयेत्तथा।
भारार्धेनाथवा शैलानितरान् परिकल्पयेत्।।
21. संवेष्ट्य सर्वान् वासोभिः सर्वानेव महोदधीन्।
चतुरश्चतुरः पात्रान् तत्तद्द्रव्येण संविशेत्।।

22. मन्दारं पारिजातं च सन्तानं हरिचन्दनम्।
मेरोरुपरि सौवर्णान् चतुर्दिक्षु निवेशयेत्।।
23. तन्मध्ये कल्पवृक्षे च सौवर्णं कमलासनम्।
ब्रह्माणं द्विभुजं देवं प्राङ्मुखं विनिवेशयेत्।।
24. मेरुशृङ्गाणि चत्वारि राजतानि प्रकल्पयेत्।
सौवर्णं मादनं प्लक्षं मन्दरे विनिवेशयेत्।।
25. हिरण्यं गरुडं जम्बुगन्धमादनपर्वते।
सौवर्णं च पुरोहंसमश्वत्थं परिकल्पयेत्।।
26. सुपार्श्वे सुरभीं हैमीं न्यग्रोधं च निवेशयेत्।
राजतानपि सर्वेषु मृगपक्षिमहीरुहः।।
27. इक्षुचन्दनखण्डानि सर्वेषु विनिवेशयेत्।।
28. द्वारेषु कुम्भौ जलवस्त्रयुक्तौ
फलैर्युतौ चन्दनखण्डयुक्तौ।
कोणेषु पूर्णं कलशं तथैव
चतुर्दिशमिक्षुरसं निधाय।।
29. कृत्वैवमद्रिप्रवरांश्च देवा-
नाराधयन् चन्दनपुष्पधूपैः।
स्वनाममन्त्रैश्च नमोऽन्तरूपै–
रभ्यर्च्य सर्वानथ विप्रमुख्यान्।।
30. सार्धं तथा गुरुणा पञ्चभिस्तैः
पुण्याहकं स्वस्तिमृद्धिं च वाच्यम्।
ततोऽत्र होमं गुरुरेव कुर्यात्
पूर्वोत्तरस्यां दिशि भूधराणाम्।।
31. अग्निं समाधाय घृतेन दध्ना
जुहोति देवाय च नाम चोक्त्वा।
तथा गिरीणामपि नाममन्त्रै–
र्दशाहुतीरधिकं चैवमेकम्।।
32. पूर्वेद्युरेवं गुरुरेव कृत्वा
निशां तथा जागरणं च कुर्यात्।

रक्षोघ्नमन्त्रांश्च जपन् स आस्ते
ततः प्रभाते विमले प्रकर्ता।।

33. प्राप्ते पुण्ये दानकाले प्रदाता
कुशोदकैस्तिलमिश्रैश्च विद्वान्।
स्नात्वा शुचिर्गुरुणा प्रोक्षितोऽसौ
तथा मन्त्रैर्वारुणैः पावमानैः।।

34. दद्यात् पुष्पाञ्जलिं तत्र मेरोः कृत्वा प्रदक्षिणम्।
संपूज्य दद्याद्विप्राय गुरवे वाहिताग्नये।।

35. यस्मात्त्वं लोकपालानां ब्रह्मणः परमेष्ठिनः।
आवासः सर्वदेवानां तस्मान्मां पाहि सर्वतः।।

36. यस्मात्त्वं क्षितिपद्मस्य कर्णिकारं महीधर।
तस्मात्त्वं सर्वदा ह्यस्मच्छ्रेयांसि प्रददस्व वै।

37. इति दद्यान्महामेरुं विप्राय विदुषे ततः।
प्रागाद्युत्तरपर्यन्तान् विप्रेभ्यः प्रतिपादयेत्।।

38. प्रत्येकमेकं विदुषां चतुर्णां प्रतिकल्पयेत्।
दद्यात् पुष्पाञ्जलिं चैव कृत्वा चापि प्रदक्षिणम्।।

39. यस्मात्त्वं मदनावासो देवानामपि पर्वतः।
संप्रीयतां मे भगवान् मन्दरः पर्वतोत्तमः।।

40. यस्मात्त्वं गरुडावासः सदा देवालयाचलः।
संप्रीयतां मे भगवान् गन्धमादनपर्वतः।।

41. यस्मिन्नश्वत्थवृक्षख्यो हंसरूपी सदा वसेत्।
तस्मात्संप्रीयतां मह्यं विपुलः पर्वतोत्तमः।।

42. सुरभिस्तिष्ठते नित्यं न्यग्रोधो मस्तके तव।
आरामो देवतानां त्वं सुपार्श्वं प्रीतिमान् भव।।

43. इत्येवं पृथिवीपद्मदानं दानोत्तमं तथा।
दत्त्वा भुङ्क्तेऽधिकान् भोगान् ब्रह्मसालोक्यमाप्नुयात्।।

44. पुण्याहं स्वस्तिमृद्धिं च वाचयेद्गुरुणा सह।
विद्वद्भिः पञ्चभिर्विप्रैर्दद्यात्तेषां तु दक्षिणाम्।।

45. दानोपदेष्ट्रे गुरवे दक्षिणां प्रतिपादयेत्।

46. दानमानसमं निष्कं जातरूपं विधानतः।
आसनं शयनं वस्त्रं पात्रं भोजनसाधनम्।।
पानीयसाधनं कांस्यं गुरवे प्रतिपादयेत्।।

47. एतद्दानेऽप्युपयुक्तं समस्तं
दद्यात्तस्मै गुरवे वस्त्रजातम्।
स्वयं भुङ्क्ते सघृतं पाणिनोक्तं
गुरून् विप्रान् भोजयेदष्टवर्गान्।।

48. एवं पुरा ऋषये नारदाय
जगत्कर्ता वाब्रवीत्पद्मयोनिः।
मया चोक्तं पृथिवीपद्मदानं
ततः किं च प्रब्रवीमि द्विजेन्द्राः।।

इति ब्रह्माण्डपुराणोक्तः पृथिवीपद्मदानविधिः।
हेमाद्रिः दानखण्डः **PP. 318-324**

The *Smṛticandrikā* (*āhnika*) (p. 201) contains a long passage with the introductory remarks—"*Viṣṇudharmottare Pulastyaḥ*". Most of the verses are identical (excepting some variations in sequece and readings) with those found in the Appendix II-C of the *Pulastyasmṛtisaṅgraha*, But the first two verses and the last one are not found in the collection of authors. They are as follows :—

विष्णुधर्मोत्तरे पुलस्त्यः—

1. गवां शतस्य विप्राणां यद्दत्तस्य भवेत्फलम्।
घृतप्रस्थेन तद्विष्णोर्भवेत् स्नानान्न संशयः।।
2. भूरिद्युम्नेन संप्राप्ता सप्तद्वीपा वसुन्धरा।
घृताढकेन गोविन्दप्रतिमास्नपनात्किल।।

....

3. दध्यादीनां विकाराणां क्षीरतः संभवो यथा।
तथैवाशेषकामानां क्षीरस्नपनतो हरेः।।

(It is to be noted that the verse 1 and 3 mentioned

above are quoted by the *Smṛtimuktāphala* (*Āhnika,* p. 387) as simply from 'Pulastya' and not as found here as '*Viṣṇudharmottare Pulastyaḥ.*' These verses from the *Smṛtimuktāphala* have been noted previously as nos. 4 and 7 as verses from Pulastya).

FOOTNOTES

Paper published in Journal of Oriental Institute, Baroda, Vol. 43, No. 3-4, March-June 1996, Issue, pp. 195-202.

Paper read at the All-India Oriental Conference (37th Session) held at Rohtak, Haryana, 26-28th Dec., 1994.

1 Shastri, Shama R.: (ed.) *Smṛticandrikā of Devaṇṇabhaṭṭa,* (*Āśaucakāṇḍa*), Oriental Library Publications Sanskrit Series, Mysore, 1921.

2. Gharpure, J.R. : (ed.) *Smṛtimuktāphala* of *Vaidyanātha Dīkṣita,* —(*Āhnikakāṇḍa*); part, II Collection of Hindu Law Texts, Bombay, 1938, (*Kālakāṇḍa* (V) and *Prāyaścittakāṇḍa* VI), *ibid.*, 1940.

3. Islampurkar, V.S. : (ed.) *Parāśaradharmasaṁhitā* or *Parāśarasmṛti,* with com. of Mādhavācārya. (*Ācārakāṇḍa*), Vol. I, Part I, Bombay University Series, Bombay, 1893,—(*Prāyaścittakāṇḍa*) Vol. II, Part II, *ibid*, 1906.

4. Gharpure, J.R.: (ed.) *Bālambhaṭṭī* of *Bālambhaṭṭa Pāyaguṇḍe*, com. on *Mitākṣarā* of *Vijñāneśvara* on *Yājñavalkya Smṛti*, Book I, *Ācārādhyāya*, Collection of Hindu Law Texts, Bombay, 1914.

5. Shiromani Bharatacandra : (ed.) *Hemādri*, or *Caturvargacintāmaṇi of Hemādri*, *Vratakhaṇḍa*, Vol. I and II, Bibliotheca India, Calcutta, 1876.—*Dānakhaṇḍa*, Chowkhamba Sanskrit Samsthan, Varanasi, reprint. 1985.

6. Bhattacharya, Jivananda Vidyasagar: (ed.) *Vīramitrodaya of Mitramiśra*, (*Vyavahāra*), Calcutta, 1875.

7. Gharpure, J.R.: (ed.) *Smṛticandrikā of Devaṇṇa Bhaṭṭa*, (*Āhnika-Vyavahāra-Śrāddha Kāṇḍas*) Collection of Hindu Law Texts, Bombay, 1918.

VIII

CRIME AND PUNISHMENT IN ANCIENT INDIA (WITH SPECIAL REFERENCE TO THE *YĀJÑAVALKYASMṚTI*)

Crime and Punishment-Introductory

Man is a social animal. He cannot live in isolation but lives in a society. A civilized society expects its every individual to follow certain rules and regulations of moral, religious, social behaviour for the well-being of the society at large. The violation or breach of certain conventional set-rules is not tolerable and and is detrimental to the general good of the society. Hence such violators of law should be punished. The King or the legal system declares punishment for them.

The breach of law which is detrimental to the well-being of the society, and which is punishable by the king is technically termed as crime. The punishment is pronounced with the ephemeral purposes of improving moral status of the individual and the society at large. But when the violation of the conventional rules is viewed from the individual point of view (*Vyaṣṭidṛṣṭyā* and not *Samaṣṭidṛṣṭyā*) it can be termed as a sin (*Pāpa*), punishable even by God in the next world in the form of obtaining births in different *yonis*. Several expiations are meant for improving psychological make-up of the sinner with personal purification and self-mortification.

All sins may not be crimes in Legal sense (e.g. *avakīrṇi*). But most of the crimes can be viewed as sins. In the absence of royal influence or his negligence towards his duty, the expiations (*Prāyaścittas*) can serve the purpose of purfication of the sinner. Since the subject of the Seminar is crime and punishment, this aspect of sin and its expiation is not taken into consideration here in this paper.

The *Yājñavalkyasmṛti*

The topic of crime and punishment will be dealt with in this paper, in the context of the *Yājñavalkyasmṛti*,which is one of the most important ancient treatises and the most concise but systematic *Smṛti*-text of great legal and historical importance.The text comprises of about 1010 verses, divided in three main divisions of *Ācāra*, *Vyavahāra* and *Prāyaścitta*, each having several subdivisions. The topic of crime and punishment has been treated in several subdivisions of the *Vyavahāra* portion. Dr. R.M. Das has made a separate study of the *Manusmṛti* from this point of view.[1] But the laws of Yājñavalkya, who is posterior to both Manu and Kauṭilya deserve to be sepcifically studied in this context; He is placed by Mm. P.V. Kane in a period between 100 A.D. to 300 A.D. With this small background and the introduction, we may now turn to the topic of crime and punishment with special reference to the study of the *Yājñavalkyasmṛti*.

The Duty of the King

In the chapter on *Rājadharma*, there is good description of the duties of the king in this connection and the nature of punishment is explained. The king should be well-versed in the science of punishment and polity *(Daṇḍanīti)* (I.311)[2]. Besides the ministers, he should also appoint a *Purohita*, who is expert in the science of polity (*daṇḍanīti*). (I.313)[3]. The kingdom is said to be having seven constituent elements— The king, the ministers, the subject, the fortress, the treasure, the *daṇḍa* (Rod), and allies (friends) (I.353)[4]. The king should properly employ the four means like *sāma*(peacful negotiations), *dāna* (presents), *bheda* (division), *daṇḍa* (punishment) in proper order. The punishment (*daṇḍa*) is the last course, when any other means is not possible or is not fruitful. (I.346).[5] For king, nobody is beyond punishment, who has failed to follow the dictates of *dharma* (I.358). Even his brother, son, a preceptor, father-in-law, or maternel uncle are not free from punishment, if they commit offence (I.358)[6]. He should observe the conduct of his officers through spies and if they are found to be involved in bribery, he should banish them from the kingdom, after confiscating their property. (I.339)[7]. He should protect the subjects from the troubles of cheats, thieves, evil-doers, villians and especially from *Kāyasthas* (the accountants/scribes). (I.336)[8]. The king should use the *daṇḍa* (punishment) against the evil-doers. His action of punishing properly the punishable and execution of capital punishment to the deserving is deemed to be equal to performance of several sacrifices. (I.359)[9].

Modes of Punishment

The king, with the help of assembly, can declare the punishment to the offender. This punishment can be of four types, according to Yājñavalkya. It is reprimand, then reproof, thirdly the fine and finally the capital or corporal punishment. (I.367)[10]. He further adds that these four should be employed separately or two and more simultaneously, in accordance with the nature of the crime. In certain cases, confiscation of the entire property and banishment are also laid down. The punishments like cutting of hand, foot, fingers, ears, nose, lips, tongue were inflicted in some cases. The crucification-impalements, burning the offender with the fire of dry grass, drowning him in water by tying him with a stone-slab, trampling him to death under the feet of bullocks—these are some of the methods referred to in the text for punishing the criminal. The *Smṛtikāra* has also mentioned the method of branding the culprit. Some kind of stigma or a mark was ordered to be made to his body, so that it would bring infamy and permanently remind him of his evil action. The fines were also of varying nature in accordance with the nature of the crime. Yājñavalkya (I.366)[11] classifies fine into *Uttama*, *madhyama* and *adhama sāhasa* and explains his own terminology as the first consisting of 1080 *Paṇas,* the middling constituting 540 *Paṇas* and the lower one accounting 270 *paṇas*. (I.366). *Paṇa* is a copper-coin, wheighing twenty *māṣas* (80 cowries). As per the varying gravity of the crime, the fine ranges from two *paṇas*, upto 1080 *Paṇas*.

Circumstances to be considered

While declaring the punishment, several circumstances were to be taken into consideration. Yājñavalkya (I.368)[12] enumerates the following circumstances 1. The place, 2. The time, 3. The capacity, 4. the age, 5. the act, and 6. the wealth; Moreover, the elements whether the crime is intentional or unintentional, whether it is the first occasion or its repetition should also be considered, while declaring punishment. The caste of the offender also was taken into consideration in many cases. When the wordly means do not lead to conclusive decision, the supernatural or divine means of ordeal is resorted to for the judgement.[13] The enumeration of above different circumstances suggests that decision about punishment varies as per these considerations and there cannot be any definite, permanent set of rules for punishment for crimes. Yājñavalkya prescribes a very prag-matic rule that when there is conflict between two *Smṛtis*, the principles of equity (*nyāya*) as determined by popular usage is superior, while the Science of Law (*dharmaśāstra*) is superior to the science of polity (*arthaśāstra*) (II.21). The rules, laid down by the *Smṛtikāras* are to be given more importance than those prescribed by the *arthaśāstrakāras*. (Political Philosophers). I.P.C. also has given general exceptions such as absence of Criminal Interest, incapacity, unsound mind, Intoxication, private defence, privileged Acts.

Classification of crimes

The topic of crime and punishment is spread over different sections of *Vyavahāra* in in the *Yājñavalkyasmṛti*. The secctions like the *Sīmāvivāda*, the *Svāmipālavivāda*, the *Asvāmivikraya*, the *Saṁvidvyatikrama*, the *Vetanādāna*, the *dyūtasamāhvaya*, the *Vākpāruṣya*, the *Daṇḍapāruṣya*, the *Sāhasa*, the *Vikrīyāsaṁpradāna*, the *Saṁbhūyasamutthāna*, the *Steya*, the *Strīsaṅgrahaṇa* and the *prakīrṇaka* contain numerous such details. These crimes can be classified under the following heads—

1. *Crime relating to living beings*—(including animals and plants) with subdivisions—1. bodily 2. psychological 3. sexual crimes.
2. *Crime relating to property*—(Movable and immovable, personal and common)
3. *Crimes relating to service and business*
4. *The crimes relating to king and social justice*
5. *Miscellaneous crimes*.

1. Crimes relating to living beings (including animals and plants)

The crimes relating to living beings may be divided in three sections (i) bodily (ii) psychological and (iii) sexual crimes. (cf. I.P.C. ch. XVI offences affecting human body which includes hurt, assault, kidnapping, sexual offence.)

(i) Bodily Crimes—If a non-brahmin causes injury to a brahmin, his limb, hand, foot etc. should be cut off. But when simply raising a weapon to kill, the punishment is the

lowest amercement and half of it only when the weapon etc. is touched for raising to kill (II.215). For raising a hand or a foot for striking, the punishment is ten and twenty *paṇas* respectively. (II.216). For raising weapon for striking each other, the middle amercement is punishment for all. (II.216). For pulling out the foot, the hair, the clothes, or the hand of the other, the fine is ten *paṇas*. If a person ties in a cloth, pulls him violently and tramples him under foot such criminal should be compelled to pay one hundred *paṇas*.(II. 217). For breaking a hand, a foot, or a tooth and for cutting an ear or nose, the middle amercement is enjoined. The same fine is enjoined for laying open a sore and for beating a person almost to death. (II.219). For restraining motion, eating, or speech, for injury to the eye etc. for a fracture to the neck, the arm or the thigh, the middle amercement is the fine (II.220). When a single person is assaulted by several persons, coming together, the fine would be double of that mentioned above (II.221). Whatever is taken away during fight should be restored and the fine of double the value of thing taken away should be paid as penalty (II.221). During the cases of bodily injury, incidental expenses, of curing, medicine, special diet etc. should be recovered. Throwing a thing in a house, causing injury to body or deprivation of life with poison, snake, etc. should be fined with 16 *Paṇas* and the middle amercement respectively. (II.222).

For giving a blow with a weapon and also for causing an abortion, the punishment is the *Uttamasāhasa*; for the killing of a man or a woman, the punishment would be the highest or the lowest as per circumstances. The wicked woman who kills a man, if not pregnant should be plunged into water after tying stone round her neck. The evil-minded woman who administers poison, sets fire or kills her husband, preceptor or her own child, the punishment for her is cutting of her ears, hands, nose and lips and she is caused to be killed by means of wild and untamed bulls (II.277-279).

Now about injury to animals and trees. For causing pain, drawing blood, cutting off their horns or limbs of lower beasts, the fine ranges from 2 *Paṇas* upwards as per the crime. For cutting off their genital organs or for causing death of them, the fine is the middle amercement and the price of the beast. In case of superior animals, the fine is double in above cases (II.225).

For cutting off the branches or the trunks or uprooting entirely the trees and also useful trees like mango etc., the fine is twenty *paṇas* and forty *paṇas* respectively. The trees growing in sacrificial place, a cemetary, a boundary, a sacred place, or a temple and also well-known trees like Pippla, Palāśa etc. the fine is double of the above (II.227-228). This shows that not only human body but even the life of animals and trees was considered precious and injury to them was a criminal offence.

(ii) Psychological Crimes—Abuse or Defamation—(cf. ch. XXI of I.P.C)—Whether true, false or in ironical words, a person abuses the other as without limbs or a sense-organ or suffering from disease, the fine is 13 and half *paṇas*. The fine of 20 *paṇas* should be paid by a person who abuses other by saying "*abhigantāsmi bhaginīm mātaram vā tava.*" This fine varies in accordance with the superior and inferior status. It is half in case of the inferier, while it is to double of the above in case of the superior. The superiority or inferiority of *varṇa* and *jāti* should also be taken into consideration. (II. 204-206). In case of the abuse of one of a superior class, the fine is two-fold, and threefold respectively, while of one of a lower class, it is reduced in the ratio of a half-respectively. For an abuse of threatening injury to the arm, neck, eye or thigh, the fine would be one hundred and fifty in case of abuse regarding injury to the foot, nose, the

hand etc. For abusing degradation from caste, the fine is the middle *sāhasa* and for an abuse involving a secondary sin, the fine is the lowest *sāhasa*. For abusing a learned *Brāhmaṇa,* the king, the Gods, the highest *sāhasa* is the fine. For abusing the castes and for abusing the village and the country, the fine is the middle and the lowest *sāhasa* respectively. (II. 207-211).

(iii) Sexual offences—Adultery with women (Ch. XVI of IPC)—Touching the upper or lower garment, the breasts, thighs, the hair or talking with them at an improper time and place or sitting together on one seat—such acts, when not permitted, a woman should pay one hundred while the man should pay two hundred as penalty. When both are prohibited their punishment is the same as for adultery. In the case of adultery of same class, *Anuloma* class and the *Pratiloma* class, the punishment is the highest amarcement, the middle amarcement and death of the man and cutting of the ear etc. of the woman respectively. For kidnapping a lady with ornaments on, the fine is the highest amarcement in the same class, but for lady without ornaments, it is the lowest amarcement. In case of a lady of superior class, death is the punishment. But if the maidens willingly going with inferior class, there is no offence, otherwise there is punishment. (II. 284-288).

For defiling a lady, the punishment is cutting off of hands, for defiling a lady of a higher class, death is a punishment. For slandering a woman, a man should pay fine of one hundred *paṇas*, while it is two hundred *paṇas* for falsely accusing her. Though intercourse with 'protected slaves' and 'kept' ladies is permissible, the fine is fifty *paṇas*. For forcible intercourse with a female slave, the fine is 10 *paṇas*. When many persons forcibly rape an unwilling female slave, the fine is twentyfour *paṇas* for each person. After accepting her fee, if a prostitute is not willing for intercourse, she should pay double the fee received; if a person, having paid the fees is not willing, no return of his fees. The fine of 20 *paṇas* is ordered, for a person, having intercourse with a woman in an improper part or with a man or for passing urine, or for having intercoruse with a female ascetic. For having intercourse with an antyā-cāṇḍāla woman, he should be branded with bad mark and banished. For an Āntya-cāṇḍāla person having intercourse with an *Ārya* woman, death is the punishment. (II. 288-294). For having intercourse with wives of king, the punishment is burning him with the fire of dry grass.

In case of intercourse with beasts, the fine is one hundred *paṇas*. For the connection with low woman or a cow the middle fine is a punishment.

(2) Crimes relating to property (Movable, Immovable/ Personal, Public)

In respect of immovable property, when there is violation of boundary or encroachment beyond the limit, or mis-appropriation of land, the fines would be *adhama*, *Uttama* and *Madhyama* type respectively. (II.196). When there is damage to crops in the field by a female buffalo, a cow or by a goat/sheep etc. the fine to owner of these beasts would be eight *māṣas,* four *māṣas* and two *māṣas* respectively (II.159). But when these eat the crop and are allowed to lie there unwarded, the fine is double of the above (II.160). In case of tresspassing the land by cattle etc., where grass or fuel is stored, the fine is the same as above. In case of an ass or a camel, the fine is as in case of a female buffalo. (II.160). Moreover, it is ordered that loss of crop of the ownee of the field be compensated. The herdsman should be beaten, (II. 161). Regarding the cattle-wealth, it stated that the herdsman when employed should componsate for the cattle, perished or lost due to this fault and pay the fine of 13 and half *paṇas*. (II. 165).

For forcibly carrying away the common public property the fine is double the value of it, but when there is denial, the fine is fourfold (II. 230). For breaking open a house which is sealed, the fine is fifty *paṇas*, while for concealing the common property, the fine is one hundred *paṇas*. (II. 232, 236). One who misappropriates the property of a *gaṇa* (a group or association), he should be deprived of all his wealth and banished from the realm by the king. One who is deputed for the business of an association, whatever he receives, should be delivered to the association if he does not deliver it, he should be made to pay eleven-fold of that (II.187, 190).

For a thief, whose charge for theft is not cleared, but was caught through suspicion, should be compelled to restore the lost article and be given the corporal punishment of a thief. The *brāhmaṇa* thief should be branded on the forehead and he be exiled from the kingdom (II.269-270). The stealers of horses and elephants should be impaled on a stake (II. 275). The pick-pockets and cut-purses should be punished by cutting their forefinger and the thumb; but for repetition of the offence, a hand and a foot be cut off for each of them. For the theft of an inferior, middling and superior articles, the fine would be as their price, but the punishment be ordered after considering the place, the time, the age and the capacity (II. 274-275).

(3) Crimes relating to service and business—

The servant, who leaves the work, without completing it, but has received the wages, he should be made to pay double of the wages. If he has not received wages, he should be made to pay the equal amount (II. 193). The master, without deciding the wages, makes the servant to work, the servant should be paid 10th part of the proceeds of trade, cattle, crop etc. (II.194). In case of less profit, the master's wish prevails but if the profit, is more, the more the servant should be paid (II.195). The wages should be paid proportionately to the work, completed (II.196). A vessel perished except the act of God or the king, the carrier be compelled to compensate for the loss. He who creates some obstruction at the outset, he should be made to pay double the wages (II.197-198). He, who denies after undertaking, should be fined the seventh part of the wages. For the denial on the way, the fine is the fourth part of the wages. For his declining in the midway, the entire amount of wages should be forfeited (II. 198).

Deception, adulteration in business—(cf. ch. XII and XIII of IPC)—The Goldsmith, who sells false gold or a butcher sells the unclean meat should be punished with the highest kind of fine and their three organs, nose, the ears and the hands be cut off. (II. 297). The persons, who make false scales, royal mandates, measures and standard coins, and also those who make use of them—both should be made to pay the highest amercement. Even the examiner of coins who deceives others by false coins should also be equally punished. The unqualified person, practising medical profession, pretending to be a doctor/physician etc. should be punished with the first, middle and the highest fine in case of lower animals, human beings and the royal persons respectively (II. 240-242). By using false measures or balance, the grocer etc. gives less by one-eighth part of it, he should be made to pay a fine of two hundrd *paṇas*. The trader, who adulterates good articles by mixing articles of inferior quality-the things like medicines, oil, salt, perfumes, food-grains, sugar etc. should be made to pay fine of 16 *paṇas*. In case articles like earth, hide, gem, yarn, iron, wood, bark or cloth, not of good quality is made to appear to be of superior quality, the fine is eight times of the sale-price. For an artificially prepared sealed casket or a valuable vessel, the fine is two to two hundred *paṇas*, as per the value of the thing. The traders, though knowing the rise and fall in price, by making mutual understanding prevail another price (not in accordance with prevailing market rates fixed by the king), they should be fined with the highest amercement. For indigenous commodities, the trader should have five percent profit and for foreign articles, the profit of 10 percent is fixed. On them, 10 percent incidental expences be added (II.244-252).

From the point of view of consumer's protection, it was ordained that one who delivers the good after receiving the price, should be compelled to deliver it with interest. For one coming from a foreign country, the delivery should be addition of the foreign profit. If the good is lost due to some accidental circumstances of God or king, before its delivery to the customer, the loss is of the seller. For selling a thing that was already sold to somebody or for selling a bad good as a good one, the fine is double the price of a thing. A rescission should not be made in the case of a trader, when he has purchased without knowing the rise and fall of prices. The fine for this is sixth part of the price. (II.254-258). The merchant who avoids the sales-tax or declares less quantity as also one who purchases such things, should be fined eight times of the value of the commodity. The taxes for land and sea articles are different. The officer charging the Land-tax for the marine one should be punished to pay ten *paṇas*. These business rules also apply to the officiating priests, farmers and artisans (II. 262-263, 265).

(4) The Crimes relating to King and Social Justice—(cf IPC. Ch. xi)

The person who adds or omits anything in the royal edict or lets free the adulter or allows the thief to escape, should be given the highest fine (II.295). The person, who speaks evil of the king, defames him or divulges his secrets, should be banished from the kingdom after cutting his tongue. (II. 302). For mounting the royal conveyance or throne, the punishment is the highest amercement. (II.303). The fine of 800 *Paṇas* is ordained for one who obeys commands of the king's enemies. (II.304).

If some wrong justice was declared which was reviewed and found otherwise, the former victorious party was to pay double the amount of fine, prescribed for the defeated party. The defeated party coming against to the court, when defeated again, was compelled to pay double amount as fine. When the king acquires a fine through injustice he should give it to brahmins, increasing it by thirty times.

(5) Miscellaneous Crimes—

There are also some general, miscellaneous crimes for which punishments were prescribed. For example, The defiling a *Brahmin* with uneatable thing, the punishment is the *uttamasāhasa*, in case of a *Kṣatriya*, it is middle one, while for a *Vaiśya*, it is lowest, for *śūdra,* the half of the lowest. (II.296). For helping a thief or a murderer with supplying him food, lodging, fire, water, counsel, implements and expenses, the punishment is the highest fine. The gamesters, using false dice or other devices should be branded and banished by the king. (II.276).

Concluding Remarks

From the above discussion of the codes of Yājñavalkya

it can be conclusively remarked that the treatment of crime and punishment in it is most systematic, and comprehensive and these codes of ancient seers have been the model of the modern framework of penal code. The exposition and enumeration of crimes is most perfect but the aspect of punishment has undergone some changes with changing times and circumstances. The corporal punishments, branding the culprit, discrimination based on caste and the supernatural element of ordeals—these are some of the aspects of it which have now become absolete. While punishment in the form of ordering of fines, banishment, forfeiture of property, which were found in ancient codes are still prevalent in the modern code. Though Yājñavalkya seems to have made a distincion between civil and criminal disputes (Yājña. II. 23), the rules, procedures and courts were not separate as in modern times.

But the question still remains. Can punishments improve the status and problem of rehabilitation of culprits in this world, where the big bulls and fraud-makers escape it by discovering some solutations through legal experts ? Our ancient seers believed more in self-mortification and the theory of *Karmavipāka*, which have more reformative and preventive value than the imposed punishments in the Modern world. Hence the stress on and creation of a society with good sense of moral and social values, leading towards social welfare and well-being of all should be our aim at all times.

FOOTNOTES

Paper read at the seminar on 'Crime and Punishment in Ancient India, held at Asiatic Society, Bombay, 29th and 28th March 1999.

1. Daś, R.M. : *Manu on Crime and Punishment,* Janaki Prakashan, Patna, 1987.
2. Yājñavalkya (Y.S.) I.311

   स्वरन्ध्रगोप्ताऽन्वीक्षिक्यां दण्डनीत्यां तथैव च।

   विनीतस्त्वथ वार्तायां त्रय्यां चैव नराधिपः।।

3. Y.S.I. 313
   पुरोहितं प्रकुर्वीत दैवज्ञमुदितोदितम्।
   दण्डनीत्यां च कुशलमथर्वाङ्गिरसे तथा।।
4. Y.S.I. 353
   स्वाम्यामात्या जनो दुर्गं कोशो दण्डस्तथैव च।
   मित्राण्येताः प्रकृतयो राज्यं सप्ताङ्गमुच्यते।।
5. Y.S.I. 346
   उपायाः साम दानं च भेदो दण्डस्तथैव च।
   सम्यक्प्रयुक्ताः सिद्ध्येयुर्दण्डस्त्वगतिका गतिः।।
6. Y.S.I.358
   अपि भ्राता सुतोऽर्घ्यो वा श्वशुरो मातुलोऽपि वा।
   नादण्ड्यो नाम राज्ञोऽस्ति धर्माद्विचलितः स्वकात्।।
7. Y.S.I.339 उत्कोचजीविनो द्रव्यहीनान्कृत्वा विवासयेन्।
   I. 338 ये राष्ट्राधिकृतास्तेषां चारैर्ज्ञात्वा विचेष्टितम्।।
8. Y.S.I.336
   चाटतस्करदुर्वृत्तमहासाहसिकादिभिः।
   पीड्यमानाः प्रजा रक्षेत्कायस्थैश्च विशेषतः।।
9. Y.S.I.359
   यो दण्ड्यान्दण्डयेद्राजा सम्यग्वध्यांश्च घातयेत्।
   इष्टं स्यात्क्रतुभिस्तेन समाप्रवरदक्षिणैः।।
10. Y.S.I.367
    धिग्दण्डस्त्वथ वाग्दण्डो धनदण्डो वधस्तथा।
    योज्या व्यस्ताःसमस्ता वा ह्यपराधवशादिमे।।
11. Y.S.I.366
    साशीतिपणसाहस्रो दण्ड उत्तमसाहसः।
    तदर्धं मध्यमः प्रोक्तस्तदर्धमधमः स्मृतः।।
12. Y.S.I.368
    ज्ञात्वापराधं देशं च कालं बलमथापि वा।
    वयः कर्म च वित्तं च दण्डं दण्ड्येषु पातयेत्।।
13. Y.S.II.22
    प्रमाणं लिखितं भुक्तिः साक्षिणश्चेति कीर्तितम्।
    एषामन्यतमाभावे दिव्यान्यतममुच्यते।।
14. Y.S.II.21
    स्मृत्योर्विरोधे न्यायस्तु बलवान्व्यवहारतः।
    अर्थशास्त्रात्तु बलवद्धर्मशास्त्रमिति स्थितिः।।

IX

TRENDS OF ASSIMILATION AND INTEGRATION IN ANCIENT INDIA *DHARMAŚĀSTRA* TRADITION

Introductory

Several traditions of Ancient India exhibit trends of assimilation and integration. The topic is viewed from several aspects, pertaining to different *śāstras*, religious creeds etc. The subjet of my paper is to deal with the trends as found in *Dharmaśāstra* tradition. The *Dharmasūtras* and the *Smṛtis* mainly constitute the ancient *Dharmaśāstra* litetature, which reflect upon such trends of ancient Indian tradition. This literature may be considered to be forming a phase which is inbetween the two traditions-the one that of Vedic culture that emphasised through *Brāhmaṇas* and *Śrautasūtras*, the Institute of sacrifices and the other one of Pauranic culture that extolled several other aspects like *vratas*, *Tīrthayātrā* etc. to be superior even to the sacrifices. The *Dharmaśāstra* tradition has exhibited the trend that has not completely neglected the sacrifical Institute, but which has been slowly whithering, as it was not much emphasised, on the contrary, some *Smṛtis* have started incorporating the Pauranic trends of *upavāsa*, *vrata*, *Tīrthayātrā* etc. This point will be more clear as we reflect more upon the trends of assimilation and integration in the *Dharmaśāstra* tradition in this paper.

The Concept of *Dharma*

The *Mīmāṁsakas* defined the *Dharma* as "*Codanā-lakṣaṇo'rtho Dharmaḥ* (*Mīmāṁsā*. sū. 1.1.2)"the *Dharma* to be object, characterised by Vedic injunctions", and the term '*codanā*' is explained as the sentence goading one for the sacrificial action. Thus they mainly understood the *Dharma* to be constituting the sacrifices.' The *Yajurvedasaṁhitā* begins with a grand concept that the Gods may impel us for the supermost-*Śreṣṭhatama* action, which is explained in *Brāhmaṇas*[2] as *yajña* to be such a supermost action-(*yajño vai śreṣṭhatamaṁ karma*). The *Vaiśeṣikas*[3] explained *Dharma* to be one that leads to the *Abhyudaya* and *Niḥśreyasa* of a person. Devala seems to endorse the same view,[4] While Vasiṣṭha[5] points out the *Niḥśreyasa* alone to be forming the main aim of *Dharma*. It needs no explanation that the *Dharmasūtras* and *Smṛtis* have given importance to *varṇāśrama-dharma* and *sadācāra*[6] i.e. good social conduct as the main aspects of *Dharma*. They mainly point out that along with Vedas, there are other sources of *Dharma* also like *Smṛti* (Tradition), conduct of the good and *svasya ātmanaḥ priyam*[7]. The *Rūḍhi* or *grāmavacanam* is also to be taken into consideration during the procedure of *vivāha* and *smaśāna*[8]. Moreover most of the *Smṛtis* have introduced the virtuous conduct to be forming the main aspect of *Dharma*[9]. Gautam[10] points out that the virtues like *ahiṁsā* etc. are more important than even the several *saṁskāras*. Manu and Yājñavalkya both give more emphasis on practising *Yamas* than *Niyamas*. Yajñavalkya[12] clearly and emphaticallv pronouces that

इज्याचारदयाहिंसायज्ञस्वाध्यायकर्मणाम्।
अयं तु परमो धर्मो यद्योगेनात्मदर्शनम्।।

Devala[13] points out the quintessence of *Dharma*—

श्रूयतां धर्मसर्वस्वं श्रुत्वा चैवावधार्यताम्।
आत्मन: प्रतिकूलानि परेषां न समाचरेत्।।

The *Mahābhārata*[14] introduces an ideal, appropriate, all-pervasive, all absorbing definition of *Dharma*.

धारणाद् धर्म इत्याहुर्धर्मो धारयते प्रजाः।
यत्स्याद् धारणसंयुक्तं स धर्म इति निश्चयः।।

Thus the above consideration would reflect upon the following facts.

(1) The sacrifices which were given more importance in the *Brāhmaṇas* and the *Śrautasūtras* have receded in importance as forming the main aspect of *Dharma*.(2) The virtues and good social conduct were more emphasised to be constituting the *Dharma*. It should be noted here that the social and religious condition may have effected this kind of change. The Jains and the Bauddhas have criticised the intricate and regorous sacrificial Institution and emphasised more upon virtues. Thus there was assimilation and integration of certain trends, while some other like sacrifices gradually receded in importance as the main aspects of *Dharma*. Thus in the explanation of the term *Dharma* and its sources, some trends of assimilation and integration are seen.

Saṁskāras

Even in the topic of the *Saṁskāras* above view prevails. Śaṅkarācārya[15] quotes a line referring to the fortyeight *Saṁskāras* *"yasyaite'ṣṭācatvāriṁśatsaṁskārāḥ."* Gautam[16] also enumerates forty sacraments and eight virtues. These sacraments included seven *haviryajña saṁsthās*,seven *somayajñasaṁsthās*, and seven *pākayajñasaṁsthās*. These were sacrifices like *vājapeya*, *Atirātra* etc. and were considered to be the part of sacraments. But in later period, these were not given much importance and only the popular sixteen sacraments were more emphasised and dealt with in details in *Smṛtis*. Thus from the point of view of *Saṁskāras* also, the sacrifices seem to have been much neglected and sixteen *Saṁskāras* were given prime importance. Even in these *Saṁskāras*, some *Saṁskāras* like *karṇavedha*, *akṣarārambha* etc. which are not found in the early Smṛtis like those of Manu and Yajñavalkya etc. were introduced among *Saṁskāras* in some Smṛtis.[17] Though several forms of marriages were in vogue, it was made compulsory by the *Smṛtikāras*[18], that the regular procedure of marriage in front of the fire be followed even in case of marriages of *Rākṣasa* and other forms. This trend was necessary to legalize the other forms of marriages. Among the four *āśramas*, the *gṛhasthāśrama* was more emphatically described and given the cardinal importance as it is on the *gṛhastha* that all other *āśramas* are dependent[19]. Here it may be noted that as the Jain and Bauddhas gave importance to medicant life, it was out of social necessity that such trend was integrated in the social system of giving importance to householder's life. Similar trend is found in the Zarostrian religion also.

It was out of practical necessity and facility that the trend of wearing a sacred thread as *Yajñopavīta* was introduced. Mm.P.V. Kane has pointed out that the wearing of upper garment was the system in earlier period which was generally replaced by a sacred thread as *yajñopavīta*.[20] Practically it is difficult to make *savya*, *apasavya* and *nivīta* several times in a particular ritual, when one is wearing the upper garment and this is more so in the *śrāddha* ceremony. It may be that these difficulties were more felt when there was introduction of the Institution of *śrāddha* with the detailed procedure incorporating numerous occasions of *savyāpa-savya*. With the beginning of this new system of wearing *yajñopavīta*, several rules came to be introduced regarding it. We find some instructions[21] regarding *yajñopavīta* even in *Manu* and *Viṣṇusmṛtis* regarding the material of it but later on it was out of ritual necessity that several rules regarding the prepa-ration, procedure of wearing, its length etc. were supple-mented by the authorities like Baudhāyana, Devala etc.[22]

Practice of *Vratas*

The *vratas* to be followed by the student of Vedic literature and by one performing the Vedic sacrifice were gradually diminishing during the centuries before the Christian era. Mm. P.V. Kane remarks[23] "In the *Gṛhya* and *Dharmasūtras* and in ancient *Smṛtis* like those of *Manu* and *Yājñavalkya* what were called *vratas* in the *Purāṇas* did not occupy any very prominent position. During the early centuries of the Christian era, Buddhism and Jainism were influential rivals of the ancient sacrificial system. In order to wean away common people from those two schisms, it is very probable that learned followers of the Vedic system hit upon the glorification of *vratas* and promised heaven and other wordly and spiritual rewards to those who performed *vratas* that were comparatively easy and within reach of all instead of sacrifices and adopted some of the practices of common folk as *vratas* e.g. *Śītalāvrata.*"The trend of performing *vratas* was extolled to the skies by *Purāṇas*, but in *Smṛtis* the trend had started emerging. Though Manu and Viṣṇu are against *vratas* for Ladies[24], Devala has clearly declared[25] that persons of all *varṇas* can be purified from sins, by performing *vratas.* Devala, Nārada, Kātyāyana etc. these *Smṛtikaras*[26] have introduced the *Ekādaśīvrata*, which it is not found in the *Manu* and *Yajñavalkya Smṛtis*.

Then several specifications regarding its observance, rules to be observed and abstained from during fast, the events that do not break the vow etc. were also considered[27]. Moreover, the various kinds of fasts like *Ekabhukta*, *Nakta* etc. were also defined and explained[28]. For the performance of the *vrata*, the decision of *tithi* was necessary. Devala's simple dictum[29] *yām tithim* etc. has become quite famous among all the digest-writers and commentators. It may be noted that this observance of *Ekādaśīvrata* must have been assimilated and integrated into the *Dharmaśāstra* tradition under the influence of *Vaiṣṇava* followers. Devala has also referred to observances of *Nāgapañcamī* on the fifth day of bright half of the *Śrāvaṇa* and also to *Gavām* krīḍam on the *Balipratipat* day i.e. on the first day of bright half of the *Kārtika*[30]. The *Viṣṇudharmasūtra* (64.6, 77.1-2) refers to the observances of *Saṅkrānti*[31]. The observances of the twelve *Saṅkrāntis* were also specifically introduced by Devala and others.[32] The auspicious period on each *Saṅkrānti* was meticulously calculated[33]. Mm. P.V.Kane observes[34], "As a matter of fact, none of the ancient *Śrauta*, *Gṛhya* or *Dharmasūtras* mentions any *rāśis* or prescribe any auspicious or inauspicious times, concerned with *rāśis* but only times in relation to *Nakṣatras*". It is to be noted that *Rāśis* were introduced under the influence of Greek astronomy. Mm. P.V.Kane's remarks regarding the observances of *Makarasaṅkrānti* are also noteworthy. He states[35], "In any case the observances and festival of *Makarasaṅkrānti* do not appear to be much older than the beginning of the Chiristian era".Thus some such *vratas*, festivals, religious observances and customs were assimilated and integrated into the *Dharmaśāstra* tradition.

Tīrthayātrā as a means of purification

Mm.P.V. Kane writes[36], "In the *Sūtras* and ancient *Smṛtis* like those of Manu and Yajñavalkya, *Tīrthas* do not occupy a very important position, but in the *Mahābhārata* and the *Purāṇas*, they are highly lauded and placed even above sacrifices." There are certain rules regarding sacrifices. They were to be practised by persons belonging to certain castes, with the help of priests with required materials in the presence of wife etc. So these could be performed by a prince or a wealthy person. The person devoid of any of these requirements was helpless. Several intricacies in the observance of them and criticism levelled against the *hiṁsā* involved in them resulted in gradual diminishing character of sacrifices. On the contrary, *Tīrthayātrā* was also eulogised to be superior and easier even to the performance of sacrifices. The *Viṣṇudharmasūtra*[37] has enumerated the *Tīrthānusaraṇam* among the various aspects, constituting the *Dharma*. Devala introduces[38] it clearly as an alternative rule-an expiation for sin. He states that the person even after perpetrating great sins can be purified from them either by the performance of great sacrifices or by visiting the holy places.This shows how the *Dharmaśāstra* tradition represents the intermediate position by introducing the new matter of *Tīrthayātrā* alternatively. While the *Purāṇas* have extolled these to an extravagant extent. In the *Mārkaṇḍeya Purāṇa*, Baladeva is said to have followed the *Tīrthayātrā* for the purification from the sin of *Brahmahatyā*[39].

Assimilation of *Sāṅkhya-yoga* in Vedic Tradition

Even *Śaṅkarācārya* has mentined that the *Sāṅkhya* system is in proximity to the Vedic tradition and is accepted even by the *śiṣṭas* like Devala etc[40]. The *Sāṅkhya* and *Yoga* systems have to some extent been accepted by the *Smṛtis* like Manu, Yajñavalkya etc. Yajñavalkya[41] propounds the realization of *Ātman* through the practice of *Yoga* to be the supreme *Dharma*. Devala, as is noted even by Śaṅkarācārya incorporated both the *Sāṅkya* and *Yoga* tenets in his *Dharmasūtra*. He has summarised the tenets of these systems on the basis of ancient inscrutable *Tantra*-works of them.[42] But it is to be noted here that what Śaṅkarācārya meant is that these Devala etc. were the *śiṣṭas* followers of Vedic tradition, but yet they assimilated and integrated these tenets in their treatises. However, the main difference between the followers of Vedic tradition and the system of *Sāṅkhya-yoga* is that the *Vaidika śiṣṭas* were not dualistic. These *śiṣṭas* also admitted the *Brahman* to be the ultimate reality. Devala like the Caraka, the *Buddhacarita*, the *Mahābhārata*[43] also propounds the ultimate position to be reached is the *Brahman*, eventhough he incorporates the *Sāṅkhya-yoga* tenets.

The Purification of persons, contaminated by *Mlecchas*:

The *Devalasmṛti*, printed in several *Smṛti*-collections[44], containing only ninety verses introduces a very new and practically important trend of purification of the persons, contaminated by *Mlecchas*. Here the sages approached Devala, the best among sages, sitting at ease on the bank of river Sindhu and asked the solution for the purification of such persons[45]. Thereupon, in his reply the sage Devala prescribed certain rules and the expiatory observances for such persons for their association with *Mlecchas* for one day upto twenty years. The expiations for ladies, ill-treated or even raped by *Mlecchas* are also laid down[46]. The assimilation and integration of this new trend of re-conversation and purification was quite necessary for the social stability and re-organisation of the Hindu society. It extends helping hand to those who were victims of forcible conversion and wish to return to their original fold. Devala has thus integrated this new trend, which can stand as an ancient authority for those social reformers, who wish to admit persons of other religion into Hinduism, not by force or lust but by their own willingness.

Some *Vyavahāra*-trends

In the *Vyavahāra* section also, certain trends were assimilated and integrated with the changing social and political situations. In the devolution of the property of the sonless, the wife and daughters are to be sepecifically admitted[47], the *Dattaka* became more acceptable among the several kinds of sons[48], the list of *divyas* which were prescribed went on increasing[49] and the punishments for crimes became more sober and humane in nature[50]. In the absence of royal influence, more and more *prāyaścittas*—the mode of self-mortification came to be emphasized than the corporal punishments[51].

Kalivarjyas—Discontinuation of some customs in Kali age

Certain customs and practices introduced in the earlier *Dharmaśāstra* works were dissimilated and disintegrated under the title of *Kalivarjyas*. Actually this aspect has been more prominently elucidated in the later digests and *Purāṇas*, but some *Smṛtis*[52] also have started incorporating these trends. The (1) *Niyoga,* (2) the numerous secondary sons except *Aurasa* and *Dattaka*, (3) offering meat and wine in the *śrāddhas,* (4) resorting to *Saṁnyāsa* and *Agnihotra.* This shows that certain customs practised in a particular period were to be discontinued in the other period. Thus considering the real sense of *Dharma,* as establishing social stability and welfare of all, the change in customs and practices was necessary. This principle needs to be considered even in the Modern Age.

Concluding Remarks

Thus the Ancient Indian *Dharmaśāstra* tradition, as reflected in the *Dharmasūtras* and *Smṛtis* exhibits some such trends of assimilation and integration. Several aspects of *Dharamśāstra* like (1) Definition denotation and connotation of the term *Dharma*. (2) the sacraments, (3) the rituals, (4) Festivals, (5) social customs and practices, (6) legal matter, (7) Expiatory rules etc. incorporate some such trends. Though the dictium '*vedo'khilo dharmamūlam* is admitted, certain practices, not traced to the *Vedas*, were introduced, assimilated and integrated through tradition. The emphasis on certain ritual practices, fasts, vows, pilgrimages, giving gifts. etc. is found in some later *Smṛtis* and these are elevated to the position superior to the performance of sacrifice. These trends might have been due to the changing social, religious and political conditions and the influence and interaction among several religious sects. Devala-a *Smṛtikāra*-has exhibited even more pragmatic and flexible outlook by assimilating even the people who were kidnapped, polluted and defiled by *Mlecchas*. He introduced a system of their re-conversion by purification. Thus in this paper, an attempt is made to present and elaborate some such aspects of *Dharma-śāstra* which are results of assimilation and integration.

FOOTNOTES

Paper presented at seminar on "Trends and Assimilation and Intergration in Ancient India" held at Deptt. of Sk., Uni. of Bombay, 9 to 11th March 1999.

1. इषे त्वोर्जे त्वा वायवस्थ देवो वः सविता प्रार्पयतु श्रेष्ठतमाय कर्मणे..............
   —*Śukla Yajurveda* 1.1
2. *Śatapatha Brāhmaṇa* 1.7.1.5; *Taittirīya Brāhmaṇa* 3.2.1
3. यतोऽभ्युदयनिःश्रेयससिद्धिः स धर्मः।—*Vaiśeṣikasūtra*-1.1
4. Wadekar, M.L.: '*Devalasmṛti-Reconstruction and Critical Study,*' Koshal Book Depot, Delhi, 1998, sr. no. 2200-2202.
5. पुरुषनिःश्रेयसार्थं धर्मजिज्ञासा —*Vasiṣṭhadharmasūtra*-1.1
6. वर्णाश्रमेतराणां नो ब्रूहि, धर्मानशेषतः।
   —*Yājñavalkyasmṛti*- 1.1 ab. cf. *Manusmṛti* I.2; 107.
7. वेदोऽखिलो धर्ममूलं स्मृतिशीले च तद्विदाम्।
   आचारश्चैव साधूनामात्मनस्तुष्टिरेव च।।–*Manusmṛti*-2.6
   श्रुतिः स्मृतिः सदाचारः स्वस्य च प्रियमात्मनः।
   –*Yājñavalkya Smṛti* 1.7 of *Manusmṛti* 2.12.
8. अनाम्नातेषु धर्मेषु..... *Manusmṛti*—12.108
   ग्रामवचनं च कुर्युः। विवाहश्मशानयोः। —*Pāraskaragṛhyasūtra* 1.8.11-12
9. धृतिः क्षमा दमोऽस्तेयं शौचमिन्द्रियनिग्रहः।
   धीर्विद्या सत्यमक्रोधो दशकं धर्मलक्षणम्।। –*Manusmṛti*-6.92
   अहिंसा सत्यमस्तेयं शौचमिन्द्रियनिग्रहः।
   एतं सामासिकं धर्मं चातुर्वर्ण्येऽब्रवीन्मनुः।। –*Manusmṛti*-10.63
   अहिंसा सत्यमस्तेयं शौचमिन्द्रियनिग्रहः।
   दानं दया दमः क्षान्तिः सर्वेषां धर्मसाधनम्।। —*Yājñavalkyasmṛti*-1.122
   सत्यमस्तेयमक्रोधो ह्रीः शौचं धीर्धृतिर्दमः।
   संयतेन्द्रियता विद्या धर्मः सार्व उदाहृतः।। —*Yājñavalkyasmṛti* 3.66

शौचं दानं तपः श्रद्धा गुरुसेवा क्षमा दया।
विज्ञानं विनयः सत्यमिति धर्मसमुच्चयः।।
—*Devalasmṛti* (Reconstructed Text, *op. cit.*) sr. no.7

क्षमा सत्यं दमः शौचं दानमिन्द्रियसंयमः।
अहिंसा गुरुशुश्रूषा तीर्थानुसरणं दया।।
आर्जवत्वमलोभश्च देवब्राह्मणपूजनम्।
अनभ्यासूया च तथा धर्मः सामान्य उच्यते।। —*Viṣṇudharmasūtra* II-16-17

अथाष्टावात्मगुणाः। दया सर्वभूतेषु क्षान्तिरनसूया शौचमनायासो मङ्गलमकार्पण्यमस्पृहेति।
– *Gautamadharmasūtra* I.8.23-24.

शौचमङ्गलनायास अनसूया स्पृहा दमः।
लक्षणानि च विप्रस्य तथा दानं दयापि च।। –*Atrismṛti* 33.

10. *Gautamadharmasūtra*- 8.25-26
11. यमान् सेवेत सततं न नित्यं नियमान्बुधः।
यमान्पतत्यकुर्वाणो नियमान्केवलान् भजन्।। —*Manusmṛti* 4.204.
12. *Yājñavalkyasmṛti* 1.8.
13. *op. cit.* sr. no. 50.
14. *Mahābhārata* 8.49.50 and 12.110.11
15. *Brahmasūtraśāṅkarabhāṣya* 3-4-34.
16. cf. no. 10 above.
17. *Vedavyāsasmṛti* 1.14, *Bṛhaspatismṛti* (Reconstructed) *Saṁskāra* 86-101, *Devalasmṛti (op. cit)*. 1.372/373
18. गान्धर्वादिविवाहेषु पुनर्वैवाहिको विधिः।
कर्त्तव्यश्च त्रिभिर्वर्णैः समयेनाग्निसाक्षिकः।।
19. ऐकाश्रम्यं तु आचार्याः। अप्रजनत्वादितरेषाम्।
—*Baudhāyanadharmasūtra* II.6-29.
also *Gautamadharmasūtra* III.1 and 35, *Manu*. 89-90, III-77.80, *Vasiṣthadharma sūtra* 8.14-17, Dakṣa II-57-60, *Viṣṇudharmasūtra* 59.29.
20. *Hist. of Dharmaśāstra* vol. II. 1 pp. 289-290.
21. *Manu*. II. 44; *Viṣṇudharmasūtra* 27.19.
22. *Devalasmṛti (op. cit.)* I.480-497, *Baudhāyanasūtra*(quot. in) *Saṁskāraratnamālā* p.188.
23. *Hist. of Dharmaśāstra* Vol. V-1 page 43
24. नास्ति स्त्रीणां पृथग्यज्ञो न व्रतं नाप्युपोषणम्।
पतिं शुश्रूषते येन तेन स्वर्गे महीयते।। —*Manusmṛti*-V.155.
पत्यौ जीवति या योषिदुपवासं व्रतं चरेत्।
आयुः सा हरते भर्तुर्नरकं चैव गच्छति।।
—*Viṣṇudharmasūtra*-25.16; *Aṅgiras* V.40.

25. *Devalasmṛti (op. cit.)* sl. No. 838
26. *Devalasmṛti (op. cit.)* 859-868

    Nārada—संक्रान्त्यामुपवासं च कृष्णैकादशिवासरे।

    चन्द्रसूर्यग्रहे चैव न कुर्यात्पुत्रवान् गृही।।

    —*Hemādri Kāla*. p. 183, *Nirṇayasindhu* p. 36

    नित्यं भक्तिसमायुक्तैर्नरैर्विष्णुपरायणैः।

    पक्षे पक्षे तु कर्तव्यमेकादश्यामुपोषणम्।।

    —*Hemādrikāla* p. 159. *Nirṇayasindhu* p.37.

    Kātyāyana— संसारसागरोत्तारमिच्छन्विष्णुपरायणः।

    ऐश्वर्यं संततिं स्वर्गं मुक्तिं वा यद्यदिच्छति।

    एकादश्यां न भुञ्जीत पक्षयोरुभयोरपि।।

    —*Hemādri-kāla*, p. 162, *Kālanirṇaya,* p.236, *Ekādaśītattva,* p. 28.
27. *Devalasmṛti* (*op. cit.*) p. 844, 859-871, 848-850.
28. *Ibid* 845-847
29. *Ibid* 828-829
30. *Ibid* 852-858
31. *Viṣṇudharmasūtra* 64.6; 77.1-2
32. *Devalasmṛti (op. cit.)* 819-825 and others like Śātātapa, Jābāli, Marīci etc. *Kṛtyakalpataru (Niyata.)* pp. 361-362, 365.
33. *Devalasmṛti (op. cit.). Ibid.*
34. *Hist. of Dharma*. Vol. V. 1 page 224
35. *Ibid.*
36. *Ibid.* Vol. IV pages 561-562.
37. *Viṣṇudharmasūtra* II. 16-17-*Tīrthānusaraṇam*
38. *Devalasmṛti (op. cit.)* 2164-2167.
39. *Mārkaṇḍeya Purāṇa* 6.35-37
40. *Brahmasūtraśāṅkarabhāṣya* I.4.26; 2.1.4.12 see comm. *Ratnaprabhā Ānanadagirīyā* on it.
41. *YājñavalkyaSmṛti* 1.8.
42. *Devalasmṛti (op. cit.)* 2210
43. *Caraka Śārira* I. 155/156, V. 21, V.33 *Buddhacarita* XII. 65, *Mahābhārata* 12.267.38.
44. *Smṛtisandharbha* III. pp. 1655-1663, *Smṛtīnām Samuccayaḥ,* pp. 85-88, *Aṣṭādaśasmṛtayaḥ* (pp. 64-67).
45. *Devalasmṛti—(Op. cit.)* 1813-1815.
46. *Ibid.* 1859-1870.
47. *Hist. of Dharmaśāstra* III pp. 702-703; 714.
48. *Ibid* Vol. III. 362
49. *Ibid* Vol. III. pp. 926-927 Śaunaka, Prajāpati, Bṛhaspati etc. *Devalasmṛti (op. cit)* sr. no. 815-817.

X

RELEVANCE OF SANSKRIT IN 21ST CENTURY
(WITH SPECIAL REFERENCE TO *DHARMAŚĀSTRA*)

Introducctory

We have already entered in the last year of the 20th century. In due course, at the end of this century, we will be entering the 21st century- the New Millenium. It is quite necessry to think about the relevance of Sanskrit in the 21st century-the coming Millenium- the topic of today's Seminar. The subject can be viewed from two points (1) Relevance of Sanskrit Language in general (2) Relevance of Sanskrit studies with reference to different *śāstras*. How far these will be relevant in the Modern world of science and Technology? Scientific inventions have no doubt contributed to the *greatest luxuries* of the human life. The computer science has facilitated many complicated issues of the modern world, but only it needs to be properly utilized and put to good purpose *by a human being*. Electronic media has brought the world quite nearer but there is danger of media being misused by the over-doses, of sex and violence on immature minds. There is invention of Atomic energy that can annihilate the entire world within no seconds if not properly utilized. There are problems of pollution and ecological imbalance. The cases of psychological disorders and mental depressions are increasing. The social, political, educational and even religious institutions are sometimes being overpowered by the leaders, hankering after selfish gains and not social welfare. Under such gloomy circumstances, we are to think and plan about the coming millenium and the relevance of Sanskrit therein. After relating about general relevance of Sanskrit, this paper aims at emphasing the relevance especially of *Dharmaśāstra* in the coming millenium.

Most of you are aware of the greatness of the Sanskrit language. (1) It is the mother of all Indian Languages, fit ot *Rāṣṭrabhāṣā* (National Language) nay even *Viśvabhāṣa* (international language) only if political issues are set aside. (2) It is the most unifying bond and force of National integration. (3) It is the most perfect language, with proper pronunciation especially quite appropriate for the modern computerised world. (4) It incorporates vast treasure of our ancient, medieval and modern Literature, exhibiting our culture and heritage. (5) It can contribute comprehensively to the history of any and every field like Religion, Philosophy, Geography, Politics, Sociology, Law, Technical Sciences, besides Astronomy, Chemitry, Medicine and Surgery, Mathematics and many other fields of modern research. From all these points of view, the Sanskrit language is most relevant even in the coming millenium.

Dharma and Ecology

The field of *Dharmaśāstra* is most pertinent in this modern world where ecological imbalance, psychological disorders and mental vices prevail. The word "*Dharma*" can not be perfectly translated in English by a term connoting and denoting all its diversified inherent contents. It is also unfortunately most misunderstood term. It does not merely connote the religion or the religious, liturgical activity of the person, like *sandhyā, pūjā* etc. This is only one of its aspects not the real, entire connotation of word. The word is to be derived from the root *Dhṛ*.

धारणाद्धर्म इत्याहुर्धर्मो धारयते प्रजाः।
यत्स्याद्धारणसंयुक्तं स धर्म इति निश्चयः।। —महा. 12.110.11

Dharma is that which sustains the entity. The sustaining element in every entity is called *Dharma*. The *Śruti* clearly declares :

धर्मो विश्वस्य जगतः प्रतिष्ठा। धर्मे सर्वं प्रतिष्ठितम्। —तै.आ. 10.79

Dharma is meant for stability and maintenance of everything. This is imporant from the point of view of modern science of ecology. The *Dharma* contributes to the ecological balance.

Dharma and Social Order

There is also significance of *Dharma* from the sociological point of view.

Man cannot live in isolation. He has to live in society. Every body wishes to live happily and peacefully. For the welfare of all members, it is necessary that certain norms and values-rules of personal and social behaviour—are to be followed, which will contribute not only to the social good but also to the individual good. Certain rules-Code of Conduct-aiming at social and personal welfare are laid down in *Dharmaśāstra*. The *Dharma* is also defined as यतोऽभ्युदय-निःश्रेयससिद्धिः स धर्मः। The *Dharma* is that by following which there can be personal and social welfare and spiritual upliftment. The *Dharmaśāstra* lays down such ideals, values and norms of social and personal behaviour that bring out personal and social well-being. (1) The rules of personal hyegine (2) Code of Conduct and Social behaviour (3) Practice of *Sāmānya Dharma*, *Yama*, *Niyamas* or *Ātmaguṇas* and social, religious festivals, for the elimination of individual psychological or mental vices like *Rāga*, *dveṣa* etc. (technically known as *Kaṣāyapācanam*) and above all (4) the practice *yoga* or *adhyātmavidyā* for the spiritual upliftment of the individual, अयं तु परमो धर्मो यद्योगेनात्मदर्शनम्— says Yājñavalkya. He also states जपयज्ञप्रसिद्ध्यर्थं विद्यां चाध्यात्मिकीं जपेत्। All these aspects of *Dharma* aim at physical, mental social, spiritual-i.e. all-round, complete and perfect development and well-being of the person and the society in turn. Persons, following ideal norms and values, with sound physical, psychological, social and spiritual background can appropriately contribute to the maintenance and welfare of the entire society. This is the idealistic attitude principally and basically aimed at and incorporated by the *Dharmśāstra* literature, if properly and genuinely understood- through the precepts and modes of behaviour enunciated by them.

Dharmaśāstra and I.P.C.

But these sociologists also knew that these are the ideals that are aimed at. But practically, it is very difficult to achieve these ideals. Hence from the practical, realistic, pragmatic point of view, they also enforced certain other norms and ideals through the chapters of *Vyavahāra*. All persons are not of equal nature. The *Bṛhadāraṇyaka* states—द्वया ह प्राजापत्याः। देवाश्चासुराश्च। The *Bhagavadgītā* expounds *Daivī* and *Āsurī Sampat*. Generally, persons are expected to follow disctates of *Dharma*, but there are also those who either do not observe and consequently transgress the rules. For such persons, the *vyavahāra* aspect of the *Dharmaśāstra* prescribing punishments for several offences, which has its parallel in the modern Indian Penal Code becomes significant. Offences can be bodily, mental or psychological (like abuse, defamation etc.), sexual (like rape, seduction etc.). For these offences, certain punishments and penalties are laid down for the maintenance of social order. There can be offences, pertaining to property-movable and immovable in the form of theft, robbery, encroachments etc. Offences regarding

Business and weights and measures are also taken note of. Businessmen may decieve customers in several ways by adulteration—even by wrong use of weights and measures etc. Now a days, there have been cases of illegal currency notes. Such cases of illegal currency were also noted in our ancient *Smṛtis* and punishments were prescribed for the culprits. There are also several other aspects of law like (1) Laws regarding marriage conditions, and divorce (2) Laws regarding adoption *(Dattaka)*, (3) Laws regarding partition and Division of property, (4) Laws, regarding *Saṁnyāsins* etc., expounded in the *Dharmaśāstra* that contain the basic principles, that are referred to and taken note of for solving the legal matters, even in modern age. Our *Yājñavalkyasmṛti* and the commentary *Mitākṣarā* on it are still held in high esteem in court of law. The decisions regarding Hindu Law, without the understanding of the Hindu Code of conduct, expounded in the *Dharmśāstra* works remain incomplete, untenable, unjustifiable.

***Dharmaśāstra* and Many fields of Knowledge**

The field of *Dharmaśāstra* is so vast that it incorporates in it aspects of different modern studies like Religion, Philosophy, Psychology, Law, Sociology, Indian Culture, History, Astronomy, Mathematics, Geometry, Geography, Education and many others. History of any of these fields is incomplete and inexhaustive, if the congnizance of views, expressed in it are not taken note of. The several aspects of *Yoga* Philosophy are quite relevant, when the significance of *Yoga* is being emphasized in the Modern world of astraunauts, placing their feet on the planet like moon.

Thus the science of *Dharma* that enforces the ecological balance of Nature, social order, stability and well-being with ideal norms and values is most pertinent for the modern world. It can guide us as to when and where the use of atomic energy or missiles is to be made. By eleminating psychological vices in the individual behaviour, it can save us from the tererrising emergence of physical and mental disorders like AIDS, heart-attack, stress, depression and many others and create a tension-free community with sound physical and mental health.

I may conclude my observations with words of sage Vyāsa who declared in the *Mahābhārata*—

ऊर्ध्वबाहुर्विरौम्येष न च कश्चिच्छृणोति माम्।
धर्मादर्थश्च कामश्च स धर्मः किं न सेव्यताम्।। —18.5.49

The *artha* and even *kāma* should be subservient to *Dharma* only. Through the practice of *Dharma*, one can obtain both *Artha* and *Kāma*. Even *Mokṣa* becomes possible through the practice of *Dharma*. This is opinion of ancient *Dharma-sūtrakāras* like Vasiṣṭha, Budha, Devala and others.

FOOTNOTES

Paper read at the seminar on "Relevance of Sanskrit in the 21st Century", held at Deptt. of Skt. Pali and Prakrit, Faculty of Arts, M.S. Uni. of Baroda, Vadodara, 22nd March 2000.

XI

A FORGOTTEN CONCEPT OF THE FORTY-EIGHT SACRAMENTS

Introductory

Among the divergent aspects of Hindu life, elucidated in the works on *Dharmaśāstra, Saṁskāras*—the sacraments occupy a very indispensable and prominent place, as they have not only been described in various *Gṛhya* and *Dharmasūtras,* but also in the metrical *Smṛtis* and *Smṛtinibandhas* (the commentaries and digests on *Dharmaśāstra*). Separate volumes and books have been written on the subject of sacraments, in which there has been great discussion about the importance, number and nature of them.From the practical point of view, they have moulded the very character and personality of Hindus, by forming the regular part of the actual life, right from the birth upto death.

Enumeration of Sacraments

Though Manu and Yājñavalkya do not enumerate the *Saṁskāras*; they have referred to them as—beginning from '*Niṣeka*' (conception) ending in '*Śmaśāna* (cremation) (*Manu* III.16 *Yājña* 1.10).[1] Gautama (1.8.14-24) has enumerated the forty sacraments and eight virtues of the soul[2]. Śaṅkha, quoted in the *Smṛticandrikā* (*Āhnika,* p.13) also refers to forty sacraments and eight virtues.[3] *Vaikhānasasmārtasūtra* (1.1) mentions eighteen *Śārīra-saṁskāras* (bodily sacraments) and twenty-two kinds of sacrifices (i.e. twentyone kinds of sacrifices, consisting of 7 *Saṁsthās*, each of *Pāka*, *Havir* and *Soma* sacrifices and five *mahāyajñas* (great sacrifices) counted as one[4]. These forty sacraments only have been referred to by most of the Modern scholars of *Dharmaśāstra*. Most of the *Dharmaśāstra* works also have laid stress mostly upon the popular sixteen sacraments.

Śaṅkarācārya's Unique reference to 48 sacraments

However it is noteworthy that Śaṅkarācārya has referred to the forty-eight sacraments in his commentary on the *Brahmasūtras*. Even MM. P.V Kane has not noticed this fact. While commenting upon the *Brahmasūtra* (3.4.34) namely "सर्वथा त एवोभयलिङ्गात्", Śaṅkarācārya explicitly remarks—

"यस्यैतेऽष्टाचत्वारिंशत्संस्कारा इत्याद्या च संस्कारप्रसिद्धिर्वैदिकेषु कर्मसु तत्संस्कृतस्य विद्योत्पत्तिमभिप्रेत्य स्मृतौ भवति"[5]

This reference clearly indicates that Śaṅkarācārya is referring here to some *Smṛti*-text that had incorporated enunciation of forty-eight sacramants, that are conducive to the wisdom of soul.

Explanation of Ānandagiri

However, the extant *Gṛhyasūtras, Dharmasūtras* and *Smṛtis* do not contain enumeration of the forty-eight sacraments. This is the highest number of sacraments ever known. While commenting upon the previously stated statement of Śaṅkarācārya, Ānandagiri tries to enumerate the forty-eight number of sacraments, in the following manner[6]—

14 —From *Garbhādhāna* upto *Vivāha*
5 —*Mahāyajñas*
21 —7 *Soma*, +7 *Haviḥ* +7 *Pāka Saṁsthās*
1 —*Anaśnatsaṁhitādhyayana*
7 —Funeral rites namely *Prāyaṇa, Japa, Utkramaṇa, Daihika, Bhasmasamūhana, Asthisañcayana, Śrādhāni*

Total-48

Anantabhaṭṭa's Enumeration

Among the *Smṛti-nibandhas*, the *Vidhāpārijata* of Anantabhaṭṭa contains explicit, reference to and enumeration of forty-eight sacraments[7]. In a quotation[7] from Yama, mentined in the same work, there is only reference to the forty-eight sacraments, while the author, Anantabhaṭṭa has also quoted two stanzas from his own collection (*māmakau Saṅgraha-ślokau*), in which they are most perfectly recorded in the following manner:—

14—	*Garbhādhāna, Puṁsavana, Sīmanta, Jātakarma, Nāmakarma, Annaprāśana, Caula, Upanayana, four Vedavratas, Samāvartana, Vivāha.*
5—	*Mahāyajñas*
21—	7 *Pāka*+7 *Haviḥ*+7 *Soma Yajñasaṁsthās.*
1—	*Anaśnatsaṁhitādhyayana*
7—	*Funeral rites, Japa, Utkramaṇa, Daihika, bhasmasamūhana, Asthisañcayana, Śrāddhāni, Sapiṇḍīkaraṇa.*
Total 48	

The *Nyāyakaṇḍalī*[8] also refers to the concept of forty-eight *Saṁskāras* in one context. The *Agnipurāṇa* (ch. 166.9[b]-17[a]) also alludes to such concept of forty-eight sacraments.[9]

It may be remarked here that originally the sacrifices were also included among the sacraments, but later on due to advent of Bauddha and Jain schools, the institution of sacrifice receeded in importance and the later metrical *Smṛtis*, generally did not even include them among the regular sacraments. Consequently, mostly the sixteen sacraments became very popular.

It is already mentioned that the reference regarding the forty eight sacraments, quoted by Śaṅkarācārya, is not traceale in the extant *Sūra* and *Smṛti* texts. It is presumable that some

Smṛti text, incorporating the enumeration of the forty-eight *saṁskāras*, might have gone into oblivion.

FOOTNOTES

Paper published in Meerut University Sanskrit Research Journal, Vol. XIII, Part II July-Decmber 1988

1. निषेकादिश्मशानान्तो मन्त्रैर्यस्योदितो विधिः।

   Acarya, Narayan Ram, ed. *Manusmṛti*, with Com, of Kullūka, Tenth ed., Nirnayasagar, Bombay, 1946, Adh. II. 16.

   निषेकादिश्मशानान्तास्तेषां वै मन्त्रतः क्रियाः।

   —*Yājñavalkya-smṛti*, with *Mitākṣara*, Venkateswar, Bombay, 1900, Adh. I, Ślo. 10.

2. गर्भाधान.......इत्येते चत्वारिंशत्संस्काराः।। 22।।

   अथाष्टावत्मगुणाः ।।23।।...

   Gokhale, Ganesh Shastri, ed, *Gautama Dharmasūtra*, with com, *Mitākṣarā* of Haradatta, Anandashram, Poona, 1910. 1.8.14-24.

3. यस्यैते चत्वारिंशत्संस्कारा अष्टावात्मगुणाश्च......

   Gharpur, J.R., ed. *Smṛticandrikā* of Devaṇṇa Bhaṭṭa (*Āhnika*, *Vyavahāra*, *Śrāddha Kāṇḍas*), Collectioa of Hindu Law Texts, Bombay, 1918, *Āhnika*, p. 13.

4. अथ निषकादिसंस्कारान्व्याख्यास्यामः।..... इत्येते चत्वारिंशद्भवन्ति।

   Caland W., ed. *Vaikhānasa-smārtasūtra*. The Asiatic Society of Bengal, Calcutta, 1927, 1.1.

5. Dhupekar, R.S. and Bakre, M.S. : ed. *Brahmasūtra-śāṅkarabhāṣ ya* with com. Ratnaprabhā, Bhāmatī, and *Nyāyanirṇaya* of Govindānanda. Vācaspati and Ānandagiri respectively, Nirnayasagar Press, Bombay, 1904, Brahm. S. 3.4 34.

6. गर्भाधानादयः सहधर्मचारिणीसंयोगान्ताश्चतुर्दश। पञ्च महायज्ञाः, सप्त सोमसंस्थाः सप्त हविःसंस्थाः, सप्त पाकसंस्था इति चत्वारिंशत्संस्काराः। अनश्नत्संहिताध्ययनं प्रायणं कर्म जप उत्क्रमणं दैहिकं भस्मसमूहनमस्थिसंचयनं श्राद्धानीत्येवमष्टाचत्वारिं-शत्संस्काराः।

7. यमः— अष्टाचत्वारिंशदेते संस्कारा विहिता द्विजे।
   य एतैः संस्कृतो विप्रो ब्रह्मलोकं स गच्छति।।

गर्भाधानमथो हि पुंसवनकं सीमान्तजातक्रिया—
नामान्नादनचौलकोपनयने वेदव्रतान्यप्युत।
चत्वारि स्नपनं विवाहकरणं पञ्चापि यज्ञा अथो
संस्थाः सप्त च सप्त सप्त गदितास्त्रिशद्दशाप्यत्र तु।।
एवं चानशनेन वेदपठनं कर्णे जपस्त्वोमिति
प्राणोत्क्रान्तिरथौर्ध्वदेहिकमतः संव्यू(वू) हनं भस्मनः।
अस्थ्नां संचयनं ततः परमपि श्राद्धानि सापिण्डकं
चत्वारिंशदिति स्मृतौ निगदिताः संस्कारका ह्यष्ट च।।

Vidyaratn, Taraprasanna, ed. *Vidhānapārijāta* of Anantabhaṭṭa, Bibliothica Indica, Calcutta, 1905, Vol. II, pp. 370-372.

8. स्ववर्णविहिताश्चाष्टचत्वारिंशत्संस्काराः। *Nyāyakaṇḍalī of Śrīdharācārya,* ed. by Jetli. J.S. and Parikh-Vasant, G. pub. by Oriental Institute of Baroda, Vadodara, 1991, p. 623.

9. *Agnipurāṇam,* ed., Jivanand Vidyasagar, Calcutta, 1882, ch. 166.9[b]-17[a]

स्यादष्टचत्वारिंशद्भिः संस्कारैर्ब्रह्मलोकगः ।। etc.

The *Agnipurāṇam* includes eight virtues among the fortyeight *Saṁskāras* and not the *antyeṣṭi Saṁskāras.*

PHILOSOPHY

XII

RĀMACANDRA PAṆḌITA'S DAŚOPANIṢAD-RAHASYA—A UNIQUE WORK

Intrdouctory

Sanskrit language has a long-standing tradition of various scholars, writing scholarly treatises on different *śāstras*. Every region of India has been gifted with talented *Paṇḍitas*, enriching the scholarly literature, in different periods of its history. Rāmacandra Paṇḍita is one of such versatile savants of Sanskrit literature, whose contribution to various *śāstras* in the form of different scholarly works has less been taken notice of by Modern researchers. In this paper, an attempt is made to introduce this great scholar from Kolhapur and his small but rare and unique work namely *Daśopaniṣadrahasya,* a treatise on *Vedānta,* which has not yet come to light and has remained in manuscript form.

Biographical Information

Rāmacandra Paṇḍita was the eldest son of the revered Siddheśvara Mahārāja of Kolhapur. Fortunately enough, we get much detailed biographical information about him and his family. His father Śrī Siddheśvara Mahārāja[1] was a great Saint and an ardent seeker of truth. He was born on the ninth day of the bright fortnight of the month of *Caitra* in year *śake* 1665 i.e. 1743 A.D. His mother's name was Godāvarī and that of his father was Rāmabhaṭṭa Bābā. He belonged to Kṛṣṇātri *gotra* of *Mādhyandinī* Recension of *Śukla Yajurveda*. It is believed that his father propitiated Lord at the self-born *(Svayambhu)* Harihareśvara temple and obtained through the grace of God, the son, who is considered to be the incarnation of Bhairava. He was given *Upanayana Saṁsakāra* at the age of five and was married also at early age but unfortunately his first wife died very early. He was again married with Bhavānībai or Bāi Mahārāja, who was a daughter of Gaṅgādhara Panta of Surangali village. He was a disciple of Guru Amṛtarāva of Aurangabad and studied *Vedas* and several *Śāstras*, under Advaitānanda at Kashi. When his Guru Advaitānanda took *Samādhi*, he teturned to Maharashtra. Thus he came in contact with three great saints namely Advaitānanda, Yogānanda and Vaikuṇṭharāya. As he was an ardent devotee of God, he obtained some miraculous powers and *Vācāsiddhi*. His grandson Śrīkṛṣṇa Paṇḍita has dilated much upon this aspect of his personality in the biography, written by him. He wrote a treatise named *Sāraṇī*. He took *Samādhi* on the sixth day of the dark fortnight of the month of *Vaiśākha* in 1801 A.D. at Kolhapur.

Rāmcandra Paṇḍita[2] was born on Sunday, the ninth day of the dark fortnight of the month of *Caitra* in *Śake* 1691 i.e. 29th April 1769. He had traditionally studied different *Śāstras* like *Vyākaraṇa*, *Nyāya*, *Dharmaśāstra*, *Alaṅkāraśāstra, Śrauta, Smārta and Mantraśāstra.* At the age of eleven, he was well-versed in the *Ṛgveda* and *Yajurveda* with *vikṛtis.* Right from his eleventh year, he started studing *Vyākarana-śāstra* under Mahādeva Śāstrī, *Nyāyaśāstra* under Narasiṁha-cārya Patykuṇḍi, *Śrautasmārta* from Raṅgabhaṭṭa Śukla and *Mantraśāstra* and *Vedāntaśāstra* from Śrī Siddheśvara (his father). He also knew *Chandaḥśāstra* and other literature like *Nāṭaka, Campū* etc. He was well-versed in different arts. He knew *Keralajyotiṣa.* He was proficient in *Saṅgīta-śāstra*, knew *Rāgarāgiṇīs* and could compose himelf some songs in those *Rāgas.* He was so much expert in swimming that he could swim the river Kṛṣṇā of Narasiṁhapur from one end upto seven hundred *Hastas* (about 12600 inches) away and return without allowing the water to touch even the *Tilaka*-mark, made on his chest. During 12 to 23 years of his life, he obtained expertise in all *Śāstras* and arts. He had an extra-ordinary physical beauty and great bodily strength. He also knew other arts like horse-riding, archery, aiming etc.

In view of his extra-ordinary intellect and scholarship, his preceptor advised him not to indulge in dispute (*Vāda-vivāda*) in *Vidvatsabhā*—assembly of scholars, as that would insult other scholars. Hence he relinquished going to assembly of scholars and followed the practical path of *Karma*, *Jñāna* and *Upāsanā* and initiated, advised disciples to follow this path and thus uplifted the ignorant people. He himself behaved like Janaka Vaideha. It is said that king of Kolhāpur, Chatrapati who had become his disciple, offered him his entire kingdom and even the title or degree of *Mahārāja*, but he had no attachment for anything. He was mercy, modesty and tranquillity incarnate. He took *Samādhi* on Sunday the 3rd day of bright fortnight of *Vaiśākha* in *Śake* 1752 (i.e. 25/4/1830).

From the present work, *Daśopaniṣadrahasya*, also his devotion to Rāma is evident as he starts with the benedictory word Rāma and thus performing *maṅgala* with the name of his own favourite deity at the outset. In the last verse also, he describes himself as a bee at the Lotus-feet of Śrīrāma. He himself informs us that he had obtained realization of unity with *Brahman* through the grace of his preceptor. The colophon of the above work gives us additional information that he was *Vidvanmukuṭālaṅkārahīravara* (supreme gem in the diadem ornament of scholars) and was *Rājayogivarya* (best among *Rājayogis*).

The following is the genealogical table[3] of the Siddheśvara family of Kolhāpur :

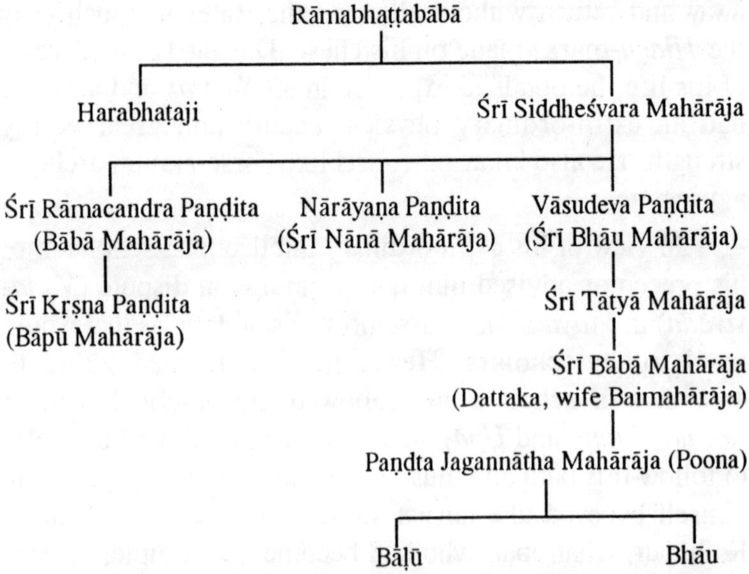

Works of Rāmacandra Paṇḍita

Rāmacandra Paṇḍita has contributed several scholarly treatises to Sanskrit and Marathi Literature.

(1) *Prātiśākhyajyotsnā* on *Vedalakṣaṇa* from the point of view of vedic grammar along with citations from *Veda*.

(2) *Baiṭha*—on *Vedalakṣaṇa*, for memorizing Vedic *Ṛks*.

(3) *Kuṇḍendu*—on *Kuṇḍalakṣaṇa*, explaining also formation of *Pīṭhas* of nine planets etc. In this work, the *Līlāvatī*, the mathematical treatise is simplified and clarified. It is useful for measuring of land as it contains also *Kṣetraphala*, mathematical devices for calculating land.

(4) *Vṛttābhirāma*—This is a work on *Chandaḥśāstra*, useful for *Sāhityaśāstra*/poets.

(5) *Īśāvāsyopaniṣad Bhāṣya*— a work on *Vedāntaśāstra*. It is a commentary on the *Īśāvāsyopaniṣad*.

(6) *Adhikaraṇasaṅgraha*—On *Vedāntaśāstra*. It is based

upon *Adhikaraṇas* of the *Brahmasūtras*, written in metrical form.

(7) *Daśopaniṣadrahasya* with commentary—a small work on *Vedāntaśāstra*. In it, Secrets of ten *Upaniṣads* are summarized in ten verses. It also contains author's own commentary on each verse.

(8) *Śrīrāmalīlāsahastranāma*—a *stotra* work in miraculous style. It contains not only the story about life and activities of Rāma, but also the *Sahastranāma*.

(9) *Rāmamahimnastotra*— a *Stotra* in praise of Rāma like the *Śivamahimnastotra*.

He has also composed other works like (10) *Śayanotsava,* (11) *Prabodhotsava,* (12) *Bhagavadgīta-gīta abhaṅga* (seven hundred *abhaṅgas* in Marathi on seven hundred *ślokas* of the *Bhagavadgītā*), (13) *Aṣṭāvakragītā-Samaślokī*.

Moreover, he was written numerous *Subhāṣitas*, *āryās*, *abhaṅgas, padas, sākīs* etc. Most of these works have still remained less-noticed and require proper study and publication.

Description of manuscript of the *Daśopaniṣadrahasya*

Of the above-mentioned works of Rāmacandra Paṇḍita, an attempt is made here to intrdouce his work namely the *Daśopaniṣadrahasya* to the world of Scholars. The present study is mainly based upon the manuscript, preserved in the private collection of Śrī Yaśavanta Mahārāja, who is present heir and successor to the *gurumahārāja*-tradition, starting from Siddeśvara Mahārāja. He favoured me by supplying the original manuscript of the above work for study and research purposes. He has also given me detailed information about the biography and contribution of Rāmacandra Paṇḍita. I am very much indebted to him for his kind jesture.

It is a complete manuscript, written in *Devanāgarī* script

containing thirteen folios, with extent of about four hundred *granthas*. It is copied on a paper of about 10.5 X 30.5 cms. size. written on both sides with margin of about three cms. on both sides and with upper and lower margin of about two cms. The handwriting of the scribe is quite clear. No information about the scribe is available. In the middle of the folios, two lines, of a *śloka* of the work are written and the commentary is written above and below it. Thus herein the *tripāṭha paddhati* of writing is followed. Enough spacc is left between the commentary and the text. so that the division of the two can be clearly understood. The two lines in the middle have about twentyfour letters each, while the commentary portion has about sixtyfour letters to a line with seven lines on each page. The margin on both sides is ruled with red pigment and some important words are also marked with red pigment. The corrections are also made with red pigment. The folios are numbered on both left and right side margins on back side. In each left hand side margin, the title '*Daśopaniṣad*' is written, while in each right hand side margin '*Rahasyaṭikā*' is written. The marginal corrections and additions are rare.

The Present work—*Daśopaniśadrahasya*

As evident from its very title, the *Daśopaniṣadrahasya* is a small but unique work on *Vedānta*, especially ten *Upaniṣads*. Here the author has summarised the esoteric teachings of each *Upaniṣad* in only single verse, composed by the author himself in *Sragdharā* metre. Thus there are in all twelve verses, first being benedictory and introductory and the last being concluding, giving details about the author and the work etc. In verses two to eleven, the secret of the following ten *Upaniṣads* is paraphrased (with slight change in sequence i.e. the *Muṇḍaka* is taken before the *Praśna*).

ईशकेनकठप्रश्नमुण्डमाण्डूक्यतित्तिरिः।
ऐतरेयं च छान्दोग्यं बृहदारण्यकं तथा।।

Another peculiarity of this work is that each verse is followed by *Svopajña Vṛtti*, written by the author himself, explaining secret, incorporated in each verse.

Verse 1—This is a benedictory and introductory verse. He first refers to his favourite deity Śrīrāma. It is imagined that Śrīrāma himself (actually the author's name is also Rāmacandra) summarizes and explains the secret of the ten *Upaniṣads* to Lakṣmaṇa, who has himself taken refuge at the feet of Rāma. He alone is qualified here for this *Vedāntaśāstra*, whose mind is purified by his own selfless deeds. After listening to the Upaniṣadic statements like *Tattvamasi* etc. from the mouth of his revered preceptor, he realizes the unity of his own self with the *Brahman* and becomes free from the cycle of birth and death and enjoys ever-lasting freedom.

Verse 2—The secret of the first viz. *Īśāvāsyopaniṣad* is given in this verse. The entire movable and immovable world appears like *rajjusarpa* on *Brahman* only, *Brahman* is within everything and outside everywhere. There is nothing in the world other than *Brahman*. It alone is there as a Puruṣa in the orb of the Sun. For him who has obtained this kind of wisdom through the grace of his preceptor, there is no craving for worldly objects (*tṛṣṇā*), doubt (*sandeho*), grief (*śoka*), infatuation (*moha*), fear, birth, old age or death.

Verse 3—The secret of the second *Upaniṣad* namely *Kena* is given here. The *Brahman* is the secret power. It is due to Its presence as *Ātman* that the mind, five *prāṇas,* sense organs like eyes, speech etc, become aware of or get knowledge of their own respective objects. Its nature cannot be said to be known and also not known. Even the Supreme Gods like Indra etc. could not comprehend its asoteric power. One who has realized such *Brahman*, obtains everlasting happiness.

Verse 4—The secret of the third *Upaniṣad*, namely the *Kaṭha* is given in this verse. The *Brahman* is minute than the minutest and greater than the greatest. It cannot be comprehended by any external means or even by the intellect. The *Brahman* resides in the intellect and is bodyless. Even the sun, the moon, and the fire shine due to its brilliance. It is bereft of all the six *bhāvavikāras*=modifications of objects and can be known by disciple only in the form of 'Existence'. A wise person, having actually comprehended the *Brahman*, through the teaching of the preceptor, obtains everlasting peace and tranquillity.

Verse 5—The essence of the fourth *Muṇḍaka Upaniṣad* is sumarised here. Just as the sparks of similar nature spring forth from the burning fire, similarly all objects come out of *Brahman* and dissolve into it. The *Brahman* is not a *Prāṇa* but is a knower of everything. *Praṇava* or *Oṅkāra* is the bow, individual soul is the arrow—both having the identical target i.e. *Brahman*. Having known the *Brahman*, one relinquishes the world of name and form and being bereft of grief, becomes one with the *Brahman*.

Verse 6—In this verse, the quintessence of the fifth-*Praśna Upaniśad* is expounded—All the sixteen *Kalās* namely *Prāṇa* (vital air), *Śraddhā* (faith), ether, air, fire, water, earth, organs, mind, food, vitaltity, penance, *Vedas, Karma*, worlds and name have originated from the *Brahman* and they all dissolve into it. The *Brahman* is the support of all. Having known the *Brahman*, one becomes free from death.

Verse 7—The gist of the *Māṇḍūkya Upaniṣad* is as follows—The waking condition, dream and deep sleep all these three are the modifications of the intellect *(mati)* but the fourth is beyond that. The *Brahman* is observer(*sākṣī*) of all of them and is devoid of qualities and impurities. Though having different appellations, the *Brahman* is the first and foremost of all the created elements, Unthinkable, the only inner soul of the entire world. The *Brahman* can be known through the *Oṅkāra*. One who has known the *Brahman*, becomes one with the *Brahman*.

Verse 8—The *Taittirīyopaniṣad* is summarised in this verse—The *Brahman* creates the entire movable and immoveable world (wherein *ākāśa*, the ether, is the first and body is the last product) and enters into and resides in it. The *Brahman* is the Lord and controller of everything. It is one and *Saccidānandarūpa* (existence, consciousness and bliss as its form). Through the advice of the preceptor, one should discriminate the *Brahman* as different from but underlying inner soul of all the sheaths beginning from the *Annamaya* etc. One who recognizes the *Brahman*, becomes very content, free from danger and all-pervading like the *Brahman*.

Verse 9—The eighth *Aitareyopaniṣad* is summarized in this verse. The Lord first creates the worlds, Lord of worlds, and all the objects of enjoyment and then enters them. He instigates everything that is movable and immovable, being inside it. One who comprehends that there is nothing else except the *Brahman*, which is one without a second and the basis of the entire world and which is consciousness itself (*prajñāna*), becomes immortal, having fulfilled all his desires.

Verse 10—The secret teaching of the *Chāndogyopaniṣad* is paraphrased in this verse. Just as by understanding the nature of clay, which is the material cause, we can know the other things like the pot, the jar etc., which are its products, similarly one should realize the *Brahman*, being constantly guided by preceptor as '*tattvamasi*'—"thou art that." This entire world, beginning from the *ākāśa* (the ether), is the *Brahman* only. One who knows that 'I am that *Brahman* and all this is not different from me,' becomes *Brahman* only and not the one, who is knower of *Brahman*.

Verse 11—The secret of the tenth and the last *Upaniṣad* i.e. the *Bṛhadāraṇyka Upaniṣad* is explained in this verse—A variety of pleasures or happiness that the living beings enjoy is merely the smallest unit (*mātrā*) of the Bliss of the *Brahman*. The world of name and form that was unmanifest before the creation has been made manifest by the lord. The *Brahman* is inner soul of everthing and controller of organs (*Hṛṣīkeśa*). This is known from the *Upaniṣad*. The *Brahman* is also all-pervading. One who knows that *'aham brahmāsmi'* 'I am *Brahman*', is absorbed in *Brahman* and his *Prāṇas* (vital breaths) do not transmigrate; they are absorbed into *Brahman* only.

Verse 12—The author concludes the work with this verse which gives important information about the author and the work. Thus Rāmacandra Paṇḍita, who is the son of Siddheśvara has composed this work in ten verses, giving the secret of ten *Upaniṣads*. Having comprehended its meaning, one who reads it, enjoys happiness through the grace of good preceptor.

Concluding Remarks

Thus we can get in a nutshell of ten verses the summary of all the ten *Upaniṣads*. This reflects upon the profound scholarship and mastery over prosody of the author. His commentary on each verse is interspersed with the citations from various authorities like the *Bhagavadgīta*, *Tāpanīyopaniṣad*, *Śruti*, *Śrirāmagītā*, *Bhagavatpāda* i.e. Śaṅkarācārya, *Aparokṣānubhūti*, *Ātharvaṇa Śruti*, *Bhāgavata*, *Muṇḍaka Upa.*, *Iśāvāsyopaniṣad, Śrīrāmahṛdaya, Praśnopaniṣad, Kāṭhaka Upaniṣad* etc. From the text and the commentary, it appears that the author had great inclination towards *Śāṅkarasiddhānta*. Owing to scarcity of time and space, it was not possible for me to go deep into the explanation and study of each verse. I, therefore, give herewith this article the entire text of the *Daśopaniṣadrahasya* along with author's commentary for the perusal of the world of scholars, who can better enjoy the greatness of the composition by going through the original.

दशोपनिषद्रहस्यम्।

सविवृति

(श्रीमत्सिद्धेश्वरसूनुश्रीमद्रामचन्द्रपण्डितविरचितम्।)

श्रीगुरुराड्विजयतेतराम्।

श्रीरामो लक्ष्मणाय स्वचरणशरणयोच एतद्रहस्यं
निष्कामैः कर्मभिः स्वैर्भवति शुचिमनो यस्य सोऽत्राधिकारी।
प्राप्य श्रीदैशिकास्याच्छ्रुतिशिर उदितैस्तत्त्वमस्यादिवाक्यैः
स्वात्मब्रह्मैक्यबोधं जनिमृतिरहितो मोदते नित्यमुक्तः।।1।।

श्रीमत्सच्चिदानन्दस्वरूपिश्रीमद्गुरुभ्यो नमः। श्रीराम इति– श्रीमद्-**भगवत्पाद**प्रणीतेषु ग्रन्थेषु श्रीदैशिकोक्तश्रुतिशिरोजन्यापरोक्षज्ञानस्यैव मुक्तिसाधन-त्वोक्तेः समस्तोपनिषदर्थविचारणाशक्तस्य विज्ञानोपयोगिदशोपनिषत्तात्पर्यबु-बोधिषया दशोपनिषद्रहस्यं दशश्लोकै रचयितुमिच्छू **रामचन्द्र**शर्मा श्रीरामाख्य-स्वेष्टदेवतानामनिर्देशात्मकं मङ्गलं कुर्वन् वक्ष्यमाणविषयं सूचयति–श्रीराम इति। श्रीर्विद्यात्मिका स्वशक्तिस्तया युक्तो रामो ब्रह्म–

"रमन्ते योगिनोऽनन्ते नित्यानन्दचिदात्मनि।
इति रामपदेनासौ परं ब्रह्माभिधीयते।।"

इति **तापनीयोक्तेः** (श्रीरामपूर्वतापिन्युपषत् 1.6) तस्य च स्वेच्छयैवालुप्त-ज्ञानैश्वर्यादिशक्तेराविर्भाव एवावतारः।

"अजोऽपि सन्नव्ययात्मा भूतानामीश्वरोऽपि सन्।
प्रकृतिं स्वामधिष्ठाय संभवाम्यात्ममायया।।"

इति भगवदुक्तेः (भ.गी. 4.6)।

स्वचरणशरणाय निजचरणयोः शरणाय प्रतिपन्नाय। अनेन स्वशरणं विना रहस्यं न वक्तव्यमिति ध्वनितम्। लक्ष्मणाय सौमित्रये। एतद्वक्ष्यमाणं रहस्यं

गुह्यं ऊचे ऊक्तवान्। एतत्किम्? निष्कामैः कामनारहितैः स्ववर्णाश्रमोदितैर्भगवदर्पितैः कर्मभिर्यस्य मनोऽन्तःकरणं शुचि शुद्धं भवति। स शुद्धचित्तः साधनचतुष्टयसंपन्नोऽत्र ज्ञानोपदेशेऽधिकारी। 'अविद्यया मृत्युं तीर्त्वा विद्ययामृतमश्नुते' इति श्रुतेः (ईशा. उप. 11) अविद्यया कर्मणा मृत्युं चित्तमलं तीर्त्वा दूरीकृत्य विद्यया ज्ञानेनामृतं मोक्षमश्नुते प्राप्नोतीत्यर्थः।

"तस्मादसक्तः सततं कार्यं कर्म समाचर।
असक्तो ह्याचरन्कर्म परमाप्नोति पूरुषः।।"

इति **भगवदुक्तेः** (भ.गी. 3.19)

कार्यमवश्यकर्तव्यं नित्यं नैमित्तिकं चासक्तः फलासक्तिरहितः सन्सततं तत्तत्काले सम्यग्यथाविध्याचर निष्कामः सन्कर्म कुर्वंश्चित्तशुद्धिद्वारा परं परमात्मानमाप्नोति न तु कर्मफलैर्बध्यते। कर्मणां चित्तशुद्धिहेतुत्वं **श्रीरामगीतायामभिहितम्।** (अध्यात्मरामा. 7.5.7)—

"आदौ स्ववर्णाश्रमवर्णिताः क्रियाः कृत्वा समासादितशुद्धमानसः।
समाप्य तत्पूर्वमुपात्तसाधनः समाश्रयेत्सद्गुरुमात्मलब्धये।। इति।

भगवत्पादैश्चैवमेवोक्तम्—

स्ववर्णाश्रमधर्मेण तपसा हरितोषणात्।

साधनं प्रभवेत्पुंसां वैराग्यादिचतुष्टयम्।। (अपरोक्षानुभूतिः 3) इति। 1. वैराग्यं, 2. विवेकः, 3. शमो दम उपरतिस्तितिक्षा श्रद्धा समाधानमिति षट्, 4 मुमुक्षुत्वं चेति साधनचतुष्टयम्। एतेषां लक्षणान्यपरोक्षानुभूत्यां द्रष्टव्यानि। सोऽधिकारी पुरुषः श्रीदैशिकास्यात् श्रीर्मोक्षसंपत्, तद्युक्तो देशिकः सद्गुरुस्तस्यास्यान्मुखकमलाद्गुरुवचनेनैववापरोक्षबोध इति भावः। उक्तं **चाथर्वणश्रुतौ**— तद्विज्ञानार्थं स गुरुमेवाभिगच्छेत्समित्पाणिः श्रोत्रियं ब्रह्मनिष्ठम्' (मुण्ड. उ. 1.2.12) इति। वेदशास्त्रार्थज्ञं ब्रह्मणि निष्ठा तात्पर्येण स्थितिर्यस्य तमपरोक्षसाक्षात्कारवन्तमित्यर्थः। **गीतायां** च— 'उपदेक्ष्यन्ति ते ज्ञानं ज्ञानिनस्तत्त्वदर्शिनः' (भ.गी. 4.3.4) इति। **भागवतेऽपि**— "तस्माद्गुरुं प्रपद्येत जिज्ञासुः श्रेय उत्तमम्। शाब्दे परे च निष्णातं ब्रह्मण्युपशमाश्रयम्।। (भा.पु. 11.4.21) इति। श्रुतिशिरःसूपनिषत्सूदितैः प्रोक्तैस्तत्त्वमस्यादिवाक्यैः 'तत्त्वमसि' (छां. 6.8.7) इत्यादि प्रमुखं येषां तैरादिशब्देन 'अहं ब्रह्मास्मि' (बृह.

1.4.10) इत्यादिवाक्यैर्महावाक्यैः स्वात्मब्रह्मैक्यबोधं स्वात्मा प्रत्यगात्मा ब्रह्म सच्चिदानन्दं जगदुत्पत्त्यादिहेतुभूतं तयोरैक्यमभेदस्तस्य बोधोऽहं ब्रह्मास्मीत्यपरोक्षसाक्षात्कारस्तं प्राप्य जनिमृतिरहितो जनिर्जन्म मृतिर्मरणं ताभ्यां रहितो वियुक्तोऽत एव नित्यमुक्तो द्वैतसम्बन्धशून्यः सन्मोदते। सहजनिजानन्दवान् भवति। 'स यो ह वै तत्परमं ब्रह्म वेद ब्रह्मैव भवति'...... 'तरति शोकम्' इति **मुण्डकश्रुतेः** (3.2.9) 'तत्र को मोहः कः शोक एकत्वमनुपश्यतः' इति **ईशावास्यश्रुतेश्च** (ईश. उप. 7)।

श्रीरामगीतायां च—"श्रद्धान्वितस्तत्त्वमसीति वाक्यतो गुरोः प्रसादादपि शुद्धमानसः।
विज्ञाय चैकात्म्यमथात्मजीवयोः सुखीभवेन्मेरुरिवाप्रकम्पनः'।
(अध्यात्मरामा. 7.5.24) इति।

श्रीरामहृदयेऽपि— "ऐक्यज्ञानं यदोत्पन्नं महावाक्येन चात्मनोः।
तदाविद्या स्वकार्यैश्च नश्यत्येव न संशयः।।"
(अध्यात्मरामा. 1.1.50) इति।

भगवद्गीतायामपि—"इदं ज्ञानमुपाश्रित्य मम साधर्म्यमागताः।
सर्गेऽपि नोपजायन्ते प्रलये न व्यथन्ति च।।" (14.2) इति-

अनेनोपनिषदुक्तज्ञानमेव मुक्तिसाधनमिति बोधितम्। तात्पर्येणानुबन्धचतुष्टयं च सूचितम्। अधिकारी त्वोक्त एव। विषय उपनिषत्प्रतिपाद्यं स्वात्मब्रह्मैक्यं संबन्धः। विषयस्य शब्दानां च प्रतिपाद्यप्रतिपादकभावः। बोधस्य मुक्तेश्च जन्यजनकभावोऽपि। प्रयोजनं निरतिशयानन्दावाप्तिरिति। एवमेव प्रतिश्लोकं बुद्ध्या विभावनीयम्।।1।।

श्रीगुरुः।

सत्ये मय्येव भातं चरमचरमतोऽन्तर्बहिश्चाहमेको
मत्तोऽन्यन्नास्ति किंचिज्जगदपि सवितुर्मण्डले पूरुषोऽहम्।
इत्थं यस्य प्रबोधो गुरुवरकरुणापाङ्गतस्तस्य तृष्णा
संदेहो मोहशोकौ भयजननजरामृत्यवो नैव सन्ति।।2।।

अथ **ईशोपनिषद्रहस्यमाह**— सत्य इति। सत्ये कालत्रयाबाधितेऽधिष्ठान-

ब्रह्मरूपे मयि प्रत्यगात्मन्येव चरं जङ्गममचरं स्थावरमुभयात्मकमखिलं जगद्रज्जौ सर्पधारादण्डादिविकल्पजातवत्, किरणेषु मृगजलवच्च भ्रान्तं मिथ्याभासविषयम्। अतः कारणादस्य जगतोऽन्तर्बहिश्चाहमेक एव सर्पादिविवर्तजालस्याधिष्ठान-भूतरज्जुवत्, मृगजलपूरस्य किरणवच्च। अत एव प्रत्यगात्मनो ब्रह्मरूपादधिष्ठानादन्यद्भिन्नं किंचिदल्पमपि जगद्विवर्तरूपं नास्ति रज्वादेः सर्पवत्। 'ईशावास्यमिदं सर्वं यत्किंच जगत्यां जगत्" (ईश. उप 1) ईश्वरेणाधिष्ठानेन मया प्रत्यगात्मना ज्ञाते नेदमखिलं जगद्विवर्तरूपमाच्छादनीयं नामरूपत्यागेनात्म-भावनया निरात्मकं भवति। किरणैर्ज्ञातैर्मृगजलमिव किरणभावनया भासमानं पूरतरङ्गादिनामरूपत्यागेनेति। पुनश्च—

"तदेजति तन्नैजति तद्दूरे तद्वन्तिके।
तदन्तरस्य सर्वस्य तदु सर्वस्यास्य बाह्यतः।।" (ईशा. उप. 5)

दूरस्थं समीपस्थं स्थावरजङ्गमं सर्वं भासमानमधिष्ठानब्रह्मरूपं सर्वस्यान्तर्बहिश्च ब्रह्मैवेति। तथा "यस्मिन्सर्वाणि भूतान्यात्मैवाभूद्विजानतः।" (ईशा. उप. 7) अत्र सर्वभूतानां स्वात्मव्यतिरिक्तत्वाभावेन सर्वात्मत्वमेव प्रतिपादितम्। किं च सवितुः सूर्यस्य मण्डले प्रकाशके बिम्बे पूरुषः पुरिशयनादन्तर्याम्यहं प्रत्यगात्मब्रह्मरूपोऽस्मि—"योऽसावादित्ये पुरुषः सोऽसा-वहम्" (ईशा. उप. 17) गीतायां च—"यदादित्यगतं तेजो जगद्भासयतेऽ-खिलम्। "यच्चन्द्रमसि यच्चाग्नौ तत्तेजो विद्धि मामकम्।।" (15.12) इति। इत्थं पूर्वोक्तप्रकारेण गुरुवरकरुणापाङ्गतो गुरुवरस्य श्रीसद्गुरोः करुणा कृपा तद्युक्तोऽपाङ्गो दृक्पातः। ततस्तेन सार्वविभक्तिकस्तसिः। यस्य पुरुषस्य प्रबोधोऽपरोक्षसाक्षात्कारोऽस्ति। तस्य फलं तस्य पुरुषस्य तृष्णा संदेहो मोहशोकौ भयजननजरामृत्यवो नैव सन्ति। तृष्णा विषयगृद्धिर्नैव। स्वातिरिक्तस्य विषयस्याभावात्। 'मा गृधः कस्यस्विद्धनम्' (ईशा. उप. 1) इत्युक्तत्वात्। संदेह उभयकोटिकं ज्ञानं, न । द्वैताभावात्। तदुक्तं—'ततो न विचिकित्सते(ति)' (ईशा. उप. 6) इति। शोकमोहौ विक्षेपावरणरूपौ न स्तः। अविद्यया नष्टत्वात्। उक्तं च—'तत्र को मोहः कः शोक एकत्वमनुपश्यतः' (ईशा. उप. 7) इति। अत एव द्वितीयत्वाभावाद्भयं भीतिर्नास्ति। 'द्वितीयाद्वै भयं भवति' (बृ. उ. 1. 4. 2) इति। जननं जन्मजरारोगादिजन्यं कार्श्यं मृत्युर्मरणम्। एते देहधर्मा नैव सन्ति। 'अकायमव्रणमस्नाविरम्'(ईशा. उप.

8) इति ब्रह्मणो देहद्वयाभावोक्तेः। ब्रह्मविदो ब्रह्मरूपत्वात्। सत्यत्वमेकत्वं स्वप्रकाशत्वं च स्वस्यानुभवतो द्वैतजन्यदोषसंपर्काभावान्निर्विकारत्वं सहजसिद्धमिति भावः।।2।।

> **स्वान्तःप्राणाक्षिवाणीप्रभृति च विषयाभासकं यस्य योगाद्**
> **यन्न प्राप्नोति चैतद्विदितमविदितं यद्भवेन्नात्मरूपम्।**
> **इन्द्राद्या देवमुख्या अपि किल न विदुर्यस्य शक्तिं निगूढां**
> **तद्बुद्धं येन सोऽसौ भवति नरवरोऽनन्तसौख्यप्रतिष्ठः।।2।।**

अथ **केनोपनिषद्रहस्यमाह**— स्वान्तःप्राणाक्षिवाणीप्रभृति स्वान्तं मनः पञ्चप्रवृत्तिर्वायुश्च। अक्षि नेत्रं वाणी वाक्। उभयं प्रभृत्यादिभूतं यस्य तत् चक्षुरादिज्ञानेन्द्रियपञ्चकं च यस्यात्मरूपस्य योगात्संबन्धात्। विषयाभासकं स्वस्वविषयोद्बोधकं भवति। मनसः संकल्पो, वायोः प्राणनादि, चक्षुरादीनां रूपग्राहकत्वं, वागादीनामुक्त्यादिक्रिया च यत्संबन्धितया भवति। 'श्रोत्रस्य श्रोत्रं मनसो मनो यद्वाचो ह वाचं स उ प्राणास्य प्राणश्च चक्षुषश्चक्षुः'। (केन.उप. 1.2) इति। श्रोत्रस्य शब्दग्राहकत्वं, मनसः संकल्पाध्यवसायसामर्थ्यं, वाचः शब्दोच्चरणं, प्राणस्य प्राणनशक्तिः, चक्षुषः रूपावभासकत्वं, ब्रह्मचैतन्याश्रयेणेति भावः। 'येन वागभ्युद्यते', 'येनाहुर्मनो मतं', 'येन चक्षूंषि पश्यति', 'येन श्रोत्रमिदं श्रुतं', 'येन प्राणः प्रणीयते', 'तदेव ब्रह्म त्वं विद्धि' (केन. उप. 1.4.8) इति च। वागिति कर्मेन्द्रियाणामुपलक्षणम्। चक्षुः श्रोत्रमिति ज्ञानेन्द्रियाणां सर्वस्यैव करणगणस्य यदर्थप्रयुक्ता प्रवृत्तिस्तद्ब्रह्मेति तात्पर्यम्। एतच्च स्वान्तादिकरणवृन्दं तु यदात्मरूपं न प्राप्नोति, न विषयी-करोति—'न तत्र चक्षुर्गच्छति, न वागगच्छति, नो मन' (केन. उप. 1.3) इति। 'यद्वाचानभ्युदितं' 'यन्मनसा न मनुते' 'यच्चक्षुषा न पश्यति' 'यच्छ्रोत्रेण न शृणोति,' 'यत्प्राणेन न प्राणिति' (केन. उप. 1.4.8) इति च करण-समुदायस्यागोचरमित्यभिप्रायः। यदात्मरूपं मनस इन्द्रियाणां चागोचरत्वाद्विदितं ज्ञातं न भवेत्, यदविदितं तज्जानामीतीच्छा जायते। आत्मरूपस्य तु त्विदं प्रत्ययागोचरत्वे सत्यहं प्रत्ययगोचरत्वात्प्रत्यक्त्वेन जिज्ञासा नोत्पद्यते। अतोऽविदितं च न भवति। 'अन्यदेव तद्विदितादथो अविदितादधि' (केन. उप. 1.3) इत्युक्तत्वात्। इन्द्राद्या इन्द्रप्रमुखा देवमुख्याः सुरश्रेष्ठा अपि यस्य निगूढां नितरां गूढां गुप्तामविज्ञेयां शक्तिं सामर्थ्यं न विदुः। किल

प्रसिद्धमितिहासेषु। अत्रेयमेतदुपनिषदुक्ताख्यायिका। ब्रह्म सामर्थ्येन धर्मविरोधिनोऽसुरान्पराभूय देवेभ्यो जयं दत्तवत्। देवास्तदविज्ञायास्माकमेवायं महिमेत्यभिमानिनो बभूवुः। तेषामभिप्रायं विदित्वा ब्रह्म तेषां दृष्टिपथे तेजोरूपं प्रादुर्बभूव। तत्किमित्यज्ञात्वा देवाश्चकिताः सन्तस्तज्जिज्ञासायाग्निं प्रेषयायासुः। स तत्समीपे गतः। ब्रह्मणा कस्त्वं किं ते सामर्थ्यमिति पृष्टोऽग्निरहं सकल-दाहनशक्तिर्ममेत्युवाच। ब्रह्मणा तृणेऽग्रतः स्थापिते तद्दग्धुमशक्तो व्रीडितः सन् तदविज्ञाय देवान्प्रत्याजगाम। एकमेव वायुर्गत्वा तेन पृष्टो वायुरहं सकलादानशक्तिर्मे इत्युक्त्वा तेनाग्रे स्थापिततृणमादातुमशक्तस्तथैव प्रत्याययौ। तत इन्द्रं प्रेरयामासुः। स यावत्समीपे गच्छति, तावत्तत्तिरोभूतम्। स तस्मिन्नेव प्रदेशे तज्जिज्ञासया तस्थौ। तत्कृपया विद्यात्मिका तच्छक्तिः स्त्रीरूपधारिणी तद्दृष्टिपथे प्रादुर्बभूव। तमिन्द्रोऽपृच्छत्— अस्मद्दृष्टिपथे प्रादुर्भूय तिरोहितं किमेतदिति। तं विद्या प्रोवाच। ब्रह्मेदमेतन्महिम्नैव भवतां विजय इति। तत इन्द्रेण ज्ञातम्। तज्ज्ञानादेवेन्द्रस्य सुरश्रेष्ठत्वमिति। तद्ब्रह्म येन पुरुषेण बुद्धं साक्षात्कृतं सोऽसौ दुर्लभो नरवरः पुरुषश्रेष्ठोऽनन्तेऽपरिमिते सौख्ये सहजनिजानन्दे प्रतिष्ठा स्थितिर्यस्य एवंभूतो भवति। 'अपहत्य पाप्मानमनन्ते स्वर्गे लोके ज्येये प्रतितिष्ठति प्रतितिष्ठति' (केन. उप. 4.9) इत्युक्तत्वात्। पाप्मानम-विद्याकामकर्मलक्षणं संसारबीजमपहत्य विधूयानन्तेऽपरिमिते स्वर्गे सुखात्मके लोक आत्मनि ज्येये सर्वश्रेष्ठे प्रतितिष्ठति प्रतिष्ठां प्राप्नोति। न पुनः संसारदुःखमापद्यत इत्यर्थः। ब्रह्मापरोक्षत्वं विना निरतिशयानन्दप्राप्तिर्नेति व्यङ्ग्यम्।।3।। श्रीः।।

सूक्ष्मात्सूक्ष्मो महीयान्महत उत धिया साधनैर्यो न लभ्यो
बुद्धिस्थो योऽशरीरो रविविधुदहना यस्य भासा विभान्ति।
षड्भिर्भावस्वभावै रहित उपसदास्तीतिरूपेण वेद्य-
स्तं साक्षात्कृत्य धीरो गुरुवचनबलाज्जायते नित्यशान्तः।।4।।

अथ **कठवल्ल्युपनिषद्रहस्यमाह**— य आत्मा सूक्ष्मादणुपरिमाणाद् वालाग्रादेरपि सूक्ष्मोऽणीयान्। महतो महत्परिमाणादाकाशादेरपि महीयान्महत्तरः। तदुक्तं-'अणोरणीयान्महतो महीयान्' (कठ. उप. 1.2.20) इति। धिया कुशाग्रबुद्ध्या साधनैः प्रवचनादिभिरुतापि यो न लभ्योऽप्राप्यः। 'नायमात्मा प्रवचनेन लभ्यो न मेधया न बहुना श्रुतेन' (कठ. उप. 1.2.23) इत्युक्तत्वात्।

प्रवचनेनोपनिषदादिपठनेन बहुना श्रुतेनानेकशास्त्राध्ययनेनेत्यर्थः। तर्हि दूरस्थः स्यान्नेत्यत आह–बुद्धिस्थो बुद्धौ हृदये स्थितोऽन्तरात्मा। 'आत्मास्य जन्तोर्निहितो गुहायाम्' (कठ. उप. 1.2.20) इत्युक्तेः। जन्तोः प्राणिनः। गुहायां बुद्धौ निहितः प्रविष्ट इत्यर्थः। अशरीरो देहद्वयशून्यः। यदुक्तम्—'अशरीरं शरीरेष्वनवस्थेष्ववस्थितम् (कठ. उप. 1.2.22) इति। अनवस्थेष्वनित्येषु शरीरेषु देवतिर्यगादिष्वशरीरं शरीरद्वयरहितमवस्थितं नित्यतयाविकृतरूपेण स्थितमित्यर्थः। रविविधुदहना सूर्यचन्द्राग्नयः। यस्यात्मनो भासा दीप्त्या विभान्ति। पदार्थप्रकाशका भवन्ति। तदुक्तं—'तमेव भान्तमनुभाति सर्वं, तस्य भासा सर्वमिदं विभाति (कठ. उप. 2.2.15)। भान्तं दीप्यमानं तं परमेश्वरमेवानुसृत्य सर्वं सूर्यादि विभाति दीप्यते। यथा जलोल्मुकाद्यग्नि-संयोगादग्निं दहन्तमनुदहति। तद्वत्। शेषं स्पष्टम्। अशरीरत्वादेव षड्भिः षट्संख्याकैर्भावस्वभावैर्भावानां पदार्थानां स्वभावैर्जायतेऽस्ति वर्धते विपरिणमतेऽपक्षीयते विनश्यतीति विकारै रहितो वियुक्तः। उक्तं च—"न जायते म्रियते वा विपश्चिन्नायं कुतश्चिन्न बभूव कश्चित्। अजो नित्यः शाश्वतोऽयं पुराणो न हन्यते हन्यमाने शरीरे।।" (कठ. उप. 1.2.19)। न जायते म्रियते वेत्यनेनाद्यन्तयोर्विकारयोः प्रतिषेधः। विपश्चिदपरिप्लुतस्वभावः। कुतश्चित्कारणान्न बभूव नोत्पन्नः। सर्वस्यादि- भूतत्वादस्माच्चान्यः कश्चिन्न बभूव।सर्वस्यापि विवर्तत्वेन स्वतः सत्त्वात्। अजो यो हि जायते, स जन्मान्तरमस्तित्वं भजते। अनेन द्वितीयविकारप्रतिषेधः। नित्योऽविचलितस्वभावः। अनेन चतुर्थविकार-प्रतिषेधः। शाश्वतः शश्वद्भवः। सर्वदैकरूपः। अनेन पञ्चमविकारप्रतिषेधः। पुराणः पुरापि नव एव न त्ववयवोपचयद्वारेणाभिनिर्वर्त्यते। अनेन तृतीयविकार-प्रतिषेधः। शरीरे शस्त्रादिभिश्छेद्यमाने सत्यत एव न हिंस्यत इत्यर्थः। गीतायां च—

न जायते म्रियते वा कदाचिन्नायं भूत्वा भविता वा न भूयः।
अजो नित्यः शाश्वतोऽयं पुराणो न हन्यते हन्यमाने शरीरे।।

(भ.गी. 2. 20)

कदाचित् कल्पादौ न जायते। कल्पान्तेऽपि न म्रियते। भूत्वोत्पद्यमानो भवितास्तित्वाश्रयो न। किं तु प्रागेव स्वतः सद्रूपः। अत्रैवाज इति हेतुत्वेन योज्यम्। शेषमुक्तार्थम्। उप समीपे हृदय एव सदावस्थात्रयेऽस्तीति रूपेण

विद्यमानत्वेन वेद्यो ज्ञेयः। एकस्यैवावस्थात्रयानुभवितृत्वादस्तित्वं सिद्धम्। तदुक्तम्—'अस्तीत्येवोपलब्धव्यः' (कठ. उप. 2.3.13) इति। अन्यथा तदधिगमानुपपत्तेः। बुद्ध्यादीनामविषयत्वात्। 'नैव वाचा न मनसा प्राप्तुं शक्यो, न चक्षुषा' (कठ. उप. 2.3.12) इत्युक्तेः। अथवोपसदोपसदनमुपस-त्संपदादित्वाद्भावे क्विप्। गुरूपसत्त्येत्यर्थः। गुरुवचनबलाद्गुरुवचनसामर्थ्येन। हेत्वर्थे पञ्चमी। तत्पूर्वोक्तमात्मानं साक्षात्कृत्यापरोक्षत्वेनाहमित्यनुभूय। उक्तं च—'न नरेणावरेणावर प्रोक्त एष सुविज्ञेयो बहुधा चिन्त्यमानः। अनन्यप्रोक्ते गतिरत्र नास्ति' (कठ. उप. 1.2.8) इति। अवरेण हीनेन प्राकृतबुद्धिना प्रोक्त एष आत्मा बहुधानेकप्रकारेण नानामतस्थैश्चिन्त्यमान अत एव नरेण सुविज्ञेयो न भवति। कथं तर्हि ज्ञेयः। अनन्येनापृथग्दर्शिना ब्रह्मात्मभूतेनाचार्येण प्रोक्ते सत्याध्यात्मनि विषयेऽगतिरनवबोधो नास्ति। श्रोतुरात्मविषयोऽवबोधो भवत्येवे- त्यर्थः। धीरो द्वन्द्वानभिभूतः। अत एव नित्य शान्तोऽनवरतसहज-शान्तियुक्तो जायते संपद्यते। 'तमात्मस्थं येऽनुपश्यन्ति धीरास्तेषां शान्तिः शाश्वती नेतरेषाम्' (कठ. उप. 2.2.13) इत्युक्तत्वात्। बुद्धिस्थमात्मानं ये साक्षात्कुर्वन्ति तेषां शान्तिर्नित्या भवतीत्यर्थः। आत्मसाक्षात्कारवतः सहजनित्यशान्तत्वमनायास- सिद्धमित्यभिप्रायः।।4।।

जायन्ते विस्फुलिङ्गा अनलत इह यद्वत्प्रदीप्तात्सरूपा-
स्तद्वत्सर्वेऽपि भावा खलु यत उदिता यान्ति यस्मिँल्लयं ते।
अप्राणः सर्वविद्यः प्रणववरधनुः स्वात्मबाणैकलक्ष्य-
स्तं जानन्नत्मरूपे त्यजति स भवति ब्रह्मरूपो विशोकः।।5।।

अथ **मुण्डकोपनिषद्रहस्यमाह**— जायन्त इति-प्रदीप्तात्समिद्धादनलतो वह्नेः सकाशात्सरूपाः समानरूपाः प्रकाशात्मका विस्फुलिङ्गा अग्निकणा यद्वद्यथा जायन्त उत्पद्यन्ते, तद्वत्तथा सर्वेऽपि सरूपाश्चैतन्यात्मका जीवा विरूपाश्च जडा देहादयो भावाः पदार्थाः। खलु निश्चयेन यतोऽक्षरात्परमात्मनः सकाशादुदिता उत्पन्नाः सुवर्णात्कटकादिवद् भिन्ना इव भासन्ते। यस्मिन्परमात्मन्यन्ते लयं यान्ति। प्राप्नुवन्ति। सुवर्णे कारणे कटकादिकार्यमिव। तदुक्तं—

"यथा सुदीप्तात्पावकाद्विस्फुलिङ्गाः सहस्रशः प्रभवन्ते सरूपाः।
तथाक्षराद्विविधाः सौम्य भावाः प्रजायन्ते तत्र चैवापि यान्ति।।"

(मुण्ड. उप. 2.1.1) इति।

"यथोर्णनाभिः सृजते गृह्णते च यथा पृथिव्यामोषधयः संभवन्ति।
यथा सतः पुरुषात्केशलोमानि तथाक्षरात्संभवतीह विश्वम्।।

(मुण्ड. उप. 1.1.7)

इति च। ऊर्णनाभिर्लूताकीटः। किंचिदपि कारणान्तरमनपेक्ष्य स्वयमेव सृजते। स्वशरीराव्यतिरिक्तान्तन्तून् बहिः प्रसारयति। कारणान्तरमनपेक्ष्योत्पादकत्वे दृष्टान्तो यथा पृथिव्यामिति। सरूपोत्पत्तौ सतः जीवतः पुरुषात्केशलोमानीति तु विरूपोत्पत्तौ। यथा दृष्टान्तत्रयवदक्षराद्ब्रह्मणः विश्वं संभवति समुत्पद्यत इत्यर्थः। यः परमात्मा प्राणः। प्राणः पञ्चाद्वृत्तिर्वायुः। स यस्य नास्ति। प्राणस्याप्यात्मकार्यत्वात्। इदं मनसोऽप्युपलक्षणम्। तस्यापि तत्कार्यत्वात्। उक्तं च—'अप्राणो ह्यमनाः शुभ्रः' (मुण्ड. उप. 2.1.2) इति। शुभ्र उपाधिरहितः। तथा 'एतस्माज्जायते प्राणो मनः सर्वेन्द्रियाणि च' (मुण्ड. उप. 2.1.3) इति। प्राणादेरुत्पत्तेः प्रागविद्यमानत्वेन तत्कारणपरमात्मनस्तद्वत्त्वं न संभवतीत्यर्थः। यः सर्ववित्सर्वं समष्टिव्यष्टिरूपेण वेत्तीति। उक्तं च—'यः सर्वज्ञः सर्ववित्' (मुण्ड. उप. 2.2.7) इति। सामान्यरूपेण सर्वं जानाति। विशेषरूपेण सर्वं वेत्तीत्यर्थः। यः प्रणववरधनुः स्वात्मबाणैकलक्ष्यः। प्रणव ॐकार एव वरं श्रेष्ठं धनुः। लक्ष्ये शरस्य प्रवेशसाधनम्। स्वात्मा प्रत्यगात्मैव बाणः प्रवेशनीयः। तयोरेको लक्ष्यो वेध्यः। 'प्रणवो धनुः शरो ह्यात्मा ब्रह्म तल्लक्ष्यमुच्यते' (मुण्ड. उप. 2.2.4) इति।। तं जानन्—'अप्रमत्तेन वेद्धव्यं शरवत्तन्मयो भवेत्' (मुण्ड. उप. 2.2.4) इत्युक्तत्वात्। सावधानतया प्रणवोपासनया प्रत्यगात्मनो ब्रह्मणा परमात्मना ऐक्यमापद्य सोऽहमित्युनुभवन् नामरूपे नामाभिधानं रूपमाकृतिः। उभयमप्यविद्याकृतं त्यजत्युभयस्माद् विमुक्तोऽहमित्यात्मनोऽनिर्वाच्यत्वमनिर्देश्यत्वं च निश्चिनोति। स एवं विद्वान् पुरुषो ब्रह्मरूपो ब्रह्मात्मकः। अत एव विशोको द्वैतदुःखरहितो भवति। 'तथा विद्वान्नामरूपाद्विमुक्तः परात्परं पुरुषमुपैति दिव्यम्।' 'स यो ह वै तत् परमं ब्रह्म वेद ब्रह्मैव भवति'....'तरति शोकम्' (मुण्ड. 3.2.8-9) इत्युक्तत्वात्। ब्रह्मत्वं विना विशोकत्वं न भवतीति रहस्यम्।।5।।

प्राणः श्रद्धा खवायुज्वलनजलधरा इन्द्रियं मानसं च
भक्तं वीर्यं तपश्चाथ सकलनिगमाः कर्मलोकाश्च नाम।

यस्माज्जाताश्च यस्मिन्विलयमुपगताः षोडशैताः कला यः
सर्वेषां संप्रतिष्ठा खलु तदधिगमाज्जायते वीतमृत्युः।।6।।

अथ **प्रश्नोपनिषद्रहस्यमाह**— प्राण इति। **प्रश्नोपनिषदो** मन्त्रात्मकमुण्डकोपनिषद्विस्तरानुवादित्वात्तत्रानुक्तं विषयं संगृह्णाति। प्राण इति— प्राणो हिरण्यगर्भः सकलप्राणिकरणाधारः। श्रद्धाखिलप्राणिनां कर्मप्रवृत्तिहेतुभूता। खमाकाशं शब्दैकगुणम्। वायुः स्वकारणगुणेन शब्देन सह स्वीयासाधारणस्पर्शवान् द्विगुणः। ज्वलनस्तेजः स्वकारणगुणाभ्यां शब्दस्पर्शाभ्यां सह स्वकीयासाधारणरूपवत्त्रिगुणम्। जलं स्वकारणगुणैः शब्दस्पर्शरूपैः सह निजासाधारणरसगुणवच्चतुर्गुणम्। धरा पृथ्वी स्वकीयगुणैः शब्दस्पर्शरूपरसैः सहात्मीयासाधारणगन्धगुणवती पञ्चगुणा। इमानि पञ्चमहाभूतन्याकाशादीनि कर्मफलोपभोगसाधनानि। इन्द्रियं द्विप्रकारमिन्द्रियजातं ज्ञानेन्द्रियपञ्चकं कर्मेन्द्रियपञ्चकं चेति। इन्द्रियमिति जात्यभिप्रायेणैकवचनम्। मानसं द्विविधेन्द्रियप्रेरकमन्तः-करणम्। भक्तमन्नं प्राणिस्थित्यर्थं व्रीहियवादिलक्षणम्। वीर्यमन्नोपभोगजन्यं सर्वकर्मसाधनं सामर्थ्यम्। तपश्च मलवतां विशुद्धिसाधनम्। अथ तपोविशुद्धान्तःकरणानां कर्मसाधनभूताः सकलनिगमा ऋग्यजुःसामाथर्वाङ्गिरसः। कर्म निगमप्रतिपाद्यमग्निहोत्रादिलक्षणम्। लोकाः कर्मसाध्यफलभूताः। नाम च तेषु सृष्टानां प्राणिनां नाम देवदत्तो यज्ञदत्त इत्यादि। एतदात्मक एव सकलसंसारः। एताः षोडशकला अवयवाः कला इव कला यस्मादात्मनो जाता मध्याह्ने किरणेभ्यो मृगजलपूर इवात्मनः। यस्मिन्नात्मनि सायाह्ने किरणेषु मृगजलपूर इवान्ते विलयमुपगताः। स्थितिसमयेऽपि य आत्मा सर्वेषां पूर्वोक्तानां सकलपदार्थानां मृगजलपूरस्य किरणा इव संप्रतिष्ठा सम्यक्प्रतिष्ठन्तेऽस्यामिति संप्रतिष्ठा। साभासाधिष्ठानमनेन स्थित्युत्पत्तिप्रलयहेतुत्वं सूचितम्। तदधिगमात्तस्यात्मनोऽधिगमात् सोऽहमित्यपरोक्षानुभवात्। वीतमृत्युर्मरणरहितः। खलु निश्चयेन जायते। यदुक्तं— "प्राणामसृजत। प्राणाच्छ्रद्धां खं वायुर्ज्योतिरापः पृथिवीन्द्रियं मनोऽन्नमन्नाद्वीर्यं तपो मन्त्राः कर्मलोका लोकेषु च नाम च" (प्रश्न. उप. 6.4)। "अरा इव रथनाभौ कला यस्मिन् प्रतिष्ठिताः। तं वेद्यं पुरुषं वेद यथा मा वो मृत्युः परिव्यथा" (प्रश्न. उप. 6.6) इति च। रथचक्रस्याक्षप्रवेशयोग्ये सच्छिद्रे काष्ठे तिर्यक्काष्ठविशेषा यथा प्रवेशितास्तदाश्रयाः। तथा यस्मिन्नेकस्मिन् षोडशकलाः स्थित्युत्पत्तिप्रलयकालेषु

प्रतिष्ठितास्तदाश्रिताः सन्ति। तं वन्दनीयं पुरुषमात्मानं यथावज्जानीथ। युष्मान्मृत्युर्मा पीडयत्विति भावः। आत्मज्ञानं विनामरत्वं नास्तीत्यर्थः।

जाग्रत्स्वप्नः सुषुप्तिस्त्रितयमपि मतेस्तद्व्यपेक्षस्तुरीयः
सर्वेषां यस्तु साक्षी गुणमलरहितोऽप्यात्तनानाभिधानः।
भूताद्योऽचिन्त्य एकः स सकलजगतः प्रत्यगीशोऽयमात्मा
ब्रह्मोङ्काराधिगम्यं विदितमिति भवेद्येव स ब्रह्मभूतः॥7॥

अथ **माण्डूक्योपनिषद्रहस्यमाह**— जाग्रदिति–जाग्रज्जागरणमिन्द्रियैर्विषय-ग्रहणलक्षणम्। स्वप्नो जाग्रद्वासनाजन्यो मानसो विषयप्रत्ययः। सुषुप्तिर्बाह्यान्त-रिन्द्रियव्यापारशून्या तमोरूपावस्था। त्रितयमिदमवस्थात्रयं मतेः (m. gloss चिदाभासस्य) मतिसंबन्धिविकारः। वस्तुतो गुणाः सत्त्वरजस्तमांसि मायायास्त एव मलो दोषस्तेन रहितः। यद्यपि स्वयमसङ्गः। तथापि तद्व्यपेक्षो गुणत्रयकल्पितावस्थारूपस्थानत्रयसंख्याव्यपेक्षया तुरीयश्चतुर्थः। तुश्चार्थे। यः साक्षी द्रष्टा दृश्याद्भिन्नो यथा घटद्रष्टा घटाद्भिन्नः। अत एवात्तनानाभिधानः। आत्तानि स्वीकृतानि मायाकल्पितान्यवस्थासाक्षित्वानुसारीणि नानाभिधानानि क्रमेण विश्वतैजसप्राज्ञेति नामानि येन सः। तदुक्तं—'सोऽयमात्मा चतुष्पात्' (माण्डू. उप. 2) इत्यादि। जाग्रतः साक्षी विश्वः, स्वप्नस्य तेजसः, सुषुप्तस्य प्राज्ञः, तुरीयः परमात्मेति तात्पर्यम्। भूतानां सकलानां हिरण्यगर्भादीनामाद्यः कारणभूत (marg. gloss अधिष्ठानभूतः) एष योनिः सर्वस्येत्युक्तत्वात्। अचिन्त्यो मनसा चिन्तितुमशक्यः। इदमुपलक्षणम्। अव्यपदेशोभ्योऽपि शब्दप्रवृत्तेर्मनःप्रवृत्तिपूर्वकत्वात्। मनोऽविषयत्वादेव शब्दाविषयत्वमनिर्वाच्य इत्यर्थः। तदुक्तम्—'अचिन्त्यमव्यपदेश्यम्' (माण्डू. उप. 7) इति। एकः परस्परविलक्षणास्ववस्थास्वेकरूपः। उक्तं च 'एकात्मप्रत्ययसारम्' (माण्डू. उप. 7) इति। जाग्रदादिस्थानेष्वकोऽयमात्मेति यः प्रत्ययस्तेनानुसारिणीयमित्यर्थः। सकलजगतः सकलप्राणिजातस्य प्रत्यगीशः प्रत्यक् चासावीशश्च। प्रत्यगहमिति गोचरः। ईशो नियन्ता च सोऽयं च प्रत्यक्त्वेनानुभूयमान आत्मैव। 'ॐकाराधि-गम्यम्'

'एतदालम्बनं श्रेष्ठमेतदालम्बनं परम्। एतदालम्बनं ज्ञात्वा ब्रह्मलोके महीयते।' इति **काठके** (कठ. उप. 1.2.17) उक्तत्वात्। ॐकारस्य

ब्रह्मवाचकत्वेन ॐकारेण ॐकारोपासनया ॐकारावयवभूताकारोकारमकार-वाच्यानां विश्वतैजसप्राज्ञानां पूर्वपूर्वस्योत्तरोत्तरस्मिन् प्रविलापनेनात्मनि पर्यवसानेन तद्रूपत्वेनाधिगम्यं ज्ञेयं ब्रह्म इति। एवं ब्रह्मैक्यं येन पुरुषेण विदितं ब्रह्मैवाहमिति साक्षात्कृतं स नरो ब्रह्मभूतो ब्रह्मरूपो भवेत्। उक्तं च—'संविशत्यात्मनात्मानं य एवं वेद' (माण्डू. उप. 12) इति। य एवं पूर्वोक्तप्रकारेण पर्यवसितं ब्रह्म वेद स आत्मना त्यक्तोपाधिना स्वरूपेणात्मानं परमात्मानं सम्यग्विशति प्रविशति। तदैक्यमाप्नोतीत्यर्थः। अभेदोपासनां विना ब्रह्मभावो नास्तीति सिद्धान्तः।।7।।

स्पृष्ट्वाकाशादिदेहावधिसकलमिदं तत्प्रविश्यान्तरस्थो
यः सर्वेषामधीशो नियमयति सदानन्दचिद्रूप एकः।
अन्नादीन्पञ्चकोशान्निजगुरुवचसा संविविच्यात्मभूतं
तं विद्वान्नित्यतृप्तः किल भयरहितो वर्तते सर्वभूतः।।8।।

अथ **तैत्तिरीयोपनिषद्रहस्यमाह**— सृष्ट्वेति-यः परमात्मा सदानन्दचिद्रूपः सत् सत्यमानन्दः सुखं चिज्ज्ञानमेतानि रूपाणि लक्षणानि यस्य सः सद्रूप आनन्दरूपश्चिद्रूप एकोऽद्वितीयः सर्वाधिष्ठानम्। न च देशः कालो वस्तु वा तदतिरिक्तं किंचिदस्ति। अनेनानन्त इति बोध्यते। 'सत्यं ज्ञानमनन्तं ब्रह्म' (तैत्ति. उप. 2.1) इति। को ह्येवान्यात्कः प्राण्याद्यदेष आकाश आनन्दो न स्यात्' (तैत्ति. उप. 2.7) इति च। यद्यद्याकाशे हार्दाकाश एष आनन्द आत्मरूपो न स्यान्न भवेत्। तर्हि प्राणापानचेष्टां कः कुर्यात्। आकाशाद्याकाशो गगनमादिर्यस्य तद्देहोऽवधिरन्तो यस्य तत्सकलं चराचरात्मकमिदं जगत्सृष्ट्वो-त्पाद्य—"तस्माद्वा एतस्मादात्मन आकाशः संभूतः। आकाशाद्वायुर्वायोर-ग्निरग्नेरापोऽद्भ्यः पृथिवी पृथिव्या ओषधय ओषधीभ्योऽन्नमन्नात्पुरुषः" (तैत्ति. उप. 2.1) इति। सर्वेषां देहानां समत्वेऽपि ज्ञानकर्मणोरधिकृतत्वेन प्राधान्यात्पुरुष एव गृहीतः। सर्वेषां ब्रह्मादीनामुत्पन्नानामधीशः प्रभुर्यस्तद्विश्वं प्रविश्यान्तरे गुहायां बुद्धौ प्रकाशत्वेन स्थितः। अन्तर्यामी सन्नन्तःप्राणान्बहिश्च वाय्वादीन्नियमति व्यवस्थया वर्तयति। तदुक्तं—"तत्सृष्ट्वा तदेवानुप्राविशत्" (तैत्ति. उप. 2.6) इति। "यो वेद निहितं गुहायां परमे व्योमन्" (तैत्ति. उप. 2.1) इति च। "भीषास्माद्वातः पवते भीषोदेति सूर्यः। भीषास्मादग्निश्चेन्द्रश्च मृत्युर्धावति पञ्चमः।" (तैत्ति. उप. 2.8) इति च। भीषा भयेनेत्यर्थः।

निजगुरुवचसा स्वस्य गुरुर्मोक्षदस्तद्वचनेन वरुणवचनेन भृगुवदन्नादीन्नन्नमयप्राण-मयमनोमयविज्ञानमयानन्दमयनामकान् पञ्चपञ्चसंख्याकान् कोशान् कोशवन्निज-रूपावरकान्संविविच्य सम्यग्विचार्य, नाहमन्नमयो देहः कार्यत्वात्, नाहं प्राणमयो वायुर्जडत्वात्, नाहं मनोमयः कामक्रोधादिविकारत्वात्, नाहं विज्ञानमयो विलयाद्यवस्थावत्त्वान्, नाहमानन्दमयः सुषुप्तिकालिकत्वेन कादाचित्कत्वादिति विवेकेन पृथक्कृत्य, तं परमात्मानमात्मभूतं प्रत्यग्रूपं विद्वान् परमात्माहमिति जानन्पुरुषः परमात्मनो ब्रह्मणः सकलजगदधिष्ठानत्वेन तद्व्यतिरिक्तस्य पदार्थस्याभावात्तद्रूपत्वेन सर्वभूतः सकलात्मक अत एव नित्यतृप्तोऽवाप्य-विषयाभावादवाप्तकामो द्वितीयाभावाद्भयरहितः सन् वर्तते तिष्ठति। उक्तं च—"एतमन्नमयमात्मानमुपसंक्रम्य, एतं प्राणमयमात्मानमुपसंक्रम्य, एतं मनोमयमात्मानमुपसंक्रम्य, एतं विज्ञानमयमात्मानमुपक्रम्य, एतमानन्दमय-मात्मानमुपसंक्रम्य, इमांल्लोकान्कामान्नी कामरूप्यमनुसंचरन्नेतत्सामगायन्नास्ते हा 3 उ हा 3 उ हा 3 उ । अहमन्नमहमन्नमहमन्नम्। अहमन्नादोऽ-3हमन्नादोऽ3हमन्नादः। अह ꣳ श्लोककृदह ꣳ श्लोककृदह ꣳश्लोककृत्। अहमस्मि प्रथमजा ऋता3स्य। पूर्वं देवेभ्योऽमृतस्य ना3माई (भायि)" (तैत्ति. उप. 3.10.5-6)। पूर्वोक्तक्रमेण पञ्चकोशानविद्याकल्पिताननात्मत्वेन विज्ञाय त्यक्त्वा निर्विकल्पमात्मानमनुभूय सार्ववर्णिकभैक्ष्यमाचरन् चेच्छावेश-धार्यनेकभूतप्रदेशान् पर्यटन्नात्मैकत्वविज्ञानफलं सर्वात्मत्वं लोकानुग्रहार्थं प्रख्यापयन्नाश्चर्यबोधकं हा3शब्दमुच्चार्य अहमन्नमहमन्नादश्च सैन्यसंघातकर्ता राजाथवा काव्यादिप्रबन्धकर्ता च मूर्तामूर्तात्मकस्य जगतः प्रथमजो हिरण्यगर्भश्च देवेभ्यः पूर्वं विद्यमानः। यदङ्गेभ्यो देवा उत्पन्नाः स विराट् च प्राणिनाममृतत्वस्याश्रयश्चाहमिति सर्वात्मबोधकान् छन्दानुच्चारयन्तिष्ठतीति तात्पर्यम्। सर्वत्र त्रिरुक्तिर्विस्मयख्यापनार्था। 'रस ꣳ ह्येवायं लब्ध्वानन्दी भवति' (तैत्ति. उप. 2.7) इति च। रसं ब्रह्मरूपं लब्ध्वा प्राप्यानुभूय, सहजनिरतिशयानन्दवान् भवति। ब्रह्मानन्दे सर्वानन्दानामन्तर्भावाद्विषय-जन्यसुखेच्छाया अभावान्नित्यतृप्त इत्यभिप्रायः। 'आनन्दं ब्रह्मणो विद्वान्न बिभेति कुतश्चन' (तैत्ति. उप. 2.9) इति चोक्तम्। आत्मज्ञानेनैव भयनिवृत्तिरित्या-कूतम्।।8।।

यो लोकाँल्लोकपालान्सकलमपि पुरा भोग्यजातं हि तेषां
सृष्ट्वान्तः संप्रविश्य स्थिरचरमखिलं प्रेरयत्यान्तरः सः।

दृष्ट्वा नात्रेषदन्यत्सकलजगदधिष्ठानरूपोऽहमेकः।
प्रज्ञानं ब्रह्म येनाधिगतमिति स नावाप्तकामोऽमृतः स्यात्।।9।।

अथ **ऐतरेयोपनिषद्रहस्यमाह**। य इति–यः परमात्मा पुरा पूर्वं लोकान् भूरादीन् लोकपालानग्न्यादीन् तेषामग्न्यादीनां सकलं भोग्यजातं च स्थितिकारण-भूतान् भोग्यपदार्थानपिश्चार्थे सृष्ट्वोत्पाद्य–'आत्मा वा' इत्युपक्रम्य' 'स ईक्षत लोकान्नु सृजा' इति। 'स इमाँल्लोकानसृजत' (ऐ. उप. 1.1-2) इति। स आत्मा लोकानुत्पादय इति विचार्य द्युलोकादीनुत्पादिवान्। अनन्तरं 'स ईक्षतेमे नु लोकान् लोकपालान्नु सृजा इति। सोऽद्भ्य एव पुरुषं समुद्धृत्यामूर्छयत्' (ऐ. उप. 1.3) इति। इमे लोका मया सृष्टा पालयितृवर्जितानभ्येयुरिति विचार्य पञ्चमहाभूतेभ्य उद्धृत्य पुरुषाकारं पिण्डमकरोत् स विराट्। तदङ्गेभ्यस्तदिच्छयाग्न्यादीनामुत्पत्तिरिति भावः। पुनश्च "स ईक्षतेमे नु लोकाश्च लोकापालाश्चान्नमेभ्यः सृजा" (ऐ. उप. 3.1) इति। सोऽपोऽभ्यपतत्ताभ्यो-ऽभितप्ताभ्यो मूर्तिरजायत। या वै सा मूर्तिरजायतान्नं वै तत् (ऐ. उप. 3.2) इति। लोकपालानां सृष्टानामन्नं विना स्थितिर्न स्यादित्यन्नमुत्पादयेति। तदिच्छयैव पञ्चमहाभूतेभ्यः शरीरधारणसमर्थं भोग्यजातमभूदिति तात्पर्यम्। अन्तः पूर्वोक्तसंघातमध्ये मूर्धद्वारेण संप्रविश्य प्रवेशं कृत्वा स्थिरं चरं स्थावरजङ्गमा-त्मकमखिलं भूतजातं प्रेरयति। स्वभावानुसारेण वर्तयति। तदुक्तं–'स ईक्षत कथं न्विदं मदृते स्यात्' (ऐ. उप. 3.11) इति। नियामकं मां विनेदं करणजातं स्वव्यापारे कथं नियतं वर्तेत इति विचारितवान्। अनन्तरं "स ईक्षत। कतरेण प्रपद्या" (ऐ. उप. 3.11) इति। "स एतमेव सीमानं विदार्यैतया द्वारा प्रापद्यत" (ऐ. उप. 3.12) इति। प्रवेशद्वारद्वयं मूर्धा प्रपदं च। तयोर्मध्ये केन द्वारेण मया प्रवेशः कर्त्तव्य इति विचार्य स्वभृत्यस्थानीयस्य क्रियाशक्तिमतः प्रवेशमार्गं प्रपदं त्यक्त्वा मूर्ध्नि केशविभागावसानस्थाने छिद्रं कृत्वा तद्द्वारेण प्रवेशं कृतवानित्यर्थः। अत्र पदार्थजाते ईषत्किंचिदप्य-न्यत्स्वातिरिक्तं न दृष्टवानवलोक्य य एकोऽद्वितीयः सकलजगदधिष्ठारूपः सकलस्य जगतो विवर्तरूपस्याधिष्ठानरूपः सत्य आश्रयः। उक्तं च–"स जातो भूतान्यभिवैख्यत्किमिहान्यं वावदिषदिति। स एतमेव पुरुषं ब्रह्म ततमपश्यत्" (ऐ. उप. 3.13) इति स भूतेषु प्रविष्टो भूतेषु मद्व्यतिरिक्तं विवेक्तव्यं न किमप्यस्तीति विचार्य कारणभूतं स्वात्मानमेव व्याप्ततमं

दृष्टवान्नित्यर्थः। आन्तरोऽन्तरात्मा सोऽहं प्रधानं ज्ञप्तिस्वरूपं सर्वप्रकाशं ब्रह्मेति येन पुरुषेणाधिगतं साक्षात्कृतं स ना पुरुषो जीवन्नेवावाप्तकामः सकलात्मकत्वात्सन्नमृतोऽमरणधर्मा स्याद्भवेन्' 'प्रज्ञानं ब्रह्म' (ऐ. उप. 5.3), इति सर्वान्कामानाप्त्वामृतः समभवदिति च। आत्मज्ञानेनैवावाप्तकामत्वमिति तत्त्वम्।।9।।

मृद्रूपे ज्ञात एतद्घटमुखमखिलं तज्जमस्यानभिन्नं
तद्वच्छ्रीदैशिकेनानुभवति सततं तत्त्वमस्येवमुक्तः।
यस्मादाकाशमुख्यं भवति जगदिदं ब्रह्म तच्चाहमस्मी-
त्येतन्मत्तो न भिन्नं स भवति मनुजो ब्रह्म न ब्रह्मवेत्ता।।10।।

अथ छान्दोग्योपनिषद्रहस्यमाह— मृद्रूप इति। मृद्रूप मृल्लक्षणे ज्ञाते विज्ञाते सत्येतत्प्रत्यक्षतोऽनुभूयमानं घटमुखं घटशरावाद्यखिलं सर्वं मृद्विकारजातं तज्जं मृदः कारणाज्जातम्। अतो मृदः सकाशाद् यद्वद्यथा न भिन्नं व्यतिरिक्तं नास्ति। यदुक्तं "यथा खलु सौम्यैकेन मृत्पिण्डेन सर्वं मृन्मयं विज्ञातं स्याद्, वाचारम्भणं विकारो नामधेयं मृत्तिकेत्येव सत्यम्" (छां. उप. 6.1.4) इति। एकेन घटादिकारणभूतेन मृत्पिण्डेन ज्ञातेन तद्विकारभूतं घटादिमृद्रूपत्वेन ज्ञातं भवति, कार्यस्य कारणानन्यत्वात्। अतो घटः शराव इत्यादीनामात्मको विकारो वागालम्बन एव न तु तत्त्वतोऽस्ति। तत्त्वतस्तु मृत्तिकैवेत्यर्थः। तद्वत्तथा श्रीदैशिकेन मोक्षप्रदगुरुणा त्वमहमिति प्रत्ययगोचरः प्रत्यगात्मा तज्जगत्कारणं सच्चिदानन्दरूपं ब्रह्म तद्रूपोऽसीत्येवमनेन प्रकारेणोक्तो बोधितः सन्नुद्दालकेन श्वेतकेतुरिवोक्तं च-"आचार्याद्धैव विदिता विद्या साधिष्ठं प्रापत्(ति)" (छां. उप. 4.9.3) इति। साधिष्ठं साधुतमत्वमपरोक्षतात्पर्यावसायित्वम्। "ऐतदात्म्यमिदꣳ सर्वं तत्सत्यꣳ स आत्मा तत्त्वमसि श्वेतकेतो'(छां. उप. 6.8.7) इति च। ब्रह्मात्मकमखिलं भूतजातं तद्ब्रह्म सत्यं तद्रूपः प्रत्यगात्मा त्वमसीत्यर्थः। यस्माद्ब्रह्मणः सकाशादाकाशमुख्यमाकाशादीदं जगद्भूतजातं भवत्युत्पद्यते। तद्ब्रह्म च ब्रह्मैवाहं प्रत्यगात्मास्मीति। अतः कारणादेतद्भूतजातं मत्तः प्रत्यगात्मनः सकाशाद्भिन्नं व्यतिरिक्तं नास्तीति सततमनवरतमनुभवति साक्षात्करोति। "सन्मूलाः सौम्येमाः प्रजाः सदायतनाः सत्प्रतिष्ठाः" (छां.उप. 6.8.4.6) इत्युक्तत्वात्। सद्ब्रह्मैव जगत उत्पत्तिस्थिति-

लयकारणमित्यभिप्रायः। स मनुजः पुरुषो ब्रह्मैव ब्रह्मरूपो भवति। ब्रह्मवेत्ता न भवति। ब्रह्मणो वाङ्मनसागोचरत्वेन तद्वेत्तृत्वासंभवात्। तथा चोक्तम्—"अथ यदास्य वाङ्मनसि संपद्यते मनः प्राणेन प्राणस्तेजसि तेजः परस्यां देवतायामथ न जानाति" (छां. उप. 6.1.2) इति। यदाविचारेण वाचो मनसि मनसः प्राणे प्राणस्य तेजसि तेजस आत्मनि लयो भवति। "तत्तेजोऽसृजत" (छां. उप. 6.2.3) इति तेजसः प्रथमविकारत्वेनाभिधानात्। आकाशवाय्वोरपि तेजस्येवान्तर्भावस्तदा न जानातीति ज्ञेयस्यान्यस्याभावात्। स्वस्य तु स्वज्ञेयत्वासंभवात्। अपरोक्षज्ञानिन एव ब्रह्माहमिति बुद्धिरुत्पद्यत इति तात्पर्यम्।।10।।

यस्यानन्दस्य मात्रा विविधसुखमिदं येन सर्वेऽपि जीवाः
प्राणन्त्यव्याकृतं प्राग्जगदिदमखिलं व्याकरोन्नामरूपैः।
अन्तर्यामी हृषीकाधिप इति विदितं व्यापकं ब्रह्म तन्ना-
हं ब्रह्मास्मीति वेत्तैति विलयमसवस्तस्य नैवोच्छलन्ति।।11।।

अथ **बृहदारण्यकोपनिषद्रहस्यमाह**— यस्येति। येन सुखेनान्देन सर्वेऽपि जीवा ब्रह्माद्याः प्राणन्ति जीवन्ति। इदं विषयजन्यं विविधं विषयभेदेन नानाप्रकारं सुखम्। जात्यभिप्रायेणैकवचनम्। आनन्दा यस्य ब्रह्मणो ब्रह्मरूपस्या-नन्दस्य मात्रालेशरूपा भवन्ति। तदुक्तम्—"एतस्यैवानन्दस्यान्यानि भूतानि मात्रामुपजीवन्ति" (बृह. उप 4.3.32) इति ब्रह्मानन्दलेशप्राप्त्यैव सर्वेषामुप-जीवनमित्यर्थः। य आत्मेदं प्रत्यक्षतोऽनुभूयमानमखिलं जगद्भूतजातं सृष्टेः पूर्वमव्याकृतमप्रग(क)टनामरूपमात्मरूपमासीत्। तन्नामरूपैर्देवदत्तयज्ञदत्तेत्या-दिनामभी रूपैर्मनुष्याद्याकृतिभिः शुक्लादिगुणैश्च व्याकरोत् प्रकटीचकार। उक्तं च—"तद्ध्येदं तर्ह्यव्याकृतमासीत्। तन्नामरूपाभ्यामेव व्याक्रियतासौ नामायमिदꣳ रूपम्" (बृह. उप. 1.4.7) इति। सृष्टेः पूर्वमव्याकृतनानाविधनामरूपं सदेकं ब्रह्मासीत्। तदेव सृष्टिकालेऽनेकनामरूपैर्व्यक्तीभावमापद्यत। यथा प्रातः स्वरूपतो विद्यमानाः किरणा मध्याह्ने भासमानजलपूरतरङ्गादिनाम-रूपैरित्यर्थः। अनेन ब्रह्मणः कालत्रयास्तित्वं सूचितम्। अन्तर्याम्यन्तः स्थित्वा प्राणादीन्नियमयति—"यः पृथिव्यां तिष्ठन्...यः पृथिवीमन्तरो यमयति" (बृह. उप. 3.7.3) इत्यादिना सर्वान्तर्यामित्वमुक्त्वा "एष त... अन्तर्याम्यमृतः"

(बृह. उप. 3.7.3) इति श्रुत्युपदिष्टत्वात्। हृषीकाधिपो हृषीकाणामिन्द्रियाणामधिपः स्वामी। यत्सत्तयेन्द्रियाणां स्वक्रियासामर्थ्यम्। "प्राणस्य प्राणमुत चक्षुषश्चक्षुरुत श्रोत्रस्य श्रोत्रं मनसो ये मनो विदुः। ते निचिक्युर्ब्रह्म पुराणमग्र्यम्" (बृह. उप. 4.4.18) इत्युक्तत्वात्। येन प्राणादीनां स्वव्यापारसामर्थ्यं यद्योगेन तद्विदुस्ते ब्रह्म निश्चयेन ज्ञातवन्त इत्यभिप्रायः। इति पूर्वोक्तशब्दद्वयविशिष्टत्वेन विदितं वेदान्तशास्त्रे प्रसिद्धम्। व्यापकं सर्वत्र कारणतानुस्यूतम्। "स वा अयं पुरुषः सर्वासु पूर्षु पुरिशयोनैनेन किंच नानावृतं नैनेन किंचनासंवृतम्" (ब्रह. उप. 2.5.18) इत्युक्तेः। सकलशरीरेषु विद्यमानो यः पुरुषोऽनेन बाह्यभूतेनानाच्छादितमन्तर्भूतेनाननुप्रविष्टं किंचिदपि भूतजातं नास्तीत्यर्थः। एतादृशं यद्ब्रह्माहं प्रत्यगात्मा। ब्रह्म सच्चिदानन्दलक्षणं सकलजगदधिष्ठानम्। तद्रूपोऽस्मीति वेत्ता विद्वान् यः पुरुषः स तत्र पूर्वोक्ते ब्रह्मणि विलयगेति, एकीभावं प्राप्नोति। तस्य विदुषोऽसवः प्राणा नैवोच्छलन्त्युत्क्रमणं नैव प्राप्नुवन्ति। तथा चोक्तम्—"न तस्य प्राणा (m. gloss प्राणशब्देनाहंब्रह्मण्येकीभावेन तिष्ठति) उत्क्रामन्त्यत्रैव समवलीयन्ते। ब्रह्मैव सन्ब्रह्माप्येति (बृह. उप. 4.4.6)" इत्यर्थः। तस्याप्तकामस्य विदुषः प्राणा नोत्क्रामन्ति। किन्तु स्वयोनौ ब्रह्मण्येव प्रलीयन्ते। स जीवन् ब्रह्मैव सन्ब्रह्माप्येति, प्रविशति, न पुनरावर्तत इत्यर्थः। ब्रह्मापरोक्ष्यं विना गतागतदुःखनिवृत्तिर्नेति गूढोऽभिसंधिः।।11।।

श्रीरामाङ्घ्र्यब्जभृंगो गुरुचरणकृपापाङ्गलब्धैक्यबोधो
यः श्रीसिद्धेशसूनुर्विरचितममुना रामचन्द्राभिधेन।
यच्छ्लोकैः पङ्क्तिसङ्ख्यैरिदमुपनिषदां सद्रहस्यं दशानां
ज्ञात्वार्थं संपठेद्योऽनुभवति स सुखं सद्गुरोः संप्रसादात्।।12।।

इतिश्रीमद्विद्वन्मुकुटालङ्कारहीरवरश्रीराजयोगिवर्यश्रीसिद्धेश्वरसूरिसूनुश्रीरामचन्द्रपण्डितविरचितं दशोपनिषद्रहस्यं समाप्तम्।।

अधुना ग्रन्थकृत्स्वनाम ग्रन्थनाम च निर्दिशति। श्रीरामेति–**यः श्रीरामाङ्घ्र्यब्जभृङ्गः** श्रीरामचरणकमलयोर्भृङ्ग इव भृङ्ग आसक्तः। **गुरुचरणकृपापाङ्गलब्धैक्यबोधः** श्रीगुरुचरणकृपादृष्ट्या लब्धः प्राप्त ऐक्यं जीवब्रह्मैक्यं तस्य बोधोऽनुभवो येन सः **श्रीसिद्धेशसूनुः** श्रीसिद्धेश्वरात्मजोऽमुना तेन **रामचन्द्राभिधेन**

रामचन्द्रशर्मणा यद्विरचितं पङ्क्तिसंख्यैर्दशसंख्याकैः श्लोकैर्दशानामीशकेन-कठमुण्डप्रश्नमाण्डूक्यतैत्तिरीयैतरेयछान्दोग्यबृहदारण्यकसंज्ञानामुपनिषदां श्रुतिशिरसां सदृजुशब्दस्वास्यानुसारि रहस्यं तात्पर्यं तदिदं प्रत्यक्षतो निर्दिष्टमर्थं ज्ञात्वा विचार्य यः पठेत्स पुरुषः सद्गुरोः संप्रसादात् श्रीगुरुप्रसादयोगेन सुखमनुभवति-नित्यसुखः सहजनिरतिशयानन्दवान्भवेत्। एतेनोपनिषदर्थविचारेण ब्रह्मानन्दी भवतीति शिवम्॥12॥

इतिश्रीमद्विद्वन्मुकुटालङ्कारहीरभूतश्रीराजयोगिवर्यश्रीमत्सिद्धेश्वरसूरिसूनु-श्रीमद्रामचन्द्रपण्डितविरचितश्रीदशोपनिषद्रहस्यस्य विवृतिः समाप्तिमगमत्॥

FOOTNOTES

Paper published in Journal of the Oriental Institute, vol. 44, Nos. 1-4, Sept. 1994-June, 1995 Issue, pp. 133-151.

1. See, Joshi, S.G.: *Bṛhanmahārāṣṭrātila Śukla Yajurvedīya Mādhyandina Brāhmaṇāncā Itihāsa*, Jalagaon, 1950, pp. 209-211.
2. I am indebted to Śrī Yaśavanta Mahārāja of Kolhapur, for supplying authentic material about Rāmacandra Paṇḍita.
3. This table is given by S.G. Joshi in his book (*op. cit.*) p. 210.

XIII

PATHWAY TO *NIḤŚREYASA*—DEVALA'S CONCEPT

Smṛtis occupy a very prominent place in the history of Ancient Indian Literature and play an important role in the cultural development. They deal with the main aim of human life, namely, the *Dharma*, with its phases of *ācāra, vyavahāra* and *prāyaścitta*. They expound the rules and restrictions, injunctions and prohibitions of ideal Hindu life. They have affected and moulded the very life and character, culture and society of Hindus for more than two thousand years. The *Smṛtis* have elucidated *Dharma* that has essentially contributed to the well-being of the entire society (*samaṣṭi*) and also to the betterment and upliftment of spiritual status of an individual (*vyaṣṭi*). *Jīvātman* or individual soul is in fact the very basis, upon which the entire structure of all the *Smṛtis*—injunctions is formulated. The entire corpus of injunctions and prohibitions become significant only when the existence of the individual soul, with its good or evil destiny, depending upon his good or evil actions, is admitted.

Devalasmṛti[1] is one of such *Smṛtis,* which has tried to depict not only the rules and regulations of ideal human society, but also the procedure of spiritual advancement and upliftment of the individual. Devala propounds that *Dharma* consists of two-fold *puruṣārtha* (goal of human life) namely, *abhyudaya* (worldly prosperity) and *niḥśreyasa* (spiritual upliftment in the form of emancipation). Devala's view can be compared with those of Budha, Kaṇāda and Śaṅkarā-cārya, who also mention *Dharma* to be for the accomplishment of *abhyudaya* and *niḥśreyasa*[2]. Vasiṣṭha[3] believes that *Dharmajiñāsā* i.e., inquiry into the nature of *Dharma* is for the *niḥśreyasa* (emancipation) of *puruṣa*; while Yājñavalkya expounds the Highest *Dharma* to be the realization of *Ātman* through the practice of *Yoga*.[4] Thus it would be seen that the *niḥśreyasa* or emancipation of the *Jīvātman* is also an important aspect of *Dharma*. It is one of the aspects of the two-fold human goal, according to Devala.

Devala expounds that the first *puruṣārtha*, i.e., aim of life, namely, *abhyudaya* or worldly prosperity, can be accomplished by the practice of *Dharma*, rules and regulations of ideal life. In the concluding portion, therefore, the author deals with the second *puruṣārtha*, namely, *niḥśreyasa*. It is explained by him in according with the ancient, inscrutable, voluminous and numerous *Tantra* works of *Sāṅkhya-yoga*, that were composed by ancient sages.[5] Devala's exposition is not based upon the extant works, but upon the more ancient and (now) extinct *Sāṅkhya-yoga Tantras*, which is clear from his statement.

According to Devala, *niḥśreyasa* is of two kinds, namely, *sānkhya* and *yoga*. Of them, the *sāṅkhya* means right understanding or realization of the twenty-five principles.[6] The knowledge of these principles is very necessary for understanding the difference between the self and not-self and consequently by obtaining discriminative knowledge the aspirant can obtain final release or emancipation. Thus it would be evident that Devala interprets the term in accordance with the stand-point of the *Sāṅkhya* philosophy and hence thinks the knowledge of twenty-four principles along with the self as necessary, while the Vedāntins do not seem to deem the knowledge of twenty-four principles to be so indispensable. According to them, by realization of one Reality only, everything becomes known (*ekenaiva vijñātena sarvaṁ vijñātaṁ bhavati*).

Accoding to Devala another way to obtain *niḥśreyasa* is *Yoga*. *Yoga* is defined as fixing or establishing (i.e., concentration of) the mind upon the intended internal entity, namely, the self, after having withdrawn it from the external objects[7]. The sense-objects surround the senses and the tendency of mind and senses towards them is quite natural and unavoidable. The withdrawing of mind from them and making it introvert requires training and practice. The practical way that aims at this objective is *yoga,* which also leads one gradually to the same purpose of emancipation. Patañjali's explanation of *Yoga*[8] cessation of mental modifications is some-what technical and different from the practical explanation given by Devala. Devala has properly pointed out the importance of turning the mind away from sense-objects and does not speak of blindly controlling the senses, without the control of the mind which has tendency to wander helter-skelter. Devala's concept is comparable to that given in the *Bhagavadgitā* (III. 6-7).

Like the *Bhagavadgitā* (V.4), Devala points out that the ultimate aim of both the above paths, namely *Sāṅkhya* and *Yoga* is the same—the attainment of emancipation (RT. Sr. No. 2208).[9] According to Devala, *apavarga* is the absolute negation or non-existance of birth, death and consequent sufferings.[10] This explanation and the use of the terms like *apavarga, atyantābhāva,* etc. suggest the influence on him of the *Nyāya-Vaiśeṣika* systems, the term *Kaivalya*, being more prevalent in the *Sāṅkhya-yoga* systems. Thus according to Devala, both *Sāṅkhya* and *Yoga* lead to the identical goal and hence there is a happy blending or judicious combination of the two, comparable to that enunciated in the *Bhagavadgītā* (V.4).

The *Jīvātman* has natural association with or attachment to the physical body, which is of three kinds, namely that of

Gods, human beings and lower beings, each of them having distinctive characteristic features which are vividly described by Devala in order to expose the troublesome, sorrowful and disgusting nature of the physical body. Such a description of it is not found in the extant *Śāṅkhya* works, which refer merely to the threefold creation viz, that of Gods, human beings and lower beings (*Sāṅkhya-kā*. 53-54, *Sāṅkhya-sū* III. 46-51)[11] But it is different and cannot be compared with the detailed elucidation of Devala.[12] Desire and aversion, pleasure and pain, hunger and thirst, activity and fear, birth and death—all these are common dispostions of all embodied beings. The realized seer finds mere tautology in this world in which the ignorant one has to return to these abodes again and again even though he has enjoyed them previously. Owing to the sense of 'I and mine', one returns to this *saṁsāra*, the transmigratory existence. 'I am not of anything' and 'nothing is mine'—this realization delivers one from bondage.[13] Thus one should try to get rid of this physical body—the abode of all calamities.

The *Jīvātman* is bound or fettered by the bondage of three kinds, the causes of which are also of three kinds and the attachment to the bondage is effected by two kinds of causes. The three kinds of bondage are *prakṛtibandha, vaikārikabandha* and *dakṣiṇābandha*. The first *(prakṛti-bandha)* is a bondage by eight principles, namely , *avyakta, mahat, ahaṅkāra* and five *tanmātras*. The second *(vaikāri-kabandha)* is the bondage of senses with the sense-objects, while the third bondage *(dakṣiṇābandha)* is caused by merits obtained through the performance of pious and charitable deeds. Devala further adds that the gods are fettered by the first one, those belonging to the particular stage of life *(āśramī,* performing pious and charitable deeds like *gṛhastha, etc.)* are bound by third one, while all others are fastened by the second bondage *(RT* 2224-26 and 2276-83).[14] In the

Sāṅkhyakārika (44) and the *Sāṅkhyasūtra* (III. 24), there is mere mention of the term *bandha,* but there is no reference to or elucidation of its three-fold nature, as is found in the *Devala-sūtras.* The *Tattvasamāsa* (21) specifically mentions the bondage to be of three kinds.[15] The *sūtra* is quite identical with that of Devala. But the small work—*Tattvasamāsa* does not explain the three-fold bondage. The commentators Vācaspati, Bhāvāgaṇeśa,[16] *etc.*, have elucidated the nature of the three-fold bondage, but these commentors, being quite posterior to Devala, cannot be presumed to have influenced Devala. The three causes of bondage are most probably *dharma*, *adharma* and *ajñāna.* The attachment to bondage is of two kinds, it is due to *ajñāna* or ignorance that the two-fold attachment for *dharma* and *adharma* arises. It is noteworthy that the *Sāṅkhyakārikā,* the *Sāṅkhyasūtra* and the *Tattavasamāsa* do not refer to these concepts.

The *Jīvātman* is generally swayed by the twelve kinds of psychological, six vocal and four bodily vices, incurring sin.[17] Of them, *moha, rāga, dveṣa* are most powerful and hence to curb and control all others, one must control these three at the outset. These are known as *kaṣāyas*. These can be curbed and eliminated by means of penance in the form of *yama, niyama*, etc., and by the realization of the Reality. The deliverance of the *Jīvātman* from these vices is called *Kaṣāyapācanam*,[18] Devala has elaborately elucidated this topic.

The *Jivātman*'s repeated attempt of bringing back and establishing the mind upon the intended object, namely, the self is known as *pratyāhāra*.[19] The mind is atomic, restless, light and forceful and hence it requires repeated attempt to control it. *Dhāraṇa* is a process of holding body, senses, mind, intellect and the self (ego), all directed towards one and the same objective only.[20] *Dhyāna* is a process of contemplation upon the *Tat* signifying the Upaniṣadic *Brahman*.[21] It is evident that Devala's explanations are somewhat different from the extant *Yogasūtras* and more akin to Vedāntic attitude.

When the aspirant is practising *Yoga* by various means mentioned previously, a number of obstacles shoot forth and obstruct his further progress in his way to obtaining perfection. They are of ten kinds according to Devala and are called *Upasargas*.[22] The *Yogasūtra* (I.30) enumerates nine *antarāyas* or obstacles and mentions supernatural powers as *Upasargas* (III. 36).[23] The treatment of Devala is somewhat different from that of the *Yogasūtra*. When the *Jīvātnam* overcomes these impediments and becomes successful in his practice of *Yoga*, the eight kinds of supernatural powers are developed in him; of which the first three viz., *aṇimā, mahimā* and *laghimā* are *śārīra* (i.e. connected with the body), while the remaining five (namely, *prāpti, prākāmya īśitva, vaśitva* and *yatra kāmāvasāyitva*) are *aindriya,* i.e., sensory according to Devala.[24] The *Yogasūtra* (III. 44) merely refers to the divine powers like *aṇimā,* etc; but no explanation of them is found therein. Vyāsa, the commentator, has explained all of them, but there is difference in their sequence in his elucidation and that of Devala.

The aspirant who is not fascinated by the alluring supernatural powers can obtain the real purpose of his spiritual endeavour, aspired for by him—such as—*sāyujya*, i.e. unity with the Divinity, *Sālokya* obtaining the world of the Divinity, *Prakṛtilaya*—absorption into the *Prakṛti* and even *Mokṣa* or emancipation in the form of cessation of repeated births.[25] The *Sāṅkhyakārikā* (45) refers only to *Prakṛtilaya*. The *Sāṅkhyasūtra* (V. 74, 76, 80 and 83) is not at all in favour of admitting *Sālokya* and *Sāyujya* kinds of liberation. The *Jivātman*, who is liberated is described as *Sāṅkhya* by Devala and is not only free from qualities, bondage, birth, old age, death and sufferings, but also obtains the Highest Infinite Bliss.[26] This is suggestive of Vedantic influence on Devala. The classical *Sāṅkhya* believes that liberataion is ultimate and complete cesation of all kinds of sufferings. There is no obtainment of positive happiness or bliss. The *Mokṣa* according to Devala is not only the cessation of sufferings but also of future birth.

The *Jīvātman* that has obtained perfection in the practice of *Yoga* can obtain knowledge of his forth-coming death through the signs or portents of approaching death. After having received the earlier intimation of his forth-coming death, he becomes well-prepared for leaving the mortal body by the Yogic method of *utkrānti* or leaving the mortal body and obtaining unity wtih the ultimate state, namely, the *Brahman*. It is the ultimate and infiite state, designated as *Sāṅkhya*, bereft of connection or contact with birth, death or other calamities.[27] This description is not in conformity with the classical *Sāṅkhya* but has its parallel in the *Sāṅkhya* accounts found in the *Caraka* (*śārīra* I. 155-156, V. 21; 33)[28] and the *Budhacarita* (*XII. 65*).[29] In the *Sāṅkhya* accounts of the *Mahābhārata* also, the *Brahman* is sometimes described as the goal of the aspirant (cf., *Mahābhārāta* cr. ed. XII. 267.38)[30] This exposition of Devala suggests his priority to the *Sāṅkhyakārikā*. Devala has borrowed the *Sāṅkhyayoga* tenets from the more ancient works of these systems, that admitted even the doctrine of the *Brahman*. Thus Devala has expounded the *Sāṅkhya-yoga* philosophy in conformity with the more ancient *Tantras* that were theistic in their attitude and somewhat akin to the Vedāntic philosophy.

In this way, Devala has expounded the entire procedure of *Jivātman*'s obtaining the Ultimate Aim, the second *puruṣārtha*, namely, *niḥśreyasa*, i.e. emancipation through the paths of *Sāṅkhya* and *Yoga*.

FOOTNOTES

Paper published in Vishveshvaranand Indological Journal, Hoshiarpur, Vol. XXVIII, Pts. i-ii, June-Dec. 1990, PP. 138-146.

1. Wadekar, Mukund Lalji, *Devalasmṛti-Reconstruction* and *Critical Study*, Ph.D. Thesis approved for Ph.D. Degree in 1983, M.S. University of Baroda, Vadodara (Published Vol. I and II by Koshal Book Depot, Delhi 1996 and 1997).
2. अथातो धर्मवर्जितत्वान्न तिर्यग्योन्यां पुरुषार्थोपदेशः। देवमनुष्ययोर्द्विविधः पुरुषार्थः। अभ्युदयो निःश्रेयसमिति। तयोरभ्युदयः पूर्वोक्तः।
   —*Devalasmṛti—Reconstructed* Text (R.T.). Sr. No. 2200-2203 quoted in *Aparārka* (AP)—Com. of Aparāditya on *Yajñavalkya Smṛti*, *Vyavahāra* and *Prāyaścittādhyāyas*. Anandashram ed., Poona, Vol. II. 1904, pp. 986-988; Aiyanagar, Rangaswami K.V., (ed.) *Kṛtyakalpataru* of Bhaṭṭa Lakṣmīdhara (KK), Gaekwad's Oriental Series, *Mokṣakāṇḍa* Vol. XIV, Baroda, 1945. p.165.
   श्रेयोऽभ्युदयसाधनो धर्मः।
   Budhasmṛti I, *Smṛtisandarbha* Collection of the *Dharmaśāstra* Texts by Maharashies, Vol. IV, Gurumandal Granthamala, Calcutta, 1953.
   यतोऽभ्युदयनिःश्रेयससिद्धिः स धर्मः।
   Vaiśeṣikasūtra of Kaṇāda, ed. Jambuvijayaji, Gaekwad's Oriental Series, Baroda, 1961, 1.1.
   द्विविधो हि वेदोक्तो धर्मः। प्रवृत्तिलक्षणो निवृत्तिलक्षणश्च। जगतः स्थितिकारणं, प्राणिनां साक्षादभ्युदयनिःश्रेयसहेतुः।
   Goyandaka, Harikrishnadas (ed.) : *Bhagavadgītā* (with *Śāṅkara-bhāṣya*) with Hindi trans, Gita Press, Gorakhpur, 13th ed., *Saṁvat* 2032, Intro. of Śaṅkarācārya.
3. अथातः पुरुषनिःश्रेयसार्थं धर्मजिज्ञासा।
   Vasiṣṭhasmṛti(I.1), *Smṛtisandrbha*, Vol. III, 1952, *op. cit.*
4. अयं तु परमो धर्मो यद्योगेनात्मदर्शनम्।
   Yājñavalkya Smṛti, I. 8b (in *Smṛtisandarbha*, Vol. III)
5. एतौ सांख्ययोगो चाधिकृत्य यैर्युक्तितः समयतश्च पूर्वप्रणीतानि विशालानि गम्भीराणि तन्त्राणीह संक्षिप्योद्देशतो वक्ष्यन्ते।—R.T., 2210 (quot. in *Ap* pp. 986-988)
6. द्विविधं निःश्रेयसम्। सांख्ययोगाविति। पञ्चविंशतितत्त्वज्ञानं सांख्यम्।
   —RT. 2204-6 (quot. in *AP.* pp. 986-988 and *KK.* p. 165)
7. विषयेभ्यो विवर्त्याभिप्रेतेऽर्थे मनसोऽवस्थापनं योगः।
   —RT 2207 (quot. in *Ap* pp. 986-988 and *KK* p. 165)

8. योगश्चित्तवृत्तिनिरोधः। – *Yogasūtra*, 1.2
Baba, Bangali; (ed.) *Yogasūtra* of *Patañjali*, with com. of Vyāsa, Eng. trans. and notes, Motilal Banarsidass. Delhi. 1976.
9. उभयत्रापवर्गः फलम्।–*RT* 2208 (quot. in *Ap* pp. 986-988, *KK* p. 165)
10. जन्ममरणदुःखयोरत्यन्ताभावोऽपवर्गः। –*RT* 2209 (quot in *KK* p. 165)
11. Mainkar. T.G. (ed.), *Sāṅkhyakārikā* of Īśvarakṛṣṇa, with com. of Gauḍapāda. Oriental Book Agency, Second revised and enlarged edition, Poona, 1972.
Bhattacharya. Ram Shankar (ed.), *Sāṅkhyasūtra*, with com. of Vijñānabhikṣu, *Tattvasamāsasūtra* with com. and *Sāṅkhyasūtra*, Bhartiya Vidya Prakashan, Varanasi, *Saṁvat* 2022.
12. तेषां त्रिविधो मूर्तिविशेषः। द्युमत्सुगन्धि...निर्मलं परमपुष्कलसुकृतनिमित्तं देवताशरीरम्। अनित्यमशुभं सर्वरोगायतनं दुःखभाजनं...नित्यसंस्कार्यं जरामरणवशमिति मानुषशरीरम्। सन्ततोद्विग्नं...दुष्कृतायतनमज्ञानमकर्मण्यमिति तिर्यग्योनिशरीरम्।
—*RT* 2264-2267 (quot. *KK*. p. 109)
13. भुक्तानि यानि तान्येव भोक्तव्यानि पुनर्नृभिः।
इति दृष्टार्थतत्त्वस्य पुनरुक्तमिदं जगत्।।
अहं ममेति चात्मानं संसारे परिवर्तते।
नाहं कश्चिन्न मे कश्चिदिति पश्यन्न बध्यते।।
–*RT* 2439-2440 (quot. *KK* p. 75 and 92)
14. त्रिविधो बन्धः। त्रयो बन्धहेतवः। द्वौ बन्धरागौ।
—*RT* 2224-26 (quot. *AP* 986-988)
प्रकृतिबन्धो वैकारिकबन्धो दक्षिणाबन्ध इति बन्धत्रयी। तत्राव्यक्तादिभिरष्टभिर्बन्धः प्रकृतिबन्धः। इन्द्रियैरिन्द्रियार्थेषु बन्धो वैकारिकबन्धः। इष्टापूर्तादिभिर्बन्धो दक्षिणाबन्धः। तत्र प्रकृतिषु बन्धो देवतानाम्। दक्षिणाभिराश्रमिणाम्। वैकारैरन्येषाम्। धर्मोऽज्ञाना(दी)नि बन्धहेतवः। —*RT* 2276-2283 (quot. *KK* p. 124)
15. त्रिविधो बन्धः। – *Tattvasamāsasūtra,* 21
16. *Sāṅkhyakārikā*, with com. *Sārabodhinī* of Shivanarayan Shastri and *Saṅkhyatattvakaumudī* of Vācaspati Miśra, Nirnayasagar Press, Bombay, 1940, com. on verse. 44.
Dvivedin, Vindhyeswariprasad, *Sāṅkhyasaṅgraha*, (*Sāṅkhyatattva-vivecana*) of Shrisimanand (Kṣemendra). *Sāṅkhyatattvayāthārthya-dīpana* of Bhāvāgaṇeśa and *Samāsasūtravyākhyā, Sarvopakāriṇī),* Chowkhamba Sanskrit Series, Benares, com. on *Sūtra* 21.
17. तत्र मोहरागद्वेषमानलोभमदशोकममत्वाहंकारभयहर्षमोघचिन्ताश्चेति द्वादश मानसाः।

ततः पुरुषवचनमपवादः पैशुन्यमनृतं वृथालापो निष्ठुरमिति वाङ्मयाः षट्।...ततो हिंसापचारः स्तेयमर्थदूषणमिति चतुर्विधाः शरीरजाः।

—*RT* 2284-2376 (quot. in *AP*. p. 222, *KK* p. 84 etc.) (also cf. Aiyangar Rangaswami K.V., *Kṛtyakalpataru* of Bhaṭṭa Lakṣmīdhara, *Gṛhastha Kāṇḍa,* Gaekwad's Oriental Series. Baroda, Vol. II. 1944, p. 354 and 393).

18. रागद्वेषमोहाः कषाया उच्यन्ते। तेषां यमनियमलक्षणेन तपसा पञ्चविधेन तत्त्वज्ञानेन चापकर्षणं कषायपाचनम्। —*RT* 2375-2376 (quot, *KK* p. 168)
19. अणुत्वाच्चापल्याल्लाघवाद् बलवत्त्वाद् वा योगभ्रष्टस्य मनसः पुनः प्रत्यानीयार्थे योजनं प्रत्याहारः। —*RT* 2408 (quot. *KK* p. 173)
20. शरीरेन्द्रियमनोबुद्ध्यात्मनां धारणाद् धारणा।
—*RT* 2409 (quot. *Ap* p. 1025, *KK* p. 174)
21. देवतायतनं शून्यागार... सर्वेन्द्रियाणि संहृत्योर्ध्वं प्राणानुद्दीर्य, मनसा तच्चिन्तनं ध्यानम्। —*RT* 2410 (quot. *KK* p. 181)
22. [अनि]ष्टाभिभवो निद्राबाधा भयानकोत्पत्तिर्ज्ञानपीडा भोगातिशयः कोपनैपुण्यमैश्वर्य-विशेषो धर्ममहत्त्वं विद्यास्थानानि यशोदीप्तिरिति योगिनां दशोपसर्गाः।
—*RT* 2411 (quot. *KK* p. 212)
23. व्याधिस्त्यानसंशयप्रमादालस्याविरतिभ्रान्तिदर्शनालब्धभूमिकत्वानवस्थितत्वानि चित्तविक्षे-पास्तेऽन्तरायाः।... ते समाधावुपसर्गा व्युत्थाने सिद्धयः।
—*Yogasūtra*, I.30, III. 36
24. अणिमा महिमा लघिमा प्राप्तिः प्राकाम्यमीशित्वं वशित्वं यत्रकामावसायित्वं चाष्टावैश्वर्यगुणाः। तेषामणिमामहिमालघिमानस्त्रयः शारीराः। प्राप्त्यादयः पञ्चैन्द्रियाः ......। —*RT* 2412-2437(quot. *KK* p. 216)
25. सायुज्यं सालोक्यं प्रकृतिलयो मोक्षश्चेति चतुर्विधं प्रयोजनम्। अपुनर्भवो मोक्षः। —*RT* 2442-2447 (quot. *KK* p. 8)
26. स तथा निवृत्तो निर्गुणश्छिन्नबन्धो जन्मजरामरणदुःखविनिर्मुक्तः परमसुखमैकान्तिक-मधिगच्छतीति साङ्ख्यम्। —*RT* 2441 (quot, *KK* p. 7)
27. एवं निर्वाणमाप्नोति योगी योगपरायणः।
दृष्टारिष्टो यतिश्रेष्ठो योगी ध्यानपरो भवेत्।।
त्यक्त्वा कलेवरं ध्यायन्परं याति महेश्वरम्।
एकान्तात्यन्तकं साङ्ख्यं परं ब्रह्म सनातनम्।।
जन्ममृत्युजराव्याधिभयसङ्गविवर्जितम्।—RT 2472-2474 (quot. *KK* p. 255)
28. गतिर्ब्रह्मविदां ब्रह्म तच्चाक्षरमलक्षणम्।
ज्ञानं ब्रह्मविदां चात्र नाज्ञस्तज्ज्ञातुमर्हति। —*Caraka-Śārīra* 1. 155-156
निवृत्तिरपवर्गस्तत्परं प्रशान्तं तदक्षरं तद्ब्रह्म स मोक्षः। —*Caraka Śārīra* V. 21

विपापं विरजः शान्तं परमक्षरमव्ययम्।
अमृतं ब्रह्मनिर्वाणं पर्यायैः शान्तिरुच्यते।। – *Caraka Śārīra* V. 33
Pade, Shankar Daji : (ed.) *Carakasaṁhitā,* Nirnayasagar Press, Bombay, 1867.

29. एतत्तत्परमं ब्रह्म निर्लिङ्गं ध्रुवमक्षरम्।
यन्मोक्ष इति तत्त्वज्ञाः कथयन्ति मनीषिणः।।
Buddhacarita of *Aśvaghoṣa*, XII 65. Clarendon Press, Cambridge, Oxford, 1892.

30. पुण्यपापक्षयार्थं हि सांख्यज्ञानं विधीयते।
तत्क्षये ह्यस्य पश्यन्ति ब्रह्मभावे परां गतिम्।।
Mahābhārata, XII. 267.38, Crit. ed., Bhandarkar Oriental Research Institute. Poona, 1933-59.

XIV

ŚAṄKARĀCĀRYA'S PREFERENCE TO THE READINGS FROM THE *MĀDHYANDINA* RECENSION

Śaṅkarācārya's commentary on the *Brahmasūtras* is full of references to and quotations from the *Śatapatha Brāhmaṇa*; This *Brāhmaṇa* belongs to the *Śukla Yajurveda* and is found in two recensions *Kāṇva* and *Mādhyandina*. Śaṅkarācārya was well-versed in both the recensions and had minutely acquinted himself with the smallest differences in readings of both the recensions. He has especially referred to the readings of the *Mādhyandina* recension, that differ from the *Kāṇva* recension at several places, while commenting on the *Brahmansūtras*.[1] Here is an attempt to collect and study all such references, where Śaṅkarācārya has specifically pointed out the difference in readings of the two recensions.

1. While explaining the *sūtra—'śrāraścobhaye' pi hi bhedenainamadhīyate*' (1.2.20), Śaṅkarācārya explains that both recensions—*Kāṇva* and *Mādhyandinas*—read this Embodied Self with difference i.e. *Kāṇvas* read as "*Yo Vijñāne tiṣṭhan*" (Br. 3.7.22)[2] while *Mādhyandinas* read—"*Yo Ātmani tiṣṭhan*" (Br. 3.7.30)[3]. He further remarks[4] that in the reading of the *Madhyandina* recension, the word *Ātman* is clearly referred to as the Embodied Self, while in the *Kāṇva* reading, the word *vijñāna* denotes the same, because the Embodied Self is indeed full of consciousness. Here Śaṅkarācārya seems to prefer to the reading of the *Mādhyandina* recension, which directly and specifically refers to *Ātman*, while in the *Kāṇva* recension, it requires explana-

tion. Moreover the reading of the *Mādhyandina* recension is more akin to his doctrine.

2. On *sūtra-Sabdādibhyo.... puruṣamapi Cainamadhīyate* (1.2.26), Śaṅkarācārya points out that some have reading *puruṣavidham* for *puruṣam* in the *sūtra*. They mean to say that the *Mādhyandinas*[5] read "*puruṣavidham puruṣe'ntaḥ pratiṣṭhitam*" (*Śata. B.* 10.6.1.11) instead of '*puruṣam puruṣe'ntaḥ Pratiṣṭhitam*'. The *Vājasaneyins* (i.e. *Kāṇvas* and *Mādhyandinas* respectively) have readings—*Puruṣam* and *Puruṣavidham*, acc. to Śaṅkarācārya. Here also Śaṅkarācārya seems to prefer to and favour the *Mādhyandina* reading as it conveys the meaning in which *puruṣavidhatvam* can be comprehended as referring to his Divine from (*adhi-daivam*) and his Form as the Embodied Self *(adhyātmam)*[6].

3. In the *Bṛhadāraṇyaka* (4.4.17)[7], the word *Pañcajanā* occurs. It is interpreted as referring to five-*prāṇa* etc. by Śaṅkarācārya in the *sūtra*, "*Prāṇādayo vākyaṣesāt* (1.4.12.). But the objector argues that the interpretation may be true in case of *Mādhyandina* recension because they read *annam* among the Prāṇas (4.2.21)[8] but the *Kāṇvas* do not read like that. As the *Mādhyandinas* do in this respect. The next *sūtra Jyotiṣaikeṣāmasatyanne* (1.4.13), contains reply to this. Though the *Kāṇvas* do not read *annam* in this context, the word *Jyotiḥ*, occurring earlier in this context is included for the calculation of the five numbers. Here Śaṅkarācārya clearly explains[9] the difference in the reading of the two recensions. The *Mādhyandinas* have enumeration of the five-*Pañcajanas-Prāṇa* etc. in the same *mantra*. They are not required to depend on the word *Jyotiḥ*, occurring in the other *mantra*. While the *Kāṇvas* do not have all the five in the same *mantra* and they have to depend upon the word *Jyotiḥ* in another *mantra*. This shows how the reading in the *Mādhyandina* recension is better than that of the *Kāṇvas*.

4. In *sūtra*, "*kāryākhyānādapūrvam*' (3.3.18) Śaṅkarācārya quotes the *Bṛhadāraṇyaka-Tadvidvāṁso Śrotriyā aśisyanta ācāmantyaśitvā cācāmantyetamevatadanamanagnam kurvanto manyante*" (Br. 6-1-14)[10] but he points out the *Kāṇvas* conclude here only, while the *Mādhyandinas* (6.3.15)[11] add one line more "*Tasmādevam vidaśiṣyannācāmedaśitvā ācāmedetameva tadanamanagnam kurute*". The difference between the two is that the *Kāṇvas* conclude with only the statement that by *ācamana,* the *prāṇa* itself is encovered or enclothed, while the *Mādhyandinas* further add the injunction. The added line, merely refers to *(anuvāda)* the earlier *ācamana* and further enjoins that one should know the encovering-enclothing of *prāṇa*, which is relevant in the context.[12] This indicates how the reading of the *Mādhyandinas* is more refined.

5. On *sūtra* "*Śamadamādyupetaḥ Syāttathāpi tu tadvidhestadaṅgatayā teṣāmavaśyānuṣṭheyatvāt*" (3.4.27), Śaṅkarācārya quotes the *Bṛhadāraṇyaka*—"*Tasmādevamvicchānto dānta uparatastitikṣuḥ samāhito bhūtvātmanyevātmānam Paśyati*" (4.4-23)[13]. The objector contends that here there is simple statement in present tense stating the fact that "he sees" *(Paśyati),* there is no injunction *(vidhi).* Śaṅkarācārya here points[14] out the difference between the readings of the *Mādhyandinas* and the *Kāṇvas.* The *Kāṇvas* here read *'Paśyati'*; but the *Mādhyandinas* explicitly read the injunction with the variant *'Paśyet'* in this very context (4.2.28)[15].

Conclusion

The *Śatapatha Brāhmaṇa* is frequently quoted and referred to by Śaṅkarācārya in the *Brahmasūtrabhāṣya* many times with words," *Vājasaneyinaḥ*", *Vājasaneyibrāhmaṇam,*" "*Vājasaneyaka*" etc. This *Vājasaneyi-śukla Yajuveda* recension has two sub-recensions-*Kāṇva* and

Mādhyandina. Both have some difference in readings. Śaṅkarācārya himself is believed to have belonged to the *Taittirīya* recension of the *Kṛṣṇa Yajurveda*[16]. But he has very meticulously noted the difference in the readings of the two recensions. This shows that Śaṅkarācārya was well-versed in the text of both the recensions and minutely studied the differences in readings also. This reflects upon his scholarship and meticulous study. Moreover, as seen above, he seems to have prefered to and favoured the variants from the *Mādhyandina* recension. These are comparatively more scientific, refined and more befitting the context than those of the *Kāṇva* recension.

FOOTNOTES

Paper published in Journal of the Oriental Institute, Vol. 47, Nos. 1-2, Sept.-Dec. 1997 Issue, p. 61-64.

1. Acharya Ram Narayan: (ed.) *The Brahmasūtra śāṅkarabhāṣya, Nirnaya Sagar* Press, Third edition, Bombay, 1948.
2. Shastri Jagadish : (ed.) *Upanisatsaṅgrahaḥ*, Motilal Banarasidass, Delhi, Reprint, 1980.
3. *Śatapatha Brāhmaṇam, Pañcamo bhāgaḥ, Bṛhadāraṇyakam*, Laksmivenkateshwar Press, Bombay, 1940.
4. अपि चोभयेऽपि हि शाखिनः काण्वा माध्यंदिनाश्चान्तर्यामिणो भेदेनैनं शारीरं पृथिव्यादिवदधिष्ठानत्वेन नियम्यत्वेन चाधीयते।—'यो विज्ञाने तिष्ठन्' (बृ. 3.7.22) इति काण्वाः। 'य आत्मनि तिष्ठन्' इति माध्यंदिनाः। 'य आत्मनि तिष्ठन्' इत्यस्मिंस्तावत्पाठे भवत्यात्मशब्दः शारीरवाचकः। 'यो विज्ञाने तिष्ठन्' इत्यस्मिन्नपि पाठे विज्ञानशब्देन शारीर उच्यते। विज्ञानमयो हि शारीरः।
5. Shastri Vamshidhar : *Śatapatha Brāhmaṇa, Dvitīyo bhāgaḥ*, Acyutagranthamala karyalaya, Kashi, *Samvat*. 1997.
6. ये तु 'पुरुषविधमपि चैनमधीयते' इति सूत्रावयवं पठन्ति, तेषामेषोऽर्थः—केवलजाठरपरिग्रहे पुरुषेऽन्तःप्रतिष्ठितत्वं केवलं स्यान्न पुरुषविधत्वम्। पुरुषविधत्वमपि चैनमधीयते वाजसनेयिनः—'पुरुषविधं पुरुषेऽन्तःप्रतिष्ठितं वेद' इति। पुरुषविधत्वं च प्रकरणाद्यदधिदैवतं द्युमूर्धत्वादि पृथिवीप्रतिष्ठितत्वान्तं, यच्चाध्यात्मं प्रसिद्धं मूर्धत्वादि चुबुकप्रतिष्ठितत्वान्तं तत्परिगृह्यते।।
7. यस्मिन्यञ्चजना आकाशश्च प्रतिष्ठितः।
तमेव मन्य आत्मानं विद्वान्ब्रह्मामृतोऽमृतम्।।

8. प्राणस्य प्राणमुत चक्षुषश्चक्षुरुत श्रोत्रस्य श्रोत्रमन्नस्यान्नं मनसो ये मनो विदुः।
9. भवेयुस्तावत्प्राणादयः पञ्चजना माध्यंदिनानाम्, येऽन्नं प्राणादिष्वामनन्ति...... माध्यंदिनानां हि समानमन्त्रपठितप्राणादिपञ्चजनलाभान्नास्मिन्मन्त्रान्तरपठिते ज्योतिष्यपेक्षा भवति। तदभावात्तु काण्वानां भवेत्यपेक्षा।
10. *Bṛhadāraṇyaka Cf. Upaniṣatsaṅgrahaḥ. op. cit.*
11. *Śatapathabrāhmaṇam*, Venkateshwar ed. *op. cit.*
12. अत एवाचमनस्याविधित्सितत्वादेतमेव तदनमनग्नं कुर्वन्तो मन्यन्त इत्यत्रैव काण्वाः पर्यवस्यन्ति, नामनन्ति 'तस्मादेवंवित्' इत्यादि। तस्मान्माध्यंदिनानामपि पाठ आचमनानुवादेनैवंवित्त्वमेव प्रकृतप्राणवासोवित्त्वं विधीयत इति प्रतिपत्तव्यम्।
13. *Upaniṣatsaṅgraha, op. cit.*
14. नन्वत्रापि शमाद्युपेतो भूत्वा पश्यतीति वर्तमानापदेश उपलभ्यते न विधिः, नेति ब्रूमः, तस्मादिदि प्रकृतप्रशंसापरिग्रहाद्विधित्वप्रतीतेः। पश्येदिति च माध्यंदिना विस्पष्टमेव विधिमधीयते।
15. *Śatapathabrāhmaṇam*, Venkateshwar ed. *op. cit.*
16. Chitrav Siddheshwar Shastri: *Madhyayugīna Caritrakośa*, Pune, 1937, p. 759.

XV

IDENTIFICATION OF SOME *SMṚTI*-CITATIONS FROM THE *BRAHMASŪTRA-ŚĀṄKARABHĀṢYA*

Śaṅkarācārya's commentary on the *Brahmasūtras*[1] abounds in citations from numerous sources, like the *Saṁhitās*, *Brāhmaṇas*, *Upaniṣads*, *Kalpasūtras*, *Smṛtis*, *Purāṇas* and schools of Indian Philosophy. The erudite editors of the commentary have taken great pains to trace these citations to their sources. Thus scholars like S.K. Belvalkar, P.V. Kane, V. Venkatachalam and others have very arduously identified numerous citations in their works.[2] However number of *Śruti* and *Smṛti* citations in the text have still remained untraced, and have not yet been identified. An attempt is, therefore, made in the present paper to identify some *Smṛti*-citations occurring in the commentary of Śaṅkarācārya on the *Brahmasūtras* which have yet remained untraced, and to trace them to their sources.

Citations in the order of textual occurrence

1. आत्मलाभान्न परं विद्यते। (I.I.17)—आप. ध. सू. 1.8.22.2

2. माया ह्येषा मया सृष्टा यन्मां पश्यसि नारद।
   सर्वभूतगणैर्युक्तं नैवं मां ज्ञातुमर्हसि।। (I.1.20; III. 2.17)
   —महाभा. 12.326.43

3. यस्याग्निरास्यं द्यौर्मूर्धा खं नाभिश्चरणौ क्षितिः।
   सूर्यश्चक्षुर्दिशः श्रोत्रं तस्मै लोकात्मने नमः।।
   (I.2. 25, I.2. 25 (second time only last quater)–
   महाभा. 12.47.44

4. सर्वेषां स तु नामानि कर्माणि च पृथक् पृथक्।
वेदशब्देभ्य एवादौ पृथक् संस्थाश्च निर्ममे।।
(I.3.28) —मनुस्मृ. 1.21

5. शूद्रश्चतुर्थो वर्ण एकजातिः। (I.3.36) —गौ. ध. सू. 2.1.51

6. न शूद्रे पातकं किंचिन्न च संस्कारमर्हति। (1.3.36)
—मनुस्मृ. 10.126

7. न शूद्रस्य मतिं दद्यात्। (1.3.38)
—वसिष्ठ ध. सू. 18.12a; मनुस्मृ. 4.80

8. द्विजातीनामध्ययनमिज्या दानम्। (1.3.38) -गौ. ध. सू. 2.1.1.

9. श्रावयेश्चतुरो वर्णान्.....। (1.3.38) —महाभा. 12. 314. 45c.

10. जगत्प्रतिष्ठा देवर्षे पृथिव्यप्सु प्रलीयते।
ज्योतिष्वापः प्रलीयन्ते ज्योतिर्वायौ प्रलीयते।। (II. 3.14)
—महाभा. 12.326. 28

11. उपलभ्याप्सु चेद्गन्धं केचिद्ब्रूयुरनैपुणाः।
पृथिव्यामेव तं विद्यादपो वायुं च संश्रितम्।। (II.3.29)
—महाभा. 12. 224.40

12. इन्द्रियाणामुपरमे मनोऽनुपरतं यदि।
सेवते विषयानेव तद्विद्यात्स्वप्नदर्शनम्।। (II.3.40)
—महाभा. 12.267.24

13. न हिंस्यात्सर्वा भूतानि।
(II. 3.48; III. 1.25)—महाभा. 3.203. 45a; 12.269. 5a; 12.316. 18a

14. वागध्यात्ममिति प्राहुर्ब्राह्मणास्तत्त्वदर्शिनः।
वक्तव्यमधिभूतं तु वह्निस्तत्राधिदैवतम्।। (II.4.14)
—महाभा. 12.301.5
(reads यथा श्रुतिनिदर्शनात् for b)

15. वर्णा आश्रमाश्च स्वकर्मनिष्ठाः प्रेत्य कर्मफलमनुभूय ततः शेषेण विशिष्टजातिकुलरूपायुःश्रुतवृत्तवित्तसुखमेधसो जन्म प्रतिपद्यन्ते। (III. 1.8)—गौ. ध. सू. 2.2.29

16. आचारहीनं न पुनन्ति वेदाः। (III.1.10)

—वसिष्ठ ध. सू. 6.6

17. योगिनस्तं प्रपश्यन्ति भगवन्तं सनातनम्। (III. 2. 24)
— महाभा. 5.45.1 ef, upto 21 ef; 5.294*.4 ; 5.297* 1; 5.299* 3; 5.300*.5; 5.301*.5

18. बीजान्यग्न्युपदग्धानि न रोहन्ति यथा पुनः।
ज्ञानदग्धस्तथा क्लेशैर्नात्मा संपद्यते पुनः।। (III. 3.32)
—महाभा. 12.204. 16; 3. App. 21 A. 223 pr. (slightly different)

19. सुरापस्य ब्राह्मणस्योष्णामासिञ्चेयुः। (III.4.30)

—गौ. ध. सू. 3.5.1

20. जप्येनैव तु संसिध्येद् ब्राह्मणो नात्र संशयः।
कुर्यादन्यन्न वा कुर्यान्मन्त्रो ब्राह्मण उच्यते।। (III. 4.38)

—मनुस्मृ. 2.87 (मैत्रो for मन्त्रो)

21. अनाश्रमी न तिष्ठेत दिनमेकमपि द्विजः। (III.4.39)

—दक्षस्मृ. 1.10 (cf. Jiva. ed.)

22. यं न सन्तं न चासन्तं नाश्रुतं न बहुश्रुतम्।
न सुवृत्तं न दुर्वृत्तं वेद कश्चित्स ब्राह्मणः।। (III.4.50)

— वसिष्ठ ध. सू. 6.40.

23. अव्यक्तलिङ्गोऽव्यक्ताचारः। (III. 4.50)

—वसिष्ठ ध. सू. 10.12

24. न हि गतिरधिकास्ति कस्यचित्
सति हि गुणे प्रवदन्त्यतुल्यताम् (III. 4.52)

— महाभा. 12.187.58

25. अण्व्यो मात्रा विनाशिन्यो दशार्धानां तु याः स्मृताः।।
ताभिः सार्धमिदं सर्वं संभवत्यनुपूर्वशः।। (IV. 2.6)

—मनुस्मृति. 1.27

26. (स्मरति ह्यापस्तम्बः।—),
"तद्यथाम्रे फलार्थे निमिते छायागन्धावनूत्पद्येते, एवं धर्मं चर्यमाण-मर्था अनूत्पद्यन्ते।" (IV. 3.14)—आप. ध. सू. 1.7.20.3.

Works Consulted

1. *Āpastambīya Dharmasūtra* (आप. ध. सू.) Ed. George Būhler, Third, ed. Bomaby Sanskrit Series, BORI, Poona, 1932.
2. *Gauama Dharamsūtra* (गौ. ध. सू.) with comm. *Mitākṣarā* of Haradatta, ed. Gasnesh Shastri Gokhale, Anandashram Sanskrit series, second ed., Poona, 1931.
3. *Manusmṛti* (मनुस्मृ.) with comm. of Kullūka, ed. Narayan Ram Acharya, 10th ed., Niryasangar press, Bombay, 1946.
4. *Mahābhārata* (महाभा.), Critical Ed., BORI, Poona, 1933-59.
5. *Śmṛtīnāṁ Samuccayaḥ*, Anandashram, Sec. ed.,Poona, 1929.
6. *Smṛtisandarbha*: Collection of the Dharmaśāstra texts by Maharshis, Vols. I-IV, Gurumandal Granthamala, Calcutta, 1952-53, Vol. III.
7. *The Pratīka-Index of the Mahābhārata*, ed. P.L. Vaidya, BORI, Poona Vols., I-IV, 1967-72.

FOOTNOTES

Paper published in The Annals of Bhandarkar Oriental Research Institute, Pune, Vol. LXIX (1988) pp. 265-267.

1. *Brahmasūtraśāṅkarabhāṣya* ed. Narayan Ram Acharya, Nirnaya-sagara Press, Third ed., Bombay, 1948.

2. S.K. Belvalkar (ed.) *The Brahmasūtras of Bādarāyana* with the commentary of Śaṅkarācārya Ch. II. quart. I and II. Second ed., Bilvakunja Publishing House Poona, 1931.

P.V. Kane, *History of Dharmaśātra*, Government Oriental series, BORI, Poona Vol. I, part I, revised and enlarged Second ed., 1968 vol. IV, *Ibid,* 1973; Vol. V-II, *Ibid,* 1977.

V. Venkatachalam "Two untraced citations in the *Brahmasūtra-bhāṣya* of Śaṅkarācārya" *Journal of Oriental Research,* Madras, Kuppuswami Sastri Reseach Institute, Siliver Jubliee Vol. 1970-71, 1971-72, Vol. XXXX-XXXXI, p. 101.

XVI

JÑĀNAMĀLĀ OF NĀGARANĀRĀYAṆA—A UNIQUE WORK OF VEDĀNTA

Introductory

The *Ācāryas* wrote commentaries on the *Prasthānatrayī* i.e. the *Upaniṣads,* the *Bhagavadgītā* and the *Brahmasūtras.* They and their disciples-followers also composed some other smaller, supplimentary treatises known as the *Prakaraṇa granthas,* expounding the esoteric Vedāntic tenets in lucid often metrical compositions. Many such works are printed. But some are still in manuscript form; one of such small *prakaraṇa granthas,* is a work of Nāgaranārāyaṇa entitled *Jñānamālā,* which is still little-known and yet unpublished, a rare manuscript of which in possession of the Oriental Institute of Baroda. In this paper, an attempt is made to introduce and bring to light and the notice of scholars interested in *Vedānta,* this small, but unique work of *Vedānta.*

A Rare manuscript in O. I. Baroda—

The *New Catalogus Catalogorum* (N.C.C.) has noted four different works, bearing the title *Jñānamālā* (1) On dealing with *Devatāpratiṣṭhā,* (2) Second dealing with the *Yogatantra,* (3) The third one on the subject of *Jyotiṣa,* (4) the fourth is the present one, the work by Nāgaranārāyaṇa. The *N.C.C.* has noted in at two places (vol. 5 pp. 120-22) and (vol. 7 pp. 332-333) as a commentary on the *Kauśītaki Brāhmaṇopaniṣat* by Nāgaranārāyaṇa. On p. 121, vol. 5 of the *N.C.C.* we notice the following information of the mss. of the said work. Baroda 3827, BORI 4 of 1879-80, CLB I, p. 56 (incl.) p. 4 *(Dīpikā)* Weber 1409 (last *kāṇḍa).*

Of these, the manuscript of this rare and unique work, deposited in the O.I. of Baroda *(called A)* is a small one, bearing acc. No. 3827, containing 109 *ślokas* in 9 folios. It is a paper ms. in *Devanāgarī* script, with good and readable handwriting. The size of the paper is 24.5 cms.×11 cms. Each page contains about seven lines and 31 to 33 letters in a line. The ms. bears title *Kauṣītaki-Upaniṣad Vyākhyā 'Jñānamālā'*, its author being Nāgaranārāyaṇa, a disciple of Rāmedrasarasvatī. The ms. has some small corrections, additions etc. noted in the margin. At two places, the ms. has become illegible due to erasions. The scribe does not make use of *avagraha* sign. The *ślokas* are all numbered properly.

The second ms. of this work is deposited in the Bhandarkar Oriental Research Institute, bearing no. 4 of 1879-80. It is a paper ms. of ten folios, having seven lines in a page and 28 letters in a line. The Oriental Institute of Baroda has produced a xerox-copy (bearing acc. no. 27319) of the above ms. The size of the xerox-copy is 21.5×10.3 cms. The name of the scribe is Govinda Paṇḍyā, belonging to *ābhyantara nāgara* caste of *Gūjarātī nāgara* brahmins. He has copied this ms. for some scholar named Jagajīvana Bhaṭṭa. The information about the time of wrinting is mentioned, but the figure of the year is not clearly legible. The word *saṁvat* is clearly readable but then 17 is seen but not the entire figure. Hence it must be somewhere in *saṁvat* 1700. It may therefore be understood to be approximately between 1644 and 1743 A.D. The scribe completed the writing on Saturday the 9th day of the dark fortnight in the month of *Māgha*.

The ms. B is not completely a copy of A. The ms. A begins with *Śrīrāmacandro Jayati;* while B begins with *Śrīgaṇeśāya namaḥ*. B. has many corrupt readings e.g.

survagre for *gurvagre, vindyāt* for *vidyāt, Pāṭhakāḥ* for *Pāṭhakaḥ, Yathāsukham* for *Sukhādikaṃ.* In most of the above cases, the reading of A are better and properly fitting the context. The ms. B completely omits the verse (no. 109) *nirguṇaghaṭanā* etc. Certain important words in the colophon are also omitted by B. i.e. B omits the words—*nāgara, Brāhmaṇa* (in *Brāhmaṇopaniṣat)* and *Jñānamālā* (the very tittle of the work). There is difference in sequence also. A reads the line *(pūrṇo'ham* etc.) as the verse 104ab, which is read after the verse 96 in B. Hence there is difference in numbering of verses in the two mss., from the verse 103 onwards.

About the author Nāgaranārāyaṇa

Unfortunately, no details about the author Nāgaranārāyaṇa are available. From the colophon, we come to know that he was one of the disciples of Śrī Rāmedrasarasvatī who was a *sannyāsin,* i.e. *Paramahaṁsa pariavrājakācārya.* He had great reverence for his preceptor as is evident from the very first line is the text.

ॐ गुरुं नत्वोपदेष्टारं वेदान्तेषु विशारदम्।

He also refers to him at another place, while referring to *guru.* सोऽयं गुरुर्गुरुः साक्षाद् राम एव न संशयः। He might have obtained esoteric teachings of *Vedānta* from him. The author seems to be not only well-versed in the *Upaniṣads,* but also was a follower of Advaitic tradition of Śaṅkarācārya. He refers in this work to the *Upaniṣads,* namely the *Bṛhadāraṇyaka,* the *Chāndogya,* the *Muṇḍaka,* the *Praśna.* He also refers to the views of Māṇḍukeya, Māṇḍavya, and Yājñavalkya. He quote lines

(1) 'ज्ञानाग्निः सर्वकर्माणि भस्मसात्कुरुतेऽर्जुन।' (भ. गी. 4.37) from the *Bhagavadgītā* (referred to as *smṛti)* to elucidate his point.

(2) so also कर्तुं नेच्छसि यन्मोहात् करिष्यस्यवशोऽपि तत्। (भ. गी. 18.80) and

(3) ब्राह्मण्याधाय कर्माणि सङ्गं त्यक्त्वा करोति यः।

लिप्यते न स पापेन पद्मपत्रमिवाम्भसा।। (भ. गी. 5.10)

Moreover,

(4) एतद्बुद्ध्वा बुद्धिमान् स्यात् कृतकृत्यश्च.........। (भ. गी. 15. 20)

He was an ardent follower of the Advaitic tradition, as in this treatise, he has paraphrased the teachings of Śaṅkarācārya in a nutshell. At the outset, while describing the *anubandha-catuṣṭaya* (fourfold preliminary requisites, he delineates the nature of the *Adhikārin* (a qualified person) as—

नित्यानित्यविवेकी सन्निहामुत्रविरक्तधीः।
शमादिषट्कसंपन्नो मुमुक्षुरधिकारवान्।।

which is in conformity with the Śaṅkarite tradition. His other explanations and exposition of Vedāntic tenets e.g. the explanation of '*Tattvamasi*' etc. is also from the same point of view. He refers to the doctrine of *vivarta* at one place in the verse—

जगत्सर्वं भोग्यजातं विवर्ततत्वादविद्यया।
तस्मादिदं परानन्दरूप आत्मा प्रकीर्तितम्।।

The author has good command over composing verses in *Anuṣṭup* (and other metres like *Upajāti* and *Āryā)*. It is noteworthy that the inscrutable Vedāntic teaching has been very lucidly presented by the author in this metrical composition, which presupposes crystal clear understanding of the tenets and good command over language and prosody. The author seems to have adequately assimilated the spiritual teachings of his precetor.

No information about the date of the author is found. The ms. of the BORI is a collection of 1879-80 A.D. The date of the scribe of BORI ms. is about 1644 to 1743 A.D. as discussed previously. The author must have flourished before round about that period. The manuscript in O.I. Baroda also seems to be an old one about two hundred years, from the paper material and mode of writing. From the colophon, it appears that he might be *ābhyantara nāgara* Brāhmin from Gujarat. He has commented upon the last part of the *Śāṅkhyāyana* or *Kauṣītaki Āraṇyaka,* which is followed by Ṛgvedins. Hence he might be a follower of *Śāṅkhyāyana* or *Kauṣītaki* school of the *Ṛgveda*. It is learnt that some *Nāgara* Brāhmins of *Sāṭhodarā* caste are followers of Ṛgvedic tradition. The author might be belonging to that caste. But these are all conjectures; no conclusive evidence to prove this is available from any internal or external sources.

The contents of the work—

The present work namely *Jñānamālā* contains one hundred nine verses, mostly in *Anuṣṭubh* metre (three verses are in different metre, one in *Āryā* and other two in *Upajāti* metre), most of them composed by the author himself, elucidating the Vedāntic tenets in a very systematic manner. As per colophon, it is a *kṛti*—a composition of Nāgara-nārāyaṇa, being the (metrical) commentary on the last portion of the *Kauṣītaki-Brāhmaṇopaniṣat*. But it should be noted here that the *Kauṣītaki Upaniṣat* or the *Kauṣītaki-Brāhmaṇo-paniṣat,* which is printed in most of the collections of the *Upaniṣads,* forms the portion of *ādhyāyas* three to six of the *Kauṣītaki/Śāṅkhāyana Āraṇyaka* and the present text *Jñānamālā* has no connection with it. The words of the author that it is the commentary on the last part of the *Kauṣītaki (brāhmaṇa)* or *Upaniṣat* are noteworthy. After a great search, it was found that it forms a metrical commentary on the last three *adhyāyas* (i.e. *adhyāyas* 13, 14 and 15) of the *Śāṅkhāyana* (also known as the *Kauṣītaki) Āraṇyaka,* which incorporate the most significant cream of the Upaniṣadic teachings. On account of its superb philosophical value, less noticed even by Vedāntic scholars, the author might have chosen this small section only as the basis or source material for his superb independent (but based upon this source) work *Jñānamālā,* giving lucid exposition and detailed comments on the significant words and phrases of the above-mentioned portion. The text of the above three *adhyāyas,* upon which the text of the *Jñānamālā* is based on is given below for ready reference and comparison, which can also reflect upon the scholarship of the author Nāgaranārāyaṇa.

शाङ्खायनारण्यकम् (ed. by Shridharshastri Pathak Anand-ashram ed, Poona, 1922, pp. 46-48)

अथ त्रयोदशोऽध्यायः।

ॐ अथातो वैराग्यसंस्कृते शरीरे ब्रह्मयज्ञनिष्ठो भवेदप पुनर्मृत्युं जयति तदु ह वा आत्मा द्रष्टव्यः श्रोतव्यो मन्तव्यो निदिध्यासितव्य इति तमेतं वेदानुवचनेन विविदिषन्ति ब्रह्मचर्येण तपसा श्रद्धया यज्ञेनानाशकेन चेति माण्डूकेयस्तस्मादेवंविच्छान्तो दान्त उपरतस्तितिक्षुः श्रद्धाक्तो भूत्वाऽऽत्मन्येवाऽऽत्मानं पश्येदिति माण्डव्यो योऽयं विज्ञानमयः पुरुषः प्राणेषु स एष नेति नेत्यात्मा न गृह्यते इदं ब्रह्मेदं क्षत्रमिमे देवा इमे वेदा इमे लोका इमानि सर्वाणि भूतानीदं सर्वं यदयमात्मा स एष तत्त्वमसीत्यात्माऽवगम्योऽहं ब्रह्मास्मीति तदेतद्ब्रह्मापूर्वमपरमनपरमनन्तरमबाह्यमयमात्मा ब्रह्म सर्वानुभूरित्यनुशासनमिति याज्ञवल्क्यस्तदेतन्नापुत्राय नानन्तेवासिनं ब्रूयादिति य इमामद्भिः परिगृहीतां वसुमतीं धनस्य पूर्णां दद्यादिदमेव ततो भूय इदमेव ततो भूय इत्यानुशासनम् तामेतामुपनिषदं वेदशिरो न यथा कथंचन वदेत्तदेतदृचाभ्युदितम्।।1।।

इति शाङ्ख्यायनारण्यके त्रयोदशोऽध्यायः।।13।।

अथ चतुर्दशोऽध्यायः।

ॐ ऋचां मूर्धानं यजुषामुत्तमाङ्गं साम्नां शिरोऽथर्वणां मुण्डमुण्ड नाधीतेऽधीते वेदमाहुस्तमज्ञं शिरश्छित्त्वाऽसौ कुरुते कबन्धम्।।1।।

स्थाणुरयं भारहारः किलाभूदधीत्य वेदं न विजानाति योऽर्थम्/योऽर्थज्ञ इत्सकलं भद्रमश्नुते नाकमेति ज्ञानविधूतपाप्मेति विधूतपाप्मेति।।2।।

इति शाङ्ख्यायनारण्यके चतुर्दशोऽध्यायः।।14।।

अथ पञ्चदशोऽध्यायः।

अथ वंशः।। नमो ब्रह्मणे नम आचार्येभ्यो गुणाख्याच्छाङ्खायनादस्माभिरधीतं गुणाख्यः शाङ्खायनः कहोलात्कोषीतकेः कहोलः कौषीतकिरुद्दालकादरुणेरुद्दालक आरुणिः प्रियव्रतात्सोमापेः प्रियव्रतः सोमापिः सोमपात्सोमपः सोमात्प्रातिवेश्यात्सोमः प्रातिवेश्यः प्रतिवेश्यात्प्रतिवेश्यो बृहद्दिवाद्बृहद्दिवः सुम्नयोः सुम्नयुरुद्दालकादुद्दालको विश्वमनसो विश्वमना व्याद्व्यश्वः साकमश्वात्साकमश्वो देवरातादेवरातो विश्वामित्राद्विश्वामित्र इन्द्रादिन्द्रः प्रजापतेः प्रजापतिर्ब्रह्मणो ब्रह्मा स्वयंभूर्नमो ब्रह्मणे नमो ब्रह्मणे।।1।।

इति शाङ्ख्यायनारण्यके पञ्चदशोऽध्यायः।।15।।

The author commences with the salutation to his preceptor. Since the *Adhyāya* begins with *Om* the commentator eulogises it in verses 2 to 12. Then the word *atha* is explained as indicating auspiciousness. The word also presupposes the *anubandha catuṣṭaya,* which is also described by the author (verses 13-20). Then follows the explanation of the phrase *vairāgya saṁskṛte śarīre brahmaniṣṭho bhavet* (verses 21-22) and also of *Apa punarmṛtyum jayati* (verse 23). All the phrases like *Tasmāduha vā ātmā draṣṭavyaḥ, śrotavyaḥ, mantavyaḥ nididhyāsitavyaḥ iti* are commented upon in verses (in 23-25). The means i.e. the *sādhanas* for obtaining knowledge of the *Brahman,* i.e. the *Brahmacarya, tapas, śraddhā, yajña, anāśaka* etc. and also by becoming *śānta, dānta, uparata, titikṣu, śraddhāvitta,* one can realize the *Ātman,* within himself only. All these means are dilated upon (verses 36-43). The nature of *Ātman* is narrated in detail, by pointing out significance of each word starting from *yo'yam Vijñānamayaḥ* upto *yadayamātmā* (44-50). When the direct meaning is incompatible as in *gaṅgāyām ghoṣaḥ,* the *lakṣaṇā* (the suggested) meaning is taken into consideration. The same is dilated upon for clarifying the meaning of '*Tattvamasi*' (verses 51-58) and thenafter also that of '*Ahaṁ brahmāsmi*' (59-61). The words—*Apūrvam, Anaparam, Anantaram Abāhyam, Ayamātmā brahma sarvānubhūḥ*—are explained in the subsequent verses (62-65). This knowledge is to be transmitted to the competent student only. It is superior even to the obtainment of the entire earth, full of wealth. This knowledge is then extolled (66-75).

Then the two passages in *Adhyāya* fourteen are commented upon in verses, that follow. The first passage *Ṛcām mūrdhānam* is explained in verses (76-78ab). The passage *sthāṇurayam* is explained in verses (78cd-81ab). In the subsequent verses the author has given a detailed explanation as to how one can become *Jñānavidhūtapāpmā*. How there can be no attachment with the bonds of all *karmas* after realization. For explainging this, he has also taken recourse to the verses from the *Bhagavadgītā* like *Jñānāgniḥ sarvakarmāṇī bhasmasāt kuruterjuna etc.* and clarified the point very properly (81cd-94ab). The final realization is *ahameva param brahma* etc. All the six *pramāṇas* then become conducive to the knowledge of the *Brahman* only (94cd-104).

The last fifteenth *adhyāya* of the *Āraṇyaka* enumerating the genealogy mentions the *guruśiṣyaparamparā*. It is explained by our author in verses (105-108). The author concludes the work with the following verse—

निर्गुणघटनाग्रथिता विशुद्धबुद्ध्या विवेकमालेयम्।
विद्याविवेकरसिकैर्विदेहविज्ञैर्धृता नित्यम्।।

Concluding Remarks—

(1) It must be noted that the author has selected a very nice portion from the *Śāṅkhāyana Āraṇyaka,* incorporating the profound philosophical speculations, for his metrical commentary.

(2) It is a metrical commentary on the said *Āraṇyaka.* It can also stand as a separate *prakaraṇagrantha* of *Vedānta,* exposing the Advaitic tradition, succinctly in the small work of 109 verses. Most of the tenets of the *Advaita Vedānta* are incorporated in it.

(3) The value of the present text lies not only in its lucidly explaining the portion of the *Āraṇyaka,* but also in simplifying and clarifying Vedāntic concepts in a nutshell.

(4) The text has hitherto remained unnoticed and unpublished. The researcher has here attempted to bring to the notice of scholars, this littleknown work of *Advaita Vedānta*.

The text of the work follows :

ज्ञानमाला

(नागरनारायणकृतिः)

[1]गुरुं नत्वोपदेष्टारं वेदान्तेषु विशारदम्।
कौषीतकिब्राह्मणान्त्यखण्डव्याख्यां करोम्यहम्।।1।।
ॐ इत्येतदुपासीत निर्गुणं प्रकृतेः परम्।
सच्चिदानन्दरूपं तल्लक्ष्यं चिन्मयविग्रहम्।।2।।
मातृकात्रयवाच्यास्य शक्ति(:) स्यात्त्रिगुणात्मिका।
ईश्वरः स च सूत्रात्मा विराडित्युच्यते बुधैः।।3।।
वासुदेवः प्रजा[2]सृ(स्र)ष्टा रुद्रः संहरणादभूत्।
व्यष्टिरध्यस्तरूपेण तत्सृष्ट्वा प्राविश[3]त्ततः।।4।।

जाग्रदिन्द्रियपर्यन्ते स्वप्नोऽभूत्कण्ठदेशतः।
[4]हृदम्बुजे सुषुप्तं तु क्रियमाण इवेक्ष्यते।।5।।
अध्यात्मं चाधिदैवं च साधिभूतं जगत्खलु।
प्रणवस्यैव वाच्यार्थो निर्विकल्पो हि लक्ष्यते।।6।।
उपासनार्थमस्यैव रूपक्लृप्तिः श्रुतिर्जगौ।
अकारो दक्षिणः पक्ष उकारस्तूत्तरः[5] स्मृतः।।7।।
मकारस्तस्य वै पुच्छमर्धमात्राशिरस्तथा।
पादौ रजस्तमस्तस्य शरीरं सत्त्वमुच्यते।।8।।
धर्मश्च दक्षिणं चक्षुर[6]धर्मश्चक्षुरुत्तरम्।
भूर्लोकः पादयोस्तस्य भुवर्लोकस्तु जानुनोः।।9।।
स्वर्लोकः कटिदेशे तु नाभिदेशे महज्जगत्।
जनलोकस्तु हृदये कण्ठदेशे तपस्ततः।।10।।
भ्रुवोर्ललाटमध्ये तु सत्यलोकव्यवस्थितिः।
सोऽहमस्मि स एवाहमिति मन्त्र(:) प्रदर्शितः।।11।।
एवमेनं समारूढो हंसयोगविचक्षणः।
न बध्यते कर्मचारी पापकोटिशतैरपि।।12।।
ॐकारस्त्वथशब्दश्च पुरा ह्वादीश्वरोद्गतौ।
मङ्गलार्थौ सदा तेन खण्डादौ सुप्रयोजितौ।।13।।
[7]निष्कामकर्मानुष्ठानशुद्धान्तःकरणो ह्ययम्।
प्रतीकोपासनायुक्ताहंग्रहैकाग्रमानसः।।14।।
नित्यानित्यविवेकी सन्निहामुत्रविरक्तधीः।
शमादिषट्कसंपन्नो मुमुक्षुरधिकारवान्।।15।।
प्रतिपाद्यं परं ब्रह्म शास्त्रं च प्रतिपादकम्।
ज्ञेयं जीवेशयोरैक्यं विषयोऽयमुदाहृतः।।16।।
सर्वानर्थनिवृत्तिस्तु परमानन्दरूपता।
चतुष्टयानुबन्धस्य परिज्ञानं प्रदर्शितम्।।17।।
साधनानन्तरं ज्ञेयमथशब्दनिरूपितम्।
अकारो वासुदेवः स्याद् थकारः कल्पितं जगत्।।18।।

अकारश्च पुनर्देवः सत्यशब्दार्थवच्छ्रुतौ।
आदौ यद्व्यापकं ब्रह्म तदेवोपरि वर्तते।।19।।
मध्येऽपि कल्पनाहीनं प्रपञ्चे सति निर्मलम्।
तत्सर्वं खल्विदं ब्रह्म नेह नानास्ति किंचन।।20।।
अतःकारणतो नित्ये वैराग्येणैव संस्कृते।
शरीरत्रितये यस्य ब्रह्मनिष्ठो भवेत्तु सः।।21।
ब्रह्मशब्दोदितो वेदस्तद्वेद्यो यज्ञपूरुषः।
यज्ञो वै विष्णुरिति च श्रुत्युक्तः परमेश्वरः।।22।।
तन्निष्ठो यः पुमान्धीरोऽपमृत्योर्जयकारकः।
एवं श्रुतीनां सिद्धान्तः सदानन्दः सुनिश्चितः।।23।।
तत्तस्मादुह वा एतदव्ययत्रितयार्थतः।
वेदत्रयान्तेषु सूक्तं हेयोपादेयवर्जितम्।।24।।
यस्य दर्शनमात्रेण सर्वं विदितमित्यसौ।
बृहदारण्यके यद्वच्छान्दोग्येऽपि तथैव तत्।।25।।
येनाश्रुतं श्रुतमिति दृष्टान्तत्रय[8]मीरितम्।
यस्मिञ्ज्ञाते जगत्सर्वं विज्ञातं भवति ध्रुवम्।।26।।
मुण्डके प्रश्नविषयेऽयमेवार्थ उदाहृतः।
अत्राप्यात्मैव द्रष्टव्यो व्यापको ज्ञानगोचरः।।27।।
कथं ज्ञानेन गम्योऽसौ तदुपायः प्रकीर्त्यते।
वेदान्तसारवाक्येभ्यो गुरुभ्यो हि निरन्तरम्।।28।।
श्रोतव्यः प्रत्यगात्मायं लिङ्गषट्कैर्विपश्चिता।
वेदान्तानां तु सर्वेषामादिमध्यावसानतः।।29।।
शुद्धात्मन्येव तात्पर्यमिति धीः श्रवणं तु तत्।
श्रौतार्थस्य विचाराख्यं मननं तु विधीयते।।30।।
ताभ्यं निर्गलिते ह्यर्थे बुद्धेः संस्थापनं तु यत्।
एकतानत्वमेतत्तु निदिध्यासनमुच्यते।।31।।
आवृत्तिश्च प्रकर्तव्या सर्वदोषापनुत्तये।
अनेकशास्त्रश्रवणादसंभावनया तथा।।32।।

विपरीतपरिज्ञानाद्विषयासाद्य लौल्यतः।
बुद्धिमान्द्यात्कु[9]तर्काच्च दुराग्रहविभावनात्।।33।।
अदृढं जायते ज्ञानं तेनावृत्तिर्विधीयते।
सर्वदुःखनिवृत्तिस्तु परमानन्दभानतः।।34।।
न तस्य प्राणगमनं संसारस्य समाप्तितः।
इतिशब्देन निर्दिष्टो ब्रह्मभावः सनातनः।।35।।
यज्ज्ञात्वा मुनयः सर्वे मुक्तिमार्गमुपागताः।
तमेतं वेदवचसा साधनैर्ज्ञातुमीप्सवः।।36।।
ब्रह्मचर्येण सततं नैष्ठिकेन जितात्मना।
तपसा देहशोषेण यतिचान्द्रायणादिना।।37।।
श्रद्धयास्तिक्यबुद्ध्या च गुरूपास्त्या विशेषतः।
यज्ञेन देवतोद्देशद्रव्यत्यागेन कर्मणा।।38।।
विषयाग्रहणेनैवानाशकेन विपश्चितः।
साधनैर्ज्ञातुमिच्छन्तीति माण्डूकेय अब्रवीत्।।39।।
माण्डव्योऽपि तथैवाह तस्माच्छान्तान्तरेन्द्रियः।
जितेन्द्रियो भवेद्दान्तो दुष्टसङ्गविवर्जितः।।40।।
उपसृत्संगमरतस्तितिक्षुश्च क्षमारतः।
भूत्वा श्रद्धावित्तयुक्तो गुरुं ब्रह्मविदां वरम्।।41।।
उपायानीतिशरणं गत्वा विन्देत्परात्परम्।
एतादृशो मुमुक्षुर्वै पश्येदात्मानमात्मनि।।42।।
निश्चयेनेति यज्ज्ञानान्मुच्यते सर्वबन्धनात्।
तज्ज्ञानं तु गुरु(:) प्राह ब्रह्मलक्षणपूर्वकम्।।43।।
योऽयं विज्ञानरूपोऽसौ वृत्तिर्ज्ञानमयो ध्रुवः।
पुरा सदा ह्यजोऽनन्तः सर्वपापविदाहकः।।44।।
पुरुष(:) पूरणाद्वापि प्राणेषु सततं स्थितः।
स एष नेति नेत्यात्मा मूर्तामूर्तविवर्जितः।।45।।
अगृह्य एव सर्वत्र भ्रमाधिष्ठाननिर्मल।
इदं ब्रह्म ब्राह्मणत्वमिदं क्षत्रं तथैव च।।46।।

इमे देवा इमे वेदा भूतानीमानि सर्वशः।
जगत्सर्वं भोग्यजातं विवर्तत्वादविद्यया।।47।।
तस्मादिदं परानन्दरूप आत्मा प्रकीर्तितम्।
स एषः सर्ववित्सर्वेश्वर(:) सर्वगुहाशयः।।48।।
सौम्य तत्त्वमसीत्येवावगम्यो भेदवर्जितः।
संसर्गार्थो न कर्तव्यो विशिष्टोऽपि च नेतरः।।49।।
एकमेवाद्वितीयं सदुच्यते द्वैतवर्जितम्।
भेदत्रयविनिर्मुक्तं सच्चिदानन्दलक्षणम्।।50।।
महागुरो ब्रह्मविदां वरिष्ठ
सर्वज्ञसंज्ञं सदिहोपदिष्टम्।
अल्पज्ञसंज्ञे मयि तत्कथंचिद्
बोधो यथार्थो हि तथा विधेहि।।51।।
एवं ब्रुवाणं सच्छिष्यं गुरुराह कृपानिधिः।
यत्र न ज्ञायते ह्यर्थो लक्षणा तत्र कीर्तिता।।52।।
सा लक्षणापि त्रिविधा जहत्स्वार्था तथा परा।
अजहल्लक्षणा ज्ञेया भागत्यागा तृतीयका।।53।।
लोके वेदे च सर्वत्र लक्षणा बोधकारिणी।
गङ्गायां घोष इत्यत्र मनो ब्रह्मेति च श्रुतौ।।54।।
जहतीलक्षणां कृत्वा तत्संबन्धी प्रगृह्यते।
श्वेतो विधावतीत्यत्र सत्यं ज्ञानमिति श्रुतौ।।55।।
अजहल्लक्षणा ज्ञेया सत्यरूपं हि लक्ष्यते।
सोऽयं पुरुष इत्यत्र तथा तत्त्वमसि श्रुतौ।।56।।
भागत्यागेन बोद्धव्यं शुद्धमेकं सनातनम्।
सर्वज्ञत्वादिकं चेशे मायया सुप्रदर्शितम्।।57।।
तथा त्वयि ह्यसर्वज्ञत्वादिकं च प्रकल्पितम्।
कल्पितांशस्य वै बाधं कृत्वात्मानं विचिन्तय।।58।।
एवं सुज्ञापितः शिष्यो निर्विकल्पं प्रपेदिवान्।
पश्चादुवाच [10]गुर्वग्रेऽहं ब्रह्मास्मि यथा भवान्।।59।।

अहंकारादिदेहान्तबाधं कृत्वावशेषितः।
तथा वै जगतो बाधं कृत्वा यदवशेषितम्॥60॥

ब्रह्माहमस्मीति हि निर्विवादं
मयानुभूतं वरसुप्रसादात्।
विज्ञानमानन्दमनन्तरूपं
अहो न जातं च सदैव भातम्॥61॥

इतः परं श्रुतिः प्राह जगदानन्दकारिणी।
तद् यो देवेषु जानाति मुनिसंघेषु यः पुनः॥62॥

मनुष्येष्वपि यो [11]विद्यात्सर्वभावं समश्नुते।
तदेतद्ब्रह्मणो रूपमपूर्वत्वात्सनातनम्॥63॥

अविनाशि त्वतो ह्यस्मात्परं नास्ति ततश्चितः।
अनन्तरमबाह्यं यत्तद्रूपं ह्यात्मनः परम्॥64॥

अयमात्मा तथा ब्रह्म सर्वाधिष्टानमद्वयम्।
सर्वानुभूरित्यनुशासनमाह श्रुतिः स्वयम्॥65॥

याज्ञवल्क्यो मुनिः प्राह ब्रह्मिष्ठः सर्ववित्तमः।
सुपुत्राय प्रवक्तव्यं सुशिष्याय विशेषतः॥66॥

न ब्रूयादन्यथा ह्यस्माद्ब्रह्मज्ञानं महत्पदम्।
य इमां धनपूर्णां वा अद्भिः परिवृतां धराम्॥67॥

दद्यात्तथा सर्ववस्तु ततो ज्ञानं विशिष्यते।
ज्ञानादेव तु कैवल्यं प्राप्यते येन मुच्यते॥68॥

यो वै भूमा तत्सुखं च नाल्पे सौख्यमनित्यतः।
इदमेव ततो भूय इति भूयोऽनुशासनम्॥69॥

दुःखाभावश्च कामाप्तिः कृतकृत्यत्वमित्यसौ।
प्राप्तप्राप्तव्यमित्येवं विद्यानन्दो हि जायते॥70॥

आनन्दजननीमेतां वेदमस्तकरूपिणीम्।
यथाकथंचन न तां [12]वदेदुपनिषद्गिरम्॥71॥

समीपस्थं यदज्ञानं जगद्विक्षेपकारणम्।
तन्नाशं नितरां कर्त्रीं स्वरूपप्रापिकां पराम्॥72॥

सच्छिष्याय प्रवक्तव्यां नान्यथा तां यथार्थदाम्।
तदेतन्नामधेयं वाग्वाचा ह्यभ्युदितं परम्।।73।।
विज्ञानं ब्रह्मसामान्यलक्षणं मूर्धलक्षणम्।
अहं ब्रह्मास्मि वचसा गुरुणानुभवः कृतः।।74।।
तत्त्वमस्यादिवाक्येन ह्युपदेशो विधीयते।
अयमात्मा परं ब्रह्म शिष्यस्यानुभवो मतः।।75।।
ऋचां मूर्धाभिधानं तु यजुषामुत्तमाङ्गकम्।
साम्नां शिरोऽथर्वणां च मुण्डमुण्डं प्रकीर्तितम्।।76।।
उत्तमाङ्गानि नाधीते पूर्वभागस्य [13]पाठकः।
तमज्ञमृषयो ह्याहुर्वेदमस्तकहा ह्यसौ।।77।।
कबन्धकर्ता वेदानां रौरवं नरकं व्रजेत्।
अयं भारहरः स्थाणुरधीत्यापि न वेत्ति यः।।78।।
वेदार्थं यो विजानाति सकलं प्राप्नुयात्फलम्।
भद्रं समश्नुते नाकमेति ज्ञानप्रसादतः।।79।।
यस्माद्विधूतपाप्मेति ह्यसुखं नैव लभ्यते।
विशेषार्थपरिज्ञानाद्गुर्वनुग्रहतो ध्रुवम्।।80।।
नाकं स्वरूपं परमं प्राप्नोत्येव न संशयः।
संचितानि दहेदाशुः ज्ञानवानाशुशुक्षणिः।।81।।
प्रारब्धपालनं लोकानुग्रहाय प्रवर्तते।
क्रियमाणस्य संस्पर्शो नैव तस्य विपश्चितः।।82।।
तस्य प्रियाश्च सुकृतमप्रिया दुष्कृतं तथा।
प्राप्नुवन्त्यनिशं ह्येवं श्रुतिसूत्रकृतोर्वचः।।83।।
यथैवमीषिकातूलमग्नौ प्रोतं [14]प्रहूयते।
एवं संचितपाप्मानः [15]प्रहूयन्ते विवेकिनः।।84।।
तावदेव चिरं तस्य प्रारब्धं परिकल्पितम्।
ब्रह्मैव सन् ततो ब्रह्म प्राप्त इत्यभिधीयते।।85।।
यथा पुष्करपर्णेऽस्मिन्नपामश्लेषणं भवेत्।
सुहृदः साधुकृत्यां च द्विषन्तः पाप्मनः फलम्।।86।।

लभन्ते विदुषो नित्यं तस्माज्ज्ञानं विभाव्यतः।
स्मृतिष्वपि तथोवाच भगवानर्जुनं प्रति।।87।।
ज्ञानाग्निः सर्वकर्माणि भस्मसात्कुरुतेऽर्जुन।
प्रारब्धकर्मवशतः प्रवृत्तिः पुरुषस्य वै।।88।।
कर्तुं नेच्छसि यन्मोहात् करिष्यस्यवशोऽपि यत्।
ब्रह्मण्याधाय कर्माणि सङ्गं त्यक्त्वा करोति यः।।89।।
लिप्यते न स पापेन पद्मपत्रमिवाम्भसा।
त्रिविधानां कर्मणां च गतिरेषा विवेकिनाम्।।90।।
एतद्बुदध्वा बुद्धिमान्स्यात्कृतकृत्यश्च सर्वदा।
एवं ये नैव जानन्ति ते यान्ति यमसादनम्।।91।।
कर्मिणो ये प्रगच्छन्ति धूमाद्रात्रिमिति क्रमात्।
कर्ममिश्रोपासका ये प्रतीकोपासनारताः।।92।।
तेऽर्चिरादिगता प्राप्य ब्रह्मलोकं प्रयान्ति च।
अहंग्रहोपासनायां रता ये ब्रह्मतत्पराः।।93।।
पुनरावृत्तिरहिता ब्रह्मलोकं प्रयान्ति ते।
यस्तु विज्ञानवान्नित्यं निर्गुणं निर्विकल्पकम्।।94।।
निरञ्जनं सदा वेत्ति तस्य कार्यं न विद्यते।
सदानन्दः सतां सेव्यः स्वयं ब्रह्मैव केवलः।।95।।
कुतो न गन्ता नागन्ता सर्वत्रायमवस्थितः।
अहमेव परं ब्रह्म शुद्धोऽहमजरोऽमरः।।96।।[16]
प्रत्यक्षं चानुमानं चोपमानं शब्दसंज्ञितम्।
अर्थापत्तिः पञ्चमं चानुपलब्धिः प्रमाणकम्।।97।।
सर्वभाने पूर्वभातं भासकं ब्रह्म लक्षयेत्।
नामरूपादिकं त्यक्त्वा प्रत्यक्षं ब्रह्म बुध्यते।।98।।
यत्कार्यं दृश्यते लोके दृष्टं तद्धि सकर्तृकम्।
क्षित्यङ्कुरादिकं कार्यं दृष्ट्वा कर्तानुमीयते।।99।।
वृत्तिज्ञानं यदा भाति तत्तुल्यं नित्यबोधकम्।
उपमानेन बोद्धव्यं शान्तादिषु [17]सुखादिकम्।।100।।

यतो वै जायते विश्वं तज्जलानीति शब्दतः।
सुखमात्यन्तिकं [18]यत्तज्ज्ञायते परमार्थतः।।101।।
अयं हि कल्पितो लोकः साधिष्ठानो भवेद्ध्रुवम्।
तदधिष्ठानभूतं सदर्थापत्त्या विवेचितम्।102।।
समाधिसुप्तिमूर्च्छादौ निर्जगद्ब्रह्मदर्शनात्।
सदा विचारयेद्विद्वान्नद्वैतं सदभावतः।।103।।
पूर्णोऽहं सच्चिदानन्दो नारायण इति स्थितः।
[19]सर्ववेदपुराणानामयमर्थः प्रदर्शितः।।104।।
अथ वंशस्य कथने माङ्गल्यं क्रियते श्रुतौ।
नमो ब्रह्मण इत्येवमाचार्येभ्यो विशेषतः।।105।।
पञ्चम्यन्तो गुरुज्ञे(ज्ञे)यः प्रथमान्तस्तु शिष्यकः।
हितमार्गप्रदर्शी यो ह्यहिताच्च निवर्तकः।।106।।
सोऽयं गुरुर्गुरुः साक्षाद्राम एव न संशयः।
अन्ते नमो ब्रह्मणे च नमो ब्रह्मण इत्यपि।।107।।
मङ्गलं च समाप्तिश्च द्विरुक्त्या सुप्रदर्शिता।
नारायणोऽहमद्वैतो नेह नानास्ति किंचन।।108।।
[20]निर्गुणघटनाग्रथिता
विशुद्धबुद्ध्या विवेकमालेयम्।
विद्याविवेकरसिकै-
र्विदेहविज्ञैर्धृता नित्यम्।।109।।

इति श्रीमत्परमहंसपरिव्राजकाचार्यश्रीरामेन्द्रसरस्वतीशिष्याभ्यन्तरना[21]-गरनारायणकृतौ कौषीतकि[22]ब्राह्मणोपनिपदन्त्यखण्डव्याख्या [23]ज्ञानमाला समाप्ता।।[24]

FOOTNOTES

Paper published in Journal of Oriental Institute, Baroda, Vol. 46, Nos. 3-4, March-June 1997 Issue, pp. 185-199. Paper read at 38th session of the All-India Oriental Conference, held at Jadavapur University of Calcutta during 28-30th Jan. 1997.

1. Begins with श्रीरामचन्द्रो जयति, B begins witn श्रीगणेशाय नमः। A and B both add before 1, ॐ.
2. A and B सृष्टा.
3. B. तमः
4. हृदेंबुजे
5. B उत्तर.
6. B अधर्मं.
7. A and B निःकाम.
8. B ईरिते.
9. A कृतः कश्चिद्.
10. B सर्वग्रे.
11. B विंद्यात्.
12. A वंदेद्.
13. B पाठकाः.
14. B प्रदूयते.
15. B प्रदूयंते.
16. B reads 104^{ab} after 96.
17. B यथासुखम्.
18. A यत्र.
19. B reads 104^{cd} and 105 as one verse No. 104 hence consecutive nos. change upto the end.
20. B omits 109.
21. B om. नागर.
22. B om. ब्राह्मण.
23. B om. ज्ञानमाला.
24. B reads after colophon—संवत् वर्षे 17 ×× माघवदि 9 शनौ आभ्यन्तरजातीयपण्ड्या श्री पं. गोविन्देत लिखितम्। यदक्षर०।। शुभं भवतु।। भट्टश्री।। जगज्जीवनार्थे लिखितम्।

EPICS AND PURĀṆA

XVII

INTERPRETATION OF THE WORD *'KAṬU'* IN THE *BHAGAVADGĪTĀ*

In the seventeenth *adhyāya* of the *Bhagavadgītā,* there is description of the three kinds of food that is agreeable to the persons of triple mentality, based upon the three kinds of *guṇas* i.e. qualities of the *prakṛti*. In the enumeration of the food, dear to the persons of Rājasic nature, the word *'kaṭu'* occurs in the following verse :

Kaṭvamlalavaṇātyuṣṇatīkṣṇarūkṣavidāhinaḥ /
āhārā rājasasyeṣṭā duḥkhaśokāmayapradāḥ //
—Bha.g. 17.9

Prof. S. Radhakrishnan translates the above verse as follows :

"The foods that are bitter, sour, saltish, very hot, pungent, harsh and burning, producing pain, grief and disease are liked by the "passionate".

This clearly shows that he has interpreted the word *'kaṭu'* in the sense of 'bitter'. Many books, incorporating traslation and/or explanation of verses of the *Bhagavadgītā,* written by different scholars are available. Many scholars like — Swami Chidbhavanand, Alladi Mahadev Shastri, Jayadayal Goyandaka, K.V. Lele, Pandurang Shastri Athawale etc. have interpreted the word *'kaṭu'* in the sense of 'bitter' only.

In the Sanskrit literature, the term *'kaṭu'* has been used in two senses i.e. (1) bitter and (2) pungent—Hence Prof. Apte has recorded the two meanings of the said word in his Dictionary.

It is presumable that the scholars, translating the verses of the *Bhagavadgītā,* were well-aware of the two kinds of meaning of the word. But yet they have taken it in the sense of 'bitter' in the context of the *Bhagavadgītā.* Harikṛṣṇadāsa Goyandakā has given the following explanation for his interpretation—

"*Neema* and *Karela* etc. fall under the category of bitter foods. Some interpret the word *'kaṭu'* as pungent and include pepper etc. in this class. But the separate mention of the word *'Tīkṣṇa'* which evidently stands for pungent foods, justifies our construing the word *'kaṭu'* as "bitter". (p. 698).

But the above statement requires consideration, his main argument being regarding the separate mention of the word *'Tīkṣṇa'*. Many scholars have also interpreted the word *'Tīkṣṇa'* in the sense of pungent, as done by him : but it is necessary to think why the word *'Tikta'* itself has not been used in the place *'tīkṣṇa'* to make the sense more clear.

Originally, the word *'Tikta'* means bitter and *'kaṭu'* means pungent. They have been used in these senses in the earlier works like *Caraka Saṁhitā* etc. But in the later period, the change is met with in Sanskrit and other Indian languages like *Kaḍu* (in Marathi), *Kedavuṁ* (in Gujarati), *Kaḍavā* (in Hindi). Similarly, *'Tikta'* has equivalent *'tikhu'* (in Gujarati), *'tikhaṭa'* (in Marathi), *tīkhā* (in Hindi)—all meaning pungent and not bitter.

In my opinion, the word *'kaṭu'* should be interpreted as 'pungent' in the context of the *Bhagavadgītā* for the following reason—

(1) The Lord is describing the three kinds of *āhāra* (food), that is liked by persons of threefold faith. Here the line is—*āhārastvapi sarvasya trividho bhavati priyaḥ.* The words '*sarvasya trividhaḥ āhāraḥ priyaḥ bhavati*—are

important. The adjectives *'sarvasya'* and *'priyaḥ'* are quite significant. It is the food that is liked by them, agreeable to them. But it appears to me to be improper to state that bitter articles are liked by the Rajasic persons. People do not generally like to eat bitter articles of food. Similarly, the word *'Iṣṭaḥ'* occurring in the above verse, (which means agreeable) is also significant and it supports the above explanation. It is the description of the articles, agreeable to Rājasic persons, hence I think, the meaning of '*kaṭu*' as bitter would not be proper. On the contrary, the meaning of '*kaṭu*' as pungent would better fit the context, as pungent articles like *Marīca* etc. are generally liked by the persons and not bitter substances. The effect also of the two kinds of articles namely of bitter and pungent nature are quite different and opposite as seen in the works of *Āyurveda*. From the point of view of effect *(paripāka)* also the pungent articles fit better as Rājasic substances than the bitter articles. The word '*kaṭu*' is employed is the sense of pungent in the early works like *Caraka Saṁhitā* etc. The *Bhagavadgītā* is also a work of ancient period and hence to interpret the word '*kaṭu*' as bitter would be improper. It is admittable that in the later Sanskrit literature, the word has been used mostly in the sense of bitter.

Śaṅkarācārya states that the word *'ati'* is to be construed with *kaṭu* etc. This would mean that *atikaṭu* (excessively *kaṭu)* articles are agreeable to Rājasic persons. If we understand *kaṭu* in the sense of bitter, the meaning—that is—excessively bitter articles are liked—would be quite improper. Instead of it, if we take it to mean as excessively pungent articles are liked by people of Rājasic nature, it would be practically quite true as we do come across such people in this world. K.V. Lele has translated the commentary of Śaṅkarācārya in Marathi. He takes the word *'atikaṭu'* in the sense of excessively bitter, which seems to be quite improper.

Now the question remains regarding the word *tīkṣṇa* of the above verse, which has been generally interpreted as pungent. The Dictionary meaning of this word is also pungent, as interpreted by them. But in the *Caraka Saṁhitā* (I. 26-89) itself, it is mentioned that the *tīkṣṇatā* is the *vīryaguṇa* (quality signifying the power) of the substance, which is again of eight kinds *(vīryam—aṣṭavidham)*. This means that according to *Caraka,* any article can be *tīkṣṇa,* not only the pungent article of food. Even the *Lavaṇa* (saltish) article also is said to be *tīkṣṇa.* Here the meaning of term *tīkṣṇa* as pungent is also not proper in the strict sense of the term.

Moreover, it is noteworthy that in the person of Rājasic nature, there is naturally the preponderance of bile—*pitta*—which is reddish in colour and he likes also such articles, that accellerate the *pitta* in the body. Hence the pungent, sour and salt etc. are conducive to that effect. On the contrary, the bitter substances subdue the bilic-*pitta*—condition of the person. *(Caraka* I. 1.65).

With complete reverence and respect for the great scholars interpreting the *Bhagavadgītā,* I have humbly to state that it would be better to interpret the *kaṭu* in the above context of the *Bhagavadgītā,* as pungent, as it is better fitting the said context which would be clear from the above explanation.

REFERENCES

1. Radhakrishnan, S., *The Bhagavadgītā* (English Translation), Sixth Indian Reprint, Blackie and Son Publishers Pvt. Ltd., Bombay, 1979.

2. Swami Chidbhavanand, *The Bhagavadgītā,* Shri Rama Krishna Tapovanam, Tirupparaitttural, Tiruchirapalli, Tamilnadu, Tenth impression, 1979.

3. Sastry Alladi Mahadev, *The Bhagavadgītā,* with Com. of Śrī Śaṅkarācārya, English Trans., Smata Books, Madras, 1979.

4. Goyandaka Jayadayal, *Śrīmad-Bhagavadgītā* with Sanskrit text and English translation, Gita Press, Gorakhpur, Third edition, 1978.

5. Lele, K. V., *Sabhāṣyaśāṅkarabhāṣya,* Marathi translation, Bombay (Adh. 13-18).

6. *Gītāmṛtam,* in Marathi, based upon lectures on *Gītā* by Shri Pandurang Shastri Athavale, Srimadbhagavadgita Pathashala, Bombay, Second edition, 1981.

7. Pade Shankar Daji, (ed.) *Cakara Saṁhitā,* Nirnaya Sagar Press, Bombay, 1867.

8. Apte, V.S., *The Practical Sanskrit-English Dictionary,* Third edition, revised and enlarged, Gopal Narayan and Co., Bombay, 1924.

XVIII

METHODOLOGY AND PRINCIPLES OF THE CRITICAL EDITION OF THE *VĀLMĪKI-RĀMĀYAṆA*

Introductory

The Critical Editions of the two great Indian epics, namely, the *Rāmāyaṇa* and the *Mahābhārata* were a Long-felt desideratum. The need for the Critical Edition (C.E.) of the *Mahābhārata* was first felt by Prof. M. Winternitz in 1897 and was first attempted by Prof. H. Luders in 1908. But the complete project was undertaken in 1919 by the Bhandarkar Oriental Research Institute, Pune. It was continued under the mature and scholarly guidance of Prof. V.S. Sukthankar and was completed in 1966. On similar lines and principles, the Oriental Institute of Baroda, undertook in 1951, the Project of the C.E. of the *Vālmīki-Rāmāyaṇa* (V.R.), with financial assistance of U.G.C. and some donors, under the General Editership of Prof. G.H. Bhatt and was completed under the General Editership of Dr. U.P. Shah in 1975. The C.E. was published in seven voluminous volumes covering one *Kāṇḍa* each namely, *Bāla, Ayodhyā, Araṇya, Kiṣkindhā, Sundara, Yuddha* and *Uttara,* each edited by such profound scholars, as Prof. G.H. Bhatt *(Bāla),* Dr. P.L. Vaidya *(Ayodhyā* and *Yuddha),* Shri P.C. Divanji *(Araṇya).* Prof. D.R. Mankad *(Kiṣkindhā),* Prof. G.C. Jhala *(Sundara)* and Dr. U.P. Shah *(Uttara).* Each volume of the C.E. incorporated in it, a detailed description of Mss., a Scholarly Introduction by each editor, a concordance of critical text with the printed Editions, the constituted critical text with the critical apparatus of each verse printed below on the same page, Appendices containing the additional passages and Lastly the critical notes. It is intended here, for the sake of general readers and beginners in the field, to deal briefly with the Methodology and Principles that were followed in preparing the C.E. of the V.R. (Critical Edition of the *Vālmīki Rāmāyaṇa).*

What is a Critical Edition

Before actually describing the methodology and principles of the Critical Edition, it is quite necessary to know what is meant by a Critical Edition.

In ancient India, there was an oral system of transmission of knowledge. Our epics and Purāṇas were no exception to that. The rhapsodists also tried to narrate the text with addition, alteration and omission of certain material for enhancing its popularity and usefulness and making it more interesting and appealing to the masses. They have added the current and popular versions and contemporary ethical, moral, religious and political ideas and beliefs. In this way the text was found narrated differently in different regions. Thus, due to local influences, the text was very much tempered with and it suffered conflation. Even when the writing method came into vogue, due to the perishability and fragility of the wrinting material, the process of copying down the manuscripts from generation to generation became quite indispensable and even during this stage, the text was undergoing changes at the hands of narrators and the copyists. Therefore, there were not only differences in the Northern and Southern traditions of the texts, but even local variations in contents and sequences of words, lines, *Ślokas, and even of sargas.*

The critical Edition is an humble attempt to remove all

such irregularities, corruptions, conflations etc. and to give as far as possible a pure, authentic, and the oldest form of the text on the basis of available authentic manuscripts of the text. To quote Prof. Sukthankar, "It is but a modest attempt to present a version of the epic as old as the extant manuscript material will permit us to reach. It only claims to be the most ancient one according to the direct line of transmission, purer than others in so far as it is free from the obvious errors of copying and spurious additions". (p. 129).

Collection of Manuscrips

As the basis of the Critical Edition is mainly the manuscripts of the text, the first necessary and pertinent task is the collection of genuine manuscripts from different regions of India, Nepal and other foreign countries. The *New Catalogus Catalogorum,* the *Catalogus Catalogorum* by Aufrecht and the published catalogues of different Institutes, Libraries and Universities can be helpful in getting information regarding manuscripts. Attempts are also made to get the original manuscripts, or their xerox, microfilm copies or even photocopies.

There being numerous manuscripts of the text, sometimes it becomes necessary to study actually the manuscripts and make a selection, so that preference can be given to pure, complete, good and different types of manuscripts, to those that are corrupt, damaged, incomplete, and similar types and those that are copies of the copy. Moreover, importance is also given to the manuscripts in scripts other than *Devanāgarī* (namely, *Śāradā, Nevārī, Maithilī, Beṅgalī, Telugu, Grantha, Malayālam* etc.), which are supposed to incorporate the regional versions of the text.

Vulgate and Collation

Among the different printed editions of the text, an

edition which is older, authentic and contains the maximum number of verses is selected as the basic text which is termed as 'Vulgate'. Each line of it is written on the top line of the specially prepared collation-sheets, having horizontal and vertical crossed lines, the space to the left side for writing *siglum* (abbreviation used for a manuscript e.g. D-1 for *Devanāgarī* manuscript No. 1) and large space to the right side for writing the additional information of each manuscript and for marginal remarks, found in the manuscripts of collation.

For the Critical Edition of the *Vālmīki Rāmāyaṇa,* the text printed by the Gujarati Printing Press, Bombay, was selected as a vulgatc. Prof. G.H. Bhatt found that there were more than two thousand manuscripts of the *Vālmīki Rāmāyaṇa,* preserved in public and private libraries in India and outside. On the principle of antiquity, purity and completeness, manuscripts belonging to different scripts were selected for collation. Even after collation, some manuscripts which were mere copies of an old manuscript were rejected. Thus, finally, the critical text of seven *Kāṇḍas* was based respectively upon, 37, 29, 32, 29, 34 and 41 manuscripts in different scripts. The oldest manuscript was in Newari script dated (C. 1020 A.D.) from the Bir Library, Kathmandu, Nepal.

Stema Codicum

On the basis of the collated material, the family relationship of different manuscripts is to be determined. This can be can be done (1) by studying the readings of the common stanzas, (2) by additions or omissions of the passages, (3) by noting the sequence in text-units. When the inter-relationship is established, an attempt is made to represent it in the form of a family tree i.e. *Stema codicum.* It was found that the *Vālmīki Rāmāyaṇa* could broadly be divided into two recesions namely Southern (S) and Northern (N) and each recension had different sub-recensions of its own. Every editor of each *kāṇḍa,* has carefully prepared and presented the *stema codicum* of manuscripts, utilized for that particular *kāṇḍa.*

Prof. G.H. Bhatt pertinently observes, "A comparative study of Northern and Southern recensions clearly shows that S has generelly preserved the text of the Vālmīki Rāmāyaṇa in an original or older form, while N. has polished the text both from the view-point of form and matter". (Introduction of *Bāla* P. XXII).

Testimonia

The evidence furnished by the commentaries and epitomes has been useful for the Critical Edition of *Vālmīki Rāmāyaṇa.* It is technically termed as *Testimonia.* The six commentaries those of (1) Varadarāja, (2) Rāmānuja, (3) Māheśvaratīrtha, (4) Govindarāja, (5) Katakayogīndra and (6) Nāgeśa Bhaṭṭa were utilized. The *Rāmopākhyāna* in the *Mahābhārata* the *Purāṇas* (like *Viṣṇu, Agni* and *Padma*) and the *Rāmāyaṇa-mañjarī* of *Kṣemendra* were also made use of. While the quotations of *Rāmāyaṇa* in several works were utilized with great caution. But, all these were given only the secondary importance in the constitution of the text.

General Principles of the Constitution of the Text

Prof. Bhatt enunciates that there are no mechanical rules which can be followed for the constitution of the text. The text cannot be re-constructed merely by the majority of manuscripts as some manuscripts, although forming minority, can represent the text in the original form. Individual cases have to be judged on their own merit. He further, remarks that a comparative study of the manuscripts in the *Mahābhārata* and the *Vālmīki Rāmāyaṇa* clearly shows that both the National Epics sail in the same boat and are entitled to the same treatment for the reconstruction of the texts. The principles enunciated by Dr. V.S. Sulthankar have been declared as very sound and recommended even for the Critical Edition of the *Rāmāyaṇa*. Prof. Bhatt followed in general the principles of Dr. Sukthankar. He also however enumerates some principles which guided him in the preparation of the Critical Edition of *Vālmīki Rāmāyaṇa* (Introduction to *Bāla,* XXXIV). They are given below :

(1) When both the Recensions N. and S. agree, the text should be accepted.

(2) When N. and S. do not agree, preference should be generally given to S. as it seems to have preserved the text in an older or original form.

But, when N. and S. do not agree and when S. presents the text in a form which does not suit the context, or which evidently appears to be absurd, preference should be given to the N. text.

(3) When a passage is omitted in both N. and S. or either of them, it creates suspicion and should, therefore, be rejected.

(4) When a passage is omitted in any version of N. or S., and if it is not necessary for the context, it should be dropped.

(5) When a passage is omitted in several manuscripts (even if not in any entire version), provided some of the manuscripts in question are not closely related and one cannot have influenced another, it should be dropped as secondary cf. 107*

(6) A way line (~~~~~~) is generally used when manuscripts of the same Recension are equally divided and keep the point moot. It is not used when S. differs from N. as S. is generally taken to represent an older form of the text than N.

(7) Emendation should be avoided, as far as possible, in favour of interpretation.

Besides these, some general rules for selection of a particular reading enunciated by Prof. Sukthankar were also followed. There is mostly an attempt to eliminate an archaism or a solecism (grammatical or metrical irregularities) of the text during the process of its transmission. They also try to simplify the readings difficult to understand. In all such cases, there is every possibility of original reading being an archaism, a solecism or a *lectio difficilior.* Such readings ate retained in the critical text.

The Critical Apparatus

When the critical text is ready, the remaining collated material like-other variants, additions, omissions, sequence of verse-units, notes regarding damaged portion, lacunae in the manuscript etc. is to be presented systematically for each verse of text—it is called critical Apparatus. Additional or substitute passages not included in the text are presented in the form of insertion, or substitute passages marked with star (*) in the Critical Apparatus. The lengthy additional passages are relegated to Appendix, with appropriate, reference, regarding their actual position in the text. When the sequence of stanzas in mss. is very complicated, it is presented in a tabular form in the apparatus, and is technically called "conspectus".

The critical apparatus of *Vālmīki Rāmāyaṇa* contains as mentioned above not only the systematic presentation of variants, but, also records the additions, omissions, alterations, notes regarding lacuna, damaged portions, sequence of stanzas, conspectus and star passages both of insertion and substitute type. The additional lengthy passages have also been relegated to the appendices of each volume.

The critical text is then compared line to line with other

printed editions and the comparative statement regarding that is presented in a tabular form is called "Concordance". The concordance of each *kāṇḍa* of the Critical Edition of *Vālmīki Rāmāyaṇa* with printed editions of Bombay, Kumbhakonam, Gorresio and Lahore has been prepared and published in each volume.

The Introductions to each volume, written by the learned editors incorporate not only the detailed information regarding the manuscript material utilized but also discussion regarding *stema codicum,* interrelationship and peculiarities of different recensions and versions. They have also dealt with contents and other distinctive issues, connected with each *Kāṇḍa.*

Concluding Remarks

Thus, after the continuous scholarly and strenous efforts of local and outside scholars for about 25 years, the complete Critical Edition of the *Vālmīki Rāmāyaṇa* was successfully brought out in 7 volumes by Oriental Institute of Baroda for the benefit of the world of scholars. It can give us the most authentic, pure and the oldest version of the *Vālmīki Rāmāyaṇa*, purely based upon the manuscript evidence, without bringing in the question of Higher Criticism. Its importance and significance can further be understood from the miraculous and outstanding findings that have been reached and several misconceptions and popular notions interpolated into it by the rhapsodists have been removed. For example, the critical text does not contain the most important and popular episode of *Lakṣmaṇa-rekhā* nor does it mention that Ahallyā was transformed into a slab of stone.

The first volume of the *Pāda Index of the Critical Edition of Vālmīki Rāmāyaṇa* has been published in 1989 by the Oriental Institute of Baroda and second one is nearing completion. Recently, the *Bare-text of the Critical Edition of Vālmīki Rāmāyaṇa* has been printed (in 1922) by the Oriental Institute.

In sum, the Critical Edition can be most useful not only to the scholars and researchers, but also to all those general readers who are genuinely interested in understanding the authentic version of the *Vālmīki Rāmāyaṇa*.

FOOTNOTES

International Seminar on "*Vālmīki Rāmāyaṇa*—Higher Criticism" organised by the Oriental Institute, Baroda, 25 to 27 Jan. 1994, Souvenir, pp. 15-20.

1. *The Critical Edition of Vālmīki Rāmāyaṇa,* pub. by Oriental Institute of Baroda in 7 volumes, 1960-1975.
2. *Critical Studies in the Mahābhārata,* by Late Dr. V.S. Sukthankar, pub. V.S. Sukthankar Memorial Edition Committee, Poona, pub. by Karnatak Publishing House, Bombay, 1944.

XIX

PROBLEMS IN CRITICALLY EDITING *PURĀṆA*-TEXTS

Introductory

The Critically Edition is an attempt to restore the text as far as possible to its original form. But this task is quite problematic in case of the Epics and Purāṇa-texts, because in case of other texts, (1) we may get an autograph (the author's own) copy or manuscript or manuscripts, not much separated from the original or having some relationship, though some what remote, with the original, but the case of Epics and Purāṇa-texts, is quite different. We can never think of getting their autographs or the immediate copies. There is ungridgable, long time-gap of about more than one thousand years between the original text and the available mss. of the Purāṇa-texts. Hence restoring them to their original form is almost an impossible task. (2) Secondly, unlike other texts, these texts have been orally transmitted from one generation to another by rhapsodists, who narrated the events, with additions, omissions, alterations and interpolations of time-honoured matter, making the material more interesting and appealing to the masses. Thus, these are a kind of floating mass of popular litereature otherwise known also as fluid texts or the transmitted texts, that incorporated the regional versions also. Hence arriving at their original form is quite difficult. (3) Thirdly, the Purāṇa-texts have undergone several revisions or redactions at the hands of the redactors and rhapsodists. For example we get a detailed reference to the successive chain or line of narrators from whom Parāśara has traditionally received the present text of the *Viṣṇupurāṇa* (6.8.43-50).

From this, it is evident that the text of the *Viṣṇupurāṇa* has been continuously handed down through oral tradition of narrators. Hence, to make a surmise about the text, that was narrated by the first narrator is quite a difficult rask. (4) by the minute study of the Purāṇa-texts only, the scholars have found that there are certain interpolations in them. For example, the *Māyāmoha* episode (VP. 3.17 and 18) or the verses about Śrī in 1.8.15-32 in the *Viṣṇupurāṇa* are regarded as interpolations.[1] Similarly, the *Mārkaṇḍeya Purāṇa* is considered to be forming five different divisions,[2] with complete interpolation of the *Devīmāhātmya* text in it. But at the present state of our knowledge of these texts, it is impossible to remove all such interpolations in them, as they are all substantiated by the manuscript evidence that is available. Thus, it is not feasible to give to the scholars, the text that is free from all interpolations, revisions, redactions etc. Hence the term "an attempt" in the present case is more significant. Moreover, it is again "an attempt" as far as possible at restoring to its supposed original form. Here again the words 'as far as possible' signify that it is an attempt as far as possible i.e. as far as our manuscript evidence can lead us to restore the text. It would be, therefore clear that by the study of manuscript evidence, we can arrive at the purest, and the most ideal form of the text. It is thus an effort to present the best and the oldest form of the text, (though not always grammatically and metrically correct one) by the study of the entire manuscript material, available in various scripts, from different regions of India. It can aim at approximation and not final decision regarding the original form of the Purāṇa-text. This is the main problem and all other problems that follow are the corrolaries or offshoots of this main problem of critical edition of the Purāṇa-texts.

While preparing the critical edition of Purāṇa-texts, one is required to face several practical difficulties to enumerate a few of them—(1) locating different mss., (2) acquiring their xerox of microfilm copies, (3) collating them on the collation-sheets, (4) preparing *stemma codicum* by finding interrelationship between mss., (5) Writing the critical apparatus of the enormous manuscript material that is collated, (6) and even printing the critical edition and its proof-reading. As all these are only the practical difficulties and not the problems in the strict sense of the term, I restrain myself from elaborating them here. The problem as I understand it, is something difficult to decision, or a knotty point requiring clarification. The above-mentioned difficulties could be overcome with appropriate academic and administrative set-up; but, there are certain problems in the way of preparing the critical editions of the Purāṇa-texts that are difficult to be solved. We have already seen the nature of the Purāṇa-texts and problems arising out of its nature. Now, we may elaborate some cases which may be termed as problems in preparing the critical editions of the Purāṇa-text, with special reference to and the examples from the work of the critical edition of the *Viṣṇupurāṇa* and the *Mārkaṇḍeya Purāṇa* that is in progress at the Oriental Institute.

(1) Problems due to regional difference in pronunciation of letter—

One problem of spelling of the words arise due to the regional difference in the pronunciation of the *dantya* and *tālavya sa.* Both forms of *Sa* are found utilized for a single word in the mss. All mss. from the North India invariably read *Śāyaka* i.e. *tālavya sa* for *dantya sa* i.e. *Sāsaka* both forms are also to be found even in the dictionaries. Hence the question arises regarding the proper use of the letter. Which *Sa* is to be used here? Many such instances can be cited from DM. e.g. *Kesarī/Keśarī, Bhuśuṇḍī/Bhusuṇḍī, Kauṣikī/Kauśikī, Khurakṣ epa/Kṣurakṣepa, Dhuta-kesaraḥ/Dhutakeśaraḥ, Somya/ Saumya;* In all these cases the selection of any kind of letter does not affect the meaning, but when we come across the variant—*Śakte* and *sakte* (DM. 11.9) it becomes a serious case as it gives rise to difference in meaning also.

(2) The language and style of the composition of the Purāṇa-texts are so simple, flexible and elastic that the metrical irregularities are found in great abundance in them. These irregularities are generally of two types. 1. Un-metrical lines *i.e.* not conforming to the rules of the composition of the metre like *Anuṣṭubh* line with sixth letter short which should have been long, for example in (1) निसर्गतो विकलाङ्गीं (VP. 3.10.17). (2) कम्बूनां चतुरशीतिः (DM. 8.4) here the suggestion to read *Caturāśītiḥ* to avoid metrical defect is also fraught with problems of interpretations. Actually, the narrator intends to convey the number eightyfour only.

(3) Similarly in बाणैरसिभिर्ऋष्टिभिः (DM. 8.61) the line is unmetrical, the fifth letter being long. Hence the variant बाणैरसिभि ऋष्टिभिः which is grammatically wrong is also found. In any case, either metrical or grammatical problem is bound to be there and there can be no solution to it.

(4) Sometimes, we also come across lines with hypermetric quarter *e.i.* वशवर्तिनश्च पञ्चैते (VP. 3.1.14). Here we get nine letters instead of eight and the variant like *vaśavartiśca* meant for improving it is also not proper as in the context other previous names are also in plural form and not in singular. Hence that hypermetric *pāda* is required to be retained in the next.

(5) The Purāṇa-texts are also full of many unpāṇinian forms and the grammatical usages, which are even supported and anthenticated by the majority of groups of mss. and hence the solitary attempts to improve these irregularities by the mss. are not taken into consideration for forming the text. For instance—लक्ष्मि लज्जे महाविद्ये श्रद्धे पुष्टि स्वधे ध्रुवे। (DM. 11.22). Though we have the variant *Puṣṭe* in some solitary mss., it could not be incorporated in the critical text, not being followed by differnt groups of mss. Similarly, in one and the same chapter, we get both forms of verbs namely *natāḥ smaḥ* and *natāḥ sma* both of them intended to convey the sense of present tense only and not the past tense. For instance the verses—भक्त्या नताः स्म विदधातु शुभानि सा नः (DM. 4.3)—here we can interpret it as *natāḥ smaḥ* but in the subsequent verse, the line is तां त्वां नताः स्म परिपालय देवि विश्वम् (DM.4.5) which can not be similarly interpreted as the word *sma* can not be understood as *smaḥ*. The commentators suggest us to take it as an indeclinable—an *avyaya* but even in that case, the meaning remains obscure and unclear. The line—वैवस्वतेऽन्तरे प्राप्ते अष्टाविंशतिमे युगे (DM. 11.41) here it should have been *aṣṭāviṁśatitame,* but we get the above form only in all the mss. Though the commentators have tried their best to explain its grammatical correctness, it is a fact that it is an *ārṣa* form (as remarked by Nāgojī Bhaṭṭa) which has to be incorporated in the Critical Text. Many such examples can be found.

(6) At many places, the lines of the text are found with hiatus in their construction and there are always attempts by the scribes to avoid such hiatus by inserting *ca, tu, hi* etc. For instance—In the above—cited quotation—वैवस्वतेऽन्तरे प्राप्ते अष्टाविंशतिमे युगे (DM.11.41)—there is a hiatus between *prāpte* and *aṣṭāviṁśatime,* but as this hiatus is found in the majority

of mss., it is to be incorporated in the critical text, though the construction with such hiatus does not sound proper to our mind. The scholars like Prof. Sukthankar have mostly preferred the epic text with the hiatus and efforts to avoid it are considered to be later improvements. Many such instances of hiatus could be cited from the Purāṇa-texts also.

(7) Sometimes, the construction of the line is so ambiguous that it becomes very difficult to interpret and understand it. Being supported by majority of groups of mss., One can not even make any improvement, while preparing the critical text. For example—उत्थाय च महासिं हं देवी चण्डमधावत। (DM. 7.20). Here two interpretations are possible—महासिंहं उत्थाय and महासिं उत्थाय हं (इति शब्दं कृत्वा) but in both cases, there are problems. In the first case, *utthāya* is required to be understood as *utthāpya* i.e. *mahāsiṁhaṁ utthyāpya* and in the second case—*Ham iti Śabdam Kṛtvā* is required to be taken as *adhyāhṛta* (understood). In fact. the construction of the line in the text itself is clumsy. Similarly, at the beginning of the *Mārkaṇḍeya Purāṇa,* we have a verse—

इति तस्य वचः श्रुत्वा मार्कण्डेयो महामुनिः।
दशाष्टदोषरहितं वक्तुं समुपचक्रमे।। —MKP. 1.18

Here both *daśāṣṭadoṣarahitaḥ* and °*rahitam* are found in mss., but if it is taken as *daśāṣṭadoṣarahitaḥ,* it will qualify Mārkaṇḍeya, but it is an improved form of the earlier word with °*rahitam.* The scribes might have thought that if *daśāṣṭadoṣarahitam*, is taken, it would qualify the listener i.e. Jaimini—दशाष्टदोषरहितं (जैमिनिं) वक्तुं समुपचक्रमे—which would be improper, as the importance is to be given to Mārkaṇḍeya and not to Jaimini, who is the listener. Hence they improved the text by making it °*rahitam,* qualifying Mārkaṇḍeya, but in reality the quarter *daśāṣṭadoṣarahitam* is to be taken adverbially in the sense—दशाष्टदोषरहितं (यस्मिन्कर्मणि

यथा स्यात्तथा) वक्तुं समुपचक्रमे। The scholars have also enumerated 18 faults of a speaker. In any case, construction here also is some what obscure and generally ordinary people who can not understand these inner implications are bound to find fault with this genuine reading. The following verse, referred to previously also requires consideration once again here—

लक्ष्मि लज्जे महाविद्ये श्रद्धे पुष्टि स्वधे ध्रुवे।
महारात्रि महाविद्ये नारायणि नमोऽस्तु ते।। —DM. 11.22

Here we have the word *Mahāvidye* in both the lines. Generally, one would not like such repetition in the same verse and hence some groups of mss., (mostly from South) improve it by reading *Mahāmāye* in the place of *Mahāvidye* in the second line, which is not at all approved by all the Northern mss. of the text. The commentators supporting the reading *Mahāvidye* in both lines, interpret the word in the second lines as *Mahā-avidye,* thus giving rise to a separate meaning. Still the problem remains as it is, as generally the readers would find the same word repeated in both lines.

(8) Interpretation is to be given preference to emendation, and we have found how the text is attempted to be interpreted without emending it. But in some solitary cases, it happens that the editor is required to emend the text, looking to the internal evidence, though not supported by the mss. For example in the line—

ऊर्जः*स्तम्भस्तथा प्राणो दत्तोलिर्ऋषभस्तथा।
निश्चरश्चार्वरीवाँश्च तत्र सप्तर्षयोऽभवन्।।—VP. 3.1.91

it was necessary to split the word into *Ūrjaḥ* and *Stambho,* to be counted as two separate names instead of one name, because there is enumeration of seven sages. If it is taken as one name, the names would be six only.

(9) There are serious problems in constituting the fourth *aṁśa* of the *Viṣṇupurāṇa* which is in prose. It contains

genealogies of sages and dynasties of kings of Kali Age. Here the mss., display so many variations in the names and spellings of the sages and kings that it becomes very difficult to decide among the array of variants available. We can appropriately prepare the pāda-Index of all the other *Aṁśa* of the *Viṣṇupurāṇa,* but preparing the pāda or line Index of this portion is also fraught with many unsoluble problems. Pāda-Index of it is in other words is an impossible task.

It would be clear from the above elaboration that there are many such problems, which arise due to the very nature of the Purāṇa-texts, as folk-literature—the literature of the masses, handled by rhapsodists, who were not expected to be good poets, linguists or grammarians. Hence even after preparing the Critical Edition on the basis of all the available oldest, purest and the best mss in different scripts, some such problems as mentioned above remain in the Constituted Text.

FOOTNOTES

Paper published in Journal of the Oriental Institute, Vol. 46, Nos. 1-2, Sept.-Dec., 1996 Issue, pp. 61-65. Read at "The Seminar on Research Methodology in Sanskrit" held at North Gujarat University, Patan, during 8-10th March, 1997.

1. Hazra, R.C. : *Studies in the Puranic Records on Hindu Rites and Customs,* Motilal Banarasidass, Delhi, Second ed., 1975, p. 21 and p. 24.
2. Pargiter, F.E. : *Mārkaṇḍeya Purāṇa*-English Translation, Introduction, P. IV and VI. DM. = *Devīmāhātmya* VP. = *Viṣṇupurāṇa*; MKP. = *Mārkaṇḍeya-puraṇa*.

XX

DESCRIPTION OF RĀMA'S LIFE IN THE *VIṢṆUPURĀṆA* –SOME OBSERVATIONS

The *Viṣṇupurāṇa* is one of the ancient and important Mahāpurāṇas. The description of the various incarnations is an important and indispensable part of the subject-matter of the *Purāṇas*. The *Viṣṇupurāṇa* also contains such descriptions but all of them are not dealt with equal importance and complete details.[1] Of the ten incarnations Rāma. Kṛṣṇa, Varāha and Paraśurāma are treated at great length, while Matsya, Kūrma ana Kalkī are briefly alluded to. Moreover, the incarnations of Nṛsiṃha and Vāmana have only cursory allusion while the incarnation of the Buddha had not yet obtained recognition.

In the fourth *aṃśa* of the *Viṣṇupurāṇa,* the genealogies of the kings of different dynasties are recorded. The entire *aṁśa* is mostly in prose. While describing the genealogies, sometimes the important and outstanding exploits of certain kings are also delineated at some length. The kings of the Ikṣvāku dynasty are mentioned. There the life of Rāma and the exploits of his brothers are narrated with some details. Prof. Wilson notes, 'This is an epitome of the *Rāmāyaṇa,* the heroic pocm of Vāmīki on the subject of Rāma's exploits'.[2] An attempt is made here to study this *Viṣṇupurāṇa* tradition of the Rāma-story and to point out the distinctive features and implications of the same, by comparing it with the Rāma-story in the Critical edition of the *Vālmīki-Rāmāyaṇa*.

The *Rāmāyṇa* is narrated in an abridged form in the prose portion of the fourth *aṁśa* of the *Viṣṇu-Purāṇa* (4.4.83-105).[3] Prof. Wilson[4] translates this portion as follows – 'The son of Khaṭvāṅga was Dīrghabāhu, his son was Raghu; his son was Aja; his son was Daśaratha. The god from whose navel the lotus springs became fourfold, as the four sons of Daśaratha, Rāma, Lakṣmaṇa, Bharata and Śatrughna, for the protection of the world. Rāma, whilst yet a boy, accompanied Viśvāmitra, to protect his sacrifice, and slew Tāḍakā. He afterwards killed Mārīca with his restless shafts; and Subāhu and others fell by his arms. He removed the guilt of Ahalyā by merely looking upon her. In the palace of Janaka, he broke with ease the mighty bow of Maheśvara and received the hand of Sītā, the daughter of the king, self-born from the earth, as the prize of his prowess. He humbled the pride of Paraśurāma, who vaunted his triumph over the race of Haihaya and his repeated slaughter of the *Kṣatriya* tribe. Obedient to the commands of his father, and cherishing no regret for the loss of sovereignty, he entered the forest, accompanied by his brother Lakṣmaṇa and by his wife. There he killed in conflict Virādha, Khara, Dūṣaṇa and other Rākṣasas, the headless giant Kabandha, and Vālī the monkey monarch. Having built a bridge across the ocean, and destroyed the whole Rākṣasa nation, he recovered his bride Sītā, whom their ten-headed king Rāvaṇa had carried off, and returned to Ayodhyā with her, after she had been purified by fire ordeal from the stigma contracted by her captivity, and had been honoured by the assembled gods, who bore witness to her virtue.

'Bharata made himself master of the Gandharvas, after destroying vast numbers of them and Śatrughna having killed Rākṣasa chief Lavaṇa, the son of Madhu, took possession of his capital Mathura. "Having thus, by their unequalled valour and might rescued the whole world from the dominion of malignant fiands, Rāma, Lakṣamaṇa, Bharata and Śatrughna reascended to heaven, and were followed by those of the people of Kośala who were fervently devoted to these partial incarnations of the Supreme Viṣṇu.

'Rāma and his brothers had each two sons. Kuśa and Lava were the sons of Rāma; those of Lakṣmaṇa were Aṅgada and Candraketu; the sons of Bharata were Takṣa and Puṣkara and Subāhu and Śūrasena were the sons of Śatrughna. The son of Kuśa was Atithi'.

Distinctive features

It would be clear from the above that the important events in the life of Rāma are recorded here.

There are some salient and distinctive features in this description of the *Viṣṇupurāṇa*. Rāma is described as *aṃśāvatāra* of the Lord. It is stated that Lord Viṣṇu Himself took the form of the four sons of Daśaratha through his own *aṃśa* (part). This point is noteworthy. P.V. Kane[5] is of the opinion that Rāma was worshipped as an incarnation of Viṣṇu at least several centuries before the birth of Christ. Kālidāsa (*Raghuvaṃśa Sarga* 10) mentions the four sons of Daśaratha as the partial incarnations of Viṣṇu. Regarding the description of this aspect in the Critical Edition of the *Rāmāyaṇa*[6], U.P. Shah's following remarks are noteworthy, 'True it is the *Rāmāyaṇa Kāṇḍas* II-VI, Rāma appears to be moral hero, while in the later books I and VII he is often depicted as an incarnation of Viṣṇu and but for very rare cases, the Critical Edition lends support to the above view; however, it must be remembered that the testimonia of *Raghuvaṁśa* shows that during the age of Kālidāsa, belief in Rāma being an incarnation of Viṣṇu had already grown.' Thus it would be clear that the *Viṣṇupurāṇa* incorporates the tradition of the *Rāmāyaṇa,* where Rāma is quite clearly regarded as the incarnation of Viṣṇu. This can also suggest the upper limit of the extant portion of the *Viṣṇupurāṇa* and the *Rāmāyaṇa* tradition, contained in it.

Secondly, the reference to the episode of Ahalyā as found in the *Viṣṇupurāṇa* is also quite significant. It is popularly and generally understood that Ahalyā, the wife of Gautama was transfomed into a stone-slab (*Śilā*) due to the curse of the sage Gautama and when Rāma came there, with the touch of His foot *(pādasparśa),* Ahalyā became purified and was again restored to her original form. But this popular belief is not traceable in the original Rāma-story as found in the Critical Edition of the *Rāmāyaṇa* and the same as found in the *Viṣṇupurāṇa*. Here in the *Viṣṇupurāṇa* it is simply stated that Rāma made her free from her blemish with his mere *darśana (darśanamātreṇaiva ahalyāmapāpām cakāra)*. Like the *Viṣṇupurāṇa*, the Critical Edition of the *Rāmāyaṇa* also does not refer to the above two aspects of the popular story, namely, that of her transformation into a stone-slab and her purification with the touch of the foot of Rāma. The verse in the Critical Edition of the *Rāmāyaṇa* is as follows:

Vāyubhakṣā nirāhārā tapyantī bhasmaśāyinī /
Adṛśyā sarvabhūtānāmāśrame 'smin nivatsyati //

—*Bāla*. 47.29

From the Critical Apparatus of this verse, it would be clear that only five mss. (all Southern G1-3 and M1.2) have the variant *śilā bhūtva* for *nirāhārā* of the critical text. In the critical edition, *(Bāla*. 48) it is mentioned that Rāma and Lakṣmaṇa both bowed down to her and Rāma did not at all touch her with His foot. *(Rāghavau tu tatastasyāḥ pādau jagṛha-tustadā—Bāla*. 48.17 ab). This may suggest that the *Viṣṇupurāṇa* text incorporates an older and pure form of the Rāma-story in which such later developments of Rāma-story had not crept in.

It is also quite remarkable that there is no reference to

Rāma's ordering exile or abandonment of Sītā, at the end of the Rāma-story found in the *Viṣṇupurāṇa*. This important event of *Sītātyāga* is not at all mentioned or referred to. The culmination of the Rāma-story as per the tradition of the *Viṣṇupurāṇa* is in the establishment of the proper order in the universe, after destruction of the evil-minded and returning to the heavenly abode along with residents of Kośala, who were devoted to His Divine nature. This may suggest the priority of *Rāmāyaṇa* tradition of the *Viṣṇupurāṇa* to the portion of the *Uttarakāṇḍa* of the *Vālmīki-Rāmāyaṇa*, that contains the *Sītātyāga* (i.e. abandonment of Sīta). It is not proper to consider that the said portion, having such a striking event has been advertently dropped or neglected in the *Viṣṇupurāṇa* tradition. In the *Uttarakāṇḍa* (*sargas* 44-49) and the *Bālakāṇḍa* (verse 3.28), there is description of and allusion to the event of the abandonment of Sītā. Kālidāsa (*sargas* 14-15) has also dealt with this aspect in the *Raghuvaṃśa*. This may suggest that the *Viṣṇupurāṇa* incorporates such a tradition of the *Rāmāyaṇa* that was anterior to these interpolations in the Rāma story.

But the exploits of Bharata and Śatrughna are mentioned in the said portion of the *Viṣṇupurāṇa*. These are found in the *Uttarakāṇḍa* of the *Vālmīki-Rāmāyaṇa* (*sargas* 53-63 and *sargas* 90-91). These episodes of the *Rāmāyaṇa* were thus known to the tradition prevalent at the time of the *Viṣṇu-purāṇa*. Moreover, there is also a reference to the *Agnidivya* by Sītā (Cf. *Yuddhakāṇḍa Sarga* 104). She has proved her chastity by entering into the fire i.e. by performing the fire-ordeal.

The *Viṣṇupurāṇa* context under consideration has clear reference to this event. P.L. Vaidya writes in his Introduction to the Critical Edition of the *Yuddha-kāṇḍa* of the *Vālmīki-Rāmāyaṇa* (p. xxxv), 'In any case, the poet Vālmīki introduced in his epic poem, an innovation of Sītā's test by fire against the epic and historical background of Vāyu assuring Rāma of Sītā's purity. This innovation among others, is thus the most striking innovation made by Vālmīki, when he decided to handle an old epic theme and gave it the shape of a poem, the first of its kind, an *ādikāvya*'. He regarded the *Rāmopākhyāna* of the *Mahābhārata* to have preceded the *Rāmāyaṇa*. U.P. Shah has again discussed the said issue and opined that 'Some early form of *Vālmīki Rāmāyaṇa* was known to the author of the *Rāmopākhyāna* and even the authors of verses of *Droṇa, Āraṇyaka* and *Śānti* (XII. 200.4) *parvans* cited above, believed that *Vālmīki's Rāmāyaṇa* preceded *Mahābhārata*'.[7] In any case, the *Viṣṇupurāṇa* envisages such a tradition of the *Rāmāyaṇa* that had already incorporated the event of purification of Sīta by entering into the fire i.e. fire-ordeal.

It is also worth-considering that the names of the sons of all the three brothers of Rāma have been mentioned in the *Viṣṇupurāṇa* context. Rāma's sons Kuśa and Lava are quite well-known. Lakṣmaṇa had two sons namely Aṅgada and Candraketu. Bharata's sons were Takṣa and Puṣkala, while those of Śatrughna were Subāhu and Śūrasena. Kuśa's son was Atithi.

The Gorakhpur edition and the Venkateshwar edition of the *Viṣṇupurāṇa* contain one more important paragraph that gives a prolonged description of the coronation or Rāma.[8] But this is not found in the Poona edition and the Bengali Edition of the *Viṣṇupurāṇa*.[9] It is also not found in most of the Mss. of the Critical Edition of the same and hence it has been omitted in the Critical text. It is naturally to be found in the star-passages of the Critical Edition. Hence its later interpolation in the text of the *Viṣṇupurāṇa* is quite evident.

Thus the Rāma-story as found in the *Viṣṇupurāṇa* is

worth-considering. R.C. Hazra[10] opines that the date of composition of the *Viṣṇnupurāṇa* falls between the end of the first and the middle of the fourth century A.D. i.e. between 100 and 350 A.D. As the *Viṣṇupurāṇa* incorporates the most pure and ancient tradition of the Rāma-story, its importance for understanding one of the ancient versions of Rāma-story is quite evident. It may be concluded that it contains the Rāma-story that was prevalent in the aforesaid period. Non-mention of *Sītātyāga* may suggest priority of the present tradition of the *Viṣṇupurāṇa*, even to the *Uttarakāṇḍa* of the Critical Edition of the *Vālmīki-Rāmāyaṇa*. The *Viṣṇupurāṇa* tradition may be regarded as prior even to the *Raghuvaṃśa of Kālidāsa*.

FOOTNOTES

Paper published in Adyar library Bulletin, Adyar, Chennai, 1993, pp. 49-57.

1. See Dayal, Thakur Harendra: *The Viṣṇupurāṇa (Social, Economic and Religious Aspects)*, Sundeep Prakashan, Delhi, 1983, pp. 215-220.
2. Wilson H.H.: (Eng. Trans.) *The Vishnu Purana – A System of Hindu Mythology and Tradition,* Punthi Pustak, Calcutta, 1972, p. 307, n. 16.
3. श्रीश्रीविष्णुपुराण, मूल श्लोक और हिन्दी अनुवादसहित, अनुवादक– श्रीमुनिलाल गुप्त, गीताप्रेस, गोरखपुर।
4. *Op. cit.*, pp. 306-308.
5. Kane, P.V.: *History of Dharmaśātra,* Bhandarkar Oriental Research Institute, Poona, 1941, Vol. II, Part II, p. 724.
6. *The Vālmīki-Rāmāyaṇa*, Critical Edition, Pub. Oriental Institute, Baroda in 7 Vols., 1960-75. *Uttarkāṇḍa* Vol. 7, Intro. p. 51.
7. *ibid.*, p. 31.
8. श्रीविष्णुमहापुराणं विष्णुचित्त्यात्मप्रकाशाख्यश्रीधरीयव्याख्याद्वयोपेतं Venkateshvar Press, Śake 1832, 98-99 and Gorakhpur ed., *op. cit.*, 98 and 99.

ततश्चाभिषेकमङ्गलं मैत्रेय वर्षशतेनापि वक्तुं न शक्यते,
संक्षेपेण श्रूयताम् ॥ 98 ॥
लक्ष्मणभरतशत्रुघ्न.........सिंहासनगत एकादशाब्दसहस्रं राज्यमकरोत्॥99॥
These lines are not found in Wilson's translation.

9. *Śrīviṣṇupurāṇam*, (text with Marathi trans.) Chitrashala Press, Poona and *Śrīviṣṇupurāṇam*, ed. Jivanand Vidyasagar, Bangavasi Press, Calcutta, 1882.

10. Hazara, R.C. : *Studies in the Puranic Records on Hindu Rites and Customs,* The University of Dacca, 1940, p. 24.

XXI

A RARE MANUSCRIPT OF THE *SAṄKETA* COMMENTARY OF THE *VIṢṆUPURĀṆA*

Purāṇas are valuable records of our ancient Indian History, Culture and Traditions. Among the eighteen *Purāṇas* the *Viṣṇupurāṇa* is one of the most ancient and important *Purāṇa*, whose text is found in a very uniform nature, through various centuries, in different manuscripts. Right from Rāmānujācāya, it has received tremendous popularity among the scholars of the *Vaiṣṇava* philosophical tradition. The wide-spread scholarly acceptance of the text can also be evident from the enormous commentatorial literature available on the said *Purāṇa*. There are more than fourteen commentaries on the *Viṣṇupurāṇa,* out of which only three are printed and the remaining are still hidden in the manuscript treasures of various institutes and libraries. The names of those commentaries are as follows :—(1) *the Svaprakāśa of Śridhara* (Venkateshwar press, Bombay, Śake 1832) (2) *the Viṣṇucittīyā of Viṣṇucitta* (Venkateshwar press Bombay, Śke 1832) (3) *the Vaiṣṇavākūtacandrikā of Ratnagarbha Bhaṭṭa* (1889 A.D.) (4) *the Viṣṇuvallabhā of Kumāra Jaya Yogin* (5) *the Citsukhī of Citsukhamuni (6) the Maṇipravālā of Veṅkaṭarāghavācārya* (7) *the Bhāvārthadīpikā of Jagannātha Pāṭhaka* (8) *Rasañjanā of Bhāṣyakārasūri* (9) *Aṁśaprakāśikā of Nīlāmbara* (10) *the Sārasaṅgraha* (11) *the commentary by Nṛhara Śrīdharapati* (12) *the commentary by Gaṅgādhara* (13) *the commentary by Nāthamuni* (14) *the commentary by Sūryakara Miśra.*

There are also some anonymous commentaries on the *Viṣṇupurāṇa*.

Commentary of Gaṅgādhara-Quite Little-known

Among the above-mentioned fourteen commentaries, there is also one commentary called *Saṅketa* by Gaṅgādhara. It is not published and the most rare and perhaps the only manuscript of it is available in the B.J. Institute, Ahmedabad. It is not mentioned in the *New Catalogus Catalogorum* or in the *Catalogus Catalogorum of Aufreutch.* No scholar seems to have ever taken notice of this rare commentary on the *Viṣṇupurāṇa.* As the commentary and its author Gaṅgādhara are quite little-known, an attempt is made in this paper to throw some light upon them with the help of the study of the available manuscript.

The Rare Manuscript in B.J. Institute, Ahmedabad

One complete manuscript of the *Saṅketa* commetary of Gaṅgādhara on the *Viṣṇupurāṇa* is deposited in the manuscript collection of the Sheth B.J. Institute of Learning and Research, Ahmedabad. It is a paper manuscript in *Devanāgarī* script, having fifty four folios. The accession No. is 2224. We get the following important information about the date of writing of the manuscript and the scribe etc.

संवत् 1438 वर्षे मार्ग सुदि 4 गुराविह श्रीमङ्गलपुरे नाणन्हीठवरसिंहेन ग्रंथार्थसंदेहभंगहेतवे अध्येतुरन्वयपावनक्षमस्य श्रीमद्विष्णुपुराणस्य षण्णामप्यंशानां गंगाधरटिप्पणीकमलेखि।

The name of the scribe was Varasiṃha from Śrīmaṅgalapura (?). It was written on Thursday, the fifth day of the bright fortnight of *Mārgaśīrṣa* in the year *saṁvat* 1438 i.e. 1382 A. D. As per the scribe, it is *ṭippaṇaka* on all the six *aṁśa*s of the *Viṣṇupurāṇa* written with a view to dispelling the doubts about the import of the text. From this, it is evident that the manuscript is not only rare but also is very old one.

Fortunately, we not only get ample information about the scribe and the manuscript but also about the author of the commentary from the post-colophon entries. The commentary commences with the salutation to Viṣṇu.

ॐ नमः श्रीविष्णवे। श्रीविष्णुं सुखचिद्रूपं प्रणम्यात्ममयं गुरुम्। संकेतः क्रियते विष्णुपुराणपदकौमुदी।।

From this, we can know the name of the commentary as the *Saṅketa*. After the colophon of the commentary on the sixth *Aṁśa*, there is most useful information about the author of the commentary. It is as follows :

वागीशानन्दशिष्यस्य शिष्यो गङ्गाधरः सुधीः।
षष्ठस्यांशस्य संकेतं पुराणे विष्णवे व्यधात्।।
चौलुक्ये जगदेकमल्लनृपतौ शास्तर्यशेषामिलां
तन्मन्त्री सकलाधिकारकुशलः श्रीवामनो राजते।
यस्तस्याखिलधर्मबोधनगुरुर्गङ्गाधरो धीनिधिः
श्रीमद्विष्णुपुराणटिप्पणमिदं तेन स्फुटं निर्मितम् ।।

It is clear from the post-colophon entries mentioned above that the commentary is called *Saṅketa*, written by Gaṅgadhāra, the disciple of the disciple of Vāgīśānanda. This is a *ṭippaṇa* i.e. a small commentary. Gaṅgādhara was a *Dharmaguru* of Śrī Vāmana, who was a minister, expert in all official duties of the king Jagadekamalla of Cāllukya race. This commentary is written by Gaṅgādhara, when this king Jagadekamalla was rulling over the entire earth. From this statement of the commentator, we can guess about the date of the commentator or the period of the composition of the commentary.

It is recorded by historians that Someśvara III, who

was given the title *Sarvajñabhūpa* or *Sarvajñacakravartī* for his extensive knowledge, composed the book, entitled- *Mānasollāsa* or *Abhilaṣitārthacintāmaṇi.* He had two sons, Taila-III and Jagadekamalla-II. Someśvara was succeded by Jagadekamall II in A.D. 1138. The period of Jagadekamalla is 1138-1151 A.D. (see *The Struggle for Empire*—Bharatiya Vidya Bhavana, Bombay, Vol. V, p. 178). It is clear that the present commentary was composed by the author during the reign of Jagadekamalla (i.e. 1138-1151 A.D.). Thus being one of the ancient commentaries on the *Viṣṇupurāṇa*, it deserves to be studied and taken notice of.

REFERENCE

Paper published in Prof. Pravin Parikh Felicitation volume, Bharatiya Vidya Prakashan, 1997, pp 282-283.

Paper read at the 10th World Sanskrit Conference, held at Tarlabalu Kendra, Bengalore, 3 to 9 Jan. 1997.

XXII

CONCEPT OF *BHAKTI* IN THE *VIṢṆUPURĀṆA*

*Purāṇa*s occupy a very indispensable place in the History of Sanskrit literature. Their importance as valuable records of customs and traditions of India has greatly been emphasised. Their study is also necessary for the proper understanding of the then prevailing Culture, Religion and Society. Of the eighteen *Purāṇa*s, the *Viṣṇupurāṇa* is one of the ancient and important *Purāṇa*s. Hence its study is very useful for understanding ancient religion and culture. The devotion or *Bhakti* is important aspect of Religion. The importance of *Bhakti* is greatly and emphatically pointed out and eulogised for the upliftment of the religious status of a devotee. In this paper, an attempt is made to elucidate the concept of *Bhakti,* as expounded in the said *Purāṇa*.

Before considering the said subject, it is necessary to understand some background. The Vedic hymns are replete with devotional fervour. While performing sacrifices, it was enjoined that the sacrificer should meditate upon the deity to whom the oblation was to be offered. With the advent of Jain and Bauddha schools of thought, the importance of sacrifices gradually diminished. Even Smṛtis, emphasised only the sixteen popular sacraments and sacrifices, which formed the part of fortyeight sacraments were not given due importance. The devotion or *Bhakti* came to be more emphasised in the works like the *Bhagavadgītā* and the *Bhaktisūtras*. *Purāṇa*s had such a background. They not only dealt with and developed the concept, but also pointed out its importance by narrating the accounts of the lives of great devotees, illustrating their extreme and utmost devotion to God.

In the *Viṣṇupurāṇa* also, the importance of the devotion has been emphasised and its superiority even to sacrifices has been emphatically and categorically advocated. By worshipping Viṣṇu with steadfast mind, the devotee obtains the complete fruit of performing the Aśvamedha sacrifice. The stories of devotees of God have been dealt with at length that illustrate the importance of *Bhakti* and it is clearly pointed out how a particular devotee, obtained the grace and favour of the Lord, with his unflinching devotion and complete surrender to the same. The story of the life of the devotee, Dhruva, which is narrated in the eleventh and the twefth *adhyāya* of the first *aṁśa* of the *Viṣṇupurāṇa* and which explains the above mentioned aspect of *Bhakti* is worth-noting from this point of view. The story of Dhruva is quite well-known and hence may not be related here at length. The main point regarding emphasis on devotional aspect should be noted here. It is narrated that by concentrating upon the Lord and by performing penance, the devotee could secure the grace of the Supreme Lord. In this chapter, it is mentioned that the sages like Marīci, Atri, Aṅgirā, Pulstya, Kratu, Pulaha and Vasiṣṭha advised Dhruva to worship Viṣṇu for obtaining the Best Position which he desired. With devotion only, one can obtain even the rare and the unaccessible salvation or *mukti*. There is nothing that cannot be obtained by worshipping Viṣṇu. Even Indra is said to have obtained his position by worshipping Viṣṇu, the Lord of the world. Dhruva then inquired what was to be meditated and how He was to be meditated upon. The sages declared him that with unwavering mind, the Lord Viṣṇu should be meditated upon.

When the Lord was pleased with devotion of Dhruva, He appeared before him. Dhruva then praised Lord with utmost fervour. The Lord here told Dhruva that by worshpping Him, the person can swiftly obtain even salvation. What to speak of such fruits like the heaven and other desired objects ?

मामाराध्य नरो मुक्तिमवाप्नोत्यविप्लम्बिताम्।
मय्यर्पितमना बाल किमु स्वर्गादिकं पदम् ॥ —I.12.89

Even in the story of the devotee Prahlāda, which is narrated in the four *adhyāyas* of first *Aṁśa* of the *Viṣṇupurāṇa* (i.e. *adhyāyas* 17–20), the same aspect of devotion to the Lord has been emphasised and here also with the delineation of the various incidents in the life of the said devotee, it is pointed out that due to the unflinching devotion to the Lord, the devotee was protected against all the different difficulties and troubles that were created by his wicked father. The devotee had completely surrendered himself to the Lord. The Lord, being pleased with the devotion of Prahlāda asked him to choose some boon. But Prahlāda desried nothing else but only the unflinching devotion to the Supreme Lord, in all his births, which he may undergo.

नाथ योनिसहस्त्रेषु येषु येषु व्रजाम्यहम्।
तेषु तेष्वच्युता भक्तिरच्युतास्तु सदा त्वयि॥ —I. 20.18

One who has obtained firm and steadfast devotion in the Lord, who is the cause or root of the entire world, why should he care for *dharma, artha, kāma?* He has actually the *mukti* or salvation at hand.

धर्मार्थकामैः किं तस्य यस्य मुक्तिः करे स्थिता।
समस्तजगतां मूले यस्य भक्तिः स्थिरा त्वयि॥ —I. 20. 27

The devotion or *bhakti,* elucidated in the above illustrations of the life of Dhruva and Prahlāda may be described as *Sakhyabhakti* (i.e. friendly devotion) to the Lord.

But it is quite curious that we also find the delineation of the devotion, which may be called as *virodhabhakti* (i.e. devotion through opposition). This aspect may be noted as the remarkable feature of this ancient *Purāṇa*. This kind of devotion has been illustrated through the description of the life of the formidable enemy of the Lord, namely Śiśupāla. In the fourth *Aṁśa* (*adhyāyas* 14 and 15), it is recorded that this Śiśupāla himself was Hiraṇyakaśyapu and Rāvaṇa in his former births and was in opposition to the Lord in those births. In his life as Śiśupala, he confronted with the Lord Śrīkṛṣṇa, and opposed Him. But while doing so, he had his mind deeply and completely engrossed in Him and hence obtained the *sāyujya mukti*. In *adhyāya* (IV. 15), Maitreya asked Parāśara through curiosity, as to how such a miracle could happen; In his reply, Parāśara again dealt with the incident of Śiśupāla's life and it is clearly explained how even while opposing the Lord, his concentration and thought-process were mainly concerned with the real nature of the Lord. Here it is emphasised that when the Lord is pleased with his devotee, He ordains the desired goal and even when displeased, while killing him, gives the incomparable Divine position.

भगवान् हि प्रसन्नो यथाभिलषितं ददाति। अप्रसन्नोऽपि निघ्नन् दिव्य-मनुपमस्थानं प्रयच्छति। —IV.14

It is also declared here that the Lord gives the fruit that is difficult to be obtained even by the Gods and *Asuras,* even when spoken of and repeatedly remembered through constant enmity. It is further emphasised here that when even through enmity, one can obtain such a Highest Position, it is but natural and assured that He ordains the Desired Goal to those who have proper devotion for Him.

भगवानिह कीर्तितः संस्मृतश्च द्वेषानुबन्धेनाखिलसुरासुरादि-दुर्लभं फलं प्रयच्छति, किमुत सम्यग्भक्तिमताम् । —IV. 15. 12

Thus we find delineation of both kinds of devotion in the *Viṣṇupurāṇa*. Moreover, the recollection or remembering the Name of the Lord has been repeatedly emphasised. The remembering of the twelve syllabled *mantra*—namely *"Om Namo Bhagavate Vāsudevāya"* has been praised and it is pointed out that whatever one obtains in *Kṛtayuga* through meditation or by sacrifices in *Tretāyuga* or by worshipping Viṣṇu in *Dvāparayuga,* is obtained by *Saṅkīrtana* or repeating or remembering the name of Lord only in *Kaliyuga*.

ध्यानन्कृते यजन् यज्ञैस्त्रेतायां द्वापरेऽर्चयन्।
यदाप्नोति तदाप्नोति कलौ संकीर्त्य केशवम्।।—VI. 2.17

The *Kali* age is very dangerous and full of many defects, but there is one great merit that one can reach the Divine, becoming free from bondage only through *Kīrtana* 'i.e. remembering the name of the Lord Kṛṣṇa).

अत्यन्तदुष्टस्य कलेरयमेको महान्गुणः।
कीर्तनादेव कृष्णस्य मुक्तबन्धः परं व्रजेत् ।। —VI. 2. 40

This aspect of *Bhakti*—is also repeatedly emphasised in the *Viṣṇupurāṇa* and it is reported to be excelling even the penance, sacrifices etc.

Thus the devotion through friendship and enmity has been described in the *Viṣṇupurāṇa* and the *Nāmasaṅkīrtana* is also very often categorically emphasised.

XXIII

THE LITTLE-KNOWN TEXT OF THE *UTTARAMĀRKAṆḌEYA PURĀṆA*

Introductory

The *Mārkaṇḍeya Purāṇa* (MKP.) is one of the ancient *Purāṇas*. The Oriental Institute of Baroda, therefore, undertook in 1986, the project of preparing the Critical Edition of it, when the work of the critical Edition of the *Viṣṇupurāṇa* was almost nearing completion. For this, the first and the most important task was that of collection of MSS. for the purposes of collation. The necessary details regarding the MSS. of the MKP. and of the *Devīmāhātmya* were collected from the *New Catalogus Catalogorum* section of the Deptt. of Sanskrit of the University of Madras. The Catalogues of different Institutes and libraries of India, Nepal and other places were also consulted for obtaining such information. The Institutes and libraries were also individually contacted for this purpose. A good response was received from them and after selection, MSS. belonging to different regions of India and Nepal, and written in different scripts were procured in the original form, or Xerox or microfilm copies for the project-work.

During this search for the MSS. of the MKP. the present researcher noticed quite a peculiar kind of a ms. in the Descriptive Catalogue of the Government Oriental MSS. Library of Madras. As per the information recorded there, the ms. contains 25 *adhyāyas* (26th incomplete) of the later part *(Uttara bhāga)* of the *Mārkaṇḍeya Purāṇa*, envisaging a dialogue between Citraketu and Mārkaṇḍeya. On reading this kind of information the curiosity for actually going through the entire contents of the work was aroused in my mind and it was found necessary to confirm, whether it had any continuing link or similarity in matter with the available text. Hence, attempts were made to procure xerox or microfilm copies of the same. In 1988, the present researcher was deputed to Madras for the same purpose. Fortunately, after a great effort, the microfilm of the said ms. could be obtained from the said Library of Madras.

But, the said ms. of the *Uttara* portion of the MKP. was in the Telugu script. Hence, with the help of one of our assistants, a *Devanāgarī* transcript of the same was got prepared. As the present text has not been taken notice of by scholars, while writing books and articles on the *Mārkaṇḍeya Purāṇa,* it is quite necessary to study the text in its connection with the said *Purāṇa*. As this subject has not been hitherto much tapped by scholars, the present researcher has made an attempt herein to introduce the general contents of the text to the world of scholars and has tried to evaluate its importance in connection with the Critical Edition of the MKP.

What is the *Uttaramārkaṇdeya Purāṇa*

There are five printed available editions of the MKP. (1) Edited by K.M. Banerjee, Bibliotheca Indica, Calcutta, Published in 1862 A.D., (2) Edited by Jivanand Vidyasagar, Calcutta, 1879 A.D., (3) With a Sanskrit Com. called *Dīpikā* on the *Devīmāhātmya* by Śantanu Cakravarti, published by Venkateshwar Press, Bombay 1910 A.D., (4) Same published with Hindi translation by Nag publishers, New Delhi, 1984, (5) Translated and edited by Mahaprabhulal Goswami, published by Institute for Puranic and Vedic Studies and Research, Naimisharanya, Sitapur, 1986 (first two Volumes are not accessible to me).

Moreover, the MKP. (1) edited by Pancanan Tarkaratna, published by Vangavasi Press, Calcutta, Fourth edition and (2) edited by Shridharatmaja Trambak Gondhalekar, Poona, Jagaddhitecchu Press, 1867 A.D. were not accessible to me.

The text printed in all the available editions of the MKP., is almost similar, excepting some differences in readings of the text, the division of *adhyāyas* and addition and omission of certain verses and the concluding portion. None of the editors seems to have consulted and even taken note of the above peculiar and distinctive kind of ms., connected with the title of the MKP. The above ms. contains the *Uttarabhāga* of the MKP., as is quite clear from the colophon of each *adhyāya* of the text. For example, the colophon of the first *adhyāya* is as follows: –

इति श्रीमार्कण्डेयपुराणे उत्तरभागे चित्रकेतुचरित्रे प्रथमोऽध्यायः।

It is evidently promulgated as the later portion of the MKP., the *pūrvabhāga* of which is understood to be complete with the last *adhyāya* of the MKP. This particular portion of the text in the ms. is considered to be added to the MKP., forming its additional and later part. It can well be described as a text containing the *Uttaramārkaṇḍeya Purāṇa*, as I feel so.

Description of the ms.

The microfilm of the above rare text is available now in the Oriental Institute of Baroda, with its accession no. 27235. It is actually the microfilm prepared from the paper ms., deposited in the Government Oriental MSS. library of Madras, bearing accession no. R. 3726. It is recorded to have been transcribed in 1921-22 from a ms. of M.R. Ry. Pudipeddi Sriramasastruluguru, S.S. Pathashala, Kamiti Library of Jami, Singavarapukota. It is a complete ms. of 106 folios (Pages 212), containing text in an incomplete form.

It is written on both sides of the country made paper of about 15 × 9 inches in size. It has about 16 letters in a line and about 20 lines in a page. The *granthasaṅkhyā* is about 2120. The handwriting is quite readable. The condition of the ms. is quite good. After the colophon of the first *adhyāya*, there is remark–

पराभवनामसंवत्सरे कार्तिके शु. 2 सोमवारम्......

Contents of the Text

This portion of the *Uttarmārkaṇḍeya Purāṇa* has a total of twentyfive *adhyāyas* and the twentysixth is left incomplete. Throughout the entire text, we come across the king Citraketu of the solar dynasty as an interlocutor and Mārkaṇḍeya as a narrator. There is a detailed narration of not only names but also sometimes exploits of the kings and their successors of the dynasties of the *Kali*-age. A brief summary of subject-matter of each *adhyāya* may be given here.

1. In the Introductory *adhyāya*, Mārkaṇḍeya is reported to be going to see Citraketu–After receiving due reception from him, he asks Citraketu about well-being of himself and his subjects. Here some teachings regarding polity are met with in this narration–thus the first chapter ends with information regarding the life of king Citraketu only.

2. and 3. Citraketu tells Mārkaṇḍeya that the *dharmas* of *Kṛta, Tretā* and *Dvāpara* ages have been listened to. Now, he wishes to know about those of *Kali*-age and also about kings of solar and lunar dynasties that protect the earth in this age. He also wants to know about the promulgators of different *Śakas.* In his reply, Mārkaṇḍeya narrates that there would be six promulgators of *Śakas* in the *Kali*-age namely– Yuddhiṣṭhira, Vikrama, Śālivāhana, Vijayābhinanda, Nāgār-juna and Kalkī. The duration of the period of each of them is then mentioned. While explaining the *Yudhiṣṭhra Śaka,*

the family of five Pāṇḍavas, their ancestors and successors are mentioned.

4. The Māgadha race, after Jarāsandha etc. is dealt with – After Bārhadrathas, Śiśumāras, Pradyotas and Nandas are described.

5. A detailed account of life and successors of Candragupta is narrated on its inquiry by Citraketu. Ten Mauryas and then twelve Śuṅgas are enumerated. The Kāṇvāyanas and Āndhras are also enlisted.

6. Seven Ābhīra kings and ten kings of Gardabha race are enumerated. The Kaliṅga kings and those of Puraṇḍa race are also noted.

7. Eleven Maunas, then Hūṇas and Yavanas are also described, along with king Śālivāhana and his descendants.

8. The King Vijaya of Lunar dynasty, his descendants, Kalkī and his descedants, 7 Āndhras, 7 Khosla Kings and those of Maurya dynasty are dealt with.

9. Description of Nāgārjuna Śaka – Nāgārjuna and his descendants, social condition in *Kali*-Age are described.

10. Origin of Kalkī, the period of beginning and end of *Kalī*-age. Devāpi will re-establish *Varṇāśramadharma* in *Kali*-age.

11. Detailed account of Bṛhadratha and his son, Bārhadratha.

12. Account of Bārhadratha continued, his descendants, Accounts of Śiṁśumāra.

13. Śiṁśumāra subdued Nandivardhana. Activities of Mahānandī and Nanda.

14. Victory of Nanda over Kings of solar and lunar dynasties.

15. Puṁsapāla and his descendants. Nanda subdued them also. Eight sons of Nanda are described.

16. Citraketu questions why Candragupta marries with ladies of four castes. Detailed answer is given by Mārkaṇḍeya.

17. Account of Candragupta continued. His victory over different kings (upto Karadaṇḍa).

18. Expeditions of Candragupta continued. His victory over kings of different regions.

19. Exploits of sons of Candragupta namely Vararuci, Vikramārka and Bhartṛhari.

20. Detailed narration of life and exploits of Vikramārka, Genealogy of Śuṅga dynasty, their expeditions and successors.

21. Rājarājanarendra and his exploits, then Kaṇvas and Āndhras.

22. Account of king Śālvivāhana, right from his birth, his victory over different regions.

23. Kāradaṇḍa, his victorious expeditions, his descendats.

24. 18 Hūṇas, Mlecchas, Rājaśekhara's victory over different kings, 14 Turuṣkas, conquering Hūṇas, Yavanas etc. by Lāṅgūlagaja king, Ten kings of Bhūmitra race, king Vijayābhinandana and his conquest over Hūṇas etc.

25. Citraketu asks Mārkaṇḍeya about king Nāgārjuna, his origin and prowess, his descendants etc. Mārkaṇḍeya explains. After Vijayābhinandana, Yavanas and Hūṇas would be powerful and would trouble the subjects. King Nāgārjuna would drive them away and would establish his sovereignty over several other kingdoms.

26. Citraketu asks regarding origin, life and prowess of Kalki, Mārkaṇḍeya starts narrating that Gods and sages went to the Abode of Viṣṇu and praised him. Here the text ends abruptly.

Distinctive Features

The text has a great historical significance, as it has dealt with the dynasties of *Kali*-age in a very detailed manner. There is, no doubt, some historical background behind narration (which resembales that of the *Viṣṇupurāṇa*, the *Matsya Purāṇa*, the *Bhāgavata Purāṇa*, etc.). It is noteworthy that it not only enumerates kings and their genealogies, but, also gives an extensive account of their life and conquests. The glimpe of gloomy social and religious atmosphere can also be comprehended from some references, during the period of atrocities by Huṇas, Yavanas, Mlecchas etc., with the entire social order quite perverted. The use of words like Bādaśahā, Navāba and clear mention of proper names like Muhammada, Tānīṣa etc. can conclusively prove the influence of Muslim culture and rule.

Probable Date and Place of Origin

From the reference to the Muslim rulers and works, mentioned above, the text can generally be placed in a period, when the Muslim rule was prevalent. It is, however, remarkable that there are some stanzas which clearly refer to four *Śaka* eras. These are—

1. सहस्त्रैकं पञ्चशतं वत्सरास्तु गते शके। 1500 Śake=1578 A.D.
2. शके गते रसशतं साहस्त्रं विंशतिद्वयम्। 1640 Śake=1718 A.D.
3. सहस्त्रं षट्शतं चैव षष्टिसंवत्सरागमे। 1660 Śake=1738 A.D.
4. सहस्त्रैकं सप्तशतं चत्वारिंशच्च वत्सराः। 1740 Śake=1818 A.D.

The last one may suggest that the text might have been composed after 1818 A.D. The repeated allusions to the kingdoms and places of pilgrimage from the South and the comparatively less to those of Northern India may be considered as suggestive of its place of origin in South India. Availability of the text from the only extant manuscript in the Telugu script and its non-availability in any other script and region suggests that its origin can be traced some where in Andhra Pradesh.

The Place of U.M. in the Cr. ed.

While preparing the critical edition of a text, it is necessary to consult all the available, different MSS. of the text, found in several regions and scripts. Therefore, when the project of the Crit. ed. of the MKP. is undertaken, it is quite essential to consult and study such a ms., clearly associated with the title of the *Purāṇa*. However, there is no link of continuity of narration or exposition between the text of the MKP. and the present text. The text has been narrated by Mārkaṇḍeya. It is only because of this that it is connected with the *Mārkaṇḍeya Purāṇa*. The text, composed by some later scholar was tagged on to the original with the frequent colophonic note of its being the *Uttarabhāga* of the original *Mārkaṇḍeya Purāṇa*. The spurious character of the text is quite evident.

The critical edition of the MKP. is to be prepared in accordance with the principles of re-constitution of the text, enunciated by the great savants in the field like Prof. V.S. Sukthankar and Prof. G.H. Bhatt. From this point of view, it is to be noted that –

The MSS. of the text from all the regions in different scripts are to be consulted and collated. When a particular portion is not found in the Southern or Northern Recension or both, it is to be considered as not being genuine. It is not to be included in the critical text, but is to be noted in the star-passages or relegated to the Appendix.

In our case, the text of the *Uttarmārkaṇḍeya Purāṇa* is neither found in any of the MSS. from Northern India consulted for the Crit. ed. nor is met with in any other mss.

in Telugu, Grantha and Malayalam scripts, collected from the Southern India.

Hence, it is to be considered as not forming the genuine part of the MKP. But, the spurious text should be relegated to the Appendix to the crit. ed., to clarify it to the world of scholars that it has also been consulted. The only intention behind writing this paper is to acquaint the world of scholars, with this little-known text, allegedly connected with the *Mārkaṇḍeya Purāṇa*.

REFERENCE

Paper published in Journal of the Oriental Institute, Vadodara, Vol. 41, Nos. 3-4, March-June 1992 Issue, pp. 219-224.

Paper read at the Seminar on "Viṣṇupurāṇa and Mārkaṇḍeya Purāṇa" held at the Oriental Institute, Vadodara, 28 to 31st July, 1993.

XXIV

ŚRĪ-LAKṢMĪ—LEGENDS AND LORES (WITH SPECIAL REFERENCE TO THE *MĀRKAṆḌEYAPURĀṆA*)

Introductory

The words Śrī and Lakṣmī referring to Goddesses are found even in the *Yajurveda Saṁhitā.*[1] The Goddess Lakṣmī is associated with several legends and lores throughout the ancient Sanskrit literature. It is really interesting to study the conceptual changes and mythological modifications that have taken place in the character and legends of Goddess Lakṣmī throughout different periods of History. The topic can be analysed from different angles of ancient treatises. Some scholars[2] especially Prof. U.N. Dhal, have made some praiseworthy attempts in this direction. The subject of the seminar is of similar nature but differs in the sense that there would be comprehensive and detailed analysis of the topic, relating only to a particular treastise. Here is an attempt to study the topic with special emphasis on findings about the Goddess Lakṣmī from the *MārkaṇḍeyaPurāṇa* (MKP). As you all know, the MKP, is one of the oldest and important ancient *Purāṇas,* conforming to the five characteristics of the *Purāṇa.* Morcover, it is also noteworthy that it incorporates the *Devīmāhātmya* (DM) also known as *Saptaśatī* or *Caṇḍīpāṭha* in thirteen *adhyāyas* (ch. 81 to 93). With this small introduction, we will now turn to the main theme regarding the Goddess Lakṣmī-legends and lores in the MKP.

1. Legends of Origin of Lakṣmī—Three Traditions

In the MKP., we come across three different traditions

regarding the origin or genesis of Lakṣmī. Herein in one context[3], Lakṣmī is said to be the daughter of Dakṣa and Prasūti. Dakṣa begot twenty-four daughters through Prasūti. Dharma married thirteen daughters out of the twenty-four daughters of Dakṣa and Prasūti. Lakṣmī was one of these thirteen daughters, given in marriage to Dharma. Darpa is the name of the son of Lakṣmī.[4] Thus, this shows that Lakṣmī's father was Dakṣa and mother was Prasūti. She had twenty-three sisters. Her husband was Dharma and Darpa was her son. Secondly, in same context, it is narrated that Khyāti, one of the twenty-four daughters of Dakṣa, was given in marriage to the sage Bhṛgu.[5] Later on in the MKP. (52,14-15), it is noted that Khyāti gave birth to Dhātā and Vidhātā and also to Śrī, who is the wife of Nārāyaṇa i.e. Viṣṇu, who himself is the Supreme God. Thus here Lakṣmī is also described to be the daughter of Bhṛgu and Khyāti and she had two brothers namely Dhātā and Vidhātā. Thus in one and the same text, we get two traditions, regarding the origin of Lakṣmī. It is noteworthy that the legends of the origin of Lakṣmī from the ocean, while it was being churned is not met with in the MKP. But only the epithet of Lakṣmī as *udadhisambhavā* is met with in Dattātreya episode.[6] But here also there seems to be some kind of discrepancy as Lakṣmī, only is described to be originating from three traditions. Dr. U.N. Dhal remarks[7] in this context, "In the primary stage of development, Lakṣmī rose as an independent deity. Then she became the consort of Dharma. But later with the development of Vaiṣṇavism, Lakṣmī was adopted to the Vaiṣṇava Pantheon and she became the consort and constant companion of Viṣṇu." He also refers to the opinion[8] of Dr. Suvira Jaiswal that Lakṣmī was admitted into the *Vaiṣṇava* pantheon during the Gupta Age (3rd-4th cent. A.D.), during which she was united with Viṣṇu.

2. Legend of Lakṣmī with Dattātreya

In the MKP. (Ch. 17), there is a unique legend relating to Lakṣmī and Dattātreya. Dattāreya is the incarnation of Viṣṇu and naturally he is associated with Lakṣmī who is his wife.[9] Dattātreya is one of the sons of Atri and Anasūyā. Here a legend is narrated : There was a terrific battle between gods and demons in which after one divine year, the Gods approached the benevolent Dattātreya. They saw Dattātreya along with Lakṣmī at his hermitage. God implored Dattātreya to rescue them from the disaster, but he pointed out that due to his association with that lady i.e. Lakṣmī, he has been contaminated. The dalliance with lady incurs blemish and this has been uninterruptedly enjoyed by him. But Gods believed him to be quite pure. The mother of the world, Lakṣmī, is absolutely stainless, just as the rays of the Sun remain stainless, whether associated with a brahmin or even a *Cāṇḍāla*.[10] On this, Dattātreya asked Gods to fetch the demons before him. Later on, while fighting with demons, the Gods reached the hermitage of Dattātreya, where they saw Dattātreya, along with his wife Lakṣmī. Here there is a good description of the Goddess Lakṣmī.[11] She is sitting to His left. She is His favourite and beautiful wife, having face like the moon, with eyes lustrous like blue lotuses, having full breasts and large hips uttering quite sweet words, endowed with all kinds of feminine virtues. The demons saw her to be the gem of ladies of the three worlds. They snatched that virtuous lady and placing her in a palanquin carried her on their heads to their abodes. Here Dattātreya pointed out to Gods that as Lakṣmī having transgressed the seven places, has ascended their heads, she would resort to someone else. On the inquiry by Gods, Dattātreya then explains[12] the seven places of Lakṣmī and their effects. (i) When Lakṣmī is stationed in foot of men, she bestows residence; (ii) when stationed on thigh, she bestows clothing and all kinds of wealth; (iii) when taking position on secret organs, she gives enjoyment of dalliance through wife; (iv) when resting on lap or bosom, she gives the fruit of good offsprings; (v) when she is placed in the heart, she bestows all cherished objects; (vi) when on neck, she adorns the neck with ornaments and brings about occasions of embracing, favourite wife, kinsmen and also those who are far away in journey; (vii) when she is abiding in the mouth, she bestows the beauty of clean Vedic recitation, obedience to his orders and good poetic genius. When on head she foresakes the person and goes to someone else. The epithet *udadhisambhavā*, born of ocean, used here for Lakṣmī is noteworthy. As the demons had carried her on their heads, they were ruined and Lakṣmī again returned to Dattātreya. In the MKP. (Ch. 19.4,7,11), Lakṣmī is mentioned as the wife of Dattātreya. She was sitting near Him, she is described as Goddess, relieving all from the mundane world.[13] Dattātreya declares that he bestows all favours of son, wife and wealth etc.[14] on one who worships him along with the Goddess Lakṣmī. Thus, in this legend, Dattātreya who is an incarnation of Viṣṇu is associated with Lakṣmī as his wife and it is advised that one should not allow Lakṣmī to ascend upon his head i.e. one's mind should not be completely overpowered with monetary considerations.

3. Lakṣmī and *Padminīvidyā*

In chapter 68 of MKP there is a description of the *Padminīvidyā,* in the dialogue between Krauṣṭuki and Mārkaṇḍeya. Krauṣṭuki wishes to know in detail the Padminī Lore, which brings about all kinds of enjoyments and also about the eight treasures that are associated with it. Earlier in ch. 66, this lore is referred to and as a result of this lore Svaroci is said to have created three cities for his children. Padminī is a lore, the presiding deity of which is Lakṣmī and all the eight treasures belong to it.[15] Padma, Mahāpadma, Makara, Kacchapa, Mukunda, Nandaka, Nīla and Śaṅkha—these are eight treasures, explained in detail by Mārkaṇḍeya in the verses that follow.[16] These are also called presiding deities of the wealth of people. The person becomes in nature and effect like that particular treasure, when looked upon by it. But it is once again emphasised that Padminī Śrī presides over all of them. The eight *Nidhis* refer to different kinds of professions or occupations that were followed for the accumulation of wealth in those days. The society seems to be quite affluent, there was very sound economic condition with plenty and prosperity. During the Gupta period, the Golden period of Indian History, these professions or occupations were followed for the accumulation of wealth. It ia termed as *Padminī Vidyā.* V.S. Agrawal remarks that during the Gupta period, an image of the Padminī Lakṣmī (or Lakṣmī, seated on lotus) was decorated in houses and was carved even on gold coins or earthen seals.[17]

4. Lakṣmī and the *Devīmāhātmya*

The thirteen chapters (81-93), forming the part of MKP are well-known as *Devīmāhātmya, Saptaśatī* or *Caṇḍīpāṭha.* All these chapters incorporate the episodes regarding the greatness of Devī and hymns in Her praise. It is traditionally understood to incorporate three *caritas,* the deities of each of them are considered to be Mahākālī, Mahālakṣmī and Mahāsarasvatī. The *Madhyamacarita,* the portion of chapters (82-84) incorporating the episode of *Mahiṣāsuravadha* is said to have Mahālakṣmī as its presiding deity. In this episode, the Goddess is described as emanating from the combination of the Lustre of all Gods, with each God giving his weapon to Her for the purposes of killing *Mahiṣāsura.* This shows that this Goddess Mahālakṣmī is possessing the lustre of all Gods. She also wields weapons of all of them. So She is also mentioned in the *Vaikārika-rahasya as aṣṭādaśabhujā, aṣṭabhujā, caturbhujā*[18] etc. In the *Devīmāhātmya,* there are several references in which Lakṣmī is explicitly referred to. Gods praise the Goddess of Sleep to be Śrī etc.[19] The Goddess Herself is in the form of Śrī in the dwellings of the fortunate people.[20] She is said to have taken resort only to the heart of enemy of Kaiṭabha i.e. Viṣṇu.[21] In the famous hymn to the Goddess, Lakṣmī is paid obeisance at two places.[22] Even in the third *carita*, the famous hymn to Nārāyaṇī, sung by Gods, the Goddess Lakṣmī is alluded to.[23] Thus all the three *caritas* of the *Devīmāhātmya* incorporate allusions to the Goddess Lakṣmī.

The supplementary portion of the *Devīmāhātmya* i.e. the three *Rahasyas,* the *Prādhānika,* the Vaikṛtika and *Mūrtirahasyas* present a very comprehensive description of the Goddess Lakṣmī. The minute inconographical details are met with here. The *Prādhānika Rahasya* explains the Goddess Mahālakṣmī to be the supermost and first principle.[24] From Her, emanated the three different couples. From *Rājasa* form, Mahālakṣmī and the couple of Brahmā and Padmā were born. Brahmā has *Trayī* or Sarasvatī as his wife. From Her *Tāmasa* form, Mahākālī and the couple Rudra and Trayīvidyā originated. Rudra married Gaurī or Umā. From Her *Sāttvika* Form, Mahāsarasvatī and the couple Viṣṇu and Umā were created. Viṣṇu married Padmā. In the *Vaikṛtika Rahaṣya* as mentioned previously, Mahālakṣmī is declared to have emanated from the bodies of all Gods. She has three qualities of *Sattva, Rajas* and *Tamas* and She is the killer of *Mahiṣa* demon.[25] The iconographical features of Mahā-lakṣmī are here narrated in detail.[26] She is here referred to as having eighteen, ten, eight and even four arms, as noted previously. She is to be worshipped with the *mantra namo devyai* etc. Lakṣmī is to be worshipped along with Viṣṇu. To her South, Mahākālī along with Gaurī and Rudra should be worshipped. To her North, Mahāsarasvatī, along with Svarā and Brahmā should be worshipped. In the *Mūrtirahasya,* the Goddess Lakṣmī is referred to as Indirā, Kamalā, Śrī and also one having the seat of the Golden Lotus.[27] The Goddess is said to confer on her devotees all desired objectives like retentive power, genius, faith, forbearance, beauty, tranquillity, nourishment and wealth.[28]

5. Stray References

In one context, the MKP mentions[29] that those dwellings where the Sun sees not the beds, and where the fire and water are constantly kept and where the lamps behold the Sun are places patronised by Lakṣmī. With control over speech, body and mind and with utmost devotion, the king is said to have offered worship to the king of kings, along with all *Nidhis,* the group of protectors of *Nidhi* and also to Lakṣmī.[30] It is to be noted that Lakṣmī is associated with Kubera also, as Lakṣmī is the presiding deity of treasures, and Kubera is Nidhīśvara, the treasurer.

6. Lakṣmī-not as Draupadi

One of the questions, discussed in the MKP., is about Draupadī. How did Draupadi become the wife of five Pāṇḍavas? Here the *Mahābhārata* (1.189.33-34) narrates that the five Indras are born as five Pāṇḍavas, while Lakṣmī is born as Draupadī, the wife of Pāṇḍavas. This shows the association of Lakṣmī with Indra. But in the later period, when Viṣṇu became more prominent and Lakṣmī became his consort, the relation of Lakṣmī with Indra went into background. Hence in the MKP, Lakṣmī is not described to be born as Draupadī, but it is Indrāṇī, the wife of Indra himself who became Draupadī, the wife of five Pāṇḍavas.[31] This incident is quite noteworthy.

7. References to Alakṣmī or Nirṛti

Alkṣmi or Nirṛti is described as wife of Mṛtyu; she had fourteen sons, who follow the dictates of Mṛtyu and attend upon men at the time of destruction.[32] It is also noted that Hiṁsā is the wife of Adharma. She had one son named Anṛta and one daughter named Nirṛti. Nirṛti begot two sons namely Naraka and Bhaya.[33] The owl is said to be the vehicle of Alakṣmī.[34] In the *Śakrādistuti* of the *Devīmāhātmya*, the Goddess is said to reside in the dwellings of the evil-minded in the form of Alakṣmī.[35] In the MKP. it is also mentioned that there is no fear of Alakṣmī, where the son worships the preceptor, the Gods and also the parents and where the spouse respects her husband.[36]

Concluding Remarks

Thus The *MārkaṇḍeyaPurāṇa* is one of the most important and oldest *Purāṇas*, incorporating also the text of the *Devīmāhātmya* in thirteen chapters. We come across several legends and lores, relating to the Goddess Lakṣmī in it. There are three legends about the origin of Lakṣmī—(i) as a Dauthter of Dakṣa and Prasūti, (ii) as a daughter of Bhṛgu and Khyāti and iii) as originating from ocean. The legend regarding her association with Dattātreya as his wife and the destruction of Demons, on her ascending their heads is quite noteworthy. The *Mārkaṇḍeypurāṇa* (ch. 65) narrates the *Padminīvidyā,* which has Lakṣmī as its presiding deity. In the *Devīmāhātmya* and other contexts of the *Purāṇa* several references to Goddess Lakṣmī (and some also to Alakṣmī) are met with. In the supplementary portion of the *Devī-māhāmya* i.e. the *Prādhānika, Vaikṛtika* and *Mūrti rahasyas,* there is detailed description of the Goddess Lakṣmī and therein several iconographical specifications are elucidated. Thus the *Mārkaṇḍeyapurāṇa* is an important and indispensable text for understanding the legends and lores, concerning the Goddess Lakṣmī.

FOOTNOTES

Paper published in Śrī-Lakṣmī. Legeneds and Lores, Proceedings of Seminar, Ananthacharya Indological Institute, Mumbai 1999, pp. 169-182.

Paper read at the National Seminar on "Śrī-Lakṣmī-Legends and Lores" held at the Ananthacharya Indological Research Institute, Mumbai, 6th and 7th March, 1999.

1. *श्रीश्च ते लक्ष्मीश्च पत्न्यौ . . . Vājasaneyisaṁhitā, (31.22).*
2. Dhal, Upendra Nath : *Goddess Lakṣmī : Origin and Development, Oriental* Publishers and Distributors. New Delhi, 1978. Hartmann Gerda : *Beitrage Zur Geschiche der Gottin Lakṣmī,* Kiel, 1933; Ray Govinda Chandra : *Prācīna Bhāratamen Lakṣmī Pratimā (eka adhyayana)* (Hindi), Varanasi, 1968. Sircar, B.C. : (ed.) : *Lakṣmī And Sarasvatī in Art and Literature,* Calcutta University, Calcutta, 1970; Choudhuri, N.N. : '*Goddess Lakṣmī in the Purana and Tantra'*, The Poona Orientalist, Vol. XIII, nos. 1/2 (1948), pp. 1-6 (an article). Coomaraswamy, A.K. : "Early Indian Iconography II, Śrī Lakṣmī,' Eastern Art, Vol. I, (1929), pp. 175-189 (an article); Motichandra : '*Padmā-Śrī - Lady of Beauty and Abundance'.* Nehru Abhinandan Grantha, Calcutta, (1949), pp. 497-513, (an article); Sivaramamurti, C. : '*Goddess Lakṣmī and Her Symbols', Journal of U.P. Historical Society,* Vol.XIV, (1941), pp. 21-24 (an article).
3. प्रसूत्यां च तथा दक्षश्चतस्रो विंशतिस्तथा।
   ससर्ज कन्यास्तासां च सम्यङ्नामानि मे शृणु।
   श्रद्धा लक्ष्मीर्धृतिस्तुष्टिः पुष्टिर्मेधा क्रिया तथा।।
   बुद्धिर्लज्जा वपुः शान्तिः सिद्धिः कीर्तिस्त्रयोदशी।
   पत्न्यर्थं प्रतिजग्राह धर्मो दाक्षयणीः प्रभुः।।

   —*Mārkaṇḍeya Purāṇa* (MKP), ed. Jivananda Vidyasagar Bhattacharya, Calcutta, 1879, 50.19-21.
4. श्रद्धा कामं श्रीश्च दर्पं नियमं धृतिरात्मजम्।।
   संतोषं च तथा तुष्टिर्लोभं पुष्टिरजायत।—MKP. 50.25-26
5. ताभ्यः शिष्टा यवीयस्य एकादश सुलोचनाः।
   ख्यातिः सत्यथ संभूतिः स्मृतिः प्रीतिस्तथा क्षमा।।
   संततिश्चानसूया च ऊर्जा स्वाहा स्वधा तथा।
   भृगुर्भवो मरीचिश्च तथा चैवाङ्गिरा मुनिः।।
   पुलस्त्यः पुलहश्चैव क्रतुश्च ऋषयस्तथा।
   वसिष्ठोऽत्रिस्तथा वह्निः पितरश्च यथाक्रमम्।।

ख्यात्याद्या जगृहुः कन्या मुनयो मुनिसत्तमाः।—MKP.50.22.5.ab

6. मृष्टानुवाक्यलावण्यमाज्ञामवितथां तथा।
मुखसंस्था कवित्वं च यच्छत्युदधिसंभवा।। —MKP.18.52

7. *Op.cit.,p.74,no.21*

8. *Ibid.*

9. इत्युक्तास्ते तदा जग्मुर्दत्तात्रेयाश्रमं सुराः।
ददृशुश्च महात्मानं तं ते लक्ष्म्या समन्वितम्।। —MKP.18.22

10. अनघेयं द्विजश्रेष्ठ ! जगन्माता न दुष्यते।
यथांशुमाला सूर्यस्य द्विजचण्डालसंगिनी।। —MKP.18.32

11. वामपार्श्वस्थितामिष्टामशेषजगतां शुभाम्।
भार्यां चास्य सुचार्वङ्गीं लक्ष्मीमिन्दुनिभाननाम्।।
नीलोत्पलाभनयनां पीनश्रोणिपयोधराम्।
गदन्तीं मधुरां भाषां सर्वैर्योषिद्गुणैर्युताम्।। —MKP.18.39, 40

12. नृणां पदे स्थिता लक्ष्मीर्निलयं संप्रयच्छति।
सक्थ्नोश्च संस्थिता वस्त्रं तथा नानाविधं वसु।।
कलत्रं गुह्यसंस्था च क्रोडस्थापत्यदायिनी।
मनोरथान्पूरयति पुरुषाणां हृदि स्थिता।।
लक्ष्मीर्लक्ष्मीवतां श्रेष्ठा कण्ठस्था कण्ठभूषणम्।
अभीष्टबन्धुदारैश्च तथाश्लेषं प्रवासिभिः।।
मृष्टानुवाक्यलावण्यमाज्ञामवितथां तथा।
मुखसंस्था कवित्वं च यच्छत्युदधिसंभवा।।
शिरोगता संत्यजति ततोऽन्यं याति चाश्रयम्। —MKP.18.49-53.ab

13. स्त्री चेयं मम पार्श्वस्था . . . . । —MKP.19.4.c.
अनघस्त्वं तथैवेयं देवी सर्वभवारणिः। —MKP.19.7.cd

14. ये च मां पूजयिष्यन्ति गन्धमाल्यादिभिर्नराः।
लक्ष्मीसमेतं गीतैश्च ब्राह्मणानां तथार्चनैः।
तेषामहं परां तुष्टिं पुत्रदारधनादिकम्।
प्रदास्याम्यवघातं च हनिष्याम्यवमन्यताम्।। —MKP.19.10-12

15. पद्मिनी नाम या विद्या लक्ष्मीस्तस्याश्च देवता।
तदाधाराश्च निधयस्तन्मे निगदतः शृणु।। —MKP.68.4

16. यत्र पद्ममहापद्मौ तथा मकरकच्छपौ।
मुकुन्दो नन्दकश्चैव नीलः शङ्खोऽष्टमो निधिः।।
सत्यामृद्धौ भवन्त्येते सिद्धिस्तेषां हि जायते।
एते ह्यष्टौ समाख्याता निधयस्तत्र क्रोष्टुके।। —MKP.68.5-6.

17. Agrawal, V.S. : *Mārkaṇḍeya Purāṇa-Eka Sāṁskṛtika Adhyayana* (Hindi), Hindustani Academy, Allahabad, First Ed; 1961,p.159.

18. खड्गपात्रशिरःखेटैरलंकृतचतुर्भुजा । –प्राधानिकरहस्यम् -9.ab

अष्टादशभुजा पूज्या सा सहस्रभुजा सती। –वैकृतिकरहस्यम् 10.ab
दक्षिणेऽष्टभुजा लक्ष्मीर्महतीति समर्चयेत् । –वैकृतिकरहस्यम् 20.cd

19. त्वं श्रीस्त्वमीश्वरी त्वं ह्रीस्त्वं बुद्धिर्बोधलक्षणा ।
लज्जा पुष्टिस्तथा तुष्टिस्त्वं शान्तिः क्षान्तिरेव च ।। —MKP.81.60

20. या श्रीः स्वयं सुकृतिनां भवनेष्वलक्ष्मीः
पापात्मनां कृतधियां हृदयेषु बुद्धिः ।
श्रद्धा सतां कुलजनप्रभवस्य लज्जा
तां त्वां नताः स्म परिपालय देवि! विश्वम् ।। —MKP.84.4

21. मेधासि देवि विदिताखिलशास्त्रसारा
दुर्गासि दुर्गभवसागरनौरसङ्गा।
श्रीः कैटभारिहृदयैककृताधिवासा
गौरी त्वमेव शशिमौलिकृतप्रतिष्ठा।। —MKP.84.10

22. कल्याण्यै प्रणतावृद्ध्यै सिद्ध्यै कुर्मो नमो नमः।
नैर्ऋत्यै भूभृतां लक्ष्म्यै शर्वाण्यै ते नमो नमः। --MKP.85.9
या देवी सर्वभूतेषु लक्ष्मीरूपेण संस्थिता।
नमस्तस्यै नमस्तस्यै नमस्तस्यै नमो नमः।। —MKP.85.26

23. लक्ष्मि लज्जे महाविद्ये श्रद्धे पुष्टि स्वधे ध्रुवे।
महारात्रि महाऽविद्ये नारायणि नमोऽस्तु ते।। —MKP.91.20

24. सर्वस्याद्या महालक्ष्मीस्त्रिगुणा परमेश्वरी।
लक्ष्यालक्ष्यस्वरूपा सा व्याप्य कृत्स्नं व्यवस्थिता।। –प्राधानिकरहस्यम्-4

25. सर्वदेवशरीरेभ्यो याविर्भूतामितप्रभा।
त्रिगुणा सा महालक्ष्मीः साक्षान्महिषमर्दिनी।। –वैकृतिकरहस्यम्-7

26. मातुलिङ्गं गदां खेटं पानपात्रं च बिभ्रती।
नागं लिङ्गं च योनिं च बिभ्रती नृप मूर्धनि।।
तप्तकाञ्चनवर्णाभा तप्तकाञ्चनभूषणा।
शून्यं तदखिलं स्वेन पूरयामास तेजसा।। –प्राधानिकरहस्यम्-5, 6.
श्वेतानना नीलभुजा सुश्वेतस्तनमण्डला।
रक्तमध्या रक्तपादा नीलजङ्घोरुरुन्मदा।।
सुचित्रजघना चित्रमाल्याम्बरविभूषणा।
चित्रानुलेपना कान्तिरूपसौभाग्यशालिनी।। –वैकृतिकरहस्यम्-८, 9.
आयुधान्यत्र वक्ष्यन्ते दक्षिणाधःकरक्रमात्।।
अक्षमाला च कमलं बाणोऽसिः कुलिशं गदा।
चक्रं त्रिशूलं परशुः शङ्खो घण्टा च पाशकः।।
शक्तिर्दण्डश्चर्म चापं पानपात्रं कमण्डलुः।
अलंकृतभुजामेभिरायुधैः कमलासनाम्।।
सर्वदेवमयीमीशां महालक्ष्मीमिमां नृप।

पूजयेत्सर्वलोकानां स देवानां प्रभुर्भवेत्।। –वैकृतिकरहस्यम्-10.cd-13.

27. कनकोत्तकान्तिः सा सुकान्तिकनकाम्बरा।
देवी कनकवर्णाभा कनकोत्तमभूषणा।
कमलाङ्कुशपाशाब्जैरलंकृतचतुर्भुजा।
इन्दिरा कमला लक्ष्मीः सा श्रीरुक्माम्बुजासना।।–मूर्तिरहस्यम्-2 and 3

28. मेधा प्रज्ञा तथा श्रद्धा धारणा कान्तिरेव च।
शान्तिः पुष्टिस्तथा लक्ष्मीरेतत्सर्वं प्रयच्छति।। –मूर्तिरहस्यम्-24

29. भास्करादृष्टशय्यानि नित्याग्निसलिलानि च।
सूर्यावलोकदीपानि लक्ष्म्या गेहानि भाजनम्।। —MKP.50.81

30. यथोक्तां साऽकरोत् पूजां राजराजस्य संयता।।
निधीनामप्यशेषाणां निधिपालगणस्य च।
लक्ष्म्याश्च परया भक्त्या यतवाक्कायमानसा।।—MKP.126.9.cd-10.

31. पञ्चधा भगवानित्थमवतीर्णः शतक्रतुः।।
तस्योत्पन्ना महाभागा पत्नी कृष्णा हुताशनात्।।
शक्रस्यैकस्य सा पत्नी कृष्णा नान्यस्य कस्यचित्।—MKP.5.23.-25.ab
लक्ष्मीश्चैषां पूर्वमेवोपदिष्टा
भार्या यैषां द्रौपदी दिव्यरूपा। —*Mahābhārata*-1.189.33-34
सृष्टा स्वयं देवपत्नी स्वयंभुवा। —*Mahābhārata*-1.189.49

32. निर्ऋतिश्च तथा चान्या मृत्योर्भार्याभवन्मुने।
अलक्ष्मीर्नाम तस्यां च मृत्योः पुत्राश्चतुर्दश।।
अलक्ष्मीपुत्रका ह्येते मृत्योरादेशकारिणः।
विनाशकालेषु नरान् भजन्त्येते शृणुष्व तान्।। —MKP.50.33-34.

33. हिंसा भार्या त्वधर्मस्य तस्यां जज्ञे तथानृतम्।
कन्या च निर्ऋतिस्तस्यां सुतौ द्वौ नरकं भयम् ।। —MKP.50.29

34. उलूकं निर्ऋतिश्चैव जग्राहातिभयावहम्।—MKP.51.68

35. cf. n. 20.

36. यत्र पुत्रो गुरोः पूजां देवानां च तथा पितुः।
पत्नी च भर्तुः कुरुते तत्रालक्ष्मीभयं कुतः।। —MKP.50.79

TECHNICAL LITERATURE

nandana.[6] Several astrological details, connected with agriculture are to be found here. Firstly, in four verses[7], the days and position of moon in *rāśis* that are favourable and unfavourable for agricultural work are mentioned. Sunday, Monday, Thursday and Friday are auspicious days, which are beneficial and bring fortune. While Tuesday, Wednesday and Saturday are inauspicious days, giving no good result. So these are to be avoided.

The *Meṣa* kills the beasts, similar is the nature of the *Vṛścika*. The *Karka* does not bring happiness and grains will not grow in the *Tulā*. The *Siṁha* destroys the crop. The *Dhana* brings about worldly calamity. There is always danger even in the *Makara* and *Kumbha rāśis*. The only auspicious *rāśis* are the *Vṛṣabha*, the *Kanyā*, the *Mithuna* and the *Mīna*. This is significant. This shows that the agricultural work should begin only on the auspicious days like Sunday, Monday, Thursday and Friday. Moreover, the moon should also be only in *rāśis* namely the *Vṛṣabha*, the *Kanyā*, the *Mithuna* and the *Mīna*, when the agricultural work is to be undertaken.

Auspicious Rites Before Starting Agriculral Work :

The agricultural work should be started on an auspicious day and good position of moon as mentioned above. The farmer should be pure and wear white dress. He should take bathe and worship as per procedure with *gandha* (sandle-paste) and flowers, the earth along with planets as also Prajāpati. He should circumambulate the sacred fire and donate ample *dakṣiṇā* to Brahmins. The black bulls should be yoked. Their faces *(mukhapārśva)* should be anointed with butter or ghee and the front part of the *phāla* (plough-share) should be touched with gold. He should first facing the North offer an *arghya* (sacred offering) with milk and then the auspicious, forunate person should start with the agricultural work.[8]

XXV

DEVALA-CITATIONS ON THE TOPIC OF AGRICULTURE

Introductory

Devala was an ancient *Dharmasūtrakāra,* referred to even by Śaṅkarācārya in his commentary on the *Brahma-sūtras.*[1] He was also a *Smṛtikāra*, whose views are profusely quoted by the commentators and digest-writers on *Dharma-śāstra.* The metrical *Smṛti*, containing merely ninety verses, dealing with the topic of purification of Hindus, contaminated by Mlecchas is a later work, ascribed to Devala.[2] The present scholar has tried to collect, compile and reconstruct the lost text of Devala, on the basis of available quotations. The reconstructed Text and its critical study have been published in two volumes.[3] Devala was also an ancient authority on *Jyotiṣa,* who is referred to and quoted even by Varāhamihira in his *Bṛhatsaṁhitā.*[4] While reconstructing the lost text of Devala on *Dharmaśāstra,* more than 80 citations of Devala, pertaining to different topics of *Jyotiṣa,* were also collected. There is a long extract of about twentyfive verses, relating to the topic of *kṛṣi* or agriculture in this collection. There are also some verses on *kṛṣi* in the portion of the Reconstructed Text of the *Devalasmṛti.*[5] Here in this paper, an attempt is made to present before the world of scholars the views of our ancient sage Devala, on the technical topic of Agriculture as is glimpsed from the available citations.

Auspicious days and *Cāndra rāśis :*

The long extract of 23 verses of Devala on agriculture, referred to above is quoted in the *Jyotistattva* of Raghu-

Characteristics of Bulls :

We have already noted that black bulls should be yoked. The bulls, whose horn is broken or whose *Khura* (hoof) is broken should be avoided. The bull, who is *vikala* (with drooping limbs) and whose tail is cut off should be avoided. Similarly, a *Kapila* (Tawny) bull should not be used. This shows that the *Kapila* bulls and bulls with physical deformity are to be avoided for agriculture.[9]

Beginning of Ploughing :

The procedure of beginning of the ploughing is also described.[10]

One should first worship the fire, Gods and the Brahmin and then begin the work of ploughing. As mentioned previously, the front part of the plough should be brushed with gold. The Vasus, Indra, Pruthu, Rāma, Moon, Parāśara, Balabhadra—these should be remembered for dispelling all calamities. Then the healthy farmer should begin the ploughing. The ploughshare etc. should be quite firm and strong, then only good result will follow otherwise calamity. Hence one should try to dispell all calamities. The one furrow brings about victory, the three bring the wealth. The five furrows give the fruit of ample crops. No more furrows should be drawn, otherwise there will be great fault.[11]

While ploughing, if a *kūrma* (tortoise) comes out, the wife of the farmer departs from this world and there is also danger from the fire. If the plough-share is broken, the farmer himself (who is the master of the plough-share) attains destruction. When there is breaking of *Īśā* (Pole of the plough), the life of the farmer himself is in danger. When there is breaking of *yuga* (yoke), *samīna* (a part of the plough) or the *yoktra* (tie or rope) the calamities respectively the death of daughter, or a son, *vyāsaṅga* (detachment) and destruction of crops occur.[12]

If one of the bull falls down, even while the ploughing is in progress, then it is attacked by such diseases like fever, descentry etc. and the agricultural work is in danger. But if one of the bulls falls down immediately after the work of ploughing or rejoices by licking the calf there is four fold better prosperity.[13]

The Showing of seeds :

The procedure of sowing seeds is also narrated is four verses. The seed, which is covered with golden water should be carried by a pure (*Śuci*) person. One should remember Indra and then he himself should sow three handfuls of seeds. Then having greeted each other, with glee, in a delightful mood, facing the East, with an auspicious pot in hand, one should recite the following two *mantras.*[14] First one is a prayer to Sītā, the earth and second is a benedictory, wishing well-being of all. These *mantras* are as follows :

त्वं वै वसुंधरे सीते बहुपुष्पफलप्रदे।
नमस्ते, मे शुभं नित्यं कृषिं मेधां शुभे कुरु।।
रोहन्तु सर्वसस्यानि काले देवः प्रवर्षतु।
कर्षकास्तु भवन्त्वग्रा धान्येन च धनेन च।।स्वाहा।। –37–38.

Comparision with the *Kṛṣiparāśara*

The *Kṛṣiparāśara*[15] is an important work in Sanskrit, dealing with the different aspects of Agriculture and astrology, connected with it. It is a systematic compilation ascribed to Parāśara, on the topic of *Kṛṣi.* It is placed between 600 A.D. to 1100 A.D. The verses, ascribed to Devala can be compared with those found in the *Kṛṣiparāśara*. Sunday is considered auspicious by Devala, while Parāśara (123) does not include Sunday like that. Similarly Devala mentions Wednesday among unfavourable days, while Parāśara (122) refers to it as favourable.[16] This difference is noteworthy. The period of Sun's entrance in various Zodiacs is also considered. Here

Parāśara (127)[17] recommends the *Vṛścika* and the *Dhana lagnas* to be auspicious, while Devala mentions position of moon in them to be inauspicious and bringing calamities. The divergent views deserve to be noted. Parāśara gives importance to *lagnas* while Devala to the position of moon. The effect of inauspicious *lagnas* namely *Karka, Siṁha, Tulā, Makara* and *Kumbha* are differently elucidated by Parāśara (128-129). They are (1) fear from acquatic creatures, (2) fear from serpents (3) danger to life (4) danger of destruction of crops, (5) fear from thieves.[17] The procedure of ploughing (130-133)[18] is mostly similar with some minor variations in readings. Here Pruthu is also included among those to be worshipped, by reading *Pruthum caiva* (131) for *Pūjayitvā,* found in Devala. Parāśara (132) notes that the plough-share is to be besmeared with honey, which is not found in Devala's description. Devala states that Vasus, Indra, Pruthu, Rāma-candra, Parāśara and Balabhadra are to be remembered, while starting ploughing. While Parāśara mentions with slight difference-Indra, Śukra, Pruthu, Rāma and Parāśara- these are to be invoked. (133) Regarding the colour of bulls Parāśara (unlike Devala) allows red and red and black bulls alternatively besides the balck bulls (134).[19] The bulls with useless hips, with ears cut off and all white bulls are to be discarded (141)[20] according to Parāśara. Devala does not mention like this. Parāśara reads that the seeds are to be sprinkled with cold water (177)[21] before sowing. While Devala reads here as *hemavāri-viliptasya* i.e. the seed is besmeared with the golden water.

Other Citations in *Dharmaśāstra* :

Among the citations of Devala, relating to *Dharma-śāstra,* compiled by the researcher, there are also about eleven verses, dealing with the topic of *kṛṣi*. In fact, the rite of *Halapravartanam* (ploughing the field) is to be found in some

Gṛhyasūtras and *Smṛtis* also.[22] Devala also has specifically described the rite of ploughing and sowing of seeds. He enjoins that at the beginning of the festival of commencement of agricultural work, the ploughshare should be properly worshipped with various *upacāras*. As per procedure, the giving of *Dakṣiṇā*, *homa* and pleasing *Brāhmaṇas* should be done. After having taken bath and well-dressed, he himself should plough the field. First, he should go to North-East direction and turning to the East, he should circumambulate and return to North-East and face that direction. The virtuous, contented, well-dressed, garlanded person should sow the powerful seed and pour water on the earth through the golden vessel, while facing East. After sowing seeds, one should take meals there only along with other Kinsmen and enjoy the festive occasion with music and drums etc.[23]

In a prose *sūtra* also, the same is explained by stating that the person, after having taken bath, decorate the bulls and he should offer meals to Brahmins. This is a meritorious act, relating to bulls. The sixth protion should be given to the king and with the fourth part, he should appease the Brahmins. Here Devala quotes two traditional verses, the import of which is as follows : This *yūpa* (sacrificial post) of sacrificers is placed here by the farmers. Hence there should be distribution of *Dakṣiṇā* in the form of food, grains and wealth without any lassitude. The farmers incur sin by ploughing fields, cutting of trees and killing insects and birds. This sin is definitely dispelled by the performance of the *Khalayaiña*. (earth-sacrifice).[24]

In last two verses[25], some prohibitions regarding bulls are prescribed. The act of sterelization and piercing of nose for cord should not be made for bulls, carrying loads. The yoking of old, sick, diseased bulls is also prohibited. The baren cow should not be made to carry the load nor should it be oppressed by heavy load. The bulls should not be driven anywhere to the mountain top.

Concluding Remarks :

Thus Devala, the ancient seer has expounded the topic of *Kṛṣi,* which is interspersed with the material relating to the religious rites and the astrological considerations. In the modern world of science and technology, it is but necessary to find out thc logical reasoning and the scientific grounds, underlying all such injuctions, by practically utilizing these and observing the results. From this point of view, the trend of *Yogeśvara Kṛṣi,* promulgated by Pt. Pandurang Shastri Athavale needs to be taken serious note of.

Besides the religious and astrological significance, there is great psychological relevance of the citations of Devala. The act of *kṛṣi* is regarded as a sacrifice. All acts like ploughing, sowing seeds etc. are to be done with pure body, cheerful and contented mind. The field *(Bhūmi) Hala* (Plough), the seed etc. are revered like divine entities. Hence the psychological rule is that whenever any act is done with contented, cheerful, peaceful mind, pure physique, and great reverence towards the act, it would definitely bring good and beneficial results than the one done with distaste, hurry and uncontented mind and inpure physique. The reverence towards the act results in performance of the act with great care and accuracy. From this point of view, Devala-citations on *Kṛṣi* are to be regarded as pertinent and relevant even today in the modern world.

FOOTNOTES

Papcr read at All-India Oriental Conference, 40th Session, Deptt. of Sanskrit, University of Madras, Chennai, 28-30th May 2000.

1. देवलप्रभृतिभिश्च कैश्चिद् धर्मसूत्रकारैःस्वग्रन्थेष्वाश्रितः।
—*Brahmasūtraśāṅkarabhāṣya*, ed. Narayan Ram Acharya, Nirnaya Sagar Press, Third ed., Bombay, 1948, I.4.26.

2. *Smṛtisandarbha,* Gurumandal Granthamala, Calcutta, 1952-53, vol. III, pp.1655-1663. *Smṛtīnām Samuccayaḥ,* Anandashram edition, second edition, Poona, 1929 pp.58-88. *Aṣṭādaśasmṛtayaḥ,* pub. by Sasta Sanskrit Sahitya Mandal, Samali, Mujaffarnagar (U.P.), *Vikrama* Sam. 1998, pp.64-67.
3. Wadekar, M.L. : *Devalasmṛti-Reconstruction and Critical study,* Vol. I (Introduction and Text) Published by Koshal Book Depot, Delhi, 1996 and Vol. II (critical study), by same publisher, 1997.
4. *Bṛhatsaṁhitā of Varāhamihira* (with com. of Bhaṭṭotpala) Vol. I and II, Benares, 1987; 11/1, 23/4, 86/1-4.
5. *Devalasmṛti op.cit.* pp.51-52.
6. *Devalasmṛti op.cit.* pp.322-324
7. गुरुसोमसूर्यशुक्राः क्षेम्याः सम्पत्कराः शुभाः
बुधार्किभूमिपुत्राश्च न भवन्ति फलप्रदाः।।
हन्ति मेषः पशून् सर्वान् स्वभावेनाथ वृश्चिकः।
कर्कटे न भवेत् सौख्यं तुलायां न प्ररोहति।।
केशरी शस्यघाती स्यात् पार्थिवोपद्रवं धनुः।
मकरे चैव कुम्भे च भयमेव विनिर्दिशेत्।।
गोस्त्रीमन्मथमौनेषु शस्यं सम्पद्यते महत्।–17-19
8. प्रशस्ते चन्द्रतारे च शुचिः शुक्लेन वाससा।
स्नात्वा गन्धैश्च पुष्पैश्च पूजयित्वा विधानतः।।
पृथ्वीं च ग्रहसंयुक्तां पूजयित्वा प्रजापतिम्।
अग्निं प्रदक्षिणीकृत्य दीयते भूरि दक्षिणा।
कृष्णौ वृषौ नियोक्तव्यौ नवनीतैर्घृतेन वा।
मुखपार्श्वं तयोर्लिप्या(म्पे)त्फालाग्रं कनकैः स्पृशेत्।।
उत्तराभिमुखो भूत्वा क्षीरेणार्घ्यं प्रदापयेत्।
ततः शुभकरः श्रीमान् कृषिकर्म समाचरेत्।।–20-23
9. वर्जयेद् भग्नशृङ्गं च क्षुरभग्नं च वर्जयेत्।
विकलं छिन्नलाङ्गूलं कपिलं वृषभं तथा।–24
10. संपूज्याग्निं द्विजं देवं कुर्याद् हलप्रवर्तनम्।
हेमनिर्घृष्टफालाग्र(ग्रं)छिन्नरेखां न कारयेत्।।
स्मर्तव्या वसवश्चेन्द्रः पृथू रामः सचन्द्रमाः।
पराशरो बलभद्रः सर्वविघ्नोपशान्तये।।–28-29
11. हलप्रवाहनं कार्यं नीरुग्भिः कृषिकर्मकैः।
हलादिभिर्दृढैः क्षेमं कुदृढैर्न शुभं वदेत्।।
वृषभा यदि मुह्यन्ति तस्य विघ्नप्रदा भवेत्।।

तस्मात्सर्वप्रयत्नेन निर्विघ्नं कारयेत्सदा।
एका जयकरी रेखा तृतीया चार्थदायिका।
पञ्चमी या भवेद् रेखा बहुशस्यफला हि सा।।
अत ऊर्ध्वं न कर्तव्यं महादोषस्ततो भवेत्।। –25-27

12. हले प्रवाह्यमाने तु कूर्म उत्पद्यते यदि।
गृहिणी म्रियते तस्य ततोऽग्नेश्च भयं भवेत्।।
लाङ्गलं भिद्यते चापि प्रभुस्तस्य विनश्यति।
ईशाभङ्गो यदा कर्तुः संशयो जीवितस्य च।।
सुतानाशो युगभङ्गे समीने म्रियते सुतः।
योक्त्रच्छेदे तु व्यासङ्गः शस्यहानिश्च जायते।–30-32

13. हले प्रवाह्यमाने तु गौरेकः प्रपतेद् यदि।
प्रपतेन्मुक्तमात्रस्तु बन्धनं स प्रपद्यते।।
ज्वरातिसाररोगेण कृषिभङ्गं विनिर्दिशेत्।
प्रवाहमात्रमुक्तस्तु ततः गौः प्रपतेद् यदि।
वत्सालीढेन नर्दन्ति ततो शस्यं चतुर्गुणम्।।–33-34

14. हेमवारिविलिप्तस्य बीजस्योन्नयतः शुचिः।
इन्द्र(न्द्रं) चित्ते निधायाथ स्वयं मुष्टित्रयं वपेत्।।
कृत्वा चान्योन्यप्रोत्साहं नर्तको हृष्टमानसः।
प्राङ्मुखः कलशं गृह्य इमं मन्त्रमुदीरयेत्।।–35-36

15. *Kṛṣiparāśara,* ed. and trans. by Girija Prasanna Majumdar and Suresh Chandra Banerji, Bibliotheca Indica, The Asiatic Society, Calcutta, 1960.

16. हलप्रसारणं कार्यं कृषकैः शस्यवृद्धये।
शुक्रेन्द्रजीववारेषु शशिजस्य विशेषतः।।
भौमार्कदिवसे चैव तथा च शनिवासरे।
कृषिकर्मसमारम्भो राज्योपद्रवमादिशेत्।। – *Kṛṣiparāśara.* 122-123.

17. वृषे मीने च कन्यायां युग्मे धनुषि वृश्चिके।
एतेषु शुभलग्नेषु कुर्याद् हलप्रसारणम्।।
मेषलग्ने पशुं हन्यात् कर्कटे जलजाद् भयम्।
सिंहे सर्पभयं चैव कुम्भे चौरभयं तथा।।
मकरे शस्यनाशः स्यात्तुलायां प्राणसंशयः।
तस्माल्लग्नं प्रयत्नेन कृष्यारम्भे विचारयेत्।।

– *Kṛṣiparāśara* 127-129.

18. शुभेऽर्के चन्द्रसंयुक्ते शुक्लयुग्मेन वाससा।
स्नात्वा गन्धैश्च पुष्पैश्च पूजयित्वा विधानतः।।

पृथिवीं ग्रहसंयुक्तां पृथुं चैव प्रजापतिम्।
अग्नेः प्रदक्षिणं कृत्वा भूरि दत्त्वा च दक्षिणाम्।
फलाग्रं स्वर्णसंयुक्तं कृत्वा मधुविलेपनम्।
अहेः क्रोडे वामपार्श्वे कुर्याद्हलप्रसारणम्।।
स्मर्तव्यो वासवः शुक्रः पृथुरामः पराशरः।
संपूज्याग्निं द्विजं देवं कुर्याद् हलप्रसारणम्।।

–*Kṛṣiparāśara* 130-133.

19. कृष्णौ वृषौ हलश्लाघ्यौ रक्तौ वा कृष्णलोहितौ।

–*Kṛṣiparāśara* 134.

20. वृषो व्यर्थकटिर्वर्ज्यश्छिन्नलाङ्गूकर्णकः।
सर्वशुक्लस्तथा वर्ज्यः कृषकैर्हलकर्मणि।।

–*Kṛṣiparāśara* 141.

21. हिमवारिनिषिक्तस्य बीजस्य तन्मनाः शुचिः।

–*Kṛṣiparāśara* 177.

22. The *Gṛhyasūtras* like Pāraskara, Kauśika, Aśvalāyana, Śāṅkhyāyana, Kauṣītaki etc. —Ram Gopal, *India of Vedic Kalpasūtras*, pp.425-427.
Parāśarasmṛti adh. II, Bṛhatparāśarasmṛti adh. V

23. यो लाङ्गले तु संपूज्य कृष्यारम्भमहोत्सवे।
गन्धैः पुष्पैस्तथा धूपैर्माल्यै रत्नैः पृथक् पृथक्।।
सदक्षिणैर्द(र्वि)धानेन होमैर्ब्राह्मणतर्पणैः।।
ततः शक्तिविमुक्तेन ब्रह्मवादेन भूरिणा।
हलयेद् वाहयेद् भूमिं स्वयं स्नातः स्वलंकृतः।।
पूर्वोत्तरां दिशं गच्छेत् क्रमात् पौरन्दरीं शुभाम्।
कृत्वा प्रदक्षिणावृत्तिमीशानाभिमुखस्ततः।।
विमुच्य वृषभं बीजं पुरुषो लक्षणान्वितः।
तुष्टः सुवासाः स्रग्वी च सुवर्णे जलसेचकः।
सुवर्णपात्रसंयुक्तं प्राङ्मुखो निर्वपेद् भुवि।।
उप्त्वा बीजं च तत्रैव भोक्तव्यं सह बन्धुभिः।
उत्सवश्चैव कर्तव्यो गीतवाद्यसमाकुलः।।

—*Devalasmṛti*, *op.cit.* no.458-462.

24. स्नात्वानुडुहोऽलंकृत्य ब्राह्मणान् भोजयेत् सौरभेयानां पुण्यमिति।
षड्भागं राज्ञे दत्त्वा पञ्चमाद् ब्राह्मणान् दत्त्वा तोषयेत्।
अथाप्यत्रोदाहरन्ति-
यूपोऽयं निहितो मध्ये मेधिनामिह कर्षकैः।
तस्मादतन्द्रितो दद्यादन्नधान्यार्थदक्षिणाः।।

भूमिं भित्त्वोषधीश्छित्त्वा हत्वा कीटपिपीलिकान्।
पुनन्ति खलयज्ञेन कर्षका नात्र संशयः।।

—*Devalasmṛti*, *op.cit.*463-466

25. पुंस्त्वोपघातं नास्ये(स्यं)वा वाहनानां न कारयेत्।
वृद्धं युग्मे न युञ्जीत जीर्णं व्याधितमेव च।।
न षण्डं वाहयेद् धेनुं न च भारेण पीडयेत्।
न वाहनीयाः शिखरे वृषभा यत्र कुत्रचित्।।

—*Devalasmṛti*, *op.cit.*467-468

XXVI

गृह्यसूत्रेषु वास्तुविज्ञानम्

पूर्वभूमिका

संहिताब्राह्मणारझण्यकोपनिषद्रूपं वैदिकं वाङ्मयम्। अस्य वैदिकवाङ्मयस्य शिक्षा, कल्पो, व्याकरणं, निरुक्तं, छन्दःशास्त्रं, ज्योतिषमिति षडङ्गानि। तेषु कल्पशब्देन कल्पसूत्राणां ग्रहणम्। कल्पसूत्रशब्देन श्रौतसूत्राणि, गृह्यसूत्राणि, धर्मसूत्राणि चेति त्रिविधानां सूत्रग्रन्थानां ग्रहणं भवति। केचन शुल्वसूत्राणामपि तत्रान्तर्भावं कुर्वन्ति। वेदवाङ्मयानुसारिणः प्रतिशाखं विभिन्ना एते सूत्रग्रन्थाः समुपलभ्यन्ते। तत्र गृह्याग्निसाध्यानां, गृहे समुपचर्यमाणानां, गृह्यसाध्यकृत्यानां, धार्मिकाचाराणां विवाहोपनयनादीनां विविधानां संस्काराणां च सूत्ररूपेण विवेचनं गृह्यसूत्रेषु संप्राप्यते। अत एव तेषामस्माकं सर्वेषां जीवनेऽतीव महत्त्वं विद्यते। डॉ. विन्टरनिट्झमहोदयेन समीचीनमेव प्रतिपादितं यदेते प्राचीनभारतीयलोकाचारप्रवर्तकाः सामयिकग्रन्थाः सन्ति। गृह्यसूत्रेषु समुपवर्णितानां पद्धतीनामाचाराणां च साम्यं, प्राचीनग्रीकरोमादिसंस्कृतिषु समुपलभ्यमानानामाचारैः सह विद्यत इति प्रतिपादयितुं शक्यमिति विदुषां मतम्। तत्र भाषाविषयकं सांस्कृतिकमपि साम्यं क्वचिद्दृश्यते। अत एव गृह्यसूत्राणामतीव महत्त्वम्। गृह्यसूत्राणां समयः प्रायेण खिस्ताब्दात्पूर्वमष्टशताब्दादारभ्य त्रिशताब्दपर्यन्तं विद्वद्भिः पाणिनेः पूर्वकालेऽनुमीयते। तत्र महामहोपाध्यायाः **पां. वा. काणेमहोदयाः** प्रमाणम्।

गृह्यसूत्राणां वास्तुविज्ञाने महत्त्वम्

गृह्यसूत्राणां वास्तुविज्ञानेऽतीव महत्त्वम्। प्राचीनभारतीयवास्तुविज्ञानविचारविषये गृह्यसूत्राणि प्रधानं प्रमाणम्। यतो प्राचीनभारतवाङ्मये सर्वप्राचीनाः सूत्ररूपेण वास्तुविज्ञानविवेचनपराः प्रमाणभूता ग्रन्थाः प्रायेण गृह्यसूत्राण्येवेति मम मतम्। वैदिकवाङ्मये प्रायेण स्वल्पमेव विवरणं, तदपि वर्णनानुगुणं, न तु स्वातन्त्र्येण वास्तुविज्ञानविषयं समुपलभ्यते। अत एव गृह्यसूत्रेषु विद्यमानं

विवरणं प्राचीनत्वेन, सुव्यवस्थितवर्णनत्वेनातीवैतिहासिकं महत्त्वं भजते। वास्तुविज्ञानविषयकसिद्धान्तप्रतिपादनपराः समुपलभ्यमाना अतिप्राचीना, आद्या वा ग्रन्था गृह्यसूत्रसणि-इत्यपि प्रतिपादयितुं शक्यम्। इदं गृह्यसूत्राणामध्ययनस्याभ्यासस्य च महत्त्वम्।

गृहस्थानां द्विविधत्वम्

देवलसदृशैः प्राचीनैर्धर्मसूत्रकारैर्गृहस्थानां द्विविधत्वं विवर्ण्यते। तथाह **देवलः—** "द्विविधो गृहस्थः। यायावरः— शालीनश्च। तयोर्यायावरः प्रवरः।" प्रेष्यचतुष्पादधनधान्ययुतः शालायां स्थायिकः षट्कर्मवृत्तिः शालीनः। यायावरो न तथा। प्रवसनशीलो नैकस्थानस्थिरः, अध्ययनयजनदानमात्रवृत्तिरसंग्रहशीलः। एतस्मादिदमनुमीयते यद्गृह्यसूत्रधर्मसूत्रयोः काले प्रायेण जनाः प्रवर्तनशीलत्वं (nomadic nature) परित्यज्य स्थानैकस्थिराः, शाला निर्माय, तासु वसन्ति स्म। अत एव गृह्यसूत्रेषु शालाकर्म-गृहनिर्माणविषयको विचारः संप्राप्यते।

वास्तुविज्ञानविषयः सामान्येन सर्वगृह्यसूत्रेषु

इदं तु पूर्वमेव प्रतिपादितं यद् गृह्यसूत्राणां प्रधानो विषयो गृह्यसाध्यानां विधीनां संस्काराणामाचाराणां च सूत्ररूपेण प्रतिपादनम्। अत एव गृहं तेषामनिवायमङ्गम्। गृहे भवानि गृह्याणि। गृहे भार्यासंयोगादुत्पन्ने गृह्याग्नौ भवानीमानि कर्माणि। गृहशब्देनात्र भार्या शाला च द्वयोरपि ग्रहणम्— "आवसथ्यादानं दारकाले दायाद्यकाले वा" इति वचनात्। अत एवेदं युक्तमेव यदेतेषु गृहनिर्माणसंबन्धी शालाकर्मविषयो वा विचारः, सिद्धान्तप्रतिपादनं वा प्रायेण सर्वेष्वेव गृह्यसूत्रेषु दरीदृश्यते। तत्र गृह्यसूत्रेषु क्वचिच्छालाकर्मरूपेण, क्वचिदगारकरणरूपेण वास्तुविज्ञानवर्णनम्। **आश्वलायन-गोभिलादिगृह्यसूत्रेषु** अवसान-भूमिपरीक्षाणादिरूपं सविस्तरं वर्णनम्। **बौधायनजैमिनीयादिषु** केवलं वास्तुशमनं, वास्तुशान्तिर्गृहशान्तिर्वा विवर्ण्यते। **कौषीतकिहिरण्यकेशीय**-सूत्रयोर्भूमिपरीक्षणं विहायागारकरणं, शालाकर्म वा वर्णितम्। **वाराहे गृह्यसूत्रे** केवलं प्रवेशविधिर्दृश्यते।

शालाकर्मणः प्रारम्भः

पारस्करगृह्यसूत्रे "पुण्याहे शालां कारयेत्" इत्येवोक्तम्। **भारद्वाजगृह्यसूत्रे** तु "शालाकर्म व्याख्यास्यामः। शालां कारयिष्यमाण आपूर्यमाणपक्षे पुण्ये

नक्षत्रे" इत्याद्युक्तम्। अस्यायमर्थः—ज्योतिषशास्त्रप्रतिपादिते शुभतिथिनक्षत्रादि-युक्तदिने गृहनिर्माणस्य शालाकर्मणो वारम्भः कर्तव्यः।

भूमिपरीक्षणम्

भूमिलक्षणं परीक्षणं वेत्यावश्यकः प्रारम्भिको विषयो वास्तुनिर्माणस्य। सा भूमिः कीदृग्लक्षणा स्वीकर्तव्येति तत्र विचार्यते। प्रायेण गृह्यसूत्रेषु "अनूषरा भूमिर्गृहीतव्या" इति प्रतिपादितम्। ऊषरभूमौ शालाकर्म न कर्तव्यम्। तादृशस्थले क्षारयुक्तभूमौ स्नानान्नपानवस्त्रक्षालनादिषु काठिन्यमनुभूयते। "भूमिर्विवादरहिता भवेत्" इत्यप्याश्वलायनेन प्रथममेव सूत्रितम्। विवादग्रस्तभूमौ गृहनिर्माणं न कर्तव्यम्। अधुना वयं Title-Clearance इति यद् वदामः। प्राचीन कालेऽप्ययं विचारो महर्षिभिः कृतः। गोभिलेनोक्तं यद् "अवसानं समं लोमशमविभ्रंशि" भवतु। यत्र आपः प्राच्य उदीच्यो वा प्रवर्तेरन्। स्थिराघातं, एकवर्णं, अशुष्कं, अमरुपरिहितं सजलं च स्थानं स्वीकर्तव्यम्। आश्वलायनदृष्ट्या ओषधिवनस्पतियुक्तं, कुशवीरणादि-संकुलमेतादृशं भूमिस्थानं स्वीकर्तव्यम्। ब्रह्मवर्चसकामेन दर्भसंमितं, बलकामेन बृहत्तृणयुतं, पशुकामेन मृदुतृणयुतं स्थानं गृहीतव्यमिति गोभिलमतम्। आश्वलायनगोभिलादिभिरेवं भूमिपरीक्षणं विहितम्।

क्षीरिण्यादिवृक्षाणां निष्कासनम्

गृहनिर्माणभूमिप्रदेशे विद्यमानाः क्षीरिणीवृक्षाः कण्टकिनः कटुवृक्षाश्च निष्कासितव्याः। अश्वत्थोदुम्बरप्रभृतयो महावृक्षा यदि वास्तुसमीपे सन्ति, तर्हि ते वास्तुविघ्नकराः, तेषां मूलानि सुदूरं भूम्यन्तर्भागं गत्वा वास्तोर्भयप्रदानि सन्ति। तेषां दूरे स्थापनार्थं सूत्रकाराणामादेशो दूरदृष्टिसमन्वितः श्रेयस्करश्चेति नात्राशङ्का। गोभिले त्वन्यत्संप्रोक्तम्— तद्यथा—

वर्जयेत्पूर्वतोऽश्वत्थं प्लक्षं दक्षिणतस्तथा।
न्यग्रोधमपराद् देशाद् उत्तराचाप्युदुम्बरम्।।
अश्वत्थादग्निभयं ब्रूयात् प्लक्षाद् ब्रूयात्प्रमायुकान् (अल्पायुषः)।
न्यग्रोधाच्छस्त्रसंपीडमक्ष्यामयमुदुम्बरात् (अक्षिरोगः)।।

अतस्तानस्वस्थानस्थान्— स्वेषु स्थानेषु तिष्ठन्तीति स्वस्थानस्थाः, न स्वस्थानस्थाा अस्वस्थानस्थाः, अन्यदिक्स्थान् कुर्वीत्। स्थानं समचतुरस्त्रं,

आयतचतुरस्त्रं वा मापयेदिति— **आश्वलायनः। गोभिलीये** तु इष्टकाकृति वर्तुलं वा वर्णितम्। **द्राह्यायणगृह्यसूत्रे** वर्णितं यद्गौरभूमिभागे ब्राह्मणो, लोहिते क्षत्रियः, कृष्णे वैश्यो गृह्यनिर्माणं कुर्यात्। **आश्वलायनेन** वैश्यस्य पीतवर्णयुतं स्थानं वर्णितम्। मधुरास्वादं सिकतायुतं सर्वेषां सामान्यम्।

गृहोत्खाताः स्तम्भस्थापनं च

तत्र उत्खातगर्तावटेत्यादिरूपाः, स्तम्भस्थापनार्था य उत्खातास्तेषां विचारोऽपि गृह्यसूत्रेषु क्रियते। तत्र तु जानुमात्रं जानुप्रमाणं गर्तं कर्तव्यमिति— **आश्वलायनः। पारस्करादिषु** चतुर्णां गर्तानामवटानां वा निर्देशः। **कौषीतकिगृह्यसूत्रे** नवस्थूणागर्तानामुल्लेखः। तत्र गर्तेषु रात्रौ जलं पूरयित्वा स्थानपरीक्षणं कार्यम्। प्रातः गर्तं यदि सोदकं तर्हि तत्स्थानं प्रशस्तम्। आर्द्रे गर्ते मध्यमम्। शुष्के गर्ते तु स्थानं गर्हितं भवति। एतेनेदं सिद्धं **यदाश्वलायन**-सिद्धान्तेन शुष्कभूमौ गृहं न कर्तव्यं, जलसंपृक्तभूमौ एव गृहं कर्तव्यमित्यर्थः। विध्यादिना पवित्रीक्रियमाणेषु उत्खातेषु स्तम्भानां समन्त्रकमारोपणं क्रियते। **पारस्करे** चतुर्णां स्तम्भानां समुल्लेखः। अनेकेषु गृह्यसूत्रेषु मध्यमस्तम्भस्य स्थूणाराजस्य वा निर्देशः। तत्र तत्र संधीनां, भित्तीनां, वंशानां च वर्णनं प्राप्यते। वंशाधानमपि समन्त्रकं क्रियते। मन्त्राणामर्थोऽपि हृद्यः, कृत्यनुरूपः शुभाशंसी, आशीर्वादात्मको दरीदृश्यते।

गृहद्वारविचारः

गृहस्य द्वारं कस्यां दिशि भाव्यमित्यस्यापि विचारो गृह्यसूत्रेषु प्राप्यते। तत्र प्रतिदिशं द्वारस्थापने किं फलं, को वा परिणाम इत्यस्य समुल्लेखो दृश्यते। तत्र **गोभिलगृह्यसूत्रे** कथितं यद् "तत्र अवसानं प्राग्द्वारं यशस्कामो, बलकामः कुर्वीत। उदग्द्वारं पुत्रपशुकामः। दक्षिणद्वारं सर्वकामः। न प्रत्यग्द्वारं कुर्वीत"। अत्र पश्चिमद्वारनिषेधो दृश्यते। अन्यगृहद्वाराभिमुखं गृहद्वारं न कर्तव्यम्। गृहं स्वावृतद्वारं कर्तव्यम्। "यथा न संलोकी स्यात्"। अत्रोद्देशोऽयं यद् बाह्यदेशस्थो गृहमध्यविद्यमानानां भक्ष्यभोज्यादीनां दर्शनक्षमो न भवतु। **कौषीतकिगृह्यसूत्रे** चतुर्णां द्वाराणामुल्लेखः।

आश्वलायनगृह्यसूत्रे शयनस्थानं, पाकशाला, सभास्थानं च गृहे कुत्र स्यादित्यस्य विवेचनं प्राप्यतें। "यत्र सर्वत आपो समेत्य प्रदक्षिणं शयनीयं

परीत्य प्राच्यः स्यन्देरन्नप्रपतत्यस्तत्सर्वसमृद्धम्। समवस्रवे भक्तशरणं कारयेत्। बह्वन्नं भवति। दक्षिणाप्रवणे सभां मापयेत्। साद्यूता ह भवति। युवानस्तस्यां कितवाः कलहिनः प्रमायुका भवन्ति। यत्र सर्वत आपः प्रस्यन्देरन्सा स्वस्त्ययनी अद्यूता च"। अस्यार्थः—गृहस्य पूर्वतः शयनीयं कृत्वा तस्य उत्तरतो पाकशालां कुर्यात्। गृहस्य उत्तरतो सभागृहं न कुर्यात्। युवानः कलहयुक्ता अल्पायुषश्च भवन्ति। अतो यत्र सर्वदिगभ्यो जलं मध्यभागं प्रति प्रवहति, एतादृशे मध्यस्थाने सभां कुर्यात्। सा कल्याणप्रदा, द्यूतरहिता च भवति।

गृहनिर्माणसमये गृहप्रवेशकाले च तत्र तत्र क्रियामाणस्य यागादिकृत्यस्यापि वर्णनं सर्वगृह्यसूत्रेषु संप्राप्यते। तत्र केचन मन्त्राः, कृत्यानि समानानि सन्ति। वास्तुशमनकृत्यस्य महत्त्वं भारद्वाजगृह्यसूत्रे प्रतिपादितम्— "यद्वास्तु गर्हितं यत्र वान्यः परिभवेत्तत्रापि सुखमासीत शमयन्वास्तु ऋतौ ऋतौ-एतद् धौम्यस्य वचनं, असितस्य तुरंगस्य च मुनेः काव्यस्य दाल्भ्यस्य। नैतद् विद्वान्पराभवेत्" जैमिनीयेऽपि कथितम्—"गृहवृद्धिमिच्छन्मासि मासि ऋतौ ऋतौ संवत्सरे संवत्सरे........गृहशान्तिं कुर्यात्"।

उपसंहारः

अत्रायं निष्कर्षः

(1) गृह्यसूत्रकाले प्राचीनार्यैः स्वकीयं प्रवसनशीलत्वं परित्यज्य शालीनत्वमङ्गीकृतम्। अतोऽतिप्राचीनं वास्तुविधानमत्र संप्राप्यते।

(2) वास्तुनिर्माणविषयकाणां मूलस्वरूपाणां सिद्धान्तानां प्रतिपादनं दरीदृश्यतेऽत्र। तत्र स्तम्भाः (Pillars), वंशाधानं, प्राग्वंशः (Beams), उत्खाताः (Trenches), द्वारदिङ्निर्णयः (Direction of main and other doors), पाकशाला-शयनीयसभागृहादीनां विचारः (Location of other Parts of house), समन्त्रकाणां विधीनां वर्णनम्-इत्याद्या आवश्यका विषया विशदीक्रियन्ते।

(3) सूत्रोक्तदिशा वास्तुप्रयोगः संक्षिप्तः, स्वल्पकालीनः, तान्त्रिकपौराणिकतत्त्वविरहितो विशुद्धश्च दरीदृश्यते। अनन्तरकालेऽनेकेषां पूर्वोत्तरकृत्यानां प्रधानेऽन्तर्भावः समभवत्।

(4) आश्वलायनगृह्यसूत्रे विवादरहितभूमेर्ग्रहणं विहितम्। आधुनिककालेऽपि तदस्माभिर्भूमिसंपादने विचार्यते।

(5) गृह्यसूत्रकाले भूमिसंपादने प्रायेण सौकर्यमासीदित्यनुमीयते,यतो हि तत्र न कोऽपि क्रयविक्रयरूप आर्थिको व्यवहारो दृश्यते।

(6) सूत्रेषु शूद्रस्य कृते कीदृशी भूमिः। कीदृग्वर्णा वा स्वीकर्तव्या इत्यस्य विचारो न प्राप्यते। अपरेषां वर्णानां कृते विचारः कृतः।

(7) सभास्थानं, पाकशाला, शयनीयमित्यादीनां वर्णनेन गृहनिर्माणक्षेत्रे समीचीना प्रगतिरनुमीयते।

अन्ते सूत्रोक्तदिशा ''शिवं वास्तु शिवं वास्तु'' इत्युक्त्वा विरम्यते।

REFERENCES

Paper published in *Surabharatī,* Baroda Sanskrit Mahavidyalaya, Annual Magazine, 1999-2000, pp. 29-33.

Paper read at the National Seminar on "*Vāstuśāstra*" held by Baroda Sanskrit Mahavidyalaya, 23-25 February 1996.